# PUBLIC REGULATION OF THE RELIGIOUS USE OF LAND

A Detailed and Critical Analysis
of a Hundred Court Cases

BY

## JAMES E. CURRY

*Of Washington, D. C.*

*Member of the Bars of the District of Columbia and of
the Supreme Courts of the United States, Puerto Rico
and Illinois, and other courts and tribunals.*

THE MICHIE COMPANY
LAW PUBLISHERS
*Charlottesville, Va.*

## PREFACE AND ACKNOWLEDGMENTS

I hope this book will be useful not only to lawyers but also to laymen. For lawyers, it will serve as a ready-reference manual of church zoning law.

It may seem paradoxical, but the reference to "laymen" includes most importantly the clergy. To them, and to building committees and other religious leaders, I hope the volume will be useful in making their own decisions and seeking public decisions as to the location and construction of religious buildings.

It will also provide zoning and planning officials with information they need in connection with applications for permits for churches and other religious buildings. Whether or not they have legal training, such officers are often required to act in a quasi-judicial capacity. It is for such purposes that I have tried to avoid technicalities, yet to analyse the problems as profoundly as possible.

I also hope the volume will receive attention from persons not directly concerned in church zoning but interested in the political science of church-state relations. The book is mainly an historical and critical analysis, in more-than-usual depth, of approximately 100 cases in which attempts to regulate the religious use of land have resulted in court decisions published in the official reports. So far as I know, no previous author has tried to bring so much of this material together. Because church and church school zoning cases are not usually classified as such in the various legal encyclopedias, digests, etc., that legal writers use as "case-finders," there is no certainty that I have found them all. If any are omitted, they may be included in supplements.

The volume differs from the usual legal text in its more critical approach to the decisions of the courts and to the opinions of legal writers. In form, it also differs. I have gone to some pains to avoid jargon. I have even omitted the long, wordy, footnotes that are usually included in such texts, repeating over and over again the official titles, volume numbers,

iii

and page numbers of cases, including abbreviations that to the lay reader are occult. Instead, I have designated each case in the main text by its reference number and by the name of the town, the state and the religion involved, e.g., the "Porterville, California, Mormon temple case." [67,71,76]

The "highlights" of all church zoning cases are set forth chronologically at page xi. Full case citations also appear in the Chronological Table of References (page 339). This arrangement is important because church zoning law changes very rapidly. The date of a decision may be as important as the principle involved. Books and articles and cases not directly involving churches are included in the same table.

In addition to the general Subject Index (page 385), which I have tried to make very complete, I have inserted separate indexes which list each case under (a) the title thereof, page 377, (b) the state involved, page 374, (c) the city, township or county involved, page 371, and (d) the religious denomination involved, page 368. Each book and article is listed alphabetically under (e) the name of the author, page 367, and (f) its title, pages 362 and 364. Articles are also listed under (g) the name of the periodical in which each appeared, page 363.

By relegating this reference information to the back of the book, I hope I have succeeded in making the main text more readable but just as usable as other similar books. The publishers plan to issue supplements or pocket parts from year to year which will keep the information up to date.

I acknowledge with deepest gratitude the help I have received from other lawyers. The manuscript was submitted, in whole or in part, to many attorneys who had appeared in church zoning cases, who had written about them, or who were otherwise competent to advise. I want to stress the magnanimity of those who responded. The only source of a lawyer's professional income is his knowledge and experience. If he shares these gratuitously, in a sense he is doing what a merchant would be doing who gave away part of his stock in trade. If my readers find this book useful, their appreciation should also be extended to these men and women.

For lack of space, I cannot acknowledge individually the assistance I received from various lawyers. I list here the attorneys who corresponded or consulted with me at greater or lesser length. This is not intended to indicate that any lawyer approved of my views. To the contrary, a few expressed spirited disagreement. Such comments were as highly appreciated as the praise received from many other correspondents. The list of lawyers, by states, is as follows:

*Alabama:* Lawrence F. Gerald, Jr., of Clanton; and Jack Crenshaw and Walter J. Knabe of Montgomery. *Arizona:* Richard G. Johnson and J. LeMar Shelley of Mesa; and Mark Wilmer of Phoenix. *California:* Paul P. Selvin of Beverley Hills; Grayson Price of Chico; Charles R. Currey of Corona del Mar; P. J. Tscharner of Glendora; William MacKenzie Brown of Los Angeles; Paul Brindel of Novato; J. Marcus Hardin and J. W. O'Neill of Oakland; Robert H. Dunlap of Pasadena; Burke E. Buford of Porterville; Jack C. Small of Redwood City; Nathaniel S. Colley of Sacramento; W. Glenn Harmon, William D. Keeler and Ronald E. Vernon of San Francisco; Charles R. Martin of San Marino; and Arthur M. Bradley, H. Roger Howell and Adrian Kuyper of Santa Ana. *Colorado:* Harry E. Smoot of Denver; Joseph W. Esch of Englewood; and Gordon C. Hinds of Pueblo. *Connecticut:* Robert Ewing and Howard J. Maxwell of Hartford. *District of Columbia:* David Cobb, Edward R. Felker, John D. Fitzgerald, Frances L. Horn, Thomas H. Ploss, and Weissbrodt, Weissbrodt and Liftin. *Florida:* F. E. Gotthardt of Miami; Milton Robbins, Marion E. Sibley, and Joseph A. Wanick of Miami Beach; and Charles W. Bryan, William R. McCown and Charles C. Whitaker II of Tampa. *Georgia:* Ross Arnold, Elmo Holt, Pierre Howard, Charles C. Hurt, and Herbert Johnson of Atlanta; and Carl T. Hudgins of Decatur. *Illinois:* Ben Copple, Andrew C. Hamilton, Jay I. Messinger, Maurice J. Nathanson, Jack Noble, and Richard W. Wattling of Chicago; Albert L. Hall of Waukegan; and William I. Caldwell of Woodstock. *Indiana:* Robert S. Anderson and Custer and Smith of Decatur; and Harvey A. Grabill, Herbert Hartman, Lester Irons, and Frank M. McHale of Indianapolis. *Iowa:* T. H. Nelson, H. F. Reynolds, and E. Marshall Thomas of Dubuque. *Kentucky:* J. W. Jones, Louis R. Ogden and Leo T. Wolford of Louisville. *Massachusetts:* Gerald A. Berlin and Charles C. Cabot of Boston. *Michigan:* Marion H. Crawmer and Thomas G. Long of Detroit; Homer Arnett of Kalamazoo; and Joseph G. O'Reilly of Lansing. *Missouri:* William H. Wyne of Clayton; William W. Cochrane, Norman T. Gordon and Harold T. Van Dyke of Kansas City; and Roberts P. Elam, John Raeburn Green and Jerome W. Sandweiss of St. Louis. *Nebraska:* Herbert M. Fitle of Omaha. *New Jersey:* Robert V. Carton of Asbury Park; M. A. Potter of Long Branch; Daniel W. Kamp of Midland Park; Samuel Allcorn, Jr., and George K. Meier, Jr., of Montclair; Worrall F. Mountain and Ralph Porzio of Morristown; Charles Handler, William Hodes, Emanuel N. Silberner and Saul J. Zucker of Newark; and William Howe Davis of Orange. *New York:* Michael Sharff of Brooklyn; Walter C. Marshall of Lynbrook; Everett J. Johns of New City; Anthony M. Farina of New Hyde Park; Edward S. Bentley, Ralph W. Crolly, Samuel Gottlieb, George L. Hubbell, Jr., Charles B. McGroddy, Jr., and Elias Rosenzweig of New York City; Edmund Clynes, Samuel Di Pasquale, Andrew L. Gilman, Donald E. Robinson, Emmett J. Schnepp, and Lucien E. Smartt of Rochester; David W. Silverman of Spring Valley; John G. Hall of Staten Island; Chester H. King, Jr., Franklin J. Schwarzer and Philip T. Young of Syracuse; and John C. Marbach of White Plains. *Ohio:* Morris Berick of Cleveland; Lawrence D. Stanley of Columbus; and Guy H. Wells of Dayton. *Oregon:* John O. Sheldahl of Oregon City; and Robert F. Maguire of Portland. *Pennsylvania:* Carl M. Kerchner of Ambridge; William S. Livengood, Jr., of Harrisburg; William F. Fox, Morris Gerber, Samuel H. High, Jr., Harry M. Sablosky and Samuel L. Sagendorph of Norristown; Gordon Cavanaugh, C. L. Cushmore, Jr., Frank F. Truscott and J. Gordon Yocum of Philadelphia; John G. Buchanan, David W. Craig, Paul C. Konnor, Owen B. McManus, Eugene B. Strassburger and Donald L. Very of Pittsburgh; and J. Frank Kelker of Rochester. *South Carolina:* Charles H. Gibbs of Charleston. *Texas:* Doren R. Eskew and Tom Gee of Austin; Bert Bader, Mike McKool and Charles H. Storey of Dallas; and Borden Seaberry of Weatherford. *Washington:* Lowell D. Sperline of East Wenatchee and James Arneil of Wenatchee. *Wisconsin:* Suel O. Arnold, Walter H. Bender, Irving B. Charne, Jack E. Keyes, Richard J. McGinn, Herbert L. Mount, Nathan Schapiro, Reynolds C.

Seitz, and Joseph J. Shutkin of Milwaukee. *West Virginia:* Truman L. Sayre of Beckley.

For valuable assistance and encouragement I also thank my wife, Alma M. Curry, J. Mel O'Rourke and Eleanor O'Rourke (my sister) of Chicago, Stanley Lichtenstein and Edmund Burke Peterson of Washington, D. C., Perry Norton of Lexington, Mass., the staff of the Law Library of the Bar Association of the District of Columbia, especially Mr. Warren Juggins, and the staff of the Law Library of Congress. The literary assistance of Carl Haessler, Ph.D., of Detroit, Michigan, was indispensable.

JAMES E. CURRY

*Washington, D. C.*

## TABLE OF CONTENTS

* These listings include only church zoning cases discussed fully herein.

** This listing includes all cases mentioned herein.

# HIGHLIGHTS OF THE CASES

This list is intended more to identify than to describe the church zoning cases. It will be useful to those of my readers (probably by no means all) who want to examine them in chronological order. Each of the cases of which the "highlights" are listed below will be discussed in much greater detail in the appropriate chapters which follow.

1922.

*Omaha, Nebraska.*[14] In a suit brought by a Presbyterian church, setback requirements were held unconstitutional as an undue limitation on property rights.

1927.

*Evanston, Illinois.*[19,23] The court held that an ordinance authorizing "colleges" should be interpreted also to include dormitories. It also refused enforcement of an amendment excluding private schools on the ground that the college had acted in good faith on the basis of the former ordinance permitting them.

1930.

*Beckley, West Virginia.*[25] Under an ordinance authorizing exclusion of any "public garage, filling station, store, or other industry of any kind or character," the court held that there was no authority to exclude a Church of God from the residential zone.

1932.

*Portland, Oregon.*[27] Because the ordinance contained an undue delegation of legislative power, the court refused to permit rejection of a permit for a Catholic school at a busy intersection.

*Winnetka, Illinois.*[34] The exclusion of a Catholic school from a residential area was forbidden because of failure of the city to show any important distinction between it and public elementary schools, which were permitted.

*Reno, Nevada.*[35] A Catholic church was refused a permit on the ground that church funerals would disturb the neighborhood. The court overruled the action on the ground that church funerals would be no more disturbing than home funerals, which were permitted.

1933.

*Grand Rapids, Michigan.*[28] The supreme court sustained a permit to a Lutheran church because "the discretion is that of the board, not the courts."

1942.

*Upper Arlington, Ohio.*[40] The refusal of a permit was overturned by
the court because of supposed representations made by the board
that the particular lot would be acceptable. The decision also contains a lengthy discussion of broad principles of church zoning, including an expression of "doubt" that a church could be excluded
from any residence district.

1943.

*Pittsburgh, Pennsylvania.*[46] The supreme court sustained a grant of a
permit for a synagogue combined with the rabbi's home.

1944.

*Sherman, Texas.*[48,49] The court ordered issuance of a permit to another
Church of God in a case where the city admitted the invalidity of its
ordinance. The court also expressed general constitutional objection
to the exclusion of churches.

1945.

*Philadelphia, Pennsylvania.*[50] A rabbi was refused a permit for a synagogue in his home. The court sustained the board because the rabbi
refused to comply with the setback requirements.

*Philadelphia, Pennsylvania.*[51] The action of the board granting a permit to another rabbi was sustained over technical objections of
neighbors based on the terms of the particular ordinance.

*Mesa, Arizona.*[53] The court voided the action of the city refusing a permit to a Catholic church. The evidence showed that other activities,
including pig-raising were permitted in the same zone.

1946.

*Atlanta, Georgia.*[55] A Baptist church obtained an injunction against
cancellation of its permit because it was attempted to be made without notice.

*Montgomery, Alabama.*[56] The refusal of a permit to a Pentecostal Holiness church was held invalid because not authorized by the particular ordinance.

*Indianapolis, Indiana.*[57] Under an ordinance authorizing churches, the
court held that a permit might also be issued for a gymnasium, amphitheater, and other incidental facilities.

1947.

*Cleveland Heights, Ohio.*[59,61] A Jewish school was refused a permit in a
residential zone on grounds of devaluation of neighboring property, etc.

*Portage Township, Michigan.*[60,63,65] A "Full Salvation Union" camp
meeting was ordered to vacate a rural area on the theory that it was

not included in the term "a church or accessory to a church," as used in the ordinance.

1948.

*Indianapolis, Indiana.*[62] Another decision by the supreme court of this state affirmed issuance of a permit to a Catholic "church," which term was construed to include a convent, priests' home, school, etc.

1949.

*Porterville, California.*[67,71,76] The California Court of Appeals ruled, on the pleadings, that an ordinance banning churches from an entire residential zone was constitutionally valid.

*Louisville, Kentucky.*[69] As a condition to the issuance of a permit for a Baptist church, the court approved a requirement for adequate off-street parking, and also required elimination of night lighting for sports.

*Decatur, Georgia.*[70] The court refused to reverse an order transferring a lot from one zone to another to permit its use as an Evangelical Lutheran church. There was evidence that there would be a decrease in the value of neighboring properties but there was also evidence to the contrary. The court held that the decision was within the discretion of the board, which should not be overruled.

*Lodi Township, New Jersey.*[78] The supreme court voided a safety provision insofar as it required reconstruction of an existing Baptist church.

1950.

*Pittsburgh, Pennsylvania.*[81] This case involved the Catholic Third Order of St. Francis of Assisi, which sought to convert a three story stable and servants' quarters in a high class estate area, into sleeping quarters for "retreatants." The zoning officials were forced to grant the permit by a lower court decision which discussed church zoning at length and made special reference to religious liberty.

*Tampa, Florida.*[83] The court reversed the city's refusal of a permit to Jehovah's Witnesses, the denial being based on noncompliance with parking space requirements. The court held that the Witnesses had "substantially" complied and were entitled to a permit.

*Bronxville, New York.*[68,74,77,82,82-A] The court of appeals refused to permit exclusion of Concordia (Lutheran) College buildings, under an ordinance requiring consent of other property owners for their construction.

1950-1.

*Atlanta, Georgia.*[72,78,91] The court held that Jehovah's Witnesses were properly refused a permit on grounds that their Kingdom Hall would cause excessive traffic problems. They later sued for a federal injunction but their suit was dismissed in the Federal Circuit Court of Appeals.

1951.

*Dover, Massachusetts.*[85] The court held that a Massachusetts law invalidating ordinances that "limit the use of land for any church or religious or . . . religious or sectarian or denominational educational purposes" was applicable even as to ordinances already in effect at the time of its adoption.

*Plandome, New York.*[87] A lower court required issuance of a permit to the Unitarians on the ground that churches could not constitutionally be excluded from an entire village where other nonresidential uses were permitted.

*Chico, California.*[88] The court of appeals sustained an order issued at the request of city authorities enjoining a group of Baptists from "carrying on or conducting a church or church functions or church services" without a permit.

1951-2.

*Newark, New Jersey.*[89,94-A] One petition of objecting neighbors, the court nullified a zoning board permit for construction of a "mikvah" which is a pool used in an Orthodox Jewish ritual. Its decision was affirmed by the appellate division. The court held that such an institution was not a "church" as that word was used in the zoning ordinance.

1951-2-3.

*Orange, New Jersey.*[86,92,99] The court held that Eastern Christian Institute, a Protestant seminary, could be excluded from a residential zone even though public and parochial grade schools and high schools were permitted in the same zone.

1952.

*Chicago, Illinois.*[93] Under an ordinance forbidding churches except on lots completely surrounded by alleys, the appellate court held that an Episcopal church, by dedicating to public use as alleys certain lands surrounding its site and owned by it could bring itself within the terms of the requirement.

*Orchard Lake, Michigan.*[94] Invoking a religious clause in the Michigan constitution, the court called "unreasonable on its face" an ordinance excluding churches and parochial schools from 90% of the village area. It required issuance of a permit for construction of a Catholic parish plant.

1953.

*Beachwood, Ohio.*[101] The court of appeals required issuance of a permit to a Jewish Temple although its membership exceeded the total population of the village, and very few synagogue members resided there.

*Dallas, Texas.*[102] The court of civil appeals upheld Dallas' refusal of a permit for a Protestant evangelistic center on application by Reverend Jack Coe. The court said that Coe's building was "more for healing and would not in fact be a church."

1954.

*Decatur, Indiana.*[104] The court refused to enforce off-street parking requirements as a condition to issuance of a permit to Jehovah's Witnesses. It said that the traffic problem could better be regulated "by traffic police, signs and other reasonable regulations" and challenged the propriety of *any* exclusion of churches from residential areas.

*Cheltenham Township, Pennsylvania.*[105] The court ordered issuance of a permit for use as a synagogue of premises already being used as a religious school. This was done over objections from neighbors, all of whom happened to be Jewish and some of whom had been members of the congregation complained against.

*Wauwatosa, Wisconsin.*[106,120] The court affirmed Wauwatosa's exclusion of a Lutheran high school, rejecting the reasoning of the Illinois court in the 1939 Winnetka Catholic case.[34] It held that there are fundamental differences between public and private education which justify different treatment thereof. This decision was refused review by the United States Supreme Court.

*Irondequoit, New York.*[107] Under the peculiar terms of the ordinance, a lower court held that the board had no authority to impose off-street parking lot requirements on a Jewish synagogue.

1954-5.

*Piedmont, California.*[115,125] The court required issuance of a permit to a Catholic school. It rejected an ordinance which forbade private schools in residential districts comprising 98.7% of the town's area although other uses were permitted in the same area. This order was issued by the same supreme court that refused review of the Porterville Mormon case, upholding total exclusion of churches from a residential area within a city.[67] The court disavowed any intention of repudiating the Porterville decision.

1955.

*Miami Beach, Florida.*[124] The court affirmed refusal of the city to permit construction of a Lutheran church although it permitted golf courses, playgrounds, parking areas, municipal buildings, etc. in the same area. It did not mention its previous decision in the 1950 Tampa case refusing to permit exclusion of a Kingdom Hall.[83]

*Morris Township, New Jersey.*[128] The court reversed the grant of a permit to Villa Walsh (Istituto Pontificio della Maestre Filippini), a papal seminary for Catholic nuns, which wanted to expand its facilities, located in a secluded spot in a rural area. The court said that such expansion would have a tendency to "subvert" sound planning and "infect" the neighborhood.

1955-56.

*Dayton, Ohio.*[122,142] The court refused a petition of neighbors asking that the parking lot permit of First Church of Christ Scientist be nullified. The court said such facilities were a "customary and incidental accessory use" for churches as authorized by the ordinance.

*Brighton, New York.*[123,131,138,149] The court required issuance of a permit for a complete Catholic parish plant on the former estate of William A. E. Drescher at 2615 East Avenue, holding that the evidence did not support the reasons assigned by the board for its refusal. The court did not forbid the regulation of religious land use or even the exclusion of churches or church schools; but it took an extremely strict view of the justifications submitted for the board's action and held each of them insufficient.

*Sands Point, New York.*[129,148] The court of appeals reversed Sands Point's refusal to permit conversion of a large mansion and 24 surrounding acres into a Jewish religious center. It rejected the contention of the board that the center's purposes were not "purely religious."

1956.

*Winston Salem, North Carolina.*[134] The Catholic bishop had obtained a permit in 1949 for conversion of a large house into a school for white children. The permit was conditioned on his agreement that no changes be made in the exterior and that no new buildings be constructed. In 1955, he conveyed the property to the Sisters of St. Joseph who applied for permission to construct new buildings and alter the old ones. The zoning board held them to the bishop's agreement and refused the permit. The court sustained the decision.

*Chicago, Illinois.*[135] The appellate court held that a Jewish synagogue and school on Hamlin Avenue in a residential zone was not in violation of the zoning ordinance, its decision being based on a technical interpretation and not involving constitutional issues.

*New Hyde Park, New York.*[137] The village law of New York required unanimous vote for adoption of any amendment to a zoning ordinance if objected to by the owners of 20% of the "land extending 100 feet from land included in the proposed change." The village adopted an amendment the purpose and effect of which was to permit construction of a Jewish school. It did not mention the school or any particular tract of land but authorized such schools in the entire village. The court held that the requirement for unanimous vote did not apply to such an amendment.

*Haltom City, Texas.*[136] The court of civil appeals held that the city was not justified in refusing a permit to Jehovah's Witnesses on the ground of additional traffic hazards, noise, and "possible" depreciation in surrounding property values. It also questioned the validity of any ordinance excluding churches from a residential area.

*West Hartford, Connecticut.*[139] The court sustained the city's refusal of a permit to a large Methodist church on the ground that it would cause traffic hazards and noise, disturb peace and quiet, and decrease the value of surrounding properties.

*South Euclid, Ohio.*[140] The court of appeals refused to permit the zoning board to exclude a Jewish synagogue. The board action had been based in part on increased traffic hazards but the court pointed out that these were Orthodox Jews forbidden by religious law to use automobiles on the Sabbath.

*Austin, Texas.*[143] The court of civil appeals refused an injunction requested by adjoining owners to prevent construction of a library for an Episcopal theological seminary. The court said that such a religious facility was not a "nuisance per se" and that the board's action would be presumed valid.

*Garden City, New York.*[150,154] The city refused a permit for a synagogue because of failure to provide adequate parking space for future needs. The lower court reversed its action, holding, in effect, that it was up to the synagogue, not up to the planning authorities, to plan for its future needs.

## 1957.

*Kansas City, Missouri.*[156] A permit for the Visitation Catholic Church's proposed parking lot was granted by the zoning board and the decision was sustained by the Kansas City Court of Appeals. The court held that strict compliance with a requirement that the lot be adjacent to the church would be an "undue hardship" on the church and therefore that the board could legally grant a variance.

*Charleston, South Carolina.*[157] The court upheld a permit to the First Baptist Church to expand its school. But it also upheld, against objections of the church, a limitation upon the enrollment thereof to 270 students.

*Bethel Borough, Pennsylvania.*[159,168] Refusal of a permit for a Kingdom Hall was upheld by the superior court. It was based upon an ordinance which forbade "any place of public assembly" within a quarter mile of any other such place. The decision was refused review in the Supreme Court of the United States.

*Tampa, Florida.*[160] The supreme court refused a permit to the Tampa, Florida, Advent Christian Church, holding that the issue was "controlled" by the decision in the 1955 Miami Beach Lutheran case.[124]

*Cheltenham Township, Pennsylvania.*[162] In a suburb called Wyncote, that had been "developed entirely for country or suburban residential living," the court required issuance of a permit for a Catholic regional high school with a capacity of 2,000 students, several convents, rectories, etc. The decision was based on a very lenient interpretation of the zoning ordinance.

*Wenatchee, Washington.*[165] The court reversed a zoning board action against Jehovah's Witnesses because it was based on a "possibility" rather than on an "actuality" or "probability" of increased traffic hazards. There was a strong dissenting opinion.

*Modesto, California.*[167] A county official had testified that the proposed Negro Baptist church would be across the street from a livestock pasture, nearby to an auto body repair shop and "as well located as any church that had been built in the community." Over technical objections of white neighbors, the court of appeals sustained the zoning board permit to the church.

*Kansas City, Missouri.*[169] The zoning board granted a permit for a Catholic church and school on 62nd Street. The dispute concerned whether the church had complied with parking requirements. By an extremely broad interpretation of the statute, the court succeeded in sustaining the permit issued to the church.

*Pelham Manor, New York.*[172,178,179,220] A series of four cases about the Pelham Jewish Center, the first three being decided on technical grounds, culminated in a decision of the intermediate court declaring unconstitutional an ordinance prohibiting places of worship in residential districts. No opinion was published.

1957-8.

*Lawrence, New York.*[173,182] An application of a Jewish group for expansion of its temple to include a swimming pool and gymnasium was rejected by the zoning board. The lower court reversed this action but its decision was in turn reversed by the appellate division. The final decision was that the congregation had filed the wrong form of action and recommended refiling. So far this has not been done.

1958.

*Chicago, Illinois.*[188] On technical grounds, the appellate court refused to review a zoning action under which the Believers in Islam were refused permission to erect a large sign.

1958-9.

*Ocean Township, New Jersey.*[180,206] A lower court sustained the township's action granting a permit for a parochial school, holding that the board was required to issue it under a section providing for "public schools". The supreme court also sustained the permit but under general discretionary provisions of the ordinance. It repudiated the lower court's dictum putting parochial and public schools on the same footing.

*Milwaukie, Oregon.*[184,200] The court upheld refusal by the city of a permit for a Kingdom Hall. It was this same court that in 1939 had required issuance of a permit for a parochial school at a busy traffic intersection. (See pages 12-13.) Allegations of religious bias were rejected as unfounded. The decision was refused review in the United States Supreme Court.

*Azusa, California.*[186,199] The court of appeals sustained exclusion of a Kingdom Hall from a residential area. It also dismissed charges of bias as unproven. The court said that it would "presume the validity and good faith of official acts". The decision was refused review in the Supreme Court of the United States.

*Miami Beach, Florida.*[189,198] Refusal of a permit to construct the Greater Miami Beach Hebrew Academy in a residential area was sustained upon the authority of the 1955 Lutheran case.[124]

1959.

*Lawrence, New York.*[191] A lower court reversed the action of the zoning board which had refused a permit to construct the Brandeis Jewish School in a residential area. With obvious reluctance, the court followed the lead of the court of appeals in the Brighton decision.[149]

*Creve Coeur, Missouri.*[192] The attempt of this middle class suburb of St. Louis to exclude a Jewish temple was invalidated. While the decision of the supreme court discussed constitutional principles at length, its basic ruling was that the state law did not authorize the zoning of land for church purposes at all.

*Tustin Heights, California.*[193,202] The court of appeals sustained exclusion of a Catholic church and school from a residential area in which public schools were permitted by state law. This decision, which was refused review by the Supreme Court of California, seems to limit the effect of the Piedmont decision [115,125] wherein the court had condemned the exclusion of a parochial school from "practically" the entire city.

*Menlo Park, California.*[194] The court of appeals reversed Menlo Park's refusal of a permit for a Kingdom Hall. The only ground assigned by the board was noncompliance with parking requirements. The court held that there was no substantial proof of such noncompliance.

*Clarkstown, New York.*[195,210,213] This decision required issuance of a permit to the Roman Catholic Missionaries of Mary for a refuge for small children. The court found it improper to forbid the use of property for the care of little children while permitting its use for the raising of little sheep and goats. The decision was affirmed by the court of appeals.

*Pueblo, Colorado.*[196] A Baptist church, erected earlier under proper permit, had added a large, bright, neon sign which the zoning commission ordered removed. The court set the order aside and said that the sign was a use that was "customary and incidental" to the original permit.

*Lake Geneva, Wisconsin.*[201] The Covenant Harbor Bible Camp at this place was using as sleeping quarters an old residence and several small cottages. The residence burned down. City officials opposed either its restoration or the construction of new cottages to replace it. The court held that the property could be restored, basing its decision on a very lenient interpretation of an ordinance forbidding reconstruction of nonconforming property destroyed to the extent of more than 50% of its value.

*Garden Grove, California.*[217] The refusal of a permit for a Kingdom Hall was sustained by the court. The dispute concerned whether there was compliance with the off-street parking requirements. There being "evidence both ways," the court sustained the action of the city.

1959-60.

*Allendale, New Jersey.*[205,219] The refusal of a permit for a Kingdom Hall was based on the alleged insufficiency of the Witnesses' provision for off-street parking. The ordinance required such parking space as would be "sufficient." When the Witnesses filed their application, this was changed to specify one space for each three seats, which is more than the Witnesses had. In spite of its suddenness, the court held that the change would be "presumed to have been done in good faith and for the public good". The decision in favor of the city was refused review by the Supreme Court of the United States.

1960.

*Philadelphia, Pennsylvania.*[216] The court angrily rejected a suit of nearby landowners to nullify a permit already issued to a Lettish Baptist church on the ground that it was issued while an amendment was pending in the city council (later adopted) that would have made its issuance illegal.

*San Marino, California.*[223,224] The court enjoined the Roman Catholic archbishop from using for parking a lot next to his church which had been used (illegally) for that purpose for years. The court also refused to order a new permit for such use, in face of the archbishop's contention that similar permits had been granted to shopping centers and other churches. The decision was refused review in the United States Supreme Court.

1960-1.

*Cazenovia, New York.*[218,234,236] The court interpreted an ordinance which authorized permits for "churches or similar places of worship," also for "parochial schools," for "rectories," and for "convents" so as to authorize what the zoning board called a "conference center" of the Episcopal archdiocese on a 36 acre estate.

1961.

*Montclair, New Jersey.*[228] The court sustained a zoning board permit for a parochial school at Lorraine Avenue and Park Street. The decision said that the authority of the case of the Catholic female seminary at Morris Township [128] had been "nullified."

*Meridian Hills, Indiana.*[229] The court held that the zoning board could not properly exclude a Catholic church, school, etc. even though residents of the area offered to acquire property for it in another nearby place. A Protestant church and a Jewish synagogue had been authorized nearby.

*Bayside, Wisconsin.*[231] The same court that had permitted exclusion of a Lutheran school from Wauwatosa [106] nullified the action of Bayside, another Milwaukee suburb, in refusing to zone a Baptist congregation's site so that it could be used as a church. The court was badly divided. Three justices held for the Baptists on the basis of one opinion. Three others held in their favor for entirely different reasons. A seventh judge was against them.

*Englewood, Colorado.*[233] The court condemned Englewood's exclusion of an Apostolic Christian church from a residence zone as an unconstitutional attempt to effect the "blanket exclusion of churches from single and double-family residence districts."

1962.

*Long Beach, New York.*[239] The zoning board of appeals granted variances to an established Jewish temple, including relaxation of the setback requirements, in order to permit expansion. Objectors' allegations that the temple had failed to prove "hardship" as required by the ordinance were overruled in the light of the "special status" of churches.

*Morris Plains Borough, New Jersey.*[241] The appellate division of the Superior Court of New Jersey reversed the action of the zoning board refusing a permit for a religious school of a Lutheran church. The decision was based on a statute, adopted while the case was on appeal, forbidding discrimination between public and private nonprofit schools.

*Modesto, California.*[245] The court sustained refusal of a permit for a Jehovah's Witnesses' Kingdom Hall, overruling contentions that the ordinance contained inadequate standards, that the Witnesses were unfairly discriminated against, and that their religious liberty was violated.

*Chicago, Illinois.*[246] The supreme court overruled the action of a board of appeals in refusing a permit for a storefront Jehovah's Witnesses' Kingdom Hall in a busy section of Chicago. It minimized the "break in the continuity of the line of small businesses" on the street, saying that such continuity would "likewise be interrupted by a dance hall, crematory, mausoleum or trade school, all uses permitted in this . . . district."

*Darien, Connecticut.*[247] In an advisory opinion, the supreme court of errors held that it was not a violation of the due process clause to discriminate between public and parochial schools by requiring the latter to obtain a special permit for establishment in a residential zone.

1963

*Montclair, New Jersey.*[248] Under a state law forbidding discrimination in favor of public schools, a Superior Court held invalid with respect to a parochial school a regulation fixing minimum play space.

# CHAPTER 1.

## GENERAL AND HISTORICAL

This subject is part of a broader one in which religion, politics and the law overlap. Al Smith's campaign for the Presidency in 1924 and 1928 evoked some rather unsavory public discussions of religio-political problems. There followed almost three decades of public reticence on the subject. This was caused by diffidence and embarrassment arising from the acrimony of the Smith campaigns and also from the direct efforts to soft pedal such discussion exerted by influential interdenominational peace-making groups like the National Conference of Christians and Jews.

This restraint had the advantage of avoiding arguments. But it had the disadvantage of postponing the solution of important problems. Perhaps it aggravated such problems. During the Kennedy-Nixon campaign of 1960, however, much of the embarassment of the Smith campaigns was dissipated. For this, thanks are due to President John F. Kennedy himself. He faced religio-political problems squarely. In fact he raised them himself. He wanted them to be discussed publicly in a fair, intelligent way. The campaign accomplished this to a considerable extent.

After Kennedy's election, religio-political and religio-legal debate was promptly revived by (a) the demands of public educators and their supporters for federal subsidies to public elementary schools and (b) the insistence of the Catholic hierarchy that some form of financial aid be given to its parochial schools. The discussion of this issue probably will continue for some time. Indirectly, it also involves financial aid that has been given in the past to Protestant and Catholic and Jewish religious hospitals and colleges, to all churches in the form of tax exemptions, assistance to foreign missions through free distribution of government-owned surplus commodities, etc., etc.

Most of the religio-political issues discussed during and after the campaign concern the propriety of financial aid to

1

religion. In my opinion, however, there are other questions in the field which have not been given enough attention and therefore have been permitted to fester. Some may be more important in the long run than the problem of financial aid. One of them is government regulation of the religious use of land, with which this book is concerned.

Inattention to this question may result from the fact that our journalists have developed a bad cold in their nose for news. To them front page attention seems warranted if some missionary is excluded from an out-of-the-way African or Asian land. Yet they relegate to the obscurity of the religious or real estate pages the news that Jehovah's Witnesses—or perhaps the Jews, or even some mainline Christian denomination—have been refused a permit to build in the same city where the newspaper is published.

When the government appropriates money for a religious purpose, people in general are being forced to support a faith not of their own choosing. The religio-political problem is then obvious. But observers seldom see the connection between the action of a local zoning board and the principle of separation of church and state. It can be understood better if we compare our own country with those in which such separation does not exist. Thus control over the Orthodox Church by the government of the Soviet Union is maintained not so much by giving or withholding money as by governmental control over the religious use of land and buildings. Likewise in Spain and Italy the discrimination against unofficial religions is effected mostly by building regulations which forbid new churches but permit the old ones of the official religion. There may be less difference than appears on the surface between government control of religious use of land and buildings and actual government ownership thereof.

How many Americans know that local officials in this country, like local officials in Spain and Russia, may control religious uses of land? Porter R. Chandler, appearing in the Brighton, New York, Catholic church and school case,[149] told the court of appeals that: "A practice whereby local administrative bodies are given a veto power over the establishment of houses of worship and schools and are empowered to pick and choose among denominational applicants runs counter to all established custom in this field, is fraught with the gravest dangers, and should not be encouraged." To what extent can this veto power be used to "establish" a single church or perhaps two or three in a particular town to the exclusion of others? Can it be used to advance atheism? On the other hand, to what extent are the claimed rights and prerogatives and the political influence of churches used to disrupt the proper functioning of government officials in connection with the community plan? To what extent is religious use of land properly subject to regulation under the zoning laws? These are important questions which I will now attempt to answer.

In America and England, land use regulation is older than the common law. In the earliest times, the police power of the state was used to protect home neighborhoods from obnoxious enterprises such as saloons, gambling houses and houses of prostitution. Later, the right to "abate a public nuisance" was used, as Canon Anson Phelps Stokes points out in his *Church and State in the United States*,[75] to exclude "certain types of business that might be demoralizing or annoying to worshippers, such as liquor saloons, fire engine houses, garages" from zones around each church. Stokes calls this arrangement a favor to religion and compares it to the aid provided by church tax exemption.

I have no doubt that church leaders endorsed these zoning laws—not then so-called—which protected the peace and quiet of their institutions. I would not be surprised if clergymen were the originators of such arrangements. They probably never dreamt that under modern zoning laws, on the basis of the same theory, churches themselves might be excluded from home neighborhoods in order to secure peace, quiet and other advantages. Yet in 1955, speaking at a conference of the American Society of Planning Officials, Rev. Walter Kloetzli, Jr., Secretary of Urban Church Planning of the National Lutheran Council said: [114] "Planners have frankly admitted to me that churches are sometimes considered 'public nuisances.' At least they complicate the problem. Some of the impressions about churches are that they devaluate property, they are a threat to public safety because of the increased traffic, and they are an intrusion on privacy. Attitudes such as these provide the undertone in which church planning is considered."

Preachers who were pleased at the closing down of saloons might turn in their graves if they were now informed, for instance, that

(a) In 1947 the Supreme Court of Michigan [60] ordered dispersal of a camp meeting of the Full Salvation Union on the outskirts of Portage on the ground that it was a public nuisance, the decision being refused review by the Supreme Court of the United States.[63,65]

(b) In 1953 on the same theory the Supreme Court of Texas [102] sustained refusal of a permit to the famous evangelist, Rev. Jack Coe, to build an evangelistic center at Dallas.

(c) In 1960 the Court of Appeals of California invoked the law of nuisance and the local zoning law to enjoin continued operation by the Catholic archbishop of parking facilities that he had maintained for many years next to his church in San Marino.[223] This decision also was refused review by the Supreme Court of the United States.[224]

(d) In 1951, a New Jersey court enjoined as a nuisance the operation of Eastern Christian Institute, a Protestant seminary on South Center Street at Orange.[86] This decision was later affirmed by the supreme court of the state.[92,99] The judge who tried the case said that "anything that unduly interferes with the exercise of a common right may be declared a nuisance and rendered abatable. . . ." The common right, he said, was "that the entire zone continue as a place for the erection and use of one family houses." He added that the "school and dormitory unduly interfere with the exercise of that right." [86:33]

(e) In 1961, according to the *Baptist and Reflector*,[237] bar owners in Oakland, California, protested the establishment of a church in their block. They won. "It's no place for a church," the bar owners complained. In the block were two bars, two liquor stores and a pool hall. One of the deacons said, "We want to put God right on the main street." One of the owners of a bar which was separated only by a wall from the proposed church hall objected, saying, "We wouldn't appreciate their message, and they wouldn't appreciate ours. The juke box would drown out the sermon."

Nuisance, like spit, seems to be a nasty word, and is seldom applied to churches as such. Yet every zoning decision by a board or a court is based on theories analogous to the law of nuisance. Such decisions often prevent construction of churches or enjoin their operation without government license.

The preceding statements should not create the false impression that in my opinion the public regulation of religious land use is an unmitigated evil. On the contrary, it is a necessity in our crowded and busy age. In certain neighborhoods, some types of churches and church activities undoubtedly partake of the nature of public nuisances. I mean this not in the same sense in which one would refer to a really disorderly "disorderly house". However, it is true to an extent that under the law can justify the refusal of church building or use permits.

Neither do I see zoning and planning officials uniformly in the role of villains and church representatives uniformly as heroes. To the contrary, in some cases, churchmen have sought permits for buildings at locations in which they did not properly belong. On occasion, they have sought to conduct in home neighborhoods religio-social and religio-commercial activities that belong in nonresidential areas. No doubt they have even sometimes abused the dignity of their calling and the sanctity of their function by invoking religious claims to attain results that are contrary to the public interest. Obviously, church zoning cases have at least two sides. This is why, in my opinion, the subject deserves book-length treatment.

In a recent issue of the *University of Pittsburgh Law Review*,[230] writing about *Church Zoning in Pennsylvania*, Richard D. Klaber said:

> Zoning is interesting because it affects large groups of people who become more than mildly interested in the particular controversy at hand. As contrasted with the average lawsuit involving two or three parties, a zoning problem usually involves at least a neighborhood, perhaps a municipality, and possibly even a geographical area. Furthermore, a zoning problem usually affects the persons involved in two sensitive areas, with a result comparable to waving a red flag in front of a bull. The areas affected are constitutional rights and the pocketbook.
>
> When the zoning problem involves a church or synagogue, the

problem is compounded. Added to the potpourri of usual questions of deprivation of property without due process, equal protection and the balancing of individual rights against the benefit of the community, is the question of the First Amendment guaranty of freedom of religion. Perhaps an accusation of bigotry or prejudice will be thrown in for added tang.

Religious support for land use regulation antedates the era when saloons were barred from the vicinity of churches. In his recent prize-winning book, *The City in History*,[226] Lewis Mumford describes how the origin of villages was found in the establishment by pagan priests of shrines and their "sacred precincts". Later, these gathering places had significance as instruments of defense by one tribe against others.

They were walled for the protection of supplies and in anticipation of siege. Thus the place was zoned off from the surrounding countryside for religious and military purposes. It could be said, I suppose, that the law of the times zoned the surrounding countryside for purposes of agriculture, etc. After the city became important as a reservoir of labor, new interior walls were constructed. In Athens eventually the Acropolis became the zone restricted to religious and military uses, the balance of the city, presumably, being zoned for residential, industrial and general uses.

Thomas More is a saint of the Catholic Church because, after serving as Lord Chancellor to Henry VIII, he gave his life in defense of papal authority. In 1516 More wrote *Utopia*,[3] which may be the first book on city planning. Thomas R. Hughes in *Towns and Town Planning*[15] calls More the "greatest of the humanists" and says that his book was the "ultimate parent of all books on town planning and kindred subjects. His visionary city was perhaps first suggested by what he had seen in Bruges and Antwerp, the most progressive cities of the age."

An early American city plan was initiated by William Penn when he founded Philadelphia as a Quaker religious project. After that there were many religious utopias in America, including the one at Zion, Illinois, which was later involved in litigation.[13] (See pages 187-91.) However, until well into the twentieth century, most of the secular-inspired cities grew up in unplanned squalor. No one could build or rent a house with any certainty that a factory would not be built next door. At least this was true of the ordinary citizen. Millionaires could make restrictive covenants with their neighbors to keep out what they considered undesirable uses and undesirable people. Multimillionaires could insulate their mansions with private parks. But the ordinary citizen was largely unprotected.

After the great immigration of the Nineties, which intensified the overcrowding of city land with tenement houses, political and religious leaders began to support the idea of municipal land use regulation under the police power. There had been no laws effectively limiting the height of slum buildings or the number of people that they might accommodate, or requiring any percentage of the land to be left unoccupied by structures. This was condemned by Rev. William Patterson, Secretary of Philadelphia's Protestant Commission on Social Service in 1914 with reference to a version of cities' origins less secular than Mumford's. He spoke to a meeting of city officials interested in planning that met in that city of William Penn. He referred [9:41] to the slums and tenements as "instruments of death and destruction" and said that they were "much more effective than the bludgeon used by Cain, who, incidentally, was the first man to found a city."

Dr. Patterson referred to testimony before a New York commission that "the greatest social evil was not direct prostitution but 'accidental prostitution' indicating that thousands of children are reared where purity is impossible." He continued:

> . . . [T]he city, originally devised by one whose hands were stained with the blood of his brother, produces one of the most modern instruments of death. And, strange as it may seem, it is only within recent years that our perception has enabled us to place the noisome tenement on the same plane with the bludgeon and poisoned dagger. . . . [T]he religious bodies of America are beginning to manifest a keener appreciation of the necessity of proper housing.
>
> The aim of all true religion is the establishment of the kingdom of God, the coming of which is the great comprehensive ideal of the church. This kingdom we believe to be not only an individual good but also a social state. The ideal city, which is to be ushered in with this final consummation, is typified in the new Jerusalem,

a holy city, a spacious city, and, in the blueprints which we have, in this city of God, we locate its very antithesis to the city which obtains in all parts of the world today. In the new description of the new Jerusalem there is no suggestion whatever of crowded quarters, of the congestion of people, or of insanitation.

At another annual meeting Rev. Dr. Newell Dwight Hillis, minister of the Plymouth Church in Brooklyn, expanded Patterson's concept of public welfare to include more than basic comforts. He said: [8:206] "We have got to the Art Age. It is not enough that things are useful, convenient, economical; they must be beautiful in addition to being useful and convenient. The next steps in American citizenship must be these, the streets that are beautiful, the houses that are beautiful, the life that is beautiful."

Neither Patterson nor Hillis spoke of churches in the same breath with tenement houses. They were not properly comparable. Then as now, church buildings were usually surrounded by ample space. Worship activities, to which people usually walked from their homes, were deemed entirely suitable in residential areas, even though industrial plants and businesses were excluded.

The speakers could not anticipate the present day when Sunday morning at church can mean a conflux of hundreds of automobiles from miles away and a congregation of thousands of people. This is also a day when churches engage in more activities than the worship of God. The house of God may include a great school, clubrooms, meeting places, ballrooms and social centers, as well as sporting and athletic facilities.

Edward M. Bassett had shared the naivete of these speakers on the problem of church zoning. He was a principal author of the first modern zoning ordinance, enacted by the city of New York two years after Patterson's speech. In 1936, Bassett wrote a book called *Zoning* about those days [36:70,200] in which he said:

When, in 1916, the framers of the Greater New York building zone resolution were discussing what buildings and uses should be excluded from residential districts, it did not occur to them that there was the remotest possibility that churches, schools and hospitals could properly be excluded from any districts. They concluded that these concomitants of civilized life had a proper place in the best and most open localities. . . .

Practically all zoning ordinances allow churches in all residence districts. It would be unreasonable to force them into business districts where there is noise and where land values are high. Some people claim that the numerous churchgoers crowd the streets, that their automobiles line the curbs, and that the music and preaching disturb the neighbors. Communities that are too sensitive to welcome churches should protect themselves by private restrictions.

Bassett might have suggested in addition that such "sensitive" people could build vast private parks around their houses, surrounded by high iron fences. Such alternatives were not available to the ordinary citizen.

The attitude of the New York City commission of 1916 seems to have been shared by courts, and even by zoning boards, for approximately 30 years. So far as reported cases indicate, it was that long before the courts got around to permitting the exclusion of churches in any case. Like the New York Building Commission, they felt that such zoning out of churches was very improper, but they shied away from the question of its legal validity.

As late as 1952, *St. John's Law Review* [95:97] could say that "the state tribunals have generally permitted charitable institutions to establish themselves in residential areas in contravention of existing zoning laws, while at the same time avoiding the issue of their constitutionality." In some cases, the article continued, "the means employed for avoiding this delicate constitutional problem are open to reproach. . . . It is noteworthy that this attitude of forbearance adopted by these courts, although evasive on the constitutional issue, did nevertheless extricate the church from the prohibition of the zoning regulations."

It was not until 1949 in the Porterville, California, Mormon church case [67,71,76] that any court squarely decided that land use regulation could be fully effective with respect to churches. In the intervening period, however, as shown in the chronological list that precedes this chapter, there were a few church zoning cases properly so called in the published reports. Generally they bespoke the extreme reluctance of the courts to permit interference with religious land use. I will mention a few examples.

At Portland, Oregon, in 1932 [27] and at Winnetka, Illinois, in 1939 [34] local Roman Catholic bishops obtained court orders requiring issuance of parochial school permits. The first of these decisions contained a vehement denunciation of the attempt to prevent construction of the school. However the decision was actually based on a technical defect in the ordinances, which contained an undue delegation of legislative power.

The Winnetka case was decided in favor of the bishop, not because it was illegal to ban a religious school as such but because the city permitted public schools in the same area from which it sought to exclude parochial schools. The court "failed to perceive" any significant difference between the two types of institution. During the same year, the Nevada court required issuance of a permit for a Catholic church in Reno.[35] The principal ground of exclusion discussed was the noise and disturbance caused by church funerals. The court overruled this contention because it saw them as no more disturbing than home funerals, which were permitted by the ordinance.

In 1942, the Supreme Court of Ohio issued its decision in the case of the Lutheran church at Upper Arlington,[40] often called a landmark case. Unlike the Reno and Winnetka cases, the decision covered many phases of church zoning law. Justice Alfred Bettman, formerly a city attorney concerned with zoning problems, displayed a wide acquaintance with the subject. He expressed, among other things, a "doubt" that churches could be constitutionally excluded from any area.

However, the actual decision in the Upper Arlington case was less significant than either of the two 1939 cases. The court's ruling was based on certain representations made by zoning officials to the church. From these representations the church concluded that a specified lot would be suitable for the project and bought it. As a result, the court held that the church could not properly be excluded. Most of Justice Bettman's observations were not necessary to the decision and therefore not binding as precedent. However, the Upper Arlington case has been cited by other courts more extensively than any other decision.

The Upper Arlington decision cited [40:521] among other things the statement quoted above from Mr. Bassett's book.[36] The statement was quoted again the following year in the Sherman, Texas, Church of God case [49:416] in which the zoning board was forced against its will to issue a permit to another Church of God. The Bassett dictum has been quoted over and over again in subsequent cases, down to and including 1961.

For instance, this passage in Mr. Bassett's book is also cited or quoted in the Mesa, Arizona, Catholic church case,[53] in a dissenting opinion in the Cleveland Heights, Ohio, Jewish case,[59:245] in the Chicago Episcopal church case,[93:920] in the South Euclid, Ohio, synagogue case,[140:179] in the Brighton, New York, Catholic church case,[149:834] in the Creve Coeur, Missouri, Jewish synagogue case,[192:455] in the Meridian Hills, Indiana, Catholic church case,[229:72] and in the Bayside, Wisconsin, Baptist church case.[231:301n.8] The last two cases were decided in 1961.

The fact that courts rely so extensively upon this now-hackneyed quotation indicates how flimsy are their decisions. Bassett would have been amazed if informed that his words would be used to support the decisions of the highest courts of the land. Bassett was a learned man, but this particular writing of his has no authority as legal precedent. Neither did Bassett intend any such result. He was not arguing or discussing a point of law but merely describing the policy views of certain planning officials who met together in the year 1916.

It would have been poor strategy at that time, when zoning legislation was untested in the courts, aggressively to exclude churches from residential zones. Nor did the circumstances of the times justify such exclusion. However, Bassett was long associated with city planners and he must have had sufficient imagination to understand that conditions in 1964 and 1965 might differ from those of 1916.

During 1945, the Supreme Court of Arizona issued a significant decision in the case of a Catholic church at Mesa.[53] There the ordinance permitted the raising of pigs and other such activities in the area. The court refused to permit exclusion of the church. During the next year, the Indianapolis

Methodist case [57] was decided in favor of the church. Constitutional issues did not arise directly but the court decided on the basis of statutory interpretation. It held that when the ordinance authorized a church it also authorized a playground, gymnasium, recreation building and outside amphitheater.

In 1947, the same Supreme Court of Ohio that had decided in favor of the Lutherans [40] sustained the exclusion of a Jewish school by the City of Cleveland Heights.[59,61] This brings us down to the year 1949 and the decision in the case of the Porterville, California, Mormon church. The court firmly held that the exclusion of churches from residential zones is constitutional and valid. This decision was refused review first in the Supreme Court of California [67] and then in the Supreme Court of the United States.[71,76]

Of course the decision was not binding on courts of other states but it represented a turning point in the history of church zoning litigation. It was the end of an era which *St. John's Law Review* [95] had called one of "forbearance" on constitutional issues and the beginning of a decade or more of lively controversy about the control of religious land use by local government.

Meanwhile, there had been some overall changes in the national scene which may have had the effect, first, of increasing the number of cases filed and, second, of increasing the number decided against churches. These changes were of at least two kinds, namely: (a) the increased use of private automobiles, and (b) the church building boom, accentuated by the "flight to the suburbs".

An example of how this change affected church zoning law is found at Milwaukie, Clackamas County, Oregon. Jehovah's Witnesses sought a permit for a Kingdom Hall. The permit was finally refused by the state supreme court in 1958. This was the same court which in 1930 had vehemently upheld the right to build a parochial school at a busy traffic intersection. In the 1958 case, the court said: [184:16,18]

> . . . [T]he impact of changing conditions upon the application of zoning ordinances and the need for flexibility require that we give close heed to the particular and controlling circumstances present in each earlier case cited and relied upon by the [congregation].

It does not follow that conditions which impelled or justified certain conclusions respecting the allowance of applications five, ten, fifteen or more years ago would result in the same holding if made today concerning the same locations in the light of currently changed conditions. This is especially true in the earlier cases where and when traffic conditions, traffic congestion and its incident dangers and annoyances were dispatched as having no validity as a reason for denying applying churches the right to build in residential areas.

Such are the impacts resulting from our rapidly changing economy, community concepts, increasing populations. All of these newer conditions are intensified, in large measure, by a drift of people from rural to urban communities, with the migrations of great numbers from one established geographical area to others far distant, leaving some towns and villages much smaller and enlarging the size of others, and leaving all with new governmental and social problems to meet, particularly in the area of transportation.

Beginning with 1940, Oregon has, in a lesser yet very noticeable way, felt the effect of such residential changes by migration, as well as by normal population growth. The federal census shows a population growth in the State of Oregon of approximately 40% from 1940 to 1950, whereas the increase in the City of Milwaukie for the same period was 180%. This knowledge gives emphasis to the oft-repeated judicial observation that every zoning case must be evaluated in terms of the particular circumstances then and there attendant.

[p. 18] . . . We take judicial notice of the extraordinary expansion in motor vehicle traffic in the State of Oregon and County of Clackamas, wherein Milwaukie is its second largest population center. From 1946, the year of the adoption of [the ordinance] to 1953, the year [the congregation] made its application to build, the registration of motor vehicles in Oregon increased 62.5%. During the same seven year period, the increase of those owned in Clackamas County was 51%. Certainly these rapid increases in population previously referred to, and these substantial increases in motor registration give emphasis to the danger of relying too heavily on the factual presentation of any earlier zoning case, be it from Oregon or other jurisdictions.

The legal conclusions of the Oregon court were based on these changes, especially with respect to traffic and transportation. Other rulings based on this factor will be discussed in Chapter 10. At this point I will go on to show how the problem of church zoning was intensified by the church building boom.

The figures for private "New Construction Put in Place" tabulated in the Construction Review of the United States Department of Commerce give a clear picture of the scope of this boom. In 1937, the year that the Winnetka school [34] and the Reno church [35] were being planned, the total "religious construction activity" in the United States amounted to 44 million dollars. By 1945, at the end of World War II, the figure had sunk to 26 million. But in 1946, after the War, it rose to 76 million, then in 1947 to 126 million, in 1948 to 251 million and in 1949 to 360 million. This was a tenfold increase between 1937 and 1949, the year when the California court decided that religious land use could be regulated even to the point of excluding churches.[67]

In the years after the Porterville decision, the religious construction figures were, successively, 409 million, 452 million, 399 million, 472 million, 593 million, 734 million, 768 million, 868 million, 863 million and 947 million. In 1960 the total of religious construction exceeded a billion dollars! The value of such construction had risen 38 fold from its low point during the War.

The private construction figures for 1961 show more being spent in the religious classification than for educational buildings, and more than for hospital and institutional buildings. The religious figures are larger than those for telephone and telegraph, and three times as great as for railroads. They are more than a third as much as for industrial and more than half as much as for farm buildings! The figures for "religious construction" do not include construction of church schools. My guess is that this figure, if it were separately available, would greatly increase the religious total. So would the expense of furnishings, which are not included in the above amounts and is estimated to be half as much as the cost of the buildings themselves.

These figures should impress my reader that in a certain sense church construction is "big business" and that the subject here under discussion has economic importance. As the number of new churches increased after 1949, so did the number of church zoning cases. There also ensued a heightened realization on the part of judges of the need for redefining the relative rights of churches and municipalities with respect to the control of religious land use. The efforts of the courts to clarify this relationship are described in the chapters which follow.

# CHAPTER 2.

## The Police Power and the Constitution

Urban land use planning in its present detailed and refined form is a comparatively new legal and political concept. During the last thirty or forty years, however, it has spread throughout the country. An urban householder today is usually conscious of the fact that his lot and that of his neighbor is "zoned for" certain uses and "zoned against" certain others.

If the land is in a "good neighborhood," it is probably zoned *for* one- and two-family residences and perhaps also for multiple apartment buildings. It is probably zoned *against* factories, stores, cabarets and drinking places, and other enterprises that might disturb the quiet enjoyment of homes and lower their value. For the same reason, a man's property may be zoned against use as a church if the courts of the state permit such regulation of religious land use.

In addition to flatly forbidding certain uses in particular neighborhoods, zoning laws often contain limitations on certain uses of land. In some cases, a particular type of enterprise is permitted only if certain conditions are met. For instance in most neighborhoods buildings of all kinds are required to be set back from the lot lines so that the land will not be overcrowded. The total number of people that may occupy a fixed amount of floor space is limited. For buildings where people assemble, ordinances often require off-street parking space.

Because we experience the advantages of zoning laws every day we gradually come to take them for granted. Because the disadvantages affect us seldom if at all we do not realize that they involve limitations on liberty. The general philosophy of the zoning laws in my opinion tends more directly toward that of the socialistic "welfare state" than do the schemes for industrial control that worried conservatives during the Great Depression.

Many are distressed about whether the government is going to "take over" control of the railroads, the banks and the

16

utilities when in fact such an eventuality would affect our daily lives comparatively little. Yet we fail to notice that the members of the local zoning board, whose names perhaps we don't even know, can exert control through land use regulations directly over one of the most important necessities of our lives—our homes.

When Rev. Newell Dwight Hillis [8] and Rev. William B. Patterson [9] addressed the National Conference on City Planning as quoted on pages 7-8 above, advocating land use regulation for the improvement of the slums, they might not have realized the awesomeness of the governmental power that they were calling down. While our government may differ in important respects from the communist, fascist, and other dictatorships, for good or for evil, it holds the same enormous power.

We know, for instance, that the power to tax can properly be called the power to destroy. We know about the government's power to condemn our land, paying us only the market value, with nothing for the inconvenience caused. Under the government's defense powers we know that it can put ordinary unoffending citizens under restraint, subject to the commands of military officers. Most relevant to our present subject is the "police power," under which the zoning laws are enacted and under which citizens may be forbidden to use their land in certain ways under pain of fine or imprisonment.

There is some misconception about the nature of the police power. The ordinary citizen is inclined to think of it as seldom affecting him personally. Alfred Bettman, former city solicitor of Cincinnati, clarified this point at a meeting of planning officials in Kansas City in 1917. Bettman is the same lawyer who a quarter-century later was a justice of the Supreme Court of Ohio. He wrote the opinion in the Upper Arlington Lutheran case [40] putting severe restraints on the police power. But at the 1917 planners' conference he was inclined to maximize rather than to minimize the proper scope of his clients' power. In his address,[10] Mr. Bettman said:

> The layman may . . . be puzzled by the constant use of the expression "police power": He may associate the word with the blue uniform and club, with the customary administration of public safety through the police court, with the arrest of the offender in

the midst of his offence, or the abatement of the noise or odor in the midst of its offense.

In truth, however, the police power is the whole field of governmental control of persons and property for the promotion of the common welfare; or perhaps, more strictly speaking, it is the whole field of governmental control, after taking out certain and special narrower species of governmental activity such as taxation and eminent domain which have names of their own. Every mode of government control over persons or property which does not fall within these technical and special provinces falls within the expression, "the police power."

"Police" is simply another variant of the old Greek "polis" and is twin brother to "politics" and "policy." It is the power to promote, guard, or regulate public health, public safety, public comfort, public prosperity, public welfare. In the language of Professor Freund, in his book on police power [*The Police Power, Public Policy and Constitutional Rights* [6:5]] "it has for its object the improvement of social and economic conditions affecting the community at large and collectively."

The scope of the police power is not limited therefore to the exercise of the particular modes or methods of the past. The mere fact that building heights were not restricted in the past does not prove that the restriction of building heights is not within the scope of the police power. The police power expands with the need of expansion. In the oft-quoted language of Mr. Justice Holmes of the Supreme Court of the United States,[7:111] "In general, police power extends to all great public needs. It may be put forth in aid of what is sanctioned by usage or held by the prevailing morality or strong and preponderant opinion to be greatly and immediately necessary to the public welfare."

Nor must we allow ourselves to conceive of the police power as engaging solely in the suppression of that which is immediately and palpably offensive or dangerous. The police power generally acts by means of restraint, but the restraint is simply the method or instrumentality, not the test of the scope of the power. The end of governmental action, whether police power or any other power, is the promotion of public welfare. The end is positive even though the form of action may be the negative one of restraint.

An iron foundry next to my residence may make such noise as to disturb the comfort and impair the comfort of myself and family. The most conservative interpreter of the Constitution will agree that the government has power to supress so immediate and obvious a nuisance. This suppression is for the purpose of promoting the health and comfort of myself and family.

By zoning the city and providing a street system corresponding to the districts adopted, the noisy industries are kept away from the immediate neighborhood of the home and the noisy classes of street traffic largely diverted from the residence district. This zoning, then, is obviously simply another example or method of this same suppression of unwholesome noise. (The promotion of public health is, of course, not the sole object of zoning. The promotion of safety and comfort by keeping heavy traffic off the streets of residence districts, the promotion of common prosperity by stabilizing and protecting property values and reducing the difficulties and expense of municipal administration and the promotion of community welfare in many other respects are within the purposes of zoning.)

A little more imagination may be required to realize this relationship between the health of the community and the unregulated location of commercial and industrial structures than to realize the relationship between the health of my family and the foundry next door but the two relationships, as well as the governmental function involved, are fundamentally identical. Constitutions do not prohibit the exercise of imagination in the process of governing. Constitutions are sufficiently elastic to permit the modern prophylactic treatment of social diseases and evils.

In 1917, Bettman obviously possessed "a little more imagination" than in 1942 when he wrote the Upper Arlington decision.[40] At neither time, however, did he look with favor on the exclusion of churches from residential zones.

If the police power does not authorize a particular regulation of religious uses, then it is because of the limitations imposed by the constitution upon its exercise. The principal limitations involved in zoning cases are:

A. The due process clause of the Fifth and Fourteenth Amendments

B. The equal protection clause of the Fourteenth Amendment, and

C. The religious liberty clause of the First Amendment.

Offhand one would expect church zoning cases to involve mainly the limitation last mentioned. For reasons which will appear in the body of this treatise, however, that clause is seldom invoked. The church usually relies instead on its right to due process of law. It is usually invoked for protection of property rather than personal rights.

The source of the limitations above mentioned is the *federal* constitution. Yet in church zoning cases they are invoked principally against *state* governments or against their instrumentalities, the cities or counties. The reason is that for most purposes the police power, under which land use is ordinarily regulated, resides in the states rather than in the federal government.

The federal constitution is a grant of enumerated powers. The federal government has no power not expressed or implied in that document. State constitutions, on the other hand, serve principally to limit the "inherent" powers of government which reside in the states. If you want to know what powers the federal government has, you must first consult the constitution. If you want to know what powers the state has, you must know what are the "natural" and traditional powers of government, then consult the state constitution to determine to what extent they are limited. One of the traditionally inherent powers of governments is the police power. This includes the authority in the public interest to regulate the use of land for religious and other purposes. In certain very limited situations, as on federally-owned lands, the government of the United States has such power. But ordinarily it is exercised by the states.

In the beginning, federal constitutional limitations applied only to the federal government and not to the states. For example, a number of the original colonies had established state churches which were not abolished by the federal constitution. Instead, they were abolished later, by state constitutional amendments.

The Fourteenth Amendment, adopted after the Civil War, is interpreted by the courts as providing due process, equal protection, and religious liberty also as against the state governments. The state constitutions also contain due process, equal protection and religious liberty provisions, usually modeled on those of the federal charter. Before analyzing the effect of these limitations on the power to regulate the religious use of land, let us briefly outline their general scope. Terms like "due process", "equal protection", and even "religious liberty" are not self-defining.

The Fifth Amendment says that "No person shall be deprived of life, liberty, or property without due process of law." The Fourteenth Amendment likewise provides that no state shall "deprive any person of life, liberty, or property without due process of law." This provision evokes the spirit of our English Common Law ancestors. A similar principle had been adopted in the Magna Charta [2] in 1215 when it forbade the imprisonment of any of the subjects of the king except by "the lawful judgment of his peers or by the law of the land."

The term "due process of law" has often been called the exact equivalent of the phrase, "law of the land," as used in the Magna Charta. It protects us from arbitrary action by government. It forbids the government to jail us, to drive us from our land, to take our money or property except by law. Such law must be in pursuance of proper powers of government (for example the police power). The police power, in turn, can be exercised by the government only, as Bettman said,[10] "to promote, guard, or regulate, public health, public safety, public comfort, public prosperity, public welfare." The Supreme Court of the United States has said that: [22:183]

> The governmental power to intervene by zoning regulations with the general rights of the landowner by restricting the character of his use is not unlimited and, other questions aside, such restriction cannot be imposed if it does not bear a substantial relation to the public health, safety, morals, or general welfare.

This is the test applied in most zoning cases, including those of churches: Is the regulation reasonably calculated to advance a substantial public purpose?

"Equal protection" is another limitation on the power to regulate religious or other use of land. It is based on the fundamental generalization contained in the Declaration of Independence as to the equality of all men. It is sometimes said that "due process" includes equal protection. At any rate, under the Fourteenth Amendment, no state may "deny to any person within its jurisdiction the Equal Protection of the Laws." This requires that all persons similarly situated be treated alike. It is a protection against unfair discrimination. In religious zoning cases, the question is whether the challenged regulation unfairly or unduly discriminates against a church and in favor of another church or some secular enterprise.

Religious liberty is the last of the three possible constitutional grounds of attack. It will be noted that the rights protected under the Fifth and Fourteenth Amendments include not only property and life but also "liberty." Religious rights are also guaranteed by implication in that clause of the First Amendment which protects freedom of speech, press and assembly. But more specifically the First Amendment provides that "Congress shall make no law respecting an establishment of religion or prohibiting the free exercise thereof." Since adoption of the Fourteenth Amendment, the courts hold that this restriction also applies fully to the states.

As interpreted by the courts, it not only prohibits any undue interference with religious expression but also, as stated by Justice Black in the Everson case,[58:15] it means that "neither a state nor the Federal Government can pass laws which aid one religion, aid all religions, or prefer one religion over another." Thus, the question that should be asked in church zoning cases is mainly whether the regulation places an undue limitation on the right to worship, the right to express religious ideas, or the right to assemble or organize for religious purposes. On rare occasions it may also be asked whether a particular regulation constitutes improper "aid" to one religion or to religion in general.

Restated very briefly, then, the principal questions to be asked are:

(a) Is the particular regulation *reasonably calculated* to serve a *substantial* public purpose?

(b) Does the regulation, or its enforcement *unduly* discriminate against the church and in favor of other property owners *similarly* situated?

(c) Does the regulation *unduly* interfere with religious liberty?

Note that the words above italicized are very general and abstract. It is quite possible for them to be applied in a particular case in accordance with the personal predilections of the judge. However, the generality or vagueness of these standards is also important to their effectiveness. This is because each of the rights guaranteed by the constitution must be subject to such limitations as are necessary to protect other rights guaranteed by the document. While the government must not, in the exercise of its police power, deprive a citizen or corporation of liberty or property, neither should an individual or corporation be permitted to impinge unduly on the rights of others.

The extremely general questions above stated are the ones to which the judges in church zoning cases have principally addressed themselves.

# CHAPTER 3.

## ABSOLUTISM IN CHURCH ZONING LAW

People seek absolutes to govern their lives and affairs because it saves them the time and effort required for thinking things through. Often what they want is peace and certainty, yet absolutisms like communism and fascism have ultimately brought to the world not peace but more turmoil and confusion.

I don't want to overemphasize, or offend anyone, but I do see a certain similarity between these vicious political absolutisms and the positions taken by many lawyers, writers and a few judges on church zoning. I don't ascribe malice to them. I know they are inspired by their own view of the public interest. But I believe they are grievously mistaken.

Church zoning absolutists are not divided into leftists and rightists as in the political world. They might more aptly be called "absolute pro-exclusionists" and "absolute anti-exclusionists." One side says that absolutely no church can be excluded from any residential zone; the other says that absolutely all churches may be excluded. The absolute anti-exclusionists, by the way, seem to make no distinction as to whether a church is excluded:

(a) in an unqualified way as by an ordinance which merely states that, in a certain zone, churches shall not be allowed, or

(b) in a qualified way as by an ordinance which provides that churches may be built in an area only if they comply with certain conditions or come within certain standards.

Both sides oversimplify. They are thinking in terms quite inconsistent with the spirit of our constitution. The emphasis in that document is on individual rights. Individuality always presupposes individual differences. This calls for more emphasis on a case-by-case treatment and less emphasis on absolute rules, either proregulation or antiregulation.

The constitution forbids government regulation of church land use if it is an undue interference with property rights,

24

for instance if it is not justified by a substantial public purpose; or if it discriminates unfairly against the church; or if it interferes unduly with the religious liberty of the church or its members. Using words like undue, substantial, unfair, one cannot arrive at an absolute rule either for or against church land use regulation. In this field as in the field of politics, absolutism creates not certainty but more confusion.

The following is a good restatement of the conflicting positions taken from Mr. Rathkopf's standard work on zoning law.[132:19-2,19-4] He says:

> The majority view takes the form of an unequivocal statement that churches may not be excluded from a residential district. *A fortiori,* a church may not be wholly excluded from within the borders of a community.
>
> The minority view is that churches are subject to zoning ordinances in the same manner and to the same extent as other uses and that if the inclusion of churches in residential districts does not fit a comprehensive plan established by the ordinances they may validly be prohibited therein as other uses legislatively found incompatible are excluded therefrom.

Mr. Rathkopf thus summarizes the *theoretical* views of many writers and some judges. I am happy to say that these extreme views have generally been kept on a theoretical plane. In almost no cases have they governed the actual decision. I am reminded of that small retail dealer who was asked during World War II what he thought of various burdensome government regulations. "They're awful," he said, "perfectly awful. And they would be even worse if I paid any attention to them."

But these absolutist rules are in my opinion "awful" even if the judges don't pay much attention to them. They are repeated over and over again in court decisions. They distract attention from the real issues and they give the whole subject of church zoning rather a fairyland quality. It is fortunate both for the churches and for city planners that neither the absolute anti-exclusion nor the absolute pro-exclusion rule is actually enforced. If they were, there would be no more call for lawsuits, for briefs, for arguments, for articles, or for books like mine than there were for free elections in Hitler Germany.

The balance of this chapter is devoted to disproving these "absolutist" theories and will be important to those familiar with the jurisprudence. Others may wish to devote less attention to this chapter and more to the chapters that follow, where I discuss what to me are sounder principles of church zoning law.

The absolute anti-exclusion theory probably had its inception from the chance paragraphs inserted by E. M. Bassett in the Russell Sage Foundation book [36] that I have quoted on pages 8-9. Bassett said that it "did not occur" to the 1916 planners to exclude churches from any zones. But, as I have said before, he was a forward-looking man. Therefore, I doubt that he was much surprised at the manner in which, six years later, planners at Euclid, Ohio, drafted that city's ordinance. I am sure that they discussed "what buildings and uses should be excluded from residential districts," as the 1916 planners had. But unlike the New York framers, it *did* occur to them to exclude churches. That is just what they did. They excluded them from two residential districts, one set aside for single-family houses and the other for such houses, plus apartment buildings.

The ordinance came before the Supreme Court of the United States in the Euclid, Ohio, zoning case [18] which later became known as the "cornerstone of modern land use zoning." The court did not pass directly on the validity of the sections excluding churches. But it did note their existence. If the exclusion of churches from residential districts was as evil as the New York City planners of 1916 thought, the Supreme Court of the United States certainly passed up an ideal opportunity to say so.*

In spite of this early record, there has been what almost seems like a campaign of learned articles to convince lawyers and the courts that any exclusion of churches from a residen-

---

* Furthermore, in 1956, an ordinance exactly similar to that of Euclid was tested by the Court of Appeals of Ohio in the South Euclid Jewish case.[140] The court held that an exception should have been made for the particular synagogue. But it took note of the exclusionary clauses and again missed an opportunity to condemn them as such.

tial area is *ipso facto* invalid. Some of the articles, it must be said, accept the rule rather than espousing it, but I have not found a single article which directly challenges it.

The following is a series of quotations from law review and encyclopedia articles which espouse, accept, or tolerate the anti-exclusion rule in one form or another. In the footnote * I have listed the church zoning cases that each article cites in support of the statement quoted. At the end of the series of quotations, beginning on page 30, I will examine each of said cases to determine to what extent they support the rule, if at all.

A. *Mississippi Law Journal*, May 1951: [84] "The courts generally agree that it is an unlawful use of the police power to bar schools, churches, or other eleemosynary institutions from residential districts because it is an unreasonable and arbitrary use of the police power and is unrelated to the health, safety, and general welfare of the public or constitutes a deprivation of property without due process of law."

B. *St. John's Law Review*, December 1952: [95:98] "A zoning ordinance, the practical effect of which is to exclude churches from the residential district, though permitting them in other parts of the community, is the type most commonly presented to the courts. The majority of those jurisdictions which have passed directly on the constitutionality of such ordinances have held them to be unconstitutional for the reason that the exclusion of a church bears no substantial relation to the public health, safety, morals or general welfare. The policy of excluding churches from residential areas though allowing them in business areas was rejected by an Ohio court as being violative of the due process clause of the state and federal constitutions. . . . The second type ordinance, less frequently

---

* Following is a list of the church zoning cases relied on (either expressly or by reference to the writings of others) in each of the articles above discussed. The article is designated by the same letter as the paragraph in the text above in which it is quoted. The cases are designated by the number that they bear in the Table of References of this book: (A) 27, 34, 49; (B) 35, 40, 49, 53, 87, 93, 94; (C) 14, 35, 40; (D) 27, 83, 107; (E) 14, 35, 40; (F) 35, 40; (G) 14, 35, 40; (H) 40, 48, 53, 83, 93; (I) 49, 53, 87, 94; (J) 35, 40, 53, 59, 62, 83, 87, 93, 94, 101, 104, 136, 148, 149; (K) 19, 27; (L) 35, 49, 53, 87; (M) 14, 25, 35, 40, 48, 49, 53, 56, 60, 81, 85, 93, 99, 101, 104, 136, 140, 148, 149, 150, 165, 171, 184, 192, 218; (N) 34, 35, 40, 49, 53, 56, 83, 87, 94, 105, 125, 136, 140, 148, 149, 165; (O) 53; (P) 87, 94; (Q) 14, 40, 99, 184; (R) 35, 87, 104, 192. See also References Nos. 235, 240, 243.

considered judicially, prohibits the erection of churches anywhere in the entire community. The courts have been unanimous in declaring this type of ordinance invalid."

C. *Michigan Law Review*, March 1955: [116:748] "With the
exception of three cases, . . . there is unanimous accord that
churches may not be excluded from residential zones. Little or
no attention is given to possible congestion, traffic hazards,
etc."

D. *St. Louis University Law Journal*, Spring 1955: [118:266]
"Courts have said that even though provisions requiring
off-street parking facilities are a valid exercise of the police
power of a municipality, the enforcement of such provisions to
prohibit building of a church is unconstitutional. The logic of
the courts in holding this to be unconstitutional is that the
application of such ordinance is arbitrary."

E. *UCLA Law Review*, April 1956: [141:390] "With the exception of . . . two cases, there is apparently unanimous
accord that churches may not be excluded from residential
areas."

F. *Minnesota Law Review*, June 1956: [144:863] ". . . [Z]on-
ing ordinances are unconstitutional when they exclude . . .
churches. . . ."

G. *Catholic Lawyer*, July 1956: [147:246] "Prior to the Porterville decision, the cases were in accord that churches could not
be excluded from residential zones, with little attention being
given to possible congestion or traffic hazards."

H. *California Law Review*, October 1956: [152:777] "In most
jurisdictions where an opinion has been expressed on the
subject, the concept prevails that churches and schools, being
concomitants of the home, may not be constitutionally prohibited in residential areas by zoning."

I. *Michigan Law Review*, February 1957: [158:601] "The clearest case of invalidity is the zoning ordinance provision which
totally excludes churches from residential areas."

J. *Brooklyn Law Review*, April 1957: [161:186] "The overwhelming weight of judicial authority in the United States
holds that the complete exclusion of churches from residential
districts by zoning regulation is an arbitrary and invalid exercise of the police power. Especially is this so where other
nonresidence uses are permitted in such districts."

K. *Notre Dame Lawyer*, August 1957: [166:628] ". . . [C]hurches may not be barred from residential zones."

L. *St. John's Law Review*, May 1958: [177:321] "[A] zoning ordinance may not wholly exclude a church or synagogue from any residential district."

M. Annotation: "Zoning Regulations as Affecting Churches", *American Law Reports:* [185:377] "General Rule that Churches Cannot be Absolutely Excluded from Residential Areas: Statement and Rationale of Rule."

N. *Villanova Law Review*, Summer 1959: [203:606] "In *Village of Euclid v. Ambler Realty Co.*[18] the supreme court . . . first declared zoning laws constitutional but it has never ruled upon their validity when they prohibit churches in residential districts. State courts, however, generally hold restrictions on the location of churches invalid. . . . Such decisions are usually not based on freedom of religion as applied to the states under the Fourteenth Amendment but rather on deprivation of property without due process of law or denial of equal protection or the statute is so construed as to permit the use."

O. *Intramural Law Review of New York University School of Law*, March 1960: [221:194] "That an ordinance totally excluding churches from residential neighborhoods is invalid has been clearly resolved."

P. *Corpus Juris Secundum:* [31:773] "It has been held that it is not a valid exercise of the zoning power to prohibit legitimate use of property anywhere within the limits of a municipality so that a zoning ordinance which excludes churches and schools from the entire municipality is invalid."

Q. *American Jurisprudence* [32§125] "A church may not, either as a matter of administrative application or enforcement of a neutrally worded enactment, validly be excluded from residential areas as an absolute and invariable rule."

R. *Catholic Lawyer*, Spring 1961: [232:151] "According to the weight of authority, churches cannot be totally excluded by a zoning ordinance from a municipality or any of its residential districts. Consequently, ordinances which either by their very terms exclude all churches, or which by their operation would cause the exclusion of a church, have been held invalid per se as applied to the particular church in controversy.

If I have chosen the above quotations from various learned writings, I do not mean to suggest that such are the only sources of views like these. Indeed, I could quote scores of similar expressions from the decisions of judges and perhaps hundreds from briefs of lawyers in church zoning cases. I will not tire my reader with any more of them. Instead, I will proceed to examine the cases cited by various of the articles above quoted and give my own views as to whether and to what extent they support the anti-exclusion rule.

1. The earliest of the church zoning cases cited in any of the articles above quoted is the 1922 Omaha, Nebraska, Presbyterian case.[14] It is mentioned by the *American Jurisprudence* article on zoning [32] which also happens to rely on the Upper Arlington, Ohio, Lutheran case.[40] In the Omaha case, the church suit was based on two points. One was the alleged invalidity of the setback requirements of the ordinance. The other was the alleged illegality of the action of the administrative officials in making their decision contingent upon the consent of the church's neighbors.

These points will be discussed fully (Chapters 6 and 20). Of importance here is the fact that the church sued, not in its capacity as a church, but in its capacity as a private landowner, the same as any other landowner. This was pointed out in the Ohio decision in which Justice Bettman said [40:522] that the Omaha case "did not turn on the fact that the proposed building was a church rather than any other type of structure."

The precedent established in this case had no effect on the churches that it did not have with equal force as to all other property owners. The case does not support the absolute anti-exclusion rule.

2. According to *The Notre Dame Lawyer* article,[166:27] the Episcopal seminary case at Evanston, Illinois,[19,23] held that churches could not be barred from residential zones. Actually, it was not a church that was attempted to be barred in the Evanston case but a college (because of a dispute regarding inclusion of a dormitory). It is true that the court held unconstitutional an amendment that would have barred the church college. However, the decision was based not on the fact that the college was religious but on the fact that it had relied in

good faith on the unamended ordinance. Therefore the amendment was held unconstitutional not in general but only with respect to a specific piece of property owned by the Episcopalians.[19:783] The case does not support the article's conclusion.

3. *The American Law Reports* annotation,[185:377] as quoted in paragraph M, above, cites the 1930 case of the Beckley, West Virginia, Church of God.[25] There the question was only whether the city council ever intended to exclude churches. The ordinance provided for exclusion from the neighborhood of any "garage, filling station, store or other industry." The court held that churches were not covered by any of these designations. The court clearly excluded consideration of the issue with respect to which the annotation cites it. The court said: [25:877] "Whether a city has constitutional authority, under legislative permission, to exclude churches from residential sections, we are clearly of the opinion that the zoning ordinance under consideration does not do so. . . ."

4. The Portland, Oregon, Catholic school case of 1932 [27] is cited in the *St. Louis University Law Journal* article [118:265] for a point with respect to off-street parking space. This problem was not even remotely referred to. The Portland case is also mentioned in *The Notre Dame Lawyer* article [166] as holding "that churches may not be barred from residential zones." It was not a church but a school that was concerned in the Portland case. The ordinance did purport to bar any "educational, religious, philanthropic, fraternal or other institutional use" which was not approved by a percentage of neighbors or voluntarily selected by the council. As set forth on pages 295-6, the court held that these consent clauses were unconstitutional. The decision does not support the absolute anti-exclusion rule.

5. The *Villanova Law Review* article [203:606] cites the 1939 Winnetka Catholic case [34] as holding "restrictions on the location of churches invalid." This was another school case. The exclusion was held invalid, not as such but because public schools were specifically permitted and because there was no showing of any distinction on the basis of which the separate classification of private schools might be justified. The absolute anti-exclusion theory was not involved in the case.

6. The Reno, Nevada, Catholic church case of 1939 [35] is

cited in several of the articles above quoted. Thus in the *Minnesota Law Review* article [144] the case is cited for the proposition that: "[Z]oning ordinances are unconstitutional when they exclude . . . churches."

The court in the Reno case was extraordinarily careful not to establish *any* general rule. It said [35:222] that "it is to be borne in mind that we do not hold the [provisions of the ordinance] invalid in their general scope or aspects, but only as to the building of the proposed church in the residential district of Reno." The principal discussion was on the question whether funerals were more "depressive" when conducted in a church than when conducted at home. (See pages 112-13.) This was the only proposed justification for the ordinance that the court discussed. The implication was that if the exclusion had been justified it could have been upheld. This is the opposite of the anti-exclusion rule.

7. In the Upper Arlington, Ohio, Lutheran case of 1942 [40] the court had reason to suspect that without admitting it the authorities were trying to exclude churches from the entire suburb. It said: [40:520] "We seriously question the constitutionality of any enactment that seeks flatly to prohibit the erection of churches in residential districts." However the next sentence said that: "We believe that under a proper and natural construction of the language of the ordinance here involved this question does not arise."

But immediately, the absolutists went to work. This decision was published in full in Volume 138 of *American Law Reports*.[41] Following it there appeared a brief, anonymous annotation entitled *Zoning Regulations Affecting Churches*. It said that "the court indicated obiter its belief that any flat exclusion of churches from residential districts would be unconstitutional." This annotation was later cited in several of the articles above quoted. An article in the *University of Detroit Law Journal* [121:436] used the same language but changed "would" to "could." Actually the court in the Upper Arlington case, did not "indicate" anything about the question of absolute anti-exclusion. It only raised a "question" about the matter. Then it said that the issue "did not arise." It clearly refrained from passing on the problem.

About five years later, the same court had an opportunity to say what it actually did believe on this issue when it was asked to review a decision of the zoning board of Cleveland Heights excluding a Jewish religious school from a single-family residence district. The belief there expressed was that such exclusion was proper.[59] Articles endorsing the absolute anti-exclusion theory practically all cite the Upper Arlington case. None of them mention what the same court said in the Cleveland Heights case. In fact only one of the articles above quoted, the one in the *Brooklyn Law Review* [161:186] even mentions the later decision. In the Cleveland Heights case,[59:244] the court said with regard to the Upper Arlington decision that "reduced to its lowest terms, the decision in that case was based upon the extremely important and unusual fact that the [church] had been misled by the zoning and village commissions of the Village of Upper Arlington."

8. The case of the Church of God at Sherman, Texas [48,49] is cited for instance in the *Michigan Law Review* [158:601] for the statement that "the clearest case of invalidity is the zoning ordinance provision which totally excludes churches from residential areas." It was impossible in this case for the court actually to establish a binding precedent to this effect. The reason was that the attorney for the city had waived the point, admitting instead that the ordinance was invalid.[48:103]

The anti-exclusion articles rely on a statement by the Texas court that was irrelevant and therefore not binding as precedent. The court said [49:417] that "to exclude churches from residential districts does not promote the health, the safety, the morals or the general welfare of the community, and to relegate them to business and manufacturing districts would conceivably result in imposing a burden upon the free right to worship and, in some instances, in prohibiting altogether the exercise of that right. An ordinance fraught with that danger will not be enforced."

Because it was irrelevant to the result this passage has validity as literature only and not as law. I pause, however, for a point that may need clarification. It matters not at all to a church whether it is kept out of an area unconditionally or "flatly" (on the one hand) or whether (on the other hand) it is excluded indirectly because conditions are imposed upon its admission which it cannot or will not meet.

In the Sherman case such conditions were imposed by the ordinance. It required, as a condition to all permits, compliance with certain "building, fire, sanitary and health laws." This seems to have been the only issue raised by the city. And on this point it was victorious. The judgment was that the church "should be allowed to comply with such requirements . . . being thereby entitled to the permit requested. Otherwise, and in the event of noncompliance the provisions of article 1011h F.A.C.S. would thereupon become available to the City of Sherman." [48:103]

If the Church of God did not comply with these regulations, it would never get its permit. In that case it would be "absolutely excluded" from the residential area. And if it did comply in the beginning, but later ceased to comply, the opinion indicates [48:100] that an injunction could be obtained to put it out of operation again. In that case, it would again be "absolutely excluded" from the residential area.

While the absolute anti-exclusionist articles all contend that a "flat" exclusion is a violation of constitutional rights, fewer of them seem to contend seriously that an indirect exclusion of churches is invalid. Is there any fundamental difference between the two types of exclusion?

9. The Mesa, Arizona, Catholic church case of 1945 [53] is cited for instance in the *Intramural Law Review* article [221:194] to support a statement which reads as follows: "That an ordinance totally excluding churches from residential neighborhoods is invalid has been clearly resolved." In the Mesa case, the ordinance did exclude churches from a residential zone. The ordinance was held unconstitutional. But what the article does not mention is that the zone from which churches were excluded was not itself purely residential.

Also authorized in that zone were schools, colleges, public libraries, public museums, art galleries, parks, swimming pools (municipal or private), athletic fields, polo fields, golf courses, farms, truck gardens, and greenhouses (provided no fertilizer was stored within fifty feet of the lot line). What especially sparked the interest of the court was that the owner of property in the residence district could maintain there not only his family, but also horses, cows and swine. The exclusion was held unconstitutional not because it was total but because it was discriminatory.

10. The Montgomery, Alabama, Pentecostal church case of 1946 [56] is cited in two of the articles quoted above. There, as in the Beckley, West Virginia, case [25] the question was not whether the city council could exclude churches from a residential zone but whether it ever intended to do so. The Montgomery City Council's ordinance provided for exclusion from such zones of any "store, filling station, automobile laundry, garage, or any other type of building to be used for commercial purposes." The court held that this language did not cover a church, which seems obvious. The case does not support the anti-exclusion rule.

11. The *American Law Reports* annotation [185] as quoted in paragraph M above, also cites the Full Salvation Union case at Portage, Michigan.[60] This case involved not a church but a camp meeting. The court held it was a nuisance and would have to go. Certainly this was a case of exclusion, and does not support the rule of anti-exclusion for which it is cited.

12. The Indianapolis, Indiana, Catholic church and school case of 1948 [62] is cited in the *Brooklyn Law Review* article,[161:186] as quoted in paragraph J above, as part of the "overwhelming weight of judicial authority in the United States" which "holds that the complete exclusion of churches from residential districts by zoning regulations is an arbitrary and invalid exercise of the police power." This case decided only that when the city council authorized "churches" its intent was broad enough to include a priests' mansion, convent, school, off-street parking, etc. Since the ordinance did not attempt to exclude churches, the court had no reason to decide, and did not decide, whether it would be in excess of the city's power to do so.

13. The *UCLA Law Review* article [141:390] says that "with the exception of Corporation v. Porterville . . . there is apparently unanimous accord that churches may not be excluded from residential areas." The *Catholic Lawyer* article [147:245] makes a similar statement. Actually, it seems that the Porterville Mormon church case of 1949 [67] was the first case in which this issue was fairly presented and fully decided. This determination was directly contrary to what these writers call an "unanimous accord."

In Porterville, there was a clarification of the issues because the area from which churches were "absolutely" excluded was purely residential. The Mormon bishop helped clarify them by refusing to present any evidence. He must have relied on the annotation [41] which misinterpreted the Upper Arlington, Ohio, Lutheran church case.[40] (See pages 32-3.) The California court refused to hold the ordinance unconstitutional "on its face." It held that the bishop, not the city, had the burden of proof. It also took judicial notice of certain aspects of church activities that have an adverse effect on the community, the abatement of which justify exclusion from a residential area. The court held the exclusion valid.

This is a good occasion for me to make clear that I disagree not only with any absolute anti-exclusion rule but also with any absolute pro-exclusion rule. There must and will be exceptions to any such rule. There are or could be houses of worship that no city could properly exclude from residential areas, whatever ordinance might be enacted. Such churches would bear a surprising resemblance to the houses of worship of the First Century, A.D.

In the Chico, California, Baptist case,[88] where the defendants were enjoined from "carrying on or conducting a church or church functions in or upon the premises" at a certain address, one of the defendants tried to convince the court that the city was trying to "regulate when and where a man may pray." The court took a different view of the facts and, also for technical reasons, dismissed the appeal and sustained the injunction. However, it seems to me very questionable whether even a permit may be required for a mere prayer meeting in a person's home which does not have any adverse effects on the neighborhood. (See page 221.)

14. The Pittsburgh, Pennsylvania, Catholic retreat house case of 1950 [81] is cited in the *American Law Reports* annotation.[185:377] There the city had granted a permit for conversion of a mansion into a church. This change was completed. Then later a permit was sought for conversion of a stable into sleeping quarters. It was to this permit that the neighbors objected. The court sustained the permit. By its ringing language it indicated that it would have insisted on issuance of almost any permit that the religious order might ask. This is obviously a strong case for the absolute anti-exclusion rule. However, its authority is subject to two qualifications. The first is that the decision was issued by a

lower court, the court of common pleas. Therefore, the decision is binding as precedent—if at all—only on the judges of that court. It does not bind other courts of Pennsylvania, let alone the courts of other states. Secondly, this case is no longer an outstanding precedent because the Supreme Court of Pennsylvania displayed an opposite attitude in the later case of the Russian Orthodox church cemetery at Ambridge.[207]

15. The 1950 case of the Tampa, Florida, Jehovah's Witnesses [83] is cited for the absolute anti-exclusion theory in several of the articles quoted. For instance the *California Law Review* article [152:777] cites it for the proposition that "churches and schools, being concomitants of the home, may not be constitutionally prohibited in residential areas by zoning." It is true that in the Tampa decision the court referred to churches as "concomitants of the home." However this premise led to no such conclusion as the one stated in the article. The principal issue in the case was whether or not the Witnesses had complied with the parking lot requirement.

The court held [83:80] that the "provisions of the ordinance were substantially complied with" and therefore required issuance of the permit. Presumably if the Witnesses had not complied they could have been excluded. This case does not support the absolute anti-exclusion theory but by implication negates it. In later cases, the courts of Florida have actually approved exclusion from residential zones of churches which fail to meet the standards or conditions laid down in the ordinance. This occurred in the Miami Lutheran case,[124] the Miami Jewish case,[189,198] and in the Tampa Advent Christian church case.[160]

16. The *American Law Reports* article,[185:377] also cites the Dover, Massachusetts, Catholic school case [85] of 1951 under the "general rule that churches cannot be absolutely excluded, etc." There is nothing general about the rule on which the decision in this case is based. Massachusetts, unlike any other state, has enacted the absolute anti-exclusion theory into statutory law.

The statute provided that "no bylaw or ordinance which prohibits or limits the use of land for any church or other religious purpose or which prohibits or limits the use of land for any religious, sectarian or denominational educational purpose shall be valid." The only issue in the case was whether ordinances were rendered invalid even though they had been adopted prior to the time the law took effect. The Supreme Judicial Court of Massachusetts properly held that they were.

17. Those articles which cite the Plandome, New York, Unitarian church case of 1951 [87] as forbidding exclusion of churches from whole municipalities are correct. Those which cite it as condemning such exclusion from individual zones are mistaken.

For instance, the *St. John's Law Review* article of 1958 [177] refers to this case as supporting the principle that "a zoning ordinance may not wholly exclude a church or synagogue from any residential district." The Plandome, New York, ordinance was like the one enforced against the Mormons of Porterville [67] in that churches were completely excluded without provision for exceptions or special permits. It was unlike Porterville in that (a) the residential area included the entire village and (b) the area was not exclusively residential. In Plandome the ordinance permitted not only residences but also "village and municipal buildings, public schools, clubhouses, railroad stations and postoffices."

This case is obviously a strong one on the side of those absolute anti-exclusionists if any who limit the application of their theory to cases in which churches are excluded from entire cities. However, this principle is not endorsed "unanimously" as claimed by the *St. John's* article.[95] At the time this article was written, this "unanimity" consisted only of this case, plus the Orchard Lake, Michigan Catholic church and school case.[94]

Aside from the substantiality of the public purpose under the due process clause it appears to me that in practically every case such total exclusion from an entire municipality would constitute an undue interference not only with freedom of worship but also with freedom of assembly. People should be able to provide themselves with reasonably convenient access to places of worship of their particular denomination. The only question is whether the courts are correct in relying on artificial municipal boundaries as an index to such accessibility.

It matters little to a churchgoer (or to a parochial school

parent) whether he or his child has to cross an imaginary boundary line on his way to school or church. The important question is how far they must travel. As time goes on, and as governments are rationalized, municipalities within metropolitan complexes will more and more merge their governmental functions. Then perhaps it will be possible to fix the limits of zones functionally and with less regard to historic subdivisions. This question is discussed again in Chapter 15 which deals with religions rights under the Constitution.

18. Several absolute anti-exclusionists also cite the Chicago Episcopalian case of 1952.[93] The Chicago ordinance provided that churches could be constructed only on lots that were completely surrounded by streets or alleys. The Episcopalian lot was surrounded on two sides by streets. As to the other two sides, the Episcopalians "made" alleys of their own, dedicating strips of their own land to the public as such. The court held only that this was a valid dedication and a compliance with the ordinance.

The court did say that any other decision "might well exclude churches" and that then the validity of the ordinance would become "questionable." This position is identical with that adopted by the Ohio court in the Upper Arlington case.[40] It expressed a doubt, not an opinion. The issue of exclusion was not involved. The judge made clear that he was not passing on it.

19. The Orchard Lake Roman Catholic case of 1952 [94] is cited in five of the articles above quoted. For instance, the *Villanova Law Review* article [203] says that "state courts . . . generally hold restrictions on the location of churches invalid," citing the Orchard Lake decision as precedent. In that case, it is true that, in the light of Michigan's peculiar constitutional provisions about religion, the court held invalid the exclusion of a church. But this was no ordinary restriction. It was an exclusion from 90% of the area of the entire city! The court held that in effect this constituted exclusion of the church from the entire municipality. This decision sustains the anti-exclusion rule but only as related to entire municipalities.

20. The Orange Township, New Jersey, Protestant seminary case [99] is cited in the *American Law Reports* annotation [185] and in *American Jurisprudence*.[32§125] The ordinance

in this case did exclude a religious institution, namely a Protestant seminary, from the residential area. The exclusion was sustained, not nullified. If the case proves anything, it is the opposite of the proposition for which it is cited.

21. The Beachwood, Ohio, Jewish case of 1953 [101] is cited in two of the articles. The Beachwood ordinance did exclude all churches from residential areas excepting those which, as found by the zoning board, would "substantially serve the public convenience and welfare" and "not substantially and permanently injure the appropriate use of neighboring property." The principal objection to the temple was that its membership was in excess of the total population of the town while very few of the members lived in Beachwood.

In spite of this the court held that the temple would serve the "public convenience and welfare," laying emphasis on the needs of the entire metropolitan area. It said, in effect, that an exception should have been made in favor of the particular applicant. It did not hold the ban on churches generally invalid.

22. The 1954 case of Jehovah's Witnesses at Decatur, Indiana,[104] is cited by only two of the articles quoted. This is a little surprising since this case is the most emphatic of the decisions espousing the absolute anti-exclusion rule. The court said that: "The law is well settled that the building of a church may not be prohibited in a residential district." It cited various cases, all of which have been covered in the preceding analysis.

It was then faced with the problem whether to enforce (a) off-street parking requirements and (b) setback requirements. The court refused to enforce the first, but did enforce the second. In order to comply, the Witnesses had to cut four feet off the front of their church which, as planned, was sixty feet deep. Thus the court refused to exclude an entire church from the district but did "exclude" the front $\frac{1}{15}$ of the proposed building. Other inconsistencies in this decision will be mentioned in other parts of this treatise.

23. The 1954 case [105] of the Jewish congregation at Melrose Park, Pennsylvania, is cited in the *Villanova Law Review* article [203:606] as quoted in paragraph N above. This ordinance excluded churches unless specifically authorized. There was

already a religious school in operation on the premises. The Jewish people wanted a permit to use the building also as a synagogue. They agreed to conform to parking lot requirements. The case had nothing to do with the validity of the exclusory feature of the ordinance. The only issue was whether the use proposed conformed to the ordinance.

The principal objection seemed to be to various disturbances, particularly the repeated playing of *Rudolph the Red-Nosed Reindeer* by children of the school. This would presumably not be affected one way or the other by the proposed additional use, and the objection was overruled.

24. The Irondequoit, New York, Jewish case of 1954 [107] is cited in the *St. Louis University Law Review* article [118:265] quoted in paragraph D above, for the proposition that "the enforcement of parking requirements to prohibit the building of a church is unconstitutional." The case held no such thing, but only that such requirements had not been authorized by the town board. The implication was clear that if they had been authorized they would have been enforced.

The ordinance authorized imposition of conditions as to size of lot, setback lines, height of buildings, etc. The board of zoning appeals attempted to tack on an additional basis of exclusion, namely inadequate parking space. The court did not hold the ordinance unconstitutional. It decided only that the zoning board could not add to its terms by requiring parking facilities.

25. Surprisingly, the Piedmont, California, Catholic school case of 1955 [115,125] is not cited in many of the articles above mentioned. Yet it contains strong arguments for the theory that religious institutions may not be excluded totally or almost totally from a municipality. Here, parochial schools were excluded from 98.7% of the total area of the village. The court invalidated the ordinance as applied to a Catholic school.

The court relied in part on the case of the Society of Sisters [17] in which the Supreme Court of the United States had upheld the right of parents to send their children to private schools against an attempt by Oregon to exclude all such schools from the state. The California court seems to have extended the scope of this parental right. It said [125:441] that parents have a right to send their children to such schools "in their immediate neighborhood." This may be a bit extreme. The better test might be "reasonable accessibility of alternative sites."

As in the Plandome Unitarian church case,[87] so also in the Piedmont case, the area from which the religious institutions were excluded was not solely residential. There were three elementary schools, one junior high school, and one high school, all public. It was on the grounds of the existence of these other nonresidential uses that the court distinguished the Piedmont case from the Porterville case [67] in which the nondiscriminatory exclusion of all churches had been upheld.

I have also discovered that there were private businesses in Piedmont that the court might have mentioned, including a drugstore, grocery store, service station and real estate office. Although, as stated, this decision has language which supports the anti-municipality-wide-exclusion rule, yet, as shown on pages 176-81, it is extremely cloudy both as to issues and as to principles of decision.

26. Three of the articles above quoted also cite the Haltom City, Texas, Jehovah's Witnesses case of 1956. There the zoning ordinance [136:703] forbade construction of churches excepting those that would "not materially injure neighboring property for residential use." It required that all churches provide one parking space for each six seats. No issue was raised as to the constitutionality of the exclusory provisions. The only question was whether the particular church had complied with the conditions laid down in the ordinance.

The principal objection seems to have been that the church's lot was too small. The court said [136:704] that "no claim is made that the size of the lot materially injures the neighboring property." It held not that the exclusory feature of the ordinance was void but that the church had complied with the conditions for admission.

In the course of the decision, the court did volunteer the following irrelevant remark:

> Since a city cannot legally exclude a church from a residential district it cannot legally accomplish the same result by denying permits. . . .

This would have been the absolute anti-exclusion theory in its most extreme—and only logical—form. The whole provision would have had to be annulled. However, the court did not stop there. The entire statement reads:

> Since a city cannot legally exclude a church from a residential district, it cannot legally accomplish the same result by denying permits *unless the reasons for refusing the permits are based on valid evidence showing that to permit a church would be detrimental to the health, safety, morals or the general welfare of the community.*

It seems to me that the portion of the above quotation that I have italicized nullifies the portion which precedes it. If, in order to be valid, the refusal is required only to advance the public welfare, etc., then the standards are no more severe in church cases than in others. At any rate, the court's dictum is of little value as precedent (a) because it did not control the outcome of the case and (b) because it is self-contradictory.

27. In the South Euclid, Ohio, Jewish synagogue case of 1956,[140] also cited in some of the articles quoted above, the ordinance did exclude churches from several residential sections. It was in the same terms as the ordinance of the City of Euclid that had been sustained by the Supreme Court of the United States in 1923.[18]

The Ohio court did not hold these exclusions invalid. It held only that, in the circumstances, an exception or variance should have been granted as authorized by the ordinance. After the synagogue application was filed, the land on which it was to be located was abruptly changed in classification from "U-2" to "U-1". U-2 was for apartment houses and U-1 was for single-family residences. Churches were made conditional uses in both areas but the pressure against them was naturally greater in the single-family zone. The change in classification must have seemed like an attempt to put the applicant at a disadvantage.

In addition, after the application was filed, the zoning board suddenly raised its parking space requirements from one space for each ten seats to one space for each four seats. The court granted the relief asked. However, it did not decide that the section banning churches from residential zones was invalid as to other cases.

28. The Brighton, New York, Catholic case [149] and the Sands Point Jewish case [148] are cited in four of the articles quoted above. It is true that in this case the zoning board action refusing the permit was overruled by the court. This was for a variety of reasons. The court said [149:837] that "[U] nder the facts presented by this record, the decisions of the planning board . . . should be annulled." But, in the sentence next following, the court disavows any intention generally to forbid exclusion of churches. It says: "That is not to say that . . . under no circumstances may they [churches, schools, etc.] ever be excluded from designated areas." In the light of this statement, it is hard to see how the absolute anti-exclusionists can take comfort from this decision.

In the Sands Point case, [148] the permit was refused on the ground that some of the purposes for which the community sought to use the land were not "strictly religious" as required by the ordinance. The court overruled this decision but its judgment was based more on statutory than constitutional considerations. In addition, the judge who wrote the Sands Point decision actually instructed the city to comply with the provisions of the ordinance which required off-street parking arrangements. If the synagogue had failed or refused to comply with the board's specifications in this respect, it would, presumably, have been absolutely excluded from the area. Thus, the Sands Point decision seems to challenge rather than to support the absolute anti-exclusion theory.

Michael Scharff's article [221] in the *Intramural Law Review of New York University Law School*, says that in view of the attitude of the court in the Brighton and Sands Point cases, it "does seem difficult to imagine any situation where the court would sustain such exclusion." With this I agree, but I further agree with Scharff when he says that "no specific declaration has come forth" to the effect that such exclusions are violations of constitutional rights.

29. The Garden City, New York, Jewish case of 1956 [150,154] is also cited in the *American Law Reports* annotation, [185:377] under the general rule that churches cannot be absolutely excluded from residential areas. It is true that in this case the zoning board denied a permit and that its action was reversed by the court (a trial court from which no appeal was taken).

However, in returning the matter to the zoning officials for further action the court stipulated that the permit should be issued "upon such proper administrative conditions as the board deems reasonable and necessary." The court itself imposed conditions restricting use of the building to the first floor thereof, prohibiting nonreligious gatherings, forbidding parking on the streets, etc. If these conditions were not complied with, then the house of worship would have been effectively "excluded from the residential area." This case hardly supports any absolute anti-exclusion rule.

30. The Wenatchee, Oregon, Jehovah's Witnesses case [165] of 1957 is likewise cited by articles quoted above although it likewise fails to support the absolute anti-exclusion rule; to the contrary, it actually negates it.

The ordinance in the Wenatchee case did exclude churches, but only if they failed to get the approval of the planning commission, based upon consideration of traffic congestion and other factors. The main reason given by the board for excluding the church was a "possible" increase in traffic. The court considered the evidence on this point insufficient. It held that the board's refusal of the permit was not justified by the evidence, and so overruled it.

The final decision of the court did not involve the validity or invalidity of the ordinance. Therefore, its discussion of that question was irrelevant. But even in this dictum the Washington court instead of endorsing the anti-exclusion rule actually criticized it sharply on the ground that [165:197] it "ignores the basic premise of modern-day zoning legislation." To the extent that these observations are precedent for any principle, they are against the absolute anti-exclusion rule.

31. *American Jurisprudence* [32§125] also cites the Milwaukie Jehovah's Witnesses case [184] of 1958. This is ridiculous. The court condemned this doctrine [184:21] as a "form of judicial favoritism" and as a "cloak of immunity." It sustained refusal of a permit. It is one of the strongest precedents to the contrary of the rule.

32. The case of the Jewish congregation at Creve Coeur, Missouri, of 1959 [192] is also cited by the *American Law Reports* annotation.[185:377] The question there was not whether churches could constitutionally be excluded from residential zones but

whether the legislature in its enabling act had intended their exclusion.

The enabling act authorized the regulation of land use only with respect to "trade, industry, residence or other purposes." The court held that this did not authorize the regulation of land for church purposes. This case was essentially similar to the Montgomery, Alabama, Pentecostal Holiness church case [56] and the Beckley, West Virginia, Church of God case.[25] In those cases it was the ordinance that was interpreted. In the Missouri case it was the enabling act. In none of these cases did the court decide that it is unconstitutional to exclude churches from residential zones.

33. The Episcopal conference center case at Cazenovia, New York,[218] decided in 1960, is also cited in the *American Law Reports* annotation.[185:377] The ordinance in that case did preclude institutions unless they fell under certain prescribed classifications. These classifications were very broad. They included not only a "church" but also a "parochial school", "convent", etc.

But in a sense they were not sufficiently broad to include what the Episcopalians wanted to establish which was a "conference center." Literally this seemed neither a church, a parochial school, nor a convent. But the Episcopalians insisted that the classifications set out in the ordinance should be interpreted broadly enough to include their center. In a very logical opinion, the court sustained this contention.

Obviously, this was purely a question of statutory interpretation. The exclusory features of the ordinance were neither challenged nor nullified. They were merely interpreted. It is improper to cite this case for the absolute anti-exclusion rule.

34. The Bayside, Wisconsin, Baptist Church case of 1960 [231] also provides support of doubtful character for both versions of the anti-exclusion rule. A total of three opinions were written. One was by Justice Fairchild. It was signed by him and two other judges. A second opinion was written by Justice Hallows and was signed by him and two other judges. A third opinion was written and signed by Justice Currie alone.

It appears, therefore, that there was a 6-1 majority of the court in favor of giving the Baptists a permit. But there was no majority in favor of any opinion. It seems to me, therefore, that none of the three opinions has any great force as precedent.

In Wisconsin, I understand, the three-man opinion prepared by Justice Fairchild is treated as the "majority opinion" and I will do the same. But my reader should not forget the qualification above noted.

The "concurring" three-man opinion written by Justice Hallows held the ordinance in effect at the time of the trial invalid because it excluded churches from particular zones. The opinion is based on cases I have discussed immediately above. I find that they fail to support the absolute anti-exclusion rule.

The "majority" three-man opinion, written by Justice Fairchild, took another tack. It held the present ordinance valid but that it could not properly be enforced against the particular church. (The reason for this will be shown on pages 68-9.) It then considered whether the ordinance previously in effect was valid. These judges held it invalid because it excluded churches from the entire community. This opinion would seem to me less objectionable. However, it might better have been based not on the totality of the exclusion of churches but on the fact that other uses, clearly just as adverse, were permitted.

Just as in Plandome [87] the town had tried to exclude churches and include clubhouses, the Bayside ordinance sought to exclude churches while specifically permitting [231:290] "any retail business." The evidence showed that there were actually "three filling stations, one retail garden store," and "five establishments maintaining bars," in operation at the time the suit was filed. It seems to me un-equal protection to permit assemblies for the purpose of drinking dry martinis, and listening to juke boxes, while forbidding assemblies for worship and prayer.

If the "majority" had based its decision on the suggested ground, the result for the Bayside Baptists would have been the same, but the court would not have created a precedent against the establishment of 100% residential towns. In my opinion, ordinances creating such towns should be deemed constitutional if there are reasonably accessible sites elsewhere for churches and other places of public assembly.

35. The alleged absolute anti-exclusion rule receives further support in the Englewood, Colorado, Apostolic Christian church case of 1961.[233] The Englewood ordinance provided [233:173] for the exclusion of churches from the one- and two-family residence districts, unless "the public interest is fully protected" and such nonresidential uses are "approved by the Board." As to the commercial and industrial districts, there was a blanket exclusion of churches. In the multi-family residence district, churches were unconditionally permitted.

The permit requested was for construction of a church in a one-family residence zone. It was rejected by the board. Such rejection was subject to legal challenge on various grounds other than the absolute anti-exclusion theory. The decision disregarded these other grounds and said: "We hold that the blanket exclusion of churches from single- and double-family residence districts, as attempted by the ordinance in question, was not in furtherance of the health, safety, morals or general welfare of the community. Even under the broadened concept of 'general welfare' . . . this ordinance cannot be upheld."

The almost incredible feature of this opinion is that it condemned a non-existent provision of the ordinance. As shown above, there was no "blanket exclusion" of churches from the single- or double-family residence district. The "blanket" exclusion was only from the commercial and industrial district. The judge who wrote the majority opinion seems not to have read carefully the ordinance he was interpreting.

The opinion is also subject to criticism because it relies inaccurately and improperly on the Wenatchee, Washington, Jehovah's Witnesses case.[165] The Colorado judge seems to have assumed that the Washington court had endorsed the absolute non-exclusion doctrine. But, as shown above, that court actually condemned the doctrine in no uncertain terms.

This completes my analysis of the articles stating the anti-exclusion rule and the cases that are supposed to support it. When lawyers and legal writers argue from cases that they have not read, or from cases they have read in only a superficial way, they make triple trouble. First, they waste their own time in making long lists of citations of irrelevant cases. Second, they waste the time of those who seek to write the exact truth and therefore must refute fallacies one by one. Third, and this I resent more than the first two, they waste the time of my readers who are forced to wade through this lengthy refutation. The price of understanding is sometimes high.

It seems to me that there is properly no absolute anti-exclusion rule such as various of the writers mentioned in the above paragraphs expound. There is an anti-exclusion rule but it is not nearly so absolute as they contend. In four or five cases that I have mentioned there is support for the theory that churches may not be completely excluded from an entire muncipality or from "practically" an entire municipality. Stated in these less-than-absolute terms, the anti-exclusion rule is more acceptable.

But even then it would be better to state the rule in another way, without reference to the arbitrary and artificial boundaries of municipalities. The better rule in my opinion would forbid the exclusion of churches from an area so large that they would be deprived of reasonably accessible alternative sites for construction.

Neither is there an absolute pro-exclusion rule. Whether a particular regulation is valid or invalid depends not on any such simple question as whether a church is a church. Instead, it depends on the more complex question whether the fundamental rights of the particular church are violated in the particular case. I will now proceed to discuss these fundamental rights in some detail.

# CHAPTER 4.

## SUBSTANTIALITY OF PURPOSE;
## BALANCING OF INTERESTS

When the due process clause is invoked—as it so often is in church zoning cases—the questions arise: is the public purpose to be served by the regulation sufficiently substantial to justify it and do the means adopted to promote these ends bear a reasonable relation to the declared purpose? Both questions must be answered affirmatively or the regulation is called arbitrary, unreasonable and capricious, and therefore unconstitutional.

The public purposes invoked to justify zoning are often expressed in terms of the advancement of general public interests such as: (1) morality, (2) health, (3) safety, (4) convenience, (5) comfort, (6) prosperity, (7) peace and quiet, and (8) general welfare. All of these purposes have been relied on in church zoning cases except the purpose first mentioned. Some of them, like "comfort," overlap others, like "peace and quiet." The last of the commonly invoked purposes, "general welfare," is a catch-all which includes the others, and a great many more.

The reader should also bear in mind that the detailed purposes of religious land use regulation described herein are only those that have been discussed in the court decisions on which the book is based. This limitation may be comparatively narrow because (a) courts which approve such regulation are inclined to say that the details of justification are an administrative rather than a judicial concern and (b) courts which disapprove such regulation are inclined to belittle any justification. There may be many reasons for regulating the religious use of land that have been approved by zoning boards but have not been invoked in published court decisions.

Each exercise of the police power must be reasonably purposeful. The courts are inclined to state, to restate and to state again in the general terms above used the purposes that they consider sound. Less often, they analyze the purposes of the zoning regulation in a more specific and concrete way. A study of the cases shows that one public purpose exceeds all others in importance as a justification for church zoning. This is the prevention of automobile traffic congestion and hazards. This and other "substantial public purposes" that have been invoked in church zoning cases will be treated in detail in Chapters 5 to 10.

When I mention any particular purpose as possibly justifying the regulation of the religious use of land, I do not mean to suggest that the use is necessarily subject to regulation for that purpose alone. Usually, a regulation is found valid for several purposes, among which are included traffic control and one or more of the other purposes mentioned below.

The justifications or stated purposes for the regulation of religious land use include those for which the police power has traditionally been used. Thus the zoning code—or building code—may require that churches be constructed under public supervision and that the heating, plumbing, electrical and other equipment, and the materials and methods of construction, shall conform to certain standards. Some courts hold that churches may not be "excluded" from any neighborhood; but even they admit that churches can be subject to reasonable "fire, police, health, and sanitary" regulations.

Sometimes churches or church institutions are excluded from particular neighborhoods (or conditions are imposed upon the granting of permits for their construction) upon the ground of the "inconvenience" or "disturbance" they might cause or the "depressiveness" of their presence; sometimes for the purpose of avoiding the noise caused by public assemblies, or the smells of auto fumes, or the bright lights of automobiles or of night-lit outdoor assemblies; sometimes for the "protection of the enjoyment of neighboring property." Corollary to that purpose is the protection of real estate values and maintenance of the tax base (composed of such values) from which public revenues are derived. Conversely, regulation is sometimes justified because the proposed use would cause an increase in the cost of public services, such as fire and police, sewer and sanitary facilities, water, etc.

An important purpose invoked to justify church zoning was described by Mr. Patterson in the speech [9] quoted on pages

7-8. This is the proper distribution of population and the prevention of concentration of buildings. It is effected by height limitations and setback standards, maximum percentages of occupancy or "proximity requirements" specially applicable to places of assembly. This purpose also justifies establishment of restricted areas from which business, industry—and sometimes churches—are excluded completely. Finally there is now a tendency of the courts to effectuate, even where it affects churches, the policy of the city beautiful advocated by Newell Dwight Hillis in 1912 in the speech [8] that I have quoted on the same page. Among the justifications for the regulation of the religious use of land is now to be found the aesthetic ideal as such.

At pages 22-3 I have said that each of the liberties guaranteed by the constitution may properly be limited in order to protect other liberties guaranteed by it. So also the public purpose that a particular regulation purports to serve may seem relatively insubstantial if there is some other proper public purpose which the regulation disserves. Among such other public purposes is the protection of the church's rights.

In determining the substantiality of the assigned purpose the court balances or weighs the harm that the regulation tries to avoid against the harm that it may cause. Most zoning cases decided in favor of churches involve this process of comparison. This gives the courts an opportunity to express their admiration of the church's high purposes and social value. However, in the very first of the church zoning cases, that of the Omaha, Nebraska, Presbyterians,[14] the court held the requirement of a set-back line invalid because it was comparatively too restrictive not of the church as such but of property owners in general.

As mentioned on page 18, Alfred Bettman had told the planners [10] that "the scope of the police power is not limited . . . to the exercise of the particular modes or methods of the past." In reliance upon such assurances as these, the legislature of Nebraska was persuaded in 1919 to adopt a comprehensive zoning enabling act. Under it,[14:618] the City of Omaha was authorized to adopt "a comprehensive zoning ordinance" including regulations "as to the height and bulk of buildings and the area of yards, courts, or open spaces." The act provided that the zoning ordinance must be "designed to secure safety from fire and other dangers and to promote the public health and welfare, including, so far as conditions may permit, provision of adequate light, air, and convenience of access."

In November of the same year, the Westminster Presbyterian Church acquired a piece of land at 35th Street and Woolworth Avenue. There was an old house on the property into which the minister, M. L. Laird, moved, using it temporarily as a manse. But plans were being prepared to replace the old house with handsome new $75,000 church. In June of 1920, the city passed its zoning ordinance. It provided, with respect to the lots located in that neighborhood, that no building should be permitted to "cover more than 25% of the area of such lot or parcel of ground." Meanwhile, the plans of the church had been finished. They provided for a building that would occupy, not just 25% of the lot, but 37½% of it.

Refused a permit, the Presbyterians sued. They did not contend that any of their rights as a church had been violated, nor that they had been unconstitutionally discriminated against, nor did they invoke either religious liberty or equal protection. Instead, they based their case on their rights as property owners the same as other property owners. They invoked the due process clause and charged by implication that the regulation had an insufficiently substantial public purpose as compared to its invasion of property rights. The court sustained the church's position. In 1952, an article in *St. John's Law Review* [95:97] would refer to this decision as "open to reproach" in that "a zoning law actively enforced over a two year period was held invalid when its provisions were employed to prevent the erection of a church."

However, there were grounds for the court's action which deserve consideration. The city engineer had testified [14:619] that he "saw no reason why the church building in question, even if it covered 37½% of [the] ground, would be a greater fire menace to the city or to its health than if only 25% were covered." In the majority opinion, Justice James R. Dean said that the "part of the ordinance which confines the building area to 25% of the lot is so restrictive that it is an unreasonable exercise of the power granted by the legislature and for that reason that part of the ordinance must be held to be invalid."

The court's deprecatory attitude toward the scope of the police power is demonstrated by an analogy that the decision used. It said that "police power . . . bears the same relation to the municipality that the principle of self-defense bears to the individual." Self-defense is a principle of which all courts take an extremely narrow view. A person may use violence against another person "in self-defense" only if threatened with attack and if there is no alternative way to protect himself from death or serious injury.

If this analogy is carried to its logical extreme, it means that Omaha was limited in its use of police power to situations in which the existence of the city was threatened. Obviously the Presbyterians were not threatening the city's existence; and, if they were, the setback requirements were not a suitable defense against such attack.

The court seems to have put into one side of the balance the church's property rights and into the other side only two of the regulation's purposes, namely fire and health protection. If the court had added to the city's side of the scales certain other purposes stated in the law such as "public welfare, including adequate light, air and convenience of access," the scales of justice might have been tipped in favor of the municipality.

The importance of such factors as those disregarded by the majority was brought out very effectively in the dissenting opinion of Justice William D. Rose. In that opinion [14:619] he said:

> The ordinance prohibiting the owners of lots from covering more than one fourth of it with buildings in residential districts had its origin in an exalted conception of city life. The goal of the city council was public improvement, leading to better, healthier, happier conditions. The rich were not to have a monopoly of beautiful surroundings with their wholesome effect upon health, morality, and usefulness. By means of the ordinance condemned, the city council meant to touch the pulse of municipal power for the general welfare. Parents and children of all classes, without regard to former environment, were to breathe pure air, at least in the streets, and see flowering shrubs around private dwellings and lis-

ten to the fluted notes of birds in hedges. To some extent, these privileges are already enjoyed in public parks.

The aesthetic features of municipal activity for the good of the public ought to be recognized and respected. Individual rights and private property must be protected, but they are not gods of government. Ownership and control of lots among urban homes are limited by the proper exercise of the police power for the general welfare. Private rights are menaced when the good of society is neglected.

When courts interfere with municipal legislation to improve conditions generally, they should point out a limitation of power fixed by the supreme law and find facts showing an unmistakable usurpation. In my opinion, the reasoning and conclusions of the majority do not meet the proper tests. When the regulatory power of the city to enact laws for the public good is considered with the individual rights of [the church] the ordinance does not seem to me to be unreasonable.

The justice who wrote this dissent was a man ahead of his time—but by only a few years. In zoning cases, especially church zoning cases, the minority opinions of one year tend to become the majority opinions of the years that follow. Thus, in 1926, four years after the Omaha decision, the Supreme Court of the United States took up the question of the constitutionality of zoning in general. It issued an opinion that sounded much more like one of Rose or Patterson or Hillis, than like the majority opinion of the Nebraska court, or the allegations of the Westminster Presbyterians of Omaha.

The leading United States Supreme Court case on land use zoning involved the Village of Euclid, a suburb of Cleveland, Ohio.[18] It was filed by a group that was more interested in industry than in preservation of the home environment. They were represented by Newton D. Baker, who had been Secretary of War under President Wilson. The village had found itself in the path of Cleveland's industrial expansion. It had decided on firm steps to preserve its residential character. It passed a comprehensive planning and zoning ordinance which made the use of land for industrial plants illegal in a large part of the village's area.

This measure disturbed not only the manufacturers who were planning to move into the suburb, but also the owners of land in Euclid whose property (so some of them claimed) was worth only one-tenth as much for suburban houses as it was for factories. The village was represented by James Metzenbaum who later wrote an outstanding textbook on zoning law.[113] The Supreme Court of the United States sustained the validity of the ordinance in general terms. At the same time it said that it would reconsider its validity from case to case as applied to specific situations. This decision was issued, not by the "New Court" that came into office after the failure of the Roosevelt "court packing" scheme, but by the conservative court that newspaper columnist Drew Pearson, in New Deal days was to call the "Nine Old Men."

Justice George M. Sutherland, formerly a top Republican political leader, known as a staunch conservative, wrote the opinion. It stated the effect and purpose of the Euclid ordinance as "the exclusion from residential areas . . . of business and trade of every sort, including hotels and apartment houses . . . in order to prevent or at least to reduce the congestion, disorder and dangers which often inhere in unregulated municipal development." Note that one of these, the reduction of congestion, was also one of the purposes of Omaha's limitation [14] on the percentage of occupancy of the Presbyterian lot. Is the prevention of "congestion, disorder and dangers" a sufficiently substantial public purpose to justify a zoning ordinance under the police power? The United States Supreme Court came to a conclusion opposite to that of the Nebraska court. It avoided the analogy to self-defense using instead another analogy based on another ancient branch of the law, the Law of Nuisance.

The supreme court cited the legal maxim, *sic utere tuo ut alienum non laedas.* (So use your own as not to injure another's property.) It said that this maxim "lies at the foundation of . . . much of the common law of nuisances" and that, ordinarily, it would "furnish a helpful clue" to determine the line which separates the "legitimate from the illegitimate function" of the police power. This was something quite different from "self-defense."

"The exclusion of places of business from residential districts," said Justice Sutherland, "is not a declaration that such places are nuisances or that they are to be suppressed as such. . . ." However, he said, the law of nuisance could be invoked "for the helpful aid of its analogy in the process of ascertaining the scope of the power. . . . Thus the question whether the power to forbid erection of a building of a particular type or for a particular use, like the question whether a particular thing is a nuisance, is to be determined not by an abstract consideration of the building . . . but by considering it in connection with the circumstances and locality. . . . A nuisance may be merely a right thing in a wrong place, like a pig in the parlor instead of the barnyard."

Thus, the Supreme Court of the United States held that the police power was available not only for "self-defense" of the state but for the broader purpose of keeping "pigs" out of municipal "parlors." The court had applied this metaphor to factories. It might also have applied it to overcrowded lots occupied by churches. The purpose of serving abstract civic values was considered sufficiently substantial to outweigh private property rights. This is a far cry from the decision in the Omaha case.

Discussing the implications of the Euclid case and other supreme court decisions in *Community Building, Techniques Science, Art* Carol Aronovici [133] says that:

> It must be admitted that zoning is, beyond question, an interference with a person's freedom to use his property as he chooses. The fundamental issue is not interference with the individual as a property owner, but rather the establishing of a reasonably clear line of demarcation between equitable property rights and the public interest.
>
> Where property is taken for a public use, compensation is provided for by constitutional guaranties. In the case of zoning, however, the property is not taken but only placed under control. This control may hinder values and profits. For actual alleged losses which may be attributed to zoning, there is no compensation. The explanation is to be found in that area of legislative power lying between the specific guaranties provided by the Constitution . . . and the unlimited, nonspecified powers vested in the states and their subsidiary lawful governments known as the "police power." The police power may be defined as the device whereby the guaranties granted to the individual by written constitutions may be socialized.

This last sentence is a sharp criticism. It implies that these extremely conservative "Nine Old Men" were guilty of having socialized 90% of the value of the land of the complaining landowners. How far can this process be carried? Aronovici says:

> How far these rights may be socialized is a matter of evolution and cannot and should not be fixed at a given time. The court seems to hold that, under the police power, there are no private rights that can be guaranteed by any constitutional provision unless such rights are not in conflict with the rights of others similarly guaranteed. This assumption rests upon the theory that the life of the state depends upon balanced social relations and any interference with this balance is subject to the so-called "police power's" control regardless of any specific infringement upon individual or property rights.

Like Dr. Aronovici, I contemplate the police power with the deepest awe but I would have to disagree with his use of the word "regardless." The courts will balance the purposes of the state against private property rights to some extent. This is demonstrated in another supreme court zoning case of 1927 affecting Cambridge, Massachusetts, and a zoning order that the city entered against one Nectow.[22] It placed a particular piece of property owned by him in a residential zone. He wanted to sell it for industrial purposes. Just as in the Euclid case [18] the court had drawn the pig-in-the-parlor concept from the ancient law of nuisances, so the court in the Cambridge case in order to give Nectow relief drew from the same source the Doctrine of Comparative Damage.

The land was bounded on one side by a railroad and on another by a factory. Presumably along at least one other boundary it fronted on a street. Before zoning, the owner had a contract to sell the land for $63,000. Then the ordinance was adopted which put the property in a residential zone. Because of the restrictions, the purchaser refused to comply with the contract. By these restrictions, business and industry of all sorts were excluded from the particular lot.

The local master in chancery who took evidence in the case had inspected the property and had reported that "no practical use can be made of the land in question for residential purposes because, among other reasons, there would not be adequate return on the amount of any investment for the development of the property." This seems to mean that the rents to be derived from residences on the land would be insufficient even to provide a return on the cost of the buildings, etc. They would return nothing at all on the value of the land. In other words, the whole value of the landowner's interest was wiped out. He was worse off, for instance, than the plaintiffs in the Euclid case [18] who (so they claimed) were wiped out to the extent of 90%.

The supreme court rejected as unconstitutional the application of the Cambridge ordinance to Nectow's property. It said that "when the due process objection is raised, it is normally required that the court weigh the harm done by the exercise of the police power against the injury to the community which it is sought to prevent by exercising this power." It added this observation: "That the invasion of the property of [Nectow] was serious and highly injurious is clearly established" and that the residential classification of Nectow's land "has no foundation in reason and is a mere arbitrary and irrational exercise of power, having no substantial relation to the public health, the public morals, the public safety, or the public welfare in its proper sense."

I don't mean to suggest that the decision with respect to the Cambridge, Massachusetts, ordinance is a complete answer to Aronovici's view. However, the court did give relief to a man the value of whose interests was "wiped out" for an insubstantial purpose. It refused relief (in the Euclid case) to landowners whose interests were wiped out to the extent of 90%. The Cambridge case shows only that Aronovici is wrong when he says that the court will sustain an exercise of the police power utterly "regardless" of infringement of property rights.

The announcement by the court in the Cambridge case that it would "weigh the harm done by the exercise of the police power against the injury to the community which it is sought to prevent" was another way of saying that it would balance the substantiality of the public purpose against the substantiality of the private injury. The "balancing of equities," also called the "comparison of conveniences" etc. is derived from the common law of nuisances. In determining whether a nuisance was to be abated, the courts traditionally gave some consideration to the injury that its abatement would cause.

This does not call for an exact weighing of one against the other. As in the Cambridge case, it is only where the injury to the landowner is very obvious and severe and the public purpose to be served is slight that such comparisons can properly sway the decision.

A public nuisance will not be enjoined if the loss and injury arising from the nuisance is "slight and inconsequential" when compared with the injurious effect of its abatement. The Cambridge case sanctions the application of similar principles to the determination whether the public purpose involved is sufficiently substantial to justify land use regulations. In general, the rule has very limited application but in the cases considered in this book it is often used by judges to defeat public regulation of religious land use. They often weigh in on the side of the church not only the injury to its property rights but also a wide variety of other factors.

The process of balancing used by the courts is not nearly so scientific as that used by the official who weighs the gold ingots that are stored at Fort Knox. That official presumably puts an ingot on one side of the scale and a legally prescribed weight on the other. He has no personal control over the weight of what he puts on either side. The decision of a court is more comparable to that of a butcher who, if he wishes, can add the weight of his hand.

If a judge hopes for a certain result he can think up either (a) any number of interests benefited by the regulation or (b) any number of interests injured by it. He is controlled only by the extent of his imagination, his ability to rationalize, and the scope of his predilections. This is not intended as an invidious comparison between judges and butchers. When the butcher does such things, he is acting illegally. When judges do them, they not only act legally but often achieve wonderful intellectual feats.

In the Tampa, Florida, Jehovah's Witnesses case of 1950,[83] the main issue was whether the Witnesses had complied with the off-street parking requirements. The court held that they had "substantially" complied with them. It could have dropped the matter at that point but it seemed to need greater support for its ruling. So it went on to say that "this is certainly a case in which the balance of convenience rule as to range of judgment might be applied."

First, the Florida judge tried to lighten the weight (or "substantiality") of the public purpose on which the city relied, which in this case was traffic safety. He did it [83:79] on the basis of the following considerations:

The street was quite wide, 30 feet.

The number of people attending church would be small.

Not all of them owned automobiles.

Religious services would be brief.

They would be held at hours when traffic would be light.

There were side streets for parking.

The court then proceeded to weight down the church's side of the scales with these considerations:

Churches, etc., are important assets to our cultural needs.

The church and school are auxiliaries of the home.

Every fundamental principle of democracy is based on the Ten Commandments and the ethics of Jesus.

The court then asked itself: "Which is the more important, to preserve and foster an attitude of respect or reverence for these institutions or throw it to the discard in order that the careless and unthinking may rip through the street with no thought for the safety of man or beast?" The scales having been carefully weighted, the answer was obvious. It was so obvious that when the same court issued a contrary opinion in the Miami Beach Lutheran church case of 1956,[124] it didn't even mention the existence of the Tampa decision.

The Tampa case [83] was a very questionable application of the rule announced in the Cambridge case.[22] The weighing of the social consequences of the regulation was more properly within the competency of the city council than within that of the court. There was no showing, as in the Cambridge case, that the property owners would suffer any real financial loss. Presumably their land could be sold or used for residential purposes for as high a value as it possessed for church use.

Although the Beachwood, Ohio, Jewish temple case [101] does not expressly mention the balancing process, it is a good example of how that process can be applied soundly. The village said that its decision was based upon evidence brought before the council that a great majority of the congregation would be nonresidents of the village. It said that the size of the congregation, exceeding by several times the population of the village, could be detrimental to the public safety, welfare, and convenience of the village.

Only 20 Beachwood families would be served by the temple while several hundred other families would be injured by it. In the village's view, the balance would therefore disfavor the religious use. The court, however, upset this calculation by placing on the temple's side of the scales an additional consideration namely the interests of the Jews of the entire metropolitan community.

The court said: ". . . [A] village which is contiguous to and a part of a great metropolitan area cannot arbitrarily refuse, within reasonable limits, to contribute its share to the general welfare of the community as a whole. The membership of a religious institution is not confined within municipal boundaries. People seek out the church of their choice without concern as to the political subdivision in which it may be located." The most telling point made by the court was in these terms: "From the evidence as to the present facilities for religious services in the village, there can be no doubt that a great majority of the 1800 residents of Beachwood attend devotional services outside its physical boundaries." The court held that "the ground for refusing the permit, that the great majority of [the congregation's] members live outside the Village of Beachwood, is without substance. . . ."

The Decatur, Indiana, Jehovah's Witnesses' Kingdom Hall case [104] is one in which it was held that off-street parking requirements were invalid because, as the court said, they would result in the exclusion of a church from a residential zone. This result was buttressed by reference to the theory of balancing of convenience. The court said [104:117] that: "We are here faced with the problem of balancing interests asserted under the police power with those under the constitutional guaranty of freedom of worship and assembly."

The court laid great stress on what it considered a burden cast by the exclusion order on the religious liberty of the Witnesses. This subject will be discussed more fully in Chapter 15. The Indiana court invoked the principle to detract from the substantiality of the public purpose assigned. It said that the safety of the public should be protected in some other way as by the use of police and signs. It suggested regulations "imposed alike on all persons using the streets in the vicinity of churches." It held that the zoning board's action would "restrict the right of worship and assembly to an extent that outweighs any benefit to the safety, health, and general welfare of the public, and in such a situation, the police power must yield to the constitutional right of freedom of worship and assembly." The court added [104:120] that:

> When under the facts in this case the welfare and safety of the people of the neighborhood is placed on the scales of justice on one side, and the right to freedom of worship and assembly is placed on the other, the balance weighs heavily on the side guaranteeing the right to peaceful assembly and to worship God according to the dictates of conscience, regardless of faith or creed.

The Brighton, New York, Catholic church and school case of 1956,[149] like the Beachwood, Ohio, Jewish case [101] mentioned above, practiced balancing without mentioning it. In considering one of the purposes assigned, namely the protection of property values from the adverse effect of the church and school, the court admitted the existence of such depreciation. However, it said [149:835] that "in view of the high purposes, and the moral value, of these institutions, mere pecuniary loss to a few persons should not bar their erection and use."

Again one of the purposes stated as justification for the refusal of the Brighton permit was maintenance of the tax base which purpose would be served by preventing the removal of the church land from the rolls. Again the court balanced various public purposes against each other. It cited the religious tax exemption law of the state. Rightly or wrongly, it interpreted this law [149:836] as meaning this: "[T]he paramount authority of this state has declared a policy that churches and schools are more important than local taxes" and "this being the case, it cannot be argued that the decision of [the city] denying this permit because of a loss of tax revenue is in furtherance of the general welfare." Thus, while the court does not couch its decision explicitly in terms of balancing, I agree with the interpretation of this decision in the article in the *Catholic Lawyer*.[204] It says that, in the Brighton case, the court "recognized that churches, like other places of assembly, produce noise, congestion and traffic hazards, but regards these as offset by the social and moral values inherent in religious institutions."

I agree with the *Catholic Lawyer* analysis of the Brighton case but I also believe that the justices laid an extremely heavy hand on the church's side of the scales of justice. The judges of the lower courts of New York have interpreted the Brighton decision as practically preventing the refusal of permits to churches. In this respect, a comment by Ralph Crolly in the *Brooklyn Law Review* [161] says that "although the court stated in effect that there may be circumstances under which churches may be excluded from designated areas, it is difficult to think of any other reason for denying an application for a church in a residence district. The board of zoning appeals is not and should not be obligated to grant a permit for a church on any spot it owns or acquires merely for the asking regardless of all conditions or circumstances."

In situations like that of New York it is fortunate, in a sense, that the balancing process can so readily bring different results depending upon the predilections of the incumbent justices. By placing new items on the opposite side of the scale, future decisions of the New York courts may possibly change the legal situation above described. In this respect, I also agree with the article in the *Catholic Lawyer* [204] which says that "the central issue in determining the validity of the zoning ordinance excluding churches has been the relation of the exclusion to the health, safety, morals or general welfare." This is the test to which I have referred as the "substantiality of the public purpose." The *Catholic Lawyer* comments on the New York decision which I have deplored, saying that:

> Courts are now going so far as to hold that such a test has no meaning at all when applied to churches because "such institutions are regarded as occupying a status different from other uses." Thus the use of such a test has so far defeated the purposes of zoning with relation to churches and also led to inconsistent results. . . . Perhaps a more consistent balancing of the social interests would result if all cases involving churches were considered on the fundamental constitutional basis of the freedom of religion. An approach to the problem on such grounds might help accomplish the purposes of zoning by validating the exclusion of churches from limited residential areas while invalidating their exclusion from entire towns.

This amounts to a suggestion that the churches cease their practice of insisting that the public purpose supporting a zoning regulation is less substantial when a church is involved than when some other institution's use of land is regulated. This may be sound advice for churches and judges alike.

While the Milwaukie, Oregon, Jehovah's Witnesses case [184] was decided in favor of the city, the court gave full recognition to the theory of balancing of interests. It said [184:19] that "the very theory of zoning is one of balancing the public interest against private interests." It quoted with approval a passage from *McQuillin on Municipal Corporations*,[66:240] saying that "the detriment to public welfare that would result if zoning restrictions were removed must be weighed against benefits that would accrue to individual property owners." The Oregon court added: "Notwithstanding that a zoning ordinance is truly an instrument designed in the public welfare, and thus superior to private property rights, it must also be reasonable and not arbitrary in reach or administration and must confer on the public benefits commensurate with its burden on private property."

The Oregon court may here be stating the balancing rule rather broadly. It depends on the meaning assigned to the word commensurate. If this word means that the public benefits arising from the regulation must be "equal in measure or extent" (Webster's *New Collegiate Dictionary*) to the burden imposed on property holders in general, if it means that, case by case, tract by tract, the benefits accruing to the public must equal the burdens imposed on the particular owners, I would call the statement an exaggeration. This would go much further than the Cambridge case [22] and much further than the tradition of the common law of nuisances. Consideration must be given to the property injury but not to that extent.

Perhaps the Oregon court was stating political rather than legal principles. Anyway, it accepted the council's determination and aptly described the complexity of the problem by saying that:

> In denying the congregation's application to build a church and predicating the denial in whole or in part upon possible traffic problems, the council considered three, rather than the usual two, points of view, to wit:

(1) Effect on the [congregation] as landowner;

(2) Effect, if any, on those owning property on residential streets in the residential zone; and

(3) The effect on the general public of the community, no matter where they resided in Milwaukie.

The court itself said: [184:7] "We are of the opinion that the council's action was, under the circumstances present here, a reasonable application of the police power."

The decision in the San Marino, California, Catholic church parking lot case,[223] which was refused review in the Supreme Court of the United States,[224] represented a return to the narrower form of the rule enunciated in the Cambridge case.[22] The city was seeking an injunction to prevent continued use of a lot adjacent to the church for parking. The archbishop filed a countersuit to require a permit for such use. He had been using the lot for parking, in defiance of the ordinance, for years. The archbishop contended that "drastic hardship would flow" from an order requiring that he cease his illegal use of the lot. The court said:

> The only "hardship" pleaded in the answer [of the archbishop] involved the loss of the beneficial use of the . . . lot to which [the Catholics] have become accustomed. . . . [T]he rights of the city in the enforcement of its zoning restriction are substantial and more than mere technical rights. The rule in this regard is stated [as follows]: . . . The doctrine of balancing conveniences is often invoked as a defense . . . where the plaintiff seeking to vindicate a technical and insubstantial right would impose an unusual hardship upon the public or the defendant. Deprivation of a substantial benefit, however, falls short of the imposition of a substantial hardship. . . . When a court of equity balances conveniences to determine that an injunction, otherwise warranted, should be withheld, its action approaches an exercise of the right of eminent domain in favor of private persons. . . . It is apparent that as a matter of law no defense of hardship was shown.

The California court also rejected the archbishop's contention that because of its long delay in enforcing the ordinance the city was estopped from doing so. The theory of balancing of equities or interests as applied by the courts in zoning cases has its origin, as stated, in the law of nuisances. Abatement of nuisances involves equitable principles. This has led, it seems, to importation into zoning law of certain other equitable principles such as estoppel. The doctrine of estoppel has little proper application against the state or its municipalities yet we find it influencing the opinions of judges in many church zoning cases.

The courts have a tendency, for instance, to invoke:

(a) in favor of a church the fact, if it exists, that at the time it purchased the land the city had given it cause to believe that the property could be used for religious purposes, or

(b) against the church the fact, if it exists, that the church acquired the property with full knowledge that its use for a religious edifice was forbidden.

Thus in the Upper Arlington, Ohio, Lutheran church case [40:521] the supreme court recited the fact that:

> Scarcely two and a half months before the special permit was finally refused, [the village officials] had by resolution determined that the very site on which [the synod] is now seeking to locate its church "would in our present judgment . . . be suitable and appropriate for the erection of churches." Although this resolution was subsequently repealed and declared to have been "advisory only" and although its adoption may not, under the circumstances, rise to the dignity of an estoppel, it does at least give a strong indication that in the minds of a majority of the village officials there was no very clear repugnancy between the erection of a church in a Class I district and the general pattern of uses prescribed in the ordinance.

By the time the same supreme court got around to deciding the Cleveland Heights, Ohio, Jewish school case, however, it came closer to defining the grounds as estoppel. It said: [59:244]

> Reduced to its lowest terms, the decision [in the Upper Arlington case] . . . was based on the extremely important and unusual fact that the [synod] had been misled by the zoning and village commissions of the Village of Upper Arlington. The [synod] had applied twice for a permit to build a church. Each application had involved a different site. The [village officials] denied both requests. Thereafter the [village officials] passed a resolution stating that certain other sites would be available for church purposes and that if an application were made for a permit to build on one of them, it would be granted.
>
> The [synod] accepted the [village officials'] suggestion in good

faith and purchased one of the recommended sites. Then an application was made for a building permit. But it, too, was denied. The [synod] then sought a writ . . . to compel the issuance of the permit on the ground that the refusal was "unreasonable, arbitrary, unwarranted, confiscatory and a restraint upon the freedom of worship." The court of appeals properly allowed the writ and the judgment was affirmed by this court.

That similar circumstances can be utilized in a reverse way was shown by the following statement:

There is no such circumstance in the instant case [of the Jewish school]. This [congregation] purchased the residence property on its own initiative and without suggestion or representation of any kind by the [city officials].

Likewise in the Miami Beach, Florida, Lutheran church case,[124] the court said: "It seems that the [church] bought the property with knowledge of the zoning restrictions. . . ."

The early case of the Episcopal seminary at Evanston, Illinois,[19] is also a good example of quasi-estoppel. The original ordinance permitted construction of colleges (including, as the court held, the dormitory around which the controversy raged). The court refused to give effect to an amendment which forbade colleges and authorized only "public institutions having the right of condemnation under the laws of eminent domain." The court said that in acquiring the property the seminary had "relied on the zoning ordinance." It added that "a publicity campaign was prepared, and in all the advertising made, it was stated that the proposed building would be located [on the tract in question]. . . . Four hundred thousand dollars had already been pledged. These pledges were all made for the erection of a building on the [premises]. . . . [T]he amendment, by depriving it of the right to make such use—which is the destruction of the only property it acquired—is unreasonable and arbitrary."

While the "opinion of the court" in the Bayside, Wisconsin, Baptist case [231] is less explicit in this respect, it is obvious that the justices who signed it, in deciding for the Baptists, relied on (a) their determination that, at the time the land was purchased, it was not legally "zoned against" churches, plus (b) certain representations made by the village board. The decision said that: "In reaching the conclusion that the action of the village board was arbitrary and capricious we have been persuaded by the . . . [proposition that] . . . plaintiff is entitled to the benefit of equitable considerations arising out of its action in reliance on the board's indication of agreement. . . ." Then, as if recognizing the impropriety of applying estoppel to a city, the court added several other "propositions" in support of its conclusion, none of which are particularly relevant to the present discussion.

In a perverse way, the Meridian Hills, Indiana, Catholic church and school case of 1961 [229] seems to have taken a cue from the San Marino, California, Catholic church parking lot decision [223] and its reference to "exercising the right of eminent domain in favor of private persons." The process by which the court reached its conclusion (however just or unjust) seems abominable. The court actually managed, in balancing the various interests, to cast the city authorities in the role of private interests and to cast the bishop in the role of a public representative. First, the court increased the weight on the bishop's side of the scale by adding to his private interests the interests of Young America. The court said: [229:42]

> The education, morally and spiritually, of children, is a matter of great public concern, and private interests, although important, should not outweigh such general public welfare.

Considering, then, the city's side of the scales, the court said: [229:44]

> Here we do not have the factor of public safety to consider but rather the private interest in protecting property from depreciation to some extent and a desire to keep the neighborhood as exclusive as possible. Such interests, although important, do not have the characteristics of general welfare as predominant as do the public interests in the moral and intellectual education of the young. Using the same rationale as that suggested in the [Decatur, Indiana,] Jehovah's Witnesses case [104] we feel the general public interest in the moral and intellectual education of the young far outweighs the private interest affected by any depreciation in the neighboring property values.

Thus, without batting an eye, the Indiana court makes the bishop a representative of the public interest and the municipality of Meridian Hills a representative of private interest, reversing their proper roles. This demonstrates the extent to which the balancing process in church zoning cases can become a feat of intellectual sleight of hand.

It is usually only by such a play upon words that the theory can be invoked to obtain special special treatment of churches as such. That is why courts cannot forever perform the legerdemain with this theory which the Indiana court performed. The due process ground, in turn, depends very much for its effectiveness on the judicial process of balancing. That is why William R. Kennedy wrote in the *Notre Dame Lawyer* of May, 1960,[222:407] that the due process ground as a defense against regulation of the religious use of land is "too vague" and one of "proven weakness." This view was also shared by Paul Brindel when he wrote in an earlier issue of the same review: [166]

> By making use of the more concrete test provided by the First Amendment provisions concerning freedom of religion, rather than the vague criterion of due process, constitutional privilege will be more readily assured and private religious organizations will realize the necessary guaranties for effective activity.

It is also shared by the author of the *Catholic Lawyer* article [204] cited in this chapter. These writers are on sound ground when they belittle the due process clause defense in church zoning cases. The question whether the religious freedom clause will avail any church any new "privileges" will be discussed in Chapter 15.

Regardless of the advice of these writers in religio-legal periodicals, however, most of the church zoning cases to date have centered upon the due process theory. They have involved the question whether the public purpose of the regulation is sufficiently substantial to justify it. Undoubtedly, in the future, churches will continue to challenge zoning actions for lack of substantiality of the purpose assigned. Therefore, I will devote the ensuing chapters (5 to 10) to a discussion, one by one, of various specific types of justification that have been invoked in church zoning cases.

# CHAPTER 5.

## JUSTIFICATIONS: A. AESTHETIC AND GENERAL

To what extent can the religious use of land be regulated, not to protect physical peace, health, or safety, but for the more general purpose of the "public welfare?" For instance, can churches be zoned out for the sole purpose of maintaining the ideal of the city beautiful as enunciated by Dr. Dwight Hillis,[8:198] or solely to distribute the various uses of land in various districts in a manner considered appropriate by the authors of the city plan?

In the Omaha Presbyterian Church case,[14:620] Justice Rose said in his dissent that "the aesthetic features of municipal activities for the good of the public ought to be recognized and respected." Rose's opinion received support in the Euclid, Ohio, decision [18] of the United States Supreme Court. But the court was careful to indicate that it was not deciding a church zoning case. Would such general or aesthetic purposes suffice in a religious case?

In the Euclid decision,[18] the supreme court referred to a business building in a residence district as a "pig in the parlor instead of the barnyard." At the same time, Justice Sutherland insisted that he was not calling businesses nuisances *per se*. It seems, then, that he was comparing businesses to pigs, not so much in the sense of their smelliness, noisiness, propensity for violence, voraciousness or filthiness, as in the sense of their inappropriateness in parlors. Could churches be compared to pigs in this regard? Or perhaps could some of them, with large schools or community centers, be so compared? Is it possible, pursuant to such an analogy, to regulate the use of church land or even to exclude churches or schools from residential areas solely on the ground that they are inappropriate or unaesthetic in such a place?

A partial answer (in the negative) is to be found in the fact that no church has ever lost a reported zoning case on purely aesthetic grounds. Another partial answer (in the affirmative) is that use regulation short of total exclusion has often been imposed on churches for aesthetic purposes and such regulations have not been challenged. I refer especially to requirements for the construction of "screens" in the form of hedges, etc.* Courts also have mentioned the aesthetic purpose as a makeweight, in addition to other purposes, to justify actual exclusion of churches from residential areas.

The word snob zoning is used in popular articles.[79,170] It is never used by juges in church zoning cases. But some of them are inclined to lift an eyebrow toward people who cluster in restricted areas for aesthetic reasons. In this respect they may reflect the attitudes of some of the people who elected them, looking upon the suburbanites and exurbanites with an attitude of condescension such as only the poor can display toward the rich.

Thus, in the Portland Catholic school case of 1932,[27] the writer of the opinion dismissed with a wave of his hand the objections of neighbors many of whom, he said, had bought their property after passage of the ordinance, had "spent large sums of money in making lawns and setting out shrubbery," and had "built a mansion thereon for a home." His opinion that this was unchristian showed through in his reference to the man who "almost 2,000 years ago . . . was born, not in a mansion, but in a manger." In the Upper Arlington Lutheran church case,[40:524] the court said that "we do not believe that it is a proper function of government to interfere in the name of the public to exclude churches from residential districts for the purpose of securing to adjacent landowners the benefit of exclusive residential restrictions." St. Johns' Law Review [95:95] compares such exclusiveness to the "bigotry of a group."

A similar attitude of condescension appeared in the quotation from Mr. Bassett,[36] quoted on pages 8-9 above, wherein he referred to people "too sensitive to welcome churches." He said they should arrange for restrictions by private deed. These sentiments are passé. There is less and less snobbishness as expressed in racial or class exclusion. In other respects, however, this is an era when, in the words of the song, the "idle poor become the idle rich." All of us now seek the sort of perquisites that used to attach only to persons of means. In the

---

* For instance, see the decisions in the Indianapolis, Indiana, Methodist church case,[57:618] the South Euclid, Ohio, Jewish synagogue case,[140:176] and the Creve Coeur, Missouri Jewish synagogue case.[192:691]

Omaha Presbyterian decision,[14:620] Justice Rose said that "rich and poor alike" should enjoy the "fluted notes of birds in hedges." He probably would not have agreed with the Oregon court [27] in imposing on either rich or poor the "prattle and laughter and merry shouts of children at play." (See page 106.)

The judicial trend will probably be toward Justice Rose's ideal which was also expressed by Rev. William B. Paterson,[9] that of a "New Jerusalem" on earth for all classes of people. In spite of the inconsistent comment above quoted this ideal was also supported by the writer of the *St. John's Law Review* article of 1952.[95:101] He said that "the only sound argument in support of legislation excluding churches from residential areas" was that "the exclusion of churches will preserve an attractive community and prevent depreciation of adjacent property values." Endorsing the aesthetic ideal, he still had to report that until then it had been legally insufficient. He said that while "the theory that aesthetic considerations are alone sufficient to justify the enactment of a zoning law has gained support in recent years," yet "the weight of authority considers aesthetic concepts merely a factor to be considered in framing a zoning ordinance and are insufficient by themselves to justify such legislation." To this writer the aesthetic argument stood alone; to him all other stated purposes of church zoning were "trivial."

In 1953, the year after the *St. John's Law Review* article, in the Protestant seminary case at Orange Township, the New Jersey Supreme Court said: [99:490]

> It is obvious from an examination of the opinion in *Euclid v. Ambler* that the United States Supreme Court has not favored the view expressed by some authorities on zoning that zoning is designed to exclude from residence districts only those activities which are injurious, but has approved the view that zoning may validly exclude noninjurious uses where reasonable city planning prompts that course. Such a basis for zoning is not a novel theory. It has been said that the primary object of zoning, often stated as the protection of public health and safety, includes "the protection of the value and usefulness of urban land, and the assurance of such orderliness in municipal growth as will facilitate the execution of the city plan and the economical provision of public services."

During 1954, the year following the decision above quoted, the United States Supreme Court wrote its opinion in *Berman v. Parker*.[111] This was neither a church case nor a zoning case but a condemnation case to which the same requirement of substantial public purpose applies. The condemnation was for purposes of urban rehabilitation in Washington, D. C. The constitutionality of the measure was challenged on the ground that its main purpose was not to improve the health of citizens nor to protect them from physical harm, but merely to improve the appearance of the nation's capital.

Justice William O. Douglas wrote the opinion which upheld the condemnation. He referred to the concept of public welfare, saying that: "The values it represents are spiritual as well as physical, aesthetic as well as monetary. It is within the power of the legislature to determine that the community shall be beautiful as well as healthy, spacious as well as clean, well-balanced as well as thoroughly patrolled. If those who govern the District of Columbia decide that the Nation's Capital shall be beautiful as well as healthy, spacious as well as clean, well balanced as well as thoroughly patrolled, there is nothing in the Fifth Amendment that stands in the way."

An excellent article [164] in the *Harvard Law Review* for June 1957, contends that this decision will alter the course of church zoning law. It says: "Much of the difficulty in cases invalidating the exclusion of churches results from courts' giving too narrow a construction to 'general welfare' and consequently taking too restrictive a view of the permissible scope of zoning. Under the view adopted by the court in the Berman case, the factors that make churches undesirable neighbors would be considered sufficient to give a municipality power to exclude them from residential neighborhoods, even though it may appear to courts and zoning authorities that there is social value in locating churches in residential areas."

The *Catholic Lawyer* article [204] of Summer 1959 takes a different view. It agrees that "the court justifies the taking of property on aesthetic considerations for the maintenance of an attractive, beautiful community." But the writer says that: "No state court has been found to have availed itself of this broad construction of public welfare as a basis for excluding churches. . . . The Berman case [111] was cited in [the West Hartford, Connecticut, Methodist Church case [139]] but the court still refused to exclude the church on grounds of public welfare."

The last part of the *Catholic Lawyer* statement is misleading to one who has not read the West Hartford Methodist church case. The court did not refuse to exclude the church but rather did exclude it. The principal ground of exclusion was a provision of the ordinance that it must not "substantially or permanently injure the use of neighboring property for residential purposes." But there was a second condition in the ordinance, namely that "the public convenience and welfare would be served by such a permit."

The court did not rely on the second ground but it did discuss the meaning of the term "public convenience." It said [139:642] that this term is not used in a colloquial manner, that it is not synonymous with "handy," and that it connotes "what is suitable or fitting." The decision then quoted the observations of Justice Douglas in the Berman case.[111] The West Hartford case was later cited by the Supreme Court of Pennsylvania in *Best v. Zoning Board*,[174] the court saying that "We are satisfied that at long last conscientious municipal officials have been sufficiently empowered to adopt reasonable zoning measures designed toward preserving the wholesome and attractive characteristics of their communities and the values of . . . property."

The "weight of authority" is interpreted in the Wenatchee, Washington, Jehovah's Witnesses case of 1957 [165] as conforming to pre-*Berman* standards. It says that the cases limit the grounds for exclusion of churches to "traffic or other hazards substantially related to public health or safety." This entirely omits "convenience" and "welfare." If this is the weight of authority, which I doubt, then I consider it mistaken. So did the Supreme Court of Washington. It decided in favor of the church, for various reasons other than the matter here under discussion, but also said that the rule above stated "may be an extreme one. It ignores the basic premise of modern day zoning legislation which emphasizes the best and most reasonable land utilization possible, considering the best interests of the entire community. It permits any church group, absent the factor of traffic hazards substantially related to public health and safety, to acquire land and to establish a church irrespective of other factors which may be of significant public interest, and normally considered and emphasized in present-day community land use planning programs."

During the same year, a trial court in New York, in the case of Temple Israel of Lawrence,[173,182] clung to the concept described above. This was presumably because of the hostile attitude displayed by the court of appeals in the Brighton case toward every suggested justification for regulation of religious land use. The application was for a $500,000 addition to a temple, to include a swimming pool and a gymnasium. The zoning board of appeals said[173:395] the structure "would be a large and massive one, completely out of keeping with the one-family dwellings on Fulton Street. It would destroy much of the charm and attractiveness of this street. It would damage the character of the district as a residential one and impair the desirability and value of the property already devoted to private residences."

The court held [173:398] that "exclusion of churches and schools from designated areas may well be justified where such situses would endanger those in attendance thereat" but that "diminution of the aesthetic, inconvenience to neighboring property owners or traffic problems, where such factors do not impair the welfare or safety of the community, are not to be considered in determining an application to erect a church, synagogue, or its accessory uses of schools, for religious training and incidental recreational facilities." The court's reference to welfare was supposedly limited here to physical welfare. The Lawrence decision was reversed by the court of appeals on technical grounds with suggestions for the filing of a different form of action. No such action has been filed.

The *Berman* decision [111] was also cited with approval in the Milwaukie, Oregon, Jehovah's Witnesses case [184:17] which also quoted the definition of "public convenience" propounded by the West Hartford decision.[139] The Milwaukie decision was based upon traffic considerations. So its mention of aesthetic considerations was probably only a makeweight.

In the Russian Orthodox cemetery case at Rochester Township, Pennsylvania,[183,207] the majority refused to include a cemetery under the classification of "religious uses" authorized in the ordinance.* The court said [207:490] that: "It is apparent from a reading of the [ordinance] in its entirety that those uses permitted therein which are not purely agricultural or purely residential are ancillary to them. . . . These general observations are helpful in delineating the scope to be given to the word 'religious.' They are helpful primarily because it is assumed that one of the basic principles of zoning, that of area homogeneity, is one of the ends sought by the zoning ordinance."

Area homogeneity is a sound purpose but it is doubtful that failure to achieve it could be called a "hazard to public health or safety." In the testimony before the zoning board in the Russian Orthodox case, there is a homely illustration of how such secular purposes can conflict with religious practices. One of the commissioners (perhaps a man who did not include in his everyday vocabulary such words as homogeneity and aesthetics) said: [207:492]

> . . . [A]s a private citizen I would like to say that a cemetery can be considered a religious function, not just an Orthodox or Catholic cemetery—any cemetery—because it does state in the Bible to bury the dead. But I cannot possibly believe that the men who drew up this zoning ordinance meant that a beautiful home should have a cemetery next door as a religious purpose.

The regulation of religious uses of land has never been sustained solely for aesthetic purposes. The question here under discussion may seem academic. However, this factor can have considerable practical significance where an attempt is made to exclude all churches, without exception, from a residential zone.

If the courts of a state recognize only actual physical dangers, like traffic hazards, as justification for the exclusion of churches, then they will require exceptions for those churches that, by providing adequate off-street parking, etc., eliminate all physical danger. On the other hand, if the courts recognize the right of cities to exclude churches from residential areas solely on the basis of inappropriateness, there is not

---

* The cemetery cases are referred to in this volume only incidentally. There is a collection of such cases in an *American Law Reports* annotation.[108] See also References Nos. 12, 47-A and 112.

much that a particular church can do to make itself appropriate.

There is some tendency—not yet very pronounced—for courts to rely on the aesthetic and general purposes in justifying religious land use regulation. For the reasons above stated, the conclusion of the *Harvard Law Review* article [164] quoted on page 74 seems quite sound. If this tendency continues, there may be more and more ordinances which unconditionally exclude churches and other religious institutions from areas designated as strictly residential.

# CHAPTER 6.

## JUSTIFICATIONS: B. SPACE, LIGHT, AIR AND EASE OF ACCESS

The need to limit heights of buildings and to surround them by open spaces was the dominant theme of progressive citizens in the days when the two clergymen, Paterson [9] and Hillis [8] made the speeches that I have quoted on pages 7-8. These requirements serve broader purposes. They serve an aesthetic purpose because overoccupation of land is ugly; they serve public health, morality, etc., because they help eliminate slums; they also help limit the cost of public services such as police and fire protection.

The reasons for light and space requirements seem seldom to apply to churches. Such institutions seldom overoccupy their land. As Justice Bettman said in the Upper Arlington case,[40:524] "Churches in fitting surroundings are an inspiration to their members and to the general public. If located in the residential district, space, perspective, greensward and trees aid in setting off the beauty of the building and thereby increasing its inspiration."

This is true partly because the land is tax exempt and therefore cheaper to the church than it would be to a private landowner. In a slum district, it is often only the church that has sufficient land comfortably to accommodate its structure. If the church steeple is high, it is for aesthetic or devotional reasons, not to accommodate larger numbers of people. This may help explain the outcome of the Omaha, Nebraska, Presbyterian church case,[14] considered on pages 52-5, where setback requirements were held invalid. In subsequent church zoning cases, however, where percentage-of-occupancy, setback, and similar requirements were under consideration they were either held to be valid or assumed to be valid.

In the first of the two synagogue cases at Philadelphia,[50] Rabbi Joseph Kurman, whose home was located at 5831 Drexel Road, began using it for religious assembly purposes. The zoning law provided that for residences the side yard must be ten feet wide. Every building other than a dwelling was required to have two side yards, "neither of which shall be less than 15 . . . feet wide." In April 1943, the Rabbi asked for a permit to use his house "as a place for conducting religious services over each weekend." The city officials refused the permit. The court upheld their decision. It did not even mention the previous contrary decision in the Omaha, Nebraska, Presbyterian church case.[14]

Neither did it give particular consideration to the fact that the use of the property was religious. Instead, it treated the enterprise as if it were a theater or other place of public assembly. The rabbi contended that the weekend services were merely an "incidental or accessory use" which should have been allowed under his residence permit. The court overruled this contention. However, the court went on to demonstrate— without actually asserting—its readiness to impose space requirements on churches. The court said:

> Since the building was used for a place of religious worship, i.e., as a synagogue, its surroundings had to conform to the [nonresidential requirements]. . . . The [rabbi] contends that the principal use of the building was for a dwelling for a single family and that the use of one room on the first floor for religious services on the weekend was merely an incidental or accessory use.
>
> The answer to that is that the mere fact that the use of the building as a place of worship is "merely incidental to some other more frequent use" does not relieve the owner from his duty to conform to the requirements of the law so far as they apply to that building when it is used for the incidental purpose.
>
> For example, if a dwelling was occasionally used as a theater, it, at the time it was so used, would have to conform to all of the requirements which relate to the maintenance of a theater. Requirements which have been violated in this case are for the protection of people who frequent such places. Those who framed [them] evidently believed that if a building was to be used for any purpose other than a dwelling, it should have two side yards, neither of which should be less than 15 feet in width.

The court added a comment on the enabling act,[50:382] saying:

> The act . . . contains . . . a list of "Purposes in View" when "such regulations" are made. Among these purposes are "to secure safety from fire, traffic and other dangers . . . to provide ade-

quate light and air, to prevent the overcrowding of land," etc. In requiring in a zoning ordinance the side yards of a church to be of the width stated, the city reasonably attempted to serve these proper "purposes." *Not* to sustain the board of adjustment . . . would be a disservice to the public welfare.

The rabbi in this case failed to ask for any special consideration under the due process clause because of the religious character of his use. The issue was not mentioned in the decision. However, the case has been cited in a subsequent Pennsylvania decision (the Bethel Borough Jehovah's Witnesses case of 1959 [159:243]) in support of the conclusion that "property used for church purposes, along with property used for other purposes, may be lawfully subjected to reasonable zoning restrictions." This is substantially correct, in my opinion, but it is not necessarily included in the language of the Philadelphia Jewish case. The case has been cited for a similar rule in other authoritative writing, such as the *Michigan Law Review*,[158:603] *Harvard Law Review*,[164] Rathkopf,[132:18-19] Metzenbaum,[113] and the decision of the Supreme Court of New Jersey in the Allendale Jehovah's Witnesses case.[205]

The requirement that a church be surrounded by adequate space arose in a slightly different form in the Chicago Episcopal church case, decided by the Appellate Court of Illinois in 1950.[93] The issue was obscured and the court's view on the subject was expressed only in dictum. But the dictum clearly sustained the propriety of space requirements for churches.

The objecting property owner, a lawyer named Vincent O'Brien, was annoyed by the prospect that the Church of the Holy Nativity would be built near his residence at 93rd and Prospect. He also may have considered slightly devious the strategy employed by the Episcopalians. The ordinance forbade construction of churches in the subdivision (which had been opened up somewhat earlier) except on lots surrounded by streets and alleys. The Episcopalians acquired a corner lot, bounded on one side by 93rd Street and on another by Prospect.

According to the official plat of the subdivision the other two sides were abutted by private residence sites. When O'Brien and his neighbors bought their land, they may have assumed, because the corner lot was not officially "surrounded by streets and alleys" that it could not be used for a church. If so they failed to anticipate the possibility of Episcopalian "do-it-yourself" alleys.

The church people went to the city council and proposed a resubdivision of their lots under which alleys were dedicated to public use out of their own land on the two sides of the tract which abutted private land. This dedication was accepted by the council. The neighbors sued to invalidate the dedication. They were unsuccessful in the lower court.

The lower court decided only that the dedication was valid. It did not interpret the zoning ordinance or the sufficiency of the dedication to comply with it. The appellate court, however, seemed desirous of settling all issues, not merely those that were properly before it. It not only sustained the lower court but also said, in dictum, that the church's procedure was a compliance with the zoning ordinance. It said: [93:920]

> The ordinance as we have interpreted it imposes a condition with respect to the site on which a church may be erected. There is no question of the city's right to exercise police power in this fashion provided the conditions are reasonably related to the public health, morals, comfort, safety, or welfare. If the purpose of the restrictions is related to . . . the necessity for a space between the church structure and adjoining property, such purpose is amply fulfilled by adequate dedication of streets and alleys on a proposed site.

Thus the court interpreted the ordinance very favorably to the church but affirmed the right of the city to impose requirements as to occupancy of space.

The case of Jehovah's Witnesses at Decatur, Indiana,[104] is distinguished mostly for its avowal of the absolute anti-exclusion doctrine. It carried that theory so far as even to invalidate off-street parking requirements because their ultimate effect, said the court, would be exclusion of the church. This phase of the case is covered in more detail at pages 125-8. However, the court held that the church had to comply with setback requirements or lose its permit. The court said: [104:118]

> We find no evidence in the record tending to show that the setback line of 18.48 feet is arbitrary or capricious as applied to [the

congregation's] property or that it places an unreasonable restriction on the freedom of worship or the right of assembly. The enforcement of this restriction will not act as a prohibition against the building of the proposed church because [the congregation] can reasonably comply with the requirements. In our judgment, [the setback requirement] is not an unreasonable regulation as applied to [the congregation's] property and is, therefore, a valid exercise of the police power in the interest of health and public welfare.

In the Jewish case at Irondequoit, New York,[107] a New York trial court also recognized the validity of set-back requirements that had been imposed on a proposed temple at 2956 St. Paul Boulevard. The ordinance did not specifically authorize a requirement with respect to off-street parking so the court invalidated a condition of the permit in that respect. However, the ordinance did provide appropriate standards with respect to "size of lot, setback and height." Under this authorization the court approved a condition in the permit under which "exterior changes shall not be made in the building without permission of the board."

The issue of space arose again in the case of the Haltom City, Texas, Jehovah's Witnesses,[136] but consideration thereof was again barred under the particular ordinance. The court considered various reasons given by the city for refusing a permit, finding them all insufficiently substantial. One of the reasons given [136:702] was "size of lot." The court rejected this justification on the same theory invoked by the New York court in rejecting the off-street parking requirement, that the ordinance did not provide for refusal of permits on such a basis.

The standard provided in the Haltom City ordinance was that the church must not "materially injure neighboring property for residential use." The court's treatment of the size-of-lot justification is equivocal as to whether constitutionality is challenged or merely statutory validity. The court said: [136:704]

> The application was denied first because of the size of lot. Under the provisions of the zoning ordinance, the size of the lot is immaterial if the building sought to be erected will not materially injure neighboring property for residential purposes. From our

understanding of the evidence, no claim is made that the size of the lot materially injures the neighboring property. The objection to the church by neighboring property owners is that they do not want any church in the neighborhood. Furthermore, there is no evidence that the size of the lot has any substantial relation to the health, morals, safety, or general welfare of the community.

If the final sentence above were applied generally it might invalidate all setback requirements in Texas. In support of it the court cited the Omaha, Nebraska, Presbyterian church case [14] which I have criticized at page 52-5.

In the Protestant evangelistic center case at Dallas, Texas,[102] the court raised the space problem in a different way. To justify the exclusion of Jack Coe's proposed edifice, the court decided that the building was not a church at all. This, said the opinion,[102:183] was because "some 2,400 square feet were [devoted] to healing rooms or prayer rooms and only 600 square feet for the auditorium or church proper." I question this as an improper attempt to regulate the distribution of space on the interior of church property between different kinds of religious activity. However, if an ordinance had been enacted requiring that not more than a certain maximum percentage of space zoned for religious use shall be used for non-religious activities, it could probably have been sustained.

In the South Euclid, Ohio, Jewish case of 1956,[140] the court ordered issuance of a permit for establishment of a small synagogue. As I have shown at page 43, the objections to the synagogue seemed rather contrived. One objection was that the lot was too small for the purpose. The court said that: [140:182]

> The zoning and planning commission asserts that it considers the six lots as too small, although an acre in total extent, upon which to erect a building of only 120 feet in length and 125 feet in depth. An examination of the maps and drawings in evidence shows only a comparatively small area for the erection of the building, leaving a comparatively large area for landscaping and parking purposes. Thus the claim that the area is too small has little or no substance in fact.

There was in this case no ordinance fixing exact setback lines or percentages of occupancy. Readers who carry slide rules will note that the percentage occupied by the building was about 25%.

In the Charleston, South Carolina, Baptist school case,[157] the central problem was interpretation of a percentage-of-occupancy requirement. The proposed church was located in the area known as "Old and Historic Charleston." The congregation had been organized in 1683 and the land, located between Tradd and Water Streets, had been bought in 1699. It was 232 years later, in 1931, that the zoning ordinance was adopted under which the percentage-of-occupancy limitations were provided.

In 1957 the Baptists asked for a permit for construction of an addition to take care of more students. Under a provision permitting variances, the board granted it. The court upheld the decision over objections of the neighbors. The principal question was whether, in computing the percentage of occupancy, such things as graves and gravestones and monuments should be counted as "buildings." The court held [157:461] that they were not to be so counted. There seems to have been no attempt to challenge the validity of the occupancy limitation as such.

Related also to the problem of space was the requirement enforced in the Jehovah's Witnesses' case at Bethel Borough, Pennsylvania.[159] There it was provided [159:241] that a "church, school auditorium, stadium and similar places of assembly" should not be "permitted within one quarter mile of each other." The court sustained the denial of a permit. It justified the proximity provisions by saying that: [159:243]

> The grouping of a number of public assembly buildings in a residential district will obviously create additional traffic hazards. The fire protection facilities of single-family residence districts are usually designed to handle fire-fighting problems presented by residences with few inhabitants. They are not normally designed to handle buildings occupied by large numbers of people.
>
> Street and traffic control facilities of a residential district are not normally prepared to handle the large concentration of people or automobiles which results from public assembly use. It is reasonable to suppose that several public assembly structures located closely together would create an additional threat to the safety of their occupants and the travelling public. Proximity requirements

are designed for the purpose of lowering the hazards which can arise from the close grouping of assembly buildings or structures which are exceptional in a residential district.

The Bethel Borough case was decided in an intermediate court and was refused review in the Supreme Court of Pennsylvania.[159] Later the same year, that court took quite a different attitude toward the application of the Catholic Archbishop of Philadelphia to build a regional high school at Wyncote in Cheltenham Township, Pennsylvania.[162] As I will show at pages 92-3 and 268-9 the entire decision was colored by an artificial interpretation of the ordinance.

In the light of this very restrictive ruling, the court [162:592] overruled the justification that "the size of this proposed high school tract of 18 acres to accommodate 1200-1600 students does not meet the requirements of the Department of Public Instruction of the Commonwealth of Pennsylvania for a public high school, which recommend that sites for high schools or secondary schools shall have a minimum area of ten acres and one additional acre for every one hundred students of ultimate enrollment over a six-year period. Under this recommendation, the tract should contain 26 acres at the least."

The court did not attack the propriety of this space requirement, but only the authority of the source from which the zoning officials sought support for it. It said [162:597] that "such recommendations are not applicable to the instant situation. They are not requirements. In many instances, the record indicates that even public school authorities are not following them and diocesan schools are not under and subject to the Department of Public Instruction. While it is idealistic and visionary to promulgate such recommendations concerning the adequacy of school sites, yet a court is not required to grant its imprimatur to such 'ideal' plans when dealing with zoning questions."

The same logic was followed in the case of the Catholic day school at Montclair, New Jersey,[228] where the court said that educational requirements as to public schools "had no controlling significance" in a zoning case. I assume, however, that valid zoning ordinances can be enacted, like the ones validated in the Philadelphia, Pennsylvania, Jewish case [50] and in the

Bethel Borough, Pennsylvania, Jehovah's Witnesses case.[159] As in the last two cases mentioned, such an ordinance may impose different space requirements on churches or schools than are imposed on residences.

The Montclair case was followed by enactment of a state law forbidding zoning ordinances to "discriminate between public and private day schools, not operated for profit, of elementary or high school grades." This statute was enforced in 1962 in favor of a Lutheran school at the Borough of Morris Plains [241] and in favor of a Catholic school at Montclair.[248] These cases will be discussed at greater length at pages 182-3.

Aside from such statutes, I would rely on the statement of E. C. Yokley on the subject in *Zoning Law and Practice*.[96] In § 163 he says that "in the early days of zoning, there were decisions holding so-called setback line provisions in ordinances invalid," but that "we may safely say . . . that it is now well settled that a municipality may, . . . as a part of a comprehensive zoning plan, establish reasonable setback or front yard requirements" and [96§165] that "legislation affecting rear and side yard requirements has, of course, met the same general approval as other area regulations." This statement is applicable also to church zoning cases.

# CHAPTER 7.

## Justifications: C. Fiscal Considerations

Alfred M. Bettman's 1917 address [10] (see page 000) included among the proper purposes of the police power the "promotion of common prosperity by stabilizing and protecting property values and reducing the difficulties and expense of municipal administration." Because it was then a minor problem, he omitted mention of another purpose: preventing the "loss of taxpayers" because of the removal of valuable land and buildings from the tax rolls. Are fiscal considerations a relevant and sufficiently substantial justification to sustain regulation of the religious use of land?

Of course, the whole subject of maintaining property value, discussed in Chapter 8, is also relevant to this matter. It is not the purpose here to discuss the propriety or impropriety of church tax exemption generally. However, it is relevant to consider certain stirrings of effort to offset the effect of such exemption by "zoning out" churches or by regulating the maximum amount of land that a church is permitted to remove from the tax rolls. These efforts have had mixed success.

It helps protect public safety, health, welfare, etc., if the government's financial position is protected either from a loss of revenue or from an increase of expense. Perhaps it would be more appropriate for the government to use its taxing power than its police power for this purpose. We will not discuss whether it is proper but only whether it is constitutional for a city to use its zoning power against churches in order to help sustain its income or decrease its expenditures.

The issue seems first to have arisen in the Beachwood, Ohio, Jewish temple case.[101] There, for various reasons, the board's decision refusing a permit was upset by the court. One of the several justifications advanced for the board's action was rejected in the following language: [101:69] "Some concern is also expressed with regard to the financial burden which will fall upon the village because of the building and operation of the

88

temple, particularly in the safety department, such financial burden being increased by the fact that the property involved will be removed from the tax duplicates."

"It has long been the policy of the State of Ohio," the court continued, "that property entirely devoted to religious, charitable or educational purposes shall be exempted from the ordinary burdens of taxation. This rule of law, which is universally recognized, is a public recognition of the importance of these voluntary organizations for the well-being of our community life. No municipal corporation can justly refuse a permit to build a church only because the property will no longer be subject to taxation." Thus the court refused to recognize the fiscal purpose as one sufficiently substantial by itself to justify the exclusion of a church from a residential neighborhood.

During the following year, however, the Supreme Court of Wisconsin decided the Wauwatosa case.[106] It sustained the exclusion of a Lutheran high school from that Milwaukee suburb. One of the court's justifications was based on fiscal considerations. In its opinion [106:46] the court said: "The projected school has many features which seriously impair the social and economic benefits to the entire community which the zoning law is designed to preserve and promote." One such impairment, said the court, was that "the school property will be taken from the tax roll, thus increasing the financial burden of the city's taxpayers. The presence of the school will lessen the taxable value of nearby homes and will deter the building of new homes in the area."

The court mentioned this matter in connection with another subject. (See pages 170-6.) Admittedly, it did not control the result. However, this statement was relevant to the question (also before the court) whether the justification was sufficient under the due process clause. While I would not be dogmatic about it, the passage above quoted probably states Wisconsin law on the question with which this chapter is concerned.

As mentioned on page 63, the fiscal purpose was one of several that the New York Court of Appeals held insufficiently substantial to justify the "zoning out" of the Catholic church, school, etc., at Brighton.[149] One of the justifications advanced for the refusal of the permit [149:830] was that "good planning requires the maintenance of larger and more expensive homes which bear higher assessed values. The board stated that it was certain that the Dreschler property [site of the church, etc.] would be subdivided and built upon, and therefore to allow a church and school at this location would result in a loss of potential tax revenue." The area from which the church was excluded was only about 12% of the total area of the town.

Discussing the "reasons advanced by the planning board to support its decision," the court of appeals entitled one part of its decision "Loss of Potential Tax Revenue." It seemed to be following the example of the Ohio court in the Beachwood Jewish temple case.[101] It said [149:836] that "Section 1 of Article XVI of the Constitution of this State provides that 'real or personal property used exclusively for religious, educational or charitable purposes, shall always be exempt from taxation, and such institutions have been granted tax exemption."

"Thus," said the court, "the paramount authority of this State has declared a policy that churches and schools are more important than local taxes, and that it is in the furtherance of the general welfare to exclude such institutions from taxation. This being the case, it cannot be seriously argued that the decision of [the city] denying this permit because of a loss of revenue is in furtherance of the general welfare. A higher authority than these boards has decreed otherwise." The court cited and quoted the decision in the Beachwood, Ohio, Jewish temple case,[101] above discussed, disregarding the contrary view of the Wisconsin court in the Wauwatosa case.[106]

Fiscal considerations present to the court the converse of the space problem discussed in Chapter 6. The area regulations there discussed have for their purpose the minimizing of the amount of space built upon. Regulations based on the fiscal purpose may seek to minimize the vacant area, thus avoiding losses of tax revenue. There is little jurisprudence with respect to such efforts, but there is some.

In the Sands Point, New York, Jewish synagogue case [148:495] the congregation owned 24 acres. The building was planned to occupy only three percent of the lot area. The board found:

(a) "that the subject premises were too large for the proposed use,"

(b) that the congregation "failed to prove that a smaller site which would serve its purposes is not available in the village," and

(c) "that the 24 acre plot is not essential for [the congregation's] strictly religious purposes."

The court held that such findings did not have "any basis in the zoning ordinance" and that they sought "in essence to impose a nonexistent duty upon the petitioner requiring it to justify the size of the site proposed in relation to the proposed use. The restrictions which are present in the ordinance with reference to the size of premises are only with respect to minimum requirements and, as we have seen, the area of the building is but 3% of the area of the site." There is an implication here that if the ordinance were properly drafted the maximum size of the lot could have been controlled.

There is a little additional information about this case not shown in the court's decision. In William Schack's article in *Commentary* for May 1957,[163] he says that while the Sands Point case was pending before the village authorities, the application was amended "to request the use of only the main building. . . . The congregation was willing to forego the use of the outdoor recreational facilities and the smaller buildings, which it was ready to place at the disposal of the village. It was even willing to consider paying taxes, though it was legally tax exempt."

Thus it appears that the question of tax exemption was rather more prominent in the case than is indicated by the court's decision. However, Schack's report is based on the situation prior to the victory of the synagogue in the court of appeals. After that, it is doubtful whether the congregation would have been so "willing to pay taxes."

In the same article, Schack refers to a case in Pittsburgh that seems never to have reached a court of last resort and is, therefore, not discussed in detail in this treatise. In that city, he says, the zoning boards withheld a building permit from Temple Emanu-el until it agreed to pay taxes on 12 of the 20 acres it had acquired as a building site, which the temple finally agreed to do "since the temple avowedly planned to use only eight of the acres for itself, reserving the rest for ultimate sale, presumably for profit."

In the Cheltenham Township, Pennsylvania, Catholic high school case of 1957,[162] the lower court found that "the expense which would be occasioned to the township by reason of the consequent widening of streets, the placement of sidewalks, and street-lighting, is a factor to be considered." The supreme court brushed off this consideration. It said: [162:597]

> What relationship this fact bears to the standards set forth for granting or refusing a special exception—the *health, morals and safety of the community*—is beyond comprehension. Any use of this site would affect consequentially the township in that it would require the widening of streets, etc. As a matter of fact, [the archdiocese] has offered of record to assume part of any attendant expense by widening at least a portion of Royal Avenue at its own expense, providing for off-highway parking and placing sidewalks along the main artery of traffic. This reason bears no substantial relation to the *only standards* which must guide the board or the court in their exercise of discretion. [Italics mine.]

Lawyers often seem to feel that a weak argument gains by overstatement. This attitude should be discarded when they go on the bench. But the justices in the highest Ohio, Pennsylvania and New York courts seem not to have done so. Thus:

(a) In the Beachwood, Ohio, Jewish temple case,[101] (see page 89) we find that the court describes church tax exemption as a "rule of law universally recognized" although in its next earlier breath it had referred to such exemption as a mere state policy changeable at any legislative session.

(b) The New York court, in the Brighton Catholic church and school case [149] says (see page 90) not that the commission's position was erroneous, which it might have been, but that it "could not be seriously argued."

(c) The Pennsylvania court, in the Cheltenham Township Catholic case [162] here discussed, refers to fiscal purposes not as insufficient, which they may have been, but as "beyond comprehension."

In the Cheltenham Township Catholic case, the conclusion of the zoning board may have been "beyond comprehension," not intrinsically but because of the justice's disinclination to comprehend. This can be demonstrated by reference to the very passage quoted above. I have italicized the words "health, morals and safety" which the court characterizes as "the only standards which must guide the board." The omission here of "general welfare" justification is important because that is the standard under which the fiscal justification can best be supported.

Does the quoted passage state the standards correctly? Obviously not. The correct standards are stated in an earlier part of the decision [162:594] and are the "promotion of the health, safety, morals *and general welfare* of the Township." (My italics) I will discuss this case again and show that in other respects the court grossly misinterpreted the same statute again. The obvious misquotation above described is sufficient to discredit the decision as a precedent on any issue.

Dr. Eugene Carson Blake, (chief administrative officer of the United Presbyterian Church in the U. S. A. and former head of the National Council of Churches of Christ in America) said recently [209] that continuation of the present church tax exemption indefinitely into the future will jeopardize not only the stability of government but the program and effectiveness of the churches themselves. He said that tax exemptions which are "proper when churches are small, poor and weak, may have highly unfortunate results for the churches and society when churches have grown large and rich."

In this connection my readers are referred to the description, at pages 14-15, of the modern billion-dollar-a-year church construction industry. These new buildings, the decorations they contain, and the land on which they are located are ordinarily tax exempt. Yet their operation is sure to increase the cost of all public services more than residential buildings would.

Dr. Blake suggested in his article that a hundred years from now, "the present pattern of religious tax exemption by federal, state, and municipal authorities, if continued, may present the state with problems of such magnitude that their only solution will be revolutionary expropriation of church properties." He pointed out that the growing wealth and property of the churches was partially responsible for the revolutionary expropriation of church property in England in the 16th Century, in France in the 18th, in Italy in the 19th, and in Mexico, Russia, Czechoslovakia and Hungary in the 20th. Those interested in church-state relations in this country, he added, dare not take for granted as "good and permanent" the religious tax exemptions now in effect in the nation, state and municipalities.

I do not here endorse Dr. Blake's views, but they highlight the importance of the subject. It may be some time before our legislators, normally so very much "on the side of God," will reduce church tax exemptions. It may not be easy for preachers, bound to meet budgets, voluntarily to pay what they do not legally owe. Can zoning regulations, perhaps, present an auxiliary method of cutting the public losses?

Few cases have passed on the question whether fiscal considerations form a sufficient justification for excluding churches from valuable lands or fixing the maximum amount of such land that can be devoted to religious purposes. The Beachwood, Ohio, Jewish temple case [101] rejected such an attempt with reference to Ohio "policy." The Brighton, New York, Catholic church and school case [149] decided the question adversely, based on an interpretation of the New York constitution. Yet in the Sands Point, New York, Jewish synagogue case [148] there is a contrary implication. The Cheltenham Township, Pennsylvania, Catholic high school case [162] decided the matter adversely, based on a misquotation of an ordinance. The Wauwatosa, Wisconsin, Lutheran high school case [106] decided the question favorably to the municipality, but in a case where this was not the principal issue. This is one of the outstanding questions of church zoning law, the judicial answer to which may become more important than it presently seems.

# CHAPTER 8.

## JUSTIFICATIONS: D. PROTECTION OF PROPERTY VALUE

As has been mentioned previously the principal present-day justification for regulation of religious land is the prevention of traffic hazards. In the beginning, the principal justification advanced for all land use regulation was protection of property values. At the National Conference on City Planning at St. Louis in 1918, Lawson Purdy (a New York attorney associated with E. M. Bassett said: [11:41]

> The courts must be educated. It is not many years ago that there were few men in this room that could make any sort of argument to sustain zoning on any principle. Now all of us think that we can make conclusive arguments to sustain some forms of zoning at least.
>
> The more I have thought of the way that we should proceed to get the courts to see what we wish them to see, the more convinced I am that we should all of us think in terms of value a great deal. Popularize the idea of preserving the value of a man's house, of a man's lot. Get that talked about. When you meet one of these judges, tell him about it, so that when, bye and bye, a case comes before him as a judge, it will be entirely familiar to him.

This sort of approach must have influenced the very conservative justices when the zoning ordinance of the Village of Euclid came before the Supreme Court of the United States in 1923.[18] It provided for exclusion of all nonresidential construction, even churches, from certain zones. The court did not consider the church phase of the ordinance directly. However, it was obvious that, to the Euclid council, the exclusion of churches was not as unthinkable as it had been a few years before to the New York Commission. As shown on pages 56-7, the justification that most appealed to the court was the protection of property from injury by quasi-nuisances.

When Mr. Purdy spoke of justifying "at least some forms of zoning," he may have implied the same ecclesiastical exceptions as Mr. Bassett. He may have given no more thought to the exclusion of churches than did the drafters of the first New

95

York zoning code. For one thing, there was substantial doubt whether the typical church did depreciate nearby property to any marked degree. It did not usually involve heavy congestion. It was not as large, nor were its activities nearly as varied, as are those of present day houses of worship. Similar observations may have been in the mind of the United States Supreme Court when it held for future decision specific cases involving particular pieces of property.

Very early, the state courts took an unfriendly view of this justification for religious land use regulation, without actually holding it invalid. In the Portland, Oregon, Catholic school case [27] the decision against the city hinged principally on the arbitrary action of the council in delegating the power to nearby neighbors to grant or deny the permit. But the matter of depreciation of property values also was presented to the court. The city contended [27:393] that the "the proposed school site is in a high class residential district in which many of the residents have expended large sums of money in improving and beautifying their property; . . . that the use of plaintiff's property for school purposes would greatly depreciate the property of other residents; that such reduction in value would result from the congregating of the children on the adjacent streets and from the inconvenience and danger of vehicular traffic, and from the noise that necessarily prevails from children at play."

It was not necessary for the court to pass on the issue of depreciation. It had decided the case on other grounds but it did refer to that issue. It restated the allegations above, adding a strong element of sarcasm. It spoke of the neighbors' homes as "mansions" and compared them with the manger of the Bible chronicle. It mentioned the "large sums of money spent in making lawns and setting out shrubbery." It said only that "this decrease in value would apply with equal force to any other residential district." The court stated no conclusion as to the propriety of justifying religious land use regulation on the basis of property value protection but made clear its hostility to such an approach.

In the Reno Roman Catholic church case [35] the standards established by law included [35:222] "conserving the value of property." The court did not hold this standard improper. It held that the evidence about funerals was insufficient, that they would not be any more bothersome if conducted in church than in private homes. There may have been other evidence as to depreciation, but if so the court disregarded it. The court may also have been influenced by the fact that there was a public school directly across the street from the site of the proposed church. At any rate, the decision rested not on the invalidity of this justification but on the lack of evidence to support it.

The same may be said of the decision in the Upper Arlington, Ohio, Lutheran church case.[40] The court refrained from challenging the validity of depreciation as a justification for church zoning. It said that "according to the testimony of a member of the Upper Arlington Zoning Commission, who most resolutely opposed the building of a church, . . . this impairment [of nearby property values] would be but a consequence of the factors already enumerated. . . . Of all non-residential uses, a small suburban church would seem to present a minimum of objections." The court obviously considered the evidence of devaluation insubstantial.

In the Church of God case of 1944 at Sherman, Texas,[48,49] the council alleged,[48:102] in support of its denial of the permit that the purpose was to "prevent . . . depreciation of at least $500 for each home or residence in this residential district." However, the court held that there was no evidence "affirmatively indicating that aforesaid residential district would be adversely affected by the contemplated uses," and therefore that "the ordinance, in such regard, must be held unreasonable." Again the court's dictum rested not on the insubstantiality of the purpose but on the insubstantiality of the evidence about it.

In the Indianapolis, Indiana, Methodist church plant case of 1946 [57] the decision went in favor of the church before the board of zoning appeals. In court the objectors seem to have raised the issue of value. The proponents of the permit had presented the evidence of three witnesses each of whom expressed the opinion that "the establishment of the church at this location would stabilize rather than deteriorate property values." On this basis, the court sustained the action of the zoning board granting the permit.

In the Pittsburgh Roman Catholic retreat house case, decided in a trial court, there was an allegation that conversion of the auxiliary building into sleeping quarters would reduce the market value of objectors' properties. First, the court challenged the sufficiency of proof on this point. It said: [81:182]

> The petitioners have argued strongly that the fair market value of their properties would be reduced to an extent of 20-75% depending upon the size of their homes and the proximity of their homes to the property of the Order. It is difficult to look into the future, especially when one deals with as intangible a matter as "the fair market value" of real estate. The real estate experts who testified for petitioners were not convincing. They did not testify to any specific instances which would indicate that the prospective purchasers were deterred or adversely influenced by the pendency of the occupancy and use permit in this case.

The experts testifying for the Franciscan Order said that the permit would not affect real estate values in the neighborhood and the judge seems to have agreed with their view. But the judge then attacked the whole theory on which this justification is based. He couched his challenge in terms not only of law but of morality, economics, and even international politics. He said [81:182] that "in connection with this phase of the case we should add the observation that property rights are not controlling when we are dealing with religious freedom as guaranteed by the constitution."

"The eternal spiritual values," this judge added, "which are inherent in the teachings of any of the great religions are more important than merely material or economic considerations. . . . History teaches that undue emphasis upon the glorification of merely material well being has always led to the drying up of the mainsprings of society and the crumbling of the state. Especially today, when our form of society is beset by a most bitter and cunning enemy, who stresses a gross and perverse form of materialism at the expense of human dignity, human worth, and human freedom, emphasis upon the ideal, the noble and the spiritual is required more than ever before."

This passage must certainly have convinced the unfortunate neighbors that their "mere material well-being" was being sacrificed in a good cause. It is the only all-out constitutional attack that I have found against this justification for religious land use regulation.

The Haltom City, Texas, Jehovah's Witnesses' Kingdom Hall case [136] was based, again, on deficiencies of evidence. The valuation witness for the city had testified only [136:705] that the church would depreciate nearby property "in a measure." Other churches had received permits even though they depreciated nearby property in a similar measure. The zoning board itself had concluded that there would be a "possible" depreciation in such values. The court said, in effect, that this was not enough. "It is true that some people prefer not to live next door to a church," the court remarked, but "the evidence falls far short of showing material injury to neighboring residential property."

Trial courts in New York on occasion have rejected this justification for zoning out churches. In the case of the Garden City, New York, Jewish center,[150] the supreme court of Nassau County held that "in view of the high purposes, and the moral value of these institutions, mere pecuniary loss to a few persons should not bar their erection and use." Relying on the Brighton, New York, Roman Catholic case,[149] decided by the court of appeals, the Nassau County supreme court said: "When the location of a church is involved, the board of appeals may not be swayed by such considerations." In the Brandeis Jewish School case at Lawrence, New York, the decision [191] followed similar reasoning.

However, it appears that the New York judicial policy is likewise based more on statutory than on constitutional grounds. Neither in the Brighton case decided by the court of appeals, nor in the Lawrence nor in the Garden City cases, decided in trial courts was there any authorization under the ordinance specifically permitting such considerations to "sway" the board. In the Brighton case the court discussed the "adverse effect upon property values." [149:835] Its conclusion was that "if such *unauthorized* (my italics) standard is allowed to prevail, the board could keep churches and private schools from locating in any place in a Class A area." The court of appeals did not say what it would have done if depreciation of nearby property values had been an authorized standard under the ordinance.

The treatment of this justification by other writers is somewhat less than exhaustive. A recent annotation in the *American Law Reports* [185] concludes that "the possible adverse effect on property values by the presence of a church in a residential zone is not of itself a sufficient ground for denying a permit for the construction of, or maintenance of, a church in such zone." As late as 1959, an article in the *Catholic Lawyer* [204] said that "depreciation of property values has not usually been a valid basis for excluding churches." The use of terms like "usually" and "of itself" makes these conclusions sufficiently equivocal to prevent direct contradiction. Their fault lies in their reliance on cases, like those above mentioned, which rejected this justification not because it was unconstitutional but because it was either (a) not authorized by the ordinance or (b) not supported by evidence. Furthermore, they fail to take any account of cases which hold the contrary. There are a number of cases directly holding that prevention of depreciation of property values is a sufficient justification for excluding churches, either of itself or in company with other factors.

In the Porterville, California, case of 1949,[67,71,76] which the Mormons tried unsuccessfully to carry to the Supreme Court of the United States, the California court took judicial notice of the fact that "a single-family residence may be much more desirable when not in an apartment house neighborhood or adjacent to a public building such as a church." The court added that "the provision in the ordinance for a single-family residential area affords an . . . inducement for the acquisition . . . of private homes." Some writers and judges have cited the Upper Arlington, Ohio, Lutheran case [40] against the validity of this justification. I disagree with this for the reasons shown on page 97, but I disagree even more positively because they refrain from mentioning the Cleveland Heights Jewish school case, a decision by the same Ohio Supreme Court that was firmly based on the depreciation factor. There the court said [59:244] that the area around the proposed school "is improved with well-kept homes, occupied in most instances by the owners" and that "there is testimony that the use of property for school purposes would substantially and permanently injure the appropriate use of the neighboring property and lower its value." The action of the zoning board in rejecting the application was sustained.

A dissenting justice, by his protest, seemed only to emphasize the grounds of the majority ruling. He said that "although . . . a number of witnesses, mostly property owners in the immediate neighborhood, testified that in their opinion the establishment of [the] school would reduce the value of surrounding real estate, I can find no tangible evidence in the record indicating that the presence of the school would adversely affect the health, safety, morals or general welfare." The dissenter obviously did not believe that depreciation of property value is adverse to the "public welfare," but the majority disagreed with him.

The Wauwatosa, Wisconsin, Lutheran high school zoning case [106] is another in which the court invoked the devaluation factor. It took judicial notice that "the presence of the school will lessen the taxable value of nearby homes and will deter the building of new homes in the area." The Lutherans were also applicants in the Miami, Florida, church case of 1955.[124] There, "one of the [city's] witnesses testified that in most instances the security value of the property would be lessened by being adjacent to a church." The court said that [124:882] "from testimony the chancellor was privileged to believe, the surrounding property would 'definitely depreciate. . . .'"

In the West Hartford, Connecticut, Methodist church case [139:641] the court used similar reasoning. It said that "the use of the premises . . . in accordance with the proposed program would change the character of these streets. . . . As a result, . . . these properties would suffer a substantial loss in value."

In the Miami Jewish school case of 1958 [189:52] the court stated the same proposition but in reverse terms. It cast the burden on the congregation of proving that the school would not devaluate other properties. The court said that "the trial court did not find, nor would the evidence support the finding, that . . . the desired prohibited use . . . as a private school would not cause loss and injury to other owners in the area."

Another strong statement in support of property devaluation as a factor in church zoning is found in the case of the

Catholic church parking lot at San Marino, California,[223] of which the archbishop also unsuccessfully sought review in the Supreme Court of the United States. The California court considered a "contention of the [archbishop] that there was no sufficient showing before the council of 'material damage or prejudice' to other property in the neighborhood from the granting of the variance." This contention, said the court, was "fully answered by reference to the transcript of the hearing. Several property owners testified that granting a variance would tend to decrease property values in the surrounding . . . zone."

The "opinion of the court" (see pages 46-7) in the Baptist case at Bayside, Wisconsin,[231] also clearly recognized property devaluation as a sound basis for zoning out churches. The decision said: [231:295] "This court has recognized that the protection of property values is an objective upon which a zoning ordinance may be grounded. . . . Whether restriction of use of a district to strictly residential use will protect property values is the type of question upon which the decision of the municipal board is accepted unless shown to be unreasonable." However, the testimony on value seemed to favor the church. A lawyer and real estate broker with twenty years' experience testified that, except for the immediately adjacent lots, values would actually be increased.

One learned article and one court decision have put a sort of reverse twist on this concept that must not be ignored. *St. John's Law Review* in an often quoted article said [95:102] that "the zoning laws themselves adversely affect some realty and, even if the existence of a church will have a similar effect, it logically follows that the depreciation caused by a church is not fatally inconsistent with zoning, and exclusion is not necessary to effectuate a comprehensive zoning plan."

This contention has the ring of logic. A legislature or council or zoning board can properly determine what kinds of buildings a district shall contain. If its determination is reasonable, property owners in the area cannot complain that their values have been lowered. This rule would apparently apply whether it is churches, factories, or residences that are included in (or excluded from) the district. The article was referring to the power of the legislature or city council to lessen the value of a man's real estate by permitting entry of undesirable neighbors.

The Indiana court carried the logic of the article a step farther and arrogated the power to itself. In the case of the Catholic "parish plant" at Meridian Hills,[229] the opinion writer started, of course, on the basis of the previously established Indiana judicial policy. As previously indicated, this policy is extremely favorable to churches. However, the evidence against the church seemed very strong.

The zoning board had rejected the permit after two or three witnesses testified "that the proposed parish plant would cause substantial and permanent injury to the property bordering upon the [archbishop's] land." A construction man said that there would be "a depreciated value" in the amount of 20%. A professional appraiser estimated the decrease in value of surrounding homes at 16 to 20%. The proposed church-school plant was a large one, estimated to cost a million dollars.

The trial court treated the testimony of these witnesses [229:41] as "but a shred of evidence" because they "gave no specific instance in which a church or school had been constructed in an area of expensive residential homes that had thereafter actually caused a depreciation in value." The supreme court added its own observation that since the archbishop acquired his site and erected a sign announcing his intention to build all of the property had increased in value, some of it as much as 100%.

Parenthetically, this indicates one of the complexities of proof with respect to market value. The court here did not seem to realize that the depreciation issue may involve not only the question (a) whether prices have gone down, but also (b) whether they have gone up less rapidly than they would have risen without the depressing factor of the church.

The important aspect of the Meridian Hills case is its adoption and expansion (without mentioning the source) of the theory above quoted from St. John's Law Review.[95] The court said: [229]

> In the Euclid case [18] it was specifically shown that the restrictions destroyed part of the value of the owner's property. Yet the showing was made that the restrictions, excluding commercial uses,

were for the general welfare, safety, and health. It would seem that the contrary would also be true—that if the use is shown to be without question for the good of the public and general welfare that no owner of private property adjacent or in the neighborhood could complain because the value of his property might be thereby depreciated to some extent, since the purpose of the zoning laws is not to protect private, personal interest, but rather to protect and promote the general public interest.

The archbishop got his permit. The court had put an ingenious turn on the logic of prior cases. I would not completely deny its validity, but in my opinion it would have been more valid if it had been used to support the decision of a zoning board. In the exercise of the police power, the legislative branch has the power to destroy the property rights of landowners in the public interest. In the Euclid case, the legislature had done just that by excluding industry. In the Meridian Hills case, however, the legislative and executive branches had refused to destroy values in a residential zone by allowing nonresidential use. The supreme court had no independent police power under which it could properly accomplish such a result.

While it is not the most important justification, protection of property value still has validity in church zoning cases, contrary to the suggestions of the other writers whom I have quoted. It may in some cases be the sole basis for excluding a church. No church should assume that it may ignore this issue if its right to a permit is challenged. Nor should a zoning board or aggrieved property owner wishing to exclude a church disregard this possible justification. The question of the extent of devaluation is deeply affected also by the type of church involved, which will be discussed at page 150.

# CHAPTER 9.

## Justifications: E. Protection of Neighbors

As a justification for public regulation of the religious use of land, "protection of enjoyment of neighboring property" ranks no higher than third. It is of less importance than either (a) traffic control or (b) maintenance of property values. Of course the three subjects are closely related. Traffic lessens property enjoyment. Loss of enjoyment may affect value. The "enjoyment" factor is subjective. It is harder to measure it than to determine, for instance, the amount of traffic or the market value of lands and buildings. Yet this factor has great social significance.

Depreciation in market value principally concerns people who are in the business of buying and selling real estate. Solid citizens buy houses, not for speculation, but to live in. If they buy a house or lot in what is supposed, under the regulations, to be a quiet, peaceful and comfortable zone, they may object to unanticipated uses of a disturbing sort nearby even if they do not decrease—or even actually if they increase—the value of their property for resale.

This problem is recognized by the New York Court of Appeals though it has ruled most consistently against the exclusion of churches and church schools. In a 1961 zoning case involving the White Plains YMCA,[227] the court said that "everyone wants churches, schools and clubs, but not in his own neighborhood." In the light of this almost universal objection, zoning boards sometimes act against religious institutions, either by exclusion or by regulation short of exclusion, in order to prevent or abate noise (see page 106), inconvenience to neighbors (see page 110), depressiveness (see page 112), disturbances of peace and comfort (see page 114) or deterioration of fire, health, and sanitary conditions (see page 115).

In reading about these different kinds of attempts to protect enjoyment of property it will become obvious that their classification is largely a matter of terminology. For instance

105

one judge may call something a disturbance which another describes as an inconvenience, etc.

## Noise

Judicial discussion of church institutions as noisemakers seems to have started, in zoning cases, in the Portland, Oregon, Catholic school case.[27] This was not the key issue but nearby owners did complain about the amount of noise that the children would make. The judge took a dim view of this charge, especially in view of other existing noises in the area.[27:395] This position seems reasonably sound. He first pointed out that the street cars ran "from early morn till dewy eve and far into the night and passed and repassed many times every hour." Automobiles, he added, were driven over the same streets "at all times of night and day." The street cars, he said, were "not noiseless" and the automobiles in operation were "not silent."

The children, on the other hand, were around only for a few hours. "It appears," said the justice sarcastically, "that the noises made by street cars and automobiles are preferable to the prattle and laughter and merry shouts of the children of a primary school, 'the playful children just let loose from school.'" He did not agree with this attitude (as restated by him) and overruled the zoning board's refusal of a permit.

The noise issue was also raised more or less parenthetically in the Reno Catholic church case.[35:219] The objection was to the use of a church bell. Since the church was across the street from a public high school, there was, perhaps, already a high noise level. The court dismissed the objections to the bell without discussing them, but the matter was given more careful attention in the Upper Arlington, Ohio, Lutheran church case [40] three years later.

One of Upper Arlington's defenses was that the church would cause increased noise. No specific noise is mentioned except the "bells or chimes." Prior to the breakdown of negotiations, there had been an agreement, satisfactory to both parties, against the use of chimes. In spite of this, the city objected in court on the grounds that the chimes would be used.

Answering, the court said that "as to increased noise, the

church authorities have expressly agreed not to install bells or chimes. People going to and from church are not customarily rowdy or boisterous. On three sides of the proposed site of the church, the neighbors would be insulated from what little disturbance there might be by a street with a minimum dedicated width of fifty feet. Moreover, the surrounding property is still largely vacant except that occupied by the telephone exchange directly across one street and three four-family apartment houses diagonally across another."

Presumably in raising the objection to the chimes, the city thought the previous agreement against them had lapsed. The court based its decision on the supposition that this agreement would be carried out. Although the court rejected the argument about noise as a basis for exclusion, by implication it imposed a condition based on protection against noise.

The Ohio Supreme Court that decided the Upper Arlington church case [40] just mentioned returned to the noise issue in the Cleveland Heights Jewish school case.[59] The testimony was that the "establishment of [the] school would result in noise and confusion." There was a strong dissent which recognized this fact but held that it would not "adversely affect the health, safety, morals or general welfare of the residents of the district."

Described in the Michigan court's decision as very noisy was the camp meeting of the so-called Full Salvation Union of Portage Township. The court said [60:300] that "the record before us indicates that the camp meetings . . . were attended with such degree of noise as to cause disturbance to others residing in the vicinity. There is testimony to the effect that such noise continued from early in the morning until approximately 4 A. M. the following day. It cannot be said that such use was within the contemplation of the ordinance." The court required destruction or removal of the whole set-up.

Perhaps the quietest of the church institutions mentioned in these cases is the retreat house maintained by the Catholic Franciscan Order in a fine residential district of Pittsburgh.[81] Persons attending such retreats are supposed to maintain silence throughout. This was a factor in granting the permit. Real estate experts had testified as to the depreciation of nearby property, using apartment buildings as examples. The court said: [81:182] "There is a vast difference between a busy apartment building with its comings and goings and the quiet atmosphere of a retreat house. These experts have given little if any consideration to the quiet dignity, the peace and good order, and to the absence of all noises and even conversation, which is of the very essence of a closed retreat." This part of the decision seems sound.

In the case of Jack Coe's evangelistic center at Dallas, Texas,[102] the court was again dealing with more flamboyant manifestations of religious spirit. There was considerable evidence of noise. In previous operations, the evidence showed that "children quartered on the premises as orphans had been heard screaming and praying" [102:183] and that "the use of the premises in 1952, when tent services were conducted, disturbed the peace and quiet of the neighborhood. Coe's own testimony showed a history and practice of healing and tent services with loud speakers and a Hammond organ." On the basis of this record, the court held that the nuisance could be enjoined, and the construction permit for a permanent building denied. In addition, as in Portage Township, Michigan,[60] the court held that Coe's institution did not come within the meaning of the word church as used in the ordinance.

Beginning in 1954 several decisions mention church noises as an important factor justifying the regulation of land for that use. The first of these was the Wauwatosa, Wisconsin, Lutheran high school case,[106] where the ordinance excluded private high schools entirely. The court [106:40] said that the city had "made it abundantly clear that respondents' projected school has many features which seriously impair the social and economic benefits to the entire community which the zoning law is designed to preserve and promote." Among those mentioned was the fact that, "Athletic events will bring noisy crowds." A fact not mentioned by the court which may have accentuated this problem was that the public high school stadium, in order to maintain Wauwatosa's aspect as a "city of homes," had been located in a nonresidential district. The importance of noise as such is also underlined by the omission of any reference to traffic hazards.

The church institutions thus far mentioned were noisy for

some special reason, such as athletic activities, outdoor meetings, or evangelistic activities. The Miami Beach Lutheran church case of 1955 [124] involved a small church of one of the "established" denominations engaged only in the usual worship practices. This was a church of the type that the Ohio court in the Upper Arlington Lutheran church case [40:524] had described as presenting "a minimum of objections." Yet the court, at least in a left-handed way, relied on noise abatement as one of the justifications for its exclusion. It spoke of the traffic problem which would result from funeral services, wedding ceremonies and other gatherings where large numbers of persons congregate about the same time and disperse about the same time, "not to mention the noise that comes from people congregating in large numbers."

A similar "established" denomination was involved in the West Hartford, Connecticut, Methodist church case in 1956.[139] Presumably it would be much quieter than football games, camp meetings and evangelistic centers. Yet it was excluded from a residential neighborhood by a decision in which the court said that there was now "very little noise" in the neighborhood, that the proposed use of the premises would change the character of the streets, and that "traffic with its attendant noise . . . will increase greatly."

In the Milwaukie, Oregon, Jehovah's Witnesses' Kingdom Hall case, noise was also mentioned as a factor.[184] The noise on which the decision was based came not so much from the congregation of people as from the congregation of automobiles. The court held [184:18] that noise, like the other factors mentioned, "is a subject bearing a substantial relation to or reasonably necessary for the protection of the public health, safety, morals and general welfare to warrant regulation through the exercise of the police power," and that this factor had "found judicial approval in 'church' zoning cases as [a] condition having a substantial relation to the public welfare."

Nonjudicial legal writings give short shrift to the factor of noise as a justification for regulation of land use for religious purposes. For instance an *American Law Reports* annotation [185] says only that "denial of a permit for construction of a church because of noise and similar inconvenience has been held arbitrary and unreasonable." Supporting this statement, it cites the Brighton, New York, Catholic church and school case.[149] It disregards the key fact that the Brighton ordinance contained no specific standards authorizing consideration of noise, inconvenience, or any similar concept as a justification.

The annotation also cites the Haltom City Jehovah's Witnesses case of 1956.[136] In that case, the question was raised but the court did not hold noise abatement an invalid justification. It held only that the alleged noisiness had not been proved. The court said [136:705] that the city "assigns 'noise' as a reason for denying the permits. The record does not support such findings insofar as the proposed religious services are concerned. The evidence is to the contrary. . . . There is no testimony that . . . outside noises will be any louder than ordinary around a small suburban church."

In the Haltom City case,[136] the court followed the lead of the Upper Arlington Lutheran high school case.[40] It treated as insignificant the noises arising from the "small suburban" church. In the Portage, Michigan, Full Salvation Union camp meeting case [60] and the Dallas, Texas, Protestant evangelistic center case [102] there was more indication of readiness to take such matters seriously where more intense religious activities were involved. That noise can be important even in considering applications from small Protestant churches is obvious from the West Hartford, Connecticut, Methodist church case [139] and the Miami, Florida, Lutheran church case.[124] Applicants for church permits cannot disregard noise as a possible argument against their admission to a quiet residential zone. Zoning boards may be justified in rejecting permits on this ground, or at least in requiring that steps be taken to minimize the number of decibels that will afflict the eardrums of the neighbors.

*"Mere Inconvenience"*

The convenience of the public is one of the standard generalities that, along with health, safety, morals and welfare, are supposed to justify use of the police power. Therefore, it is a little disconcerting to find, in a number of church zoning cases, passages which refer to "mere" inconvenience as insufficient to justify such regulation.

In the Pittsburgh, Pennsylvania, Catholic retreat house case,[81:184] the court said that, in religious cases, "the threat to the health, good order and morals of the community must be a very real, substantial and tangible one. Mere inconvenience is not enough." However, the Pittsburgh case should be read in connection with the case of the Russian Orthodox cemetery case at Rochester Township, where the highest court of the same state took quite a different attitude.[207]

Again in the Haltom City, Texas, Jehovah's Witnesses case,[136] "mere" inconvenience to neighbors was said not to be a "valid reason to deny to a church the right to exist in a residential district. It is hard to visualize a church being constructed in a residential district without inconveniencing someone. To restrict churches to areas where no one would be inconvenienced would be in effect excluding churches from residential districts. The maintenance of churches is such a valuable right that their existence will not be denied because of mere inconvenience to neighbors."

This sort of statement was repeated in the Brighton, New York, Catholic church and school case.[149:836] There the court said that "noise and other inconveniences have been held to be insufficient grounds upon which to deny a permit to a church or a parochial school." Supporting this rule with respect to a church, the court cited the Upper Arlington, Ohio, Lutheran church case.[40] I see nothing in that decision with reference to "convenience" or "inconvenience" as such. Furthermore, the result in the Upper Arlington case flowed not from insubstantiality of purpose but from the city's misrepresentations. (See pages 67-8.

The New York court also cites the Portland, Oregon, Catholic school case.[27] That decision did discuss the inconvenience of having children about, of whom, said the good justice, are the Kingdom of Heaven. The court said [27:395] there was "no virtue in the argument that children will trespass on private property in the vicinity of the school" because "there is a sufficient remedy at law to prevent such a trespass." The court did not mention the practical difficulty of collecting damages from every tyke who might hit a baseball over a fence.

Since these cases refer so often to "mere" inconvenience as being insufficient, they are hard to controvert. Some inconveniences may be so "mere" that they would not justify the exercise of the police power. But these decisions should not be construed as negating the abatement of "inconvenience" entirely as a justification for regulation of religious land use. Bear in mind the statement in the West Hartford, Connecticut, Methodist case [139:642] that the term is not used in a colloquial manner, that it is not synonymous with "handy" and that it connotes that which is suitable or fitting." The concept of convenience overlaps the aesthetic ideals described in Chapter 5 and the "depressiveness" discussed in the following paragraphs.

*"Depressiveness"*

For complex psychological reasons some activities of churches, such as funerals, are quite distasteful to the "captive" spectator. The plaintiffs in the Reno, Nevada, Catholic church case emphasized this point, or at least so the judge made it seem. This was the only neighborly objection to the church to which the court gave direct attention. The court said: [35:222] "[The city] urges that funerals at the proposed new church would have a depressing effect on nearby residents." Deprecating the evidence on this point, the court cited a previous federal decision involving an old ladies' home. In it the court had said:

> The owner of the adjoining duplexes testified that having an old ladies' home as an immediate neighbor would . . . affect his morals [morale?] to have it referred to as the old ladies' home next door. . . . Certainly the fact that aged people may have a depressing effect on some people is not sufficient to exclude such people [the old ladies?] from a district. There is no limit to the causes that may depress people, but they do not furnish a basis for support of a restriction as to use of one's property.
>
> What was said . . . with respect to the noise and annoyance incident to the operation of a grocery store in a residential district would apply a *priori* to the so-called "depressing influence" of elderly residents, *viz:* it could disturb or impair the comfort of only highly sensitive persons. But laws are not made to suit the acute sensibilities of such persons. It is with common humanity— the average of the people—that police laws must deal. A lawful and ordinary use of property is not to be prohibited because repugnant to the sentiments of a particular class.

After quoting this language the Nevada court said: [35:222] "Death is a part of our existence and is as natural as life. We are unable to perceive why a church funeral service, reverently conducted as such services uniformly are, should have a more depressing effect on the normal person than one held at a private residence." It neglected to mention that funerals are frequent events in churches while in private homes they occur only "once in a lifetime." Yet there are firm grounds for sympathy with the court's general observations. Judges cannot concede too much to the psychological quirks of individuals or classes when contraposed to the rights of others. Many have a sort of "allergy" to certain religions and their practices, based perhaps on religious beliefs of their own.* For instance, the mere proximity of Jehovah's Witnesses sometimes gives rise to individual and mass psychoses. Such human weaknesses must not be indulged.

The psychological-depressiveness argument as applied to church funerals is probably now less relevant. Funerals now increase traffic hazards so substantially that the depressiveness factor pales by comparison. Private funeral chapels are restricted, generally, to business zones. However, the lighthearted attitude of the Nevada court could still in a sense be compared with the small boy's whistling as he walks past a country graveyard at night. The abhorrence of death and its trappings will continue. It may have been an important factor in the case of the Russian Orthodox cemetery at Rochester Township, Pennsylvania.[207] There the court upheld exclusion of a church cemetery. The reason, as stated by one commissioner, was that he "could not possibly believe that the men who drew up this zoning ordinance meant that a beautiful home should have a cemetery next door as a religious purpose."

A rather amusing variation of the psychological theme turns up in connection with the application of a Jewish congregation to use as a synagogue a school property already in operation at Cheltenham Township, Pennsylvania. The court said: [105] "The principal protestant appears to be Mrs.

---

* According to William F. Buckley, an Oriental appeared at a religious banquet, turned to his neighbor at the table and said: "My miserable superstition is Buddhism. May I ask what is yours?"

Scherr, who lives across the street from the premises in question." Mrs. Scherr was a "protestant" but not a Protestant. She had been a member of the Jewish congregation against which she was protesting.

The decision says that "she strenuously objects to the children playing outdoors and listening to records of nursery rhymes, in particular 'Rudolph the Red-Nosed Reindeer.'" The judge may have been overindulging his sense of humor when he emphasized the particular song. However, many readers will sympathize with this lady's attitude as reported. Yet the fact that the Rudolph song got on Mrs. Scherr's nerves was not considered a proper reason for refusing the permit. For one thing, the song was perpetrated by the children in the school (the permit for which was not in issue) and not in the proposed religious services.

*Disturbances of the Peace*

Neighbors, of course, might be annoyed by various church activities. The incidence of such annoyance is as unlimited as the inventiveness of recreation directors. In the Porterville, California, Mormon temple case, the court upheld [67:825] the total exclusion of churches as an "inducement for the acquisition and occupation of private homes where the owners thereof may live in comparative peace, comfort and quiet." In the Louisville, Kentucky, Baptist church case [69] the lower court approved a building permit but only on condition that the planned night lighting for athletic activities be eliminated. In the Wauwatosa, Wisconsin, Lutheran high school case, night lighting was one of the reasons justifying exclusion of the school. The court said [106:46] it would "interfere with the peace and comfort of the neighborhood."

The whole subject of traffic control, discussed at greater length in Chapter 10, relates to disturbances of the peace. As shown on pages 130-1, the court in the Bethel Borough, Pennsylvania, Jehovah's Witnesses case [159] emphasized that traffic control is not exercised "merely to cater to the convenience of owners and operators of motor vehicles." Its purpose, said the court, includes "freeing the streets of the . . . often intolerable conditions of traffic congestion." This is to be compared with the view of the Oregon court in the Portland Catholic school case [27] which believed that children needed defense against the drivers of automobiles, also with that of the Florida court in the Tampa Jehovah's Witnesses case [83] which was solicitous for the carriage horse.

### Police, Fire, Health and Sanitary Regulations

In the Bethel, Pennsylvania, Jehovah's Witnesses case [159] above mentioned the court also said that the evils which the law sought to remedy "affect conditions for . . . operation of fire and police forces, etc.," and therefore that "its justification stems directly from the exercise of the police power which is the supreme power of government." The expansion of our concepts of police power to include zoning and planning does not spell the end of the purposes for which that power had previously been exercised. Long before modern land planning began, we had police regulations with respect to building materials, fire hazards, sanitation, safety, health, etc. Even those who contend most strongly against the zoning regulation of churches will admit that regulations are proper when directed toward such important ends.

If safety, fire and sanitary regulations are incorporated into the zoning code, they may provide that building permits shall not be issued except on advance guaranty of compliance with such provisions. The permit may contain conditions as to future compliance with general regulations or with special requirements recited in the permit. If the conditions are violated, the permit may be made subject to cancellation. Continuance of the use may then be prosecuted or abated as a nuisance (and the church or church school thereby "excluded").

There are enough disasters even in the "established" churches to make such provisions relevant. However, the groups most directly affected are the so-called store front churches, such as the Church of God at Sherman, Texas. According to the decision in that case,[48:101] the congregation was occupying a building 30 or 40 feet wide and 40 feet long. "Presumably built for a filling station, it had since been used as a garage, then as a Helpy Selfy laundry, with the proprietor living there part time; but had been vacant for some two years before trial."

The new pastor, it appears, had run an extension cord to the outside and had put up a sign designating the church and the kind of services held. "Seemingly no attempt was made to comply with city requirements relative to fire, sanitation and health, Reverend Sims stating to Police Chief Tribble, after differences had arisen, that 'he didn't recognize any law but God's.' " The city authorities tried to prevent Sims from using the place for a church at all. The court rebuked this policy and ordered issuance of the permit but only upon compliance with fire, safety, sanitary and health laws. It said: [48:102] "Otherwise and in event of noncompliance, the provisions of Article 1011h, V.A.C.S. would thereupon become available to the city of Sherman." This was the section providing for injunctions.

The Montgomery, Alabama, Pentecostal Holiness church case [56] concerned a similar dispute as to sanitary, police and health regulations. The permit was made conditional on compliance therewith. There was a similar problem in the Portage, Michigan, case, [60] involving the Full Salvation Union. In that case the camp meeting was dispersed. In the Baptist school case at Charleston, South Carolina, [157] the evidence indicated a hazard of fire if the proposed addition to the school was constructed. The board accordingly imposed a restriction on the number of students who might attend the school. A Kingdom Hall of Jehovah's Witnesses was excluded from its proposed location in Bethel, Pennsylvania, [159:243] the court saying, among other things, that "the fire protection facilities of single-family residential districts are usually designed to handle the fire-fighting problems presented by residences with few inhabitants. They are not normally designed to handle buildings occupied by large numbers of people."

In the case of the Lacordaire Catholic day school at Montclair, New Jersey, [228] the need for fire protection operated in favor of the permit. The sisters were occupying three floors of an ancient residence. As stated in the decision of the New Jersey Supreme Court, [228:390] the Montclair fire department had inspected the school's premises and had made various recommendations. These included the suggestion that the use for student activities of any floor above the first be discontinued and that "the sisters presently housed on the third floor be moved to the second floor." The sisters then sought a variance to enable construction of a new two story building on the premises. There were a number of objections all of which were overruled. The variance granted by the zoning board was upheld. The court was obviously interested in, among other things, the additional fire protection that the new building would provide.

This chapter has disposed of a number of minor justification that are invoked from time to time for regulation of the religious use of land. The next chapter will deal with the principal justification so invoked, namely the prevention of traffic hazards and congestion.

# CHAPTER 10.

## JUSTIFICATIONS: F. TRAFFIC CONTROL

Referring to a recent church zoning case, Bishop Fred Corson of the Methodist Church said: "There are apparently militant atheists in this country who want to deny Christians their basic rights." [211] In 1957, *St. John's Law Review*,[95:103] referring to zoning in general, said: "If such legislation [excluding churches] were upheld, it would be theoretically possible to legislate this country into atheism."

Writing in the *American Mercury* of November, 1959,[212] however, Rev. Ralph I. Yarnell, General Secretary of the American Council of Christian Churches, blames the bans on church construction on "ministerial associations that are part of the National Council of the Churches of Christ in the U. S. A." He says that they seek such prohibitions "by their cooperation with and pressure upon city councils and planning commissions."

I have no confirmation of Dr. Yarnell's views; but neither do I believe that an atheist bloc in American public life has been responsible for the zoning out of a single church. When religious uses of land are regulated under zoning laws, it is usually done in good faith for purely public purposes and after exceedingly sympathetic consideration of the rights and interests of the church. Where malice exists, then, as described in Chapter 14, it is instigated not by rationalists but by local people of religious convictions so deep that they can brook no others. I was inclined at first to agree with the views above quoted. I had a vague impression that the increased willingness to enact and enforce religious land use regulations reflected a trend toward anticlericalism or secularism. A more thorough study of the church zoning cases convinces me that no such trend exists.

The one factor that more than any other has reconciled reluctant courts to the necessity for regulating religious use of land is the increase in automobile traffic. It is reinforced by tremendous population changes and by the religious building boom. The reasons for the change are entirely objective. If the horse-and-buggy conditions of the past had continued to prevail, judges and zoning officials would now be just as loath as ever to permit such regulation. In his day, as E. M Bassett [36] said, people complained that churchgoers' automobiles "lined the curbs." Now it is not the lining of the curbs (they are already lined with residents' cars) but the jamming of the streets' entire width. The importance of traffic is made crystal clear in the long quotation at pages 12-13 from the Oregon court's decision in the Milwaukie Jehovah's Witnesses case.[184]

The issue of traffic congestion is now involved, directly or indirectly, in most church zoning cases. Even courts devoted to what I have called the "absolute anti-exclusion" doctrine are recognizing the necessity for reasonable control in the interests of traffic safety. To show how this judicial attitude has developed, one need only review a few of the cases in which the issue is discussed.

In the Euclid case of 1926,[18] the whole concept of comprehensive land use zoning was put to the constitutional test. However, the court argued the importance of traffic considerations by saying that zoning regulations "are sustained, under the complex conditions of our day, for reasons analogous to those which justify traffic regulations which, before the advent of the automobile and rapid transit street railways, would have been condemned as fatally arbitrary and unreasonable."

In 1930, in the Beckley, West Virginia, Church of God case,[25] the traffic problem was mentioned. The city charged, among other things, that the church "would materially interfere with traffic." The court recited some of the surrounding conditions, such as the width of the street and the availability of space for parking in the area, and said that "from these facts, the contention was without basis." The charge not having been proved, it was unnecessary for the court to pass on its validity as a justification for denial of the permit.

The traffic issue was again raised, in a secondary way, in the 1932 Catholic school case at Portland, Oregon.[27] The case was decided on other grounds but the court took occasion to comment on an allegation by the city that the proposed school was to be located at the intersection of a streetcar line and a busy automobile traffic artery. Three fourths of the children would have to cross at least one of the thoroughfares to go to and from school. The proposed playground would front on one of the busy streets.

"They complain," said the court,[27:394] "that it will be dangerous for the children to cross those through streets. That matter may be easily remedied by compelling vehicular traffic to slow down at a designated crossing." The judge felt it was better to slow down traffic than to require the archbishop to build his school in a safer place. This attitude may have been the result in part of (a) sentiment toward streetcar and automobile operators that was characteristic of middle-aged non-drivers, and (b) the judge's affection for children.

The judge said that streetcars run "from early morning to dewy eve and far into the night." Automobiles, he said, "in operation are not silent. They are driven over those streets at all times of the day and night." Referring to the noises of children, on the other hand, he said: "Children were ever so. They were so nearly 2000 years ago when a Man who was born not in a mansion but in a manger said: 'Suffer little children and forbid them not to come unto Me; for of such is the Kingdom of Heaven.'" Twenty-six years later, the traffic issue was brought more squarely before the same court. This time it did not attempt to "slow down" the march of automotive progress. Instead, it required Jehovah's Witnesses to build their Kingdom Hall elsewhere. (See pages 131-3.)

Although Justice Bettman, who wrote the Upper Arlington, Ohio, Lutheran church decision of 1942,[40] was associated with planners, he shared some of the ideas of the Oregon justice. Bettman had been city attorney of Cincinnati and in 1917 he had spoken from the same platform with E. M. Bassett. The long dictum in the Upper Arlington case reflects this point of view. Yet the justice carefully refrained from holding that traffic control cannot justify religious land use regulation. In the preliminary negotiations between the Lutheran synod and the city officials, the latter had insisted upon the maintenance of a percentage of any church site as a parking lot. The Lutherans had agreed to this condition. In light of this agreement, the court said: [40:523]

> The objection that there will be possible traffic congestion caused by persons congregating for religious services has been

expressly repudiated, in similar circumstances, as a ground for refusing to permit the erection of a church in a residential district.

The repudiation, Bettman indicated, was contained in the Beckley, West Virginia, Church of God case.[25] In this respect Bettman was mistaken. The West Virginia court had not repudiated the assigned purpose of lessening traffic hazards. It had held only that there was no proof of such hazards. Bettman's mistake was verbal only. In his decision he likewise refrained from repudiating this justification. He based his decision also on lack of evidence. He said:

> Here it appears that the church site is not only bounded by streets but that there has also been an express agreement to set aside 25% of the lot for a parking space, an area sufficient to accommodate 60 automobiles. Any perceptible increase in traffic which might result from attendance at a church seating only 250 persons would occur mostly on Sunday morning, a time when ordinary traffic would be greatly diminished, and any danger to children going to and from school entirely eliminated.

In 1941, in *Cox v. New Hampshire*,[39] the Supreme Court of the United States decided a case between the city government of Manchester and Jehovah's Witnesses. It was not a church permit but a parade permit that was involved. About 90 members of the sect had started out from a Kingdom Hall, in four or five groups, on what they called an "information march." Each marcher carried a sign reading "Religion is a Snare and a Racket," and "Serve God and Christ, the King." They handed out printed leaflets announcing a meeting.

They had no parade permit. They were prosecuted for violating a state law requiring one. The Supreme Court of the United States upheld their conviction, saying:

> The authority of a municipality to impose regulations in order to assure the safety and convenience of the people in the use of public highways has never been regarded as inconsistent with civil liberties, but rather as one of the means of safeguarding the good order upon which they ultimately depend. The control of travel on the streets is the most familiar illustration of this recognition of social needs. Where a restriction of the use of highways in that relation is designed to promote the public convenience in the interests of all, it cannot be disregarded by the attempted

exercise of some civil right which in other circumstances would be entitled to protection.

One would not be justified in ignoring the familiar red traffic light because he thought it his religious duty to disobey the municipal command or sought by that means to direct public attention to an announcement of his opinions. As regulation of the use of streets for parades and processions is a traditional exercise of control by local government, the question in a particular case is whether that control is exerted so as not to deny or unwarrantedly abridge the right of assembly and opportunity for communication of thought and discussion of public questions immemorially associated with resort to public places.

The Cox case did not refer to property rights, as most church zoning cases do, but rather to the rights of religion, speech, and assembly, that are more precious to the citizen and the courts alike.

The Porterville, California, Mormon temple decision of March 1949,[67] was also based in part upon the traffic-control justification. This case was decided on the pleadings, neither side presenting evidence. The court took judicial notice of certain facts. It said that "it is a matter of common knowledge that people in considerable numbers assemble in churches, that parking and traffic problems exist where crowds gather." Thus, it held that for the purpose, among others, of controlling traffic, a church could be entirely excluded from a residential area.

In the case of the Broadway Baptist Church at Louisville, Kentucky,[69] there was a zoning regulation requiring off-street parking. The case went to the court of appeals on a procedural issue. In returning the case to the lower court for further proceedings, the court called attention to the off-street parking provisions and approved them. It said: [69:862] "There is also in the case the issue of the adequacy of provisions for off-street parking, which is one of the fixed conditions to granting a permit." At another point,[69:863] speaking of "traffic hazards, off-street parking," etc., the court said: "The commission has the power to require proper and suitable arrangements, which in the present case we have no doubt can be made."

In the Atlanta, Georgia, Jehovah's Witnesses case of 1950,[72,78] the Witnesses contended that they had complied with the off-street parking requirements and, if they had not, that such requirements were a violation of their "constitutional rights respecting the use of property and the right to worship." [72:582] The case was remanded to the court of appeals,[78] which considered the difference of opinion as to whether the ordinance had been complied with. The court sustained the city's view that compliance had not been made. It said:

> Under the constitution of this state and the enabling act, the City of Atlanta has a broad authority as to zoning, and in the establishment of districts and regulations, classification may be on any basis "relevant to the promotion of the public health, safety, order, morals, convenience, prosperity or welfare. . . . The court will not control this discretion unless it is manifestly abused. . . . Under the record before this court in the present case, it does not appear that there was an abuse of the discretion and judgment vested in the board of zoning appeals in determining that it was undesirable to permit the location of a church at the proposed site in that it would likely create a serious traffic problem, considering the number of vehicles that would be brought into the area and the number of those which could be parked off the street and around the proposed building.

The court did not refer directly to the due process clause under which substantiality of public purpose is required. But by its reference to "public health, safety," etc., it is obvious that this standard was in its mind.

Only eight months later a case substantially similar to the Atlanta, Georgia, case [78] was submitted to the Supreme Court of Florida. This one was decided in the opposite way. The court required issuance of a permit to the Tampa congregation of Jehovah's Witnesses.[83] It first decided that the Witnesses had "substantially complied" with the off-street parking requirements. This should have settled the problem, but the court felt called upon also to suggest another possibility. It said in effect that even if the violation had been proved traffic control was not a sufficient justification for religious land use regulation. It said: [83:79]

> It is a matter of common knowledge that traffic hazards about the church are of unusually rare occurrence, much less rare than they are in the home or out on the highway. For every traffic injury on the highway about the church, you can chalk up hundreds

of them from slips in the bathroom. Perhaps the traffic department should require more non-skid mats on the floor.

The court obviously meant "less frequent" not "less rare." The dictum in the Tampa case, like the decision in the Porterville Mormon temple case,[67] was based less on facts supported by evidence than on facts judicially noticed. The difference between the two decisions was that they took judicial notice of directly opposite facts. The Florida decision took judicial notice of the absence of traffic hazards around churches. The Mormon decision took judicial notice of their presence. Each court insisted that the facts as stated were "matters of common knowledge."

In the Tampa decision there also are found traces of the same "pedestrian" attitude as that of the judge in the Portland case.[27] As pointed out at page 61, the court in the Tampa case referred to automobile drivers generally as the "careless and unthinking" who "rip through the streets with no thought for the safety of man or beast." It added: [83:79]

> When exposed to the illuminating power of common sense, the regulation drawn in question has very little to sustain it. Drive through any municipality in this country between the Atlantic and the Pacific about 11 A. M. and 7 P. M. on Sundays and 7 P. M. on Wednesdays and you will find hundreds of cars parked along the street adjacent to churches. To undertake the prohibition of this practice would be futile. There is no showing here that a different rule should govern [the Tampa Jehovah's Witnesses.]

The common knowledge about church traffic conditions upon which the Florida court based its dictum seems to have been about as permanent as the tandem bicycle. Only five years later the same court, including the justice who wrote the words above quoted, expressed a contrary view on the application of the Lutheran Church of the Epiphany in Miami Beach.[124] There, the exclusion of a church from a residential area was upheld on the ground, among others, that "evidently the property is located on a state highway, often heavily travelled. . . . The effect of the rezoning of the property would be a genuine traffic problem which would result from funeral services, wedding ceremonies, and other gatherings where large numbers of persons congregate about the same time and disperse about the same time. . . ."

In the Chicago Episcopal church case of 1952,[93] where the ordinance required each church site to be surrounded by alleys, the court also dealt, incidentally, with traffic control as a justification for church zoning. It said that "the ordinance as we have interpreted it imposes a condition with respect to the sites on which a church may be erected." It added: "There is no question of the city's right to exercise police power in this fashion . . . if the purpose of the restriction is related to the traffic requirements which may be created. . . ."

In the case of the Decatur, Indiana, Jehovah's Witnesses,[104] the question of the validity of off-street parking requirements was more directly raised than it had ever been before. The court made the following general statement: [104:119]

> If the refusal of the zoning board to grant a variance results in the exclusion of a church from a residential district, such action is illegal and must be reversed.

If this statement is read out of context, it clearly bars the imposition of any conditions with which a religious application is unable or unwilling to comply. However, in the sentence immediately following, such a generality is controverted. The court contradicts itself by saying:

> If the regulation requiring off-street parking for churches in proportion to the number of seats in the church is to be sustained, it must be upon the ground that the benefit to the public health, morals, general welfare and safety outweighs the restriction which such regulation places upon the right of freedom of worship and assembly.

This statement seems to place no greater burden upon the zoner in church cases than in other cases. The last statement clearly contemplates that a church may be barred for failure or refusal to comply with reasonable regulations. Since the two statements conflict, neither is worth very much as a precedent.

One phase of the Decatur case must have made a deep impression on the court. It does not appear on the face of the decision but requires a little computation. The court said [104:116] that the dimensions of the lot were 66 by 108 feet. This means that its total area was 7128 square feet. The amount of off-street parking space required by the ordinance was 6250 square feet, leaving the Witnesses only 878 square feet (a) to construct their building and (b) to comply with the setback requirements. This space was not even enough for the building which, as the decision states, was 34 by 60 feet, giving it an area of 2040 square feet. The setback requirements were 18.48 feet, presumably on two sides.

This is why the court concluded that the enforcement of the off-street parking requirement would "result in the exclusion of the church." There is a flaw in this reasoning. What made the construction impossible at that place was not only the regulation but also the fact that the Witnesses had bought too small a lot. One wonders what the court's attitude would have been if the Witnesses, instead of buying a lot with 7,128 square feet, had bought one with only 2,040 square feet. In that case, would the court have permitted the Kingdom Hall to be built flush with the street and alley and flush with the neighboring property lines? Any other decision would in such a case have "resulted in the exclusion of a church."

The court ended by enforcing the setback requirements (because that left the Witnesses enough land for their building) and refusing enforcement to the off-street parking requirements (because their land was insufficient for that purpose). The saving grace of the decision is the care with which the judges limit its effect as a precedent. Thus (at page 120) the court says (my italics) *"under the facts in this case,* the welfare and safety of the people of the neighborhood is placed in the scales of justice, etc." On the same page the court says that "we believe the fact situation *now before us* squares with that before the Supreme Court of Florida, etc." (referring to the Tampa, Florida, Jehovah's Witnesses case.[83]) Again on the same page the court says that *"under the set of facts in this particular case,* the application on this provision would . . . restrict the right of freedom of worship, etc." On the following page, the court says that: "In our judgment [the ordinance] as it has been *applied to appellee's property in the factual situation before us* contravenes the First and Fourteenth Amendments . . . , etc." and that "those provisions are *unconstitutional in their application to appellee's particular property."* The court did *not* hold the parking requirements unconstitutional as applied to other properties.

Of interest, however, is the Indiana court's general evaluation of traffic control as a justification for religious land use regulation. Like the justices in the Portland, Oregon, Catholic school case [27] and the Tampa, Florida, Jehovah's Witnesses case,[83] this justice was more inclined to slow down traffic than to slow down a religious group. The court said:

> It is no doubt true that automobile traffic often chokes the streets and endangers both the general and the travelling public. However, it is rarely, if ever, that people entering or leaving a church cause or contribute to traffic accidents. It would seem reasonable to assume that if regulation is necessary in the interests of the safety, convenience and welfare of the general public, that should be regulated which has a direct effect upon such general welfare. This can be, and is, done generally by traffic police, signs, and other reasonable regulations imposed alike upon all persons using the streets in the vicinity of churches, without undue interference with the right of worship and freedom of assembly.

This attitude evokes considerable sympathy if one is old enough to recall the day when we were not quite sure that the automobile had come to stay. But a more forward-looking attitude was expressed in the minority opinion signed by two of the five judges. Like Justice Rose's opinion in the Omaha Presbyterian case,[14:619] this was to become the basis of at least two later majority opinions, both of which were refused review in the United States Supreme Court.* The dissenting judges in the Decatur case [104:122] said the following:

> Our city streets are too often choked with automobiles and automobile traffic, which endanger the general public as well as the travelling public, because cities were planned for horse and buggy transportation. What might have been an unreasonable exercise of the police power in the day of the Model T may be clearly valid now under the growing menace of the automobile, which has been taking an annual toll of more than 40,000 killed and over a million injured. . . .
>
> It is quite evident that the members of the [congregation] could be killed just as dead going to and from church as going to and from a theater or a basketball game. It is a proper exercise of the police power to protect [the congregation's] members from their own negligence as well as from the negligence of the travelling

---

* The Milwaukie, Oregon, Jehovah's Witnesses case [184,200] and The Bethel Borough, Pennsylvania, Jehovah's Witnesses case.[159,168]

> public. There would be just as much logic in holding that the
> members of the [congregation] when going to church were not
> required to comply with traffic regulations as in holding that the
> [congregation] is not required to make reasonable provisions for
> lessening of the traffic hazards by off-street parking.

The dissent expressly suggested no analogy to the Supreme
Court's logic in the Cox case [39] (see pages 121-2), but the
similarity of the argument is clear. Finally, the dissent put its
finger directly on the most glaring inconsistency of the majority view. It said:

> If it was a proper exercise of the police power for the city, by its
> zoning ordinance, to require the [congregation] to comply with
> the average setback line of the residences, which only has a very
> remote bearing on traffic hazards, a fortiori, it was a reasonable
> exercise of the police power to require [the congregation] to
> provide space for 25 cars to park off the streets.

In the Irondequoit, New York, Jewish case of 1954 [107] the
court rejected off-street parking requirements but only because they were not authorized by the ordinance. It said that
"had the ordinance provided that one of the standards
. . . was that suitable parking facilities be provided, such a
provision would have been a valid delegation of authority." In
the Dayton, Ohio, Christian Science parking lot case,[122,142] the
court ruled that parking facilities had become so universal
that they should be considered a "customarily incidental or
accessory use" in connection with a church.

The Haltom City, Texas, Jehovah's Witnesses case [136] was
decided in favor of the Witnesses. However, again, it was
because the parking lot requirements were "substantially
complied with." The West Hartford, Connecticut, Methodist
church case [139] justified refusal of the permit on grounds,
among others, of traffic congestion, saying [139:643] that if it were
granted, "traffic, with its attendant danger and noise, will
increase greatly."

In the South Euclid, Ohio, case,[140] as will be shown in
Chapter 11, the city, at the time of the Jewish application,
suddenly increased its requirements from one space for each
ten seats to one for each four. The court did not invalidate this
requirement as applied to other institutions but required

issuance of a special permit for the synagogue, saying: [140:176] "It is stipulated that members of the [synagogue] are adherents of the Orthodox segment of the Jewish faith and as such they are prohibited from performing any manner of labor on the Sabbath and on holidays and using any form of transportation except walking to the place where the religious services are held on those days. . . . Because they adhere to this faith, their places of worship must be within walking distance of their homes." The court also pointed out how wide the street was, etc., and said [140:181] that the allegation respecting traffic was "without substance in fact." Again, the court held not that the allegation was improper but that it was unproved.

In the leading New York case of the Roman Catholic parish at Brighton,[149] the issue of traffic dangers was also raised. The court held it irrelevant not because regulation of traffic is an insufficient purpose under the due process clause but [149:836] because "no such policy or standard was declared in the statute." The court also cited with approval certain of the cases mentioned above, interpreting them to hold that "it is arbitrary and unreasonable to deny a permit to church or parochial school because of possible traffic hazards that may be created." However, this conclusion is inconsistent, in my opinion, with the Sands Point Jewish case [148] decided the same day.

In the Sands Point case, an important consideration was approval of the "size and location of parking and recreation areas." The court did not invalidate this requirement. On the contrary, it required the zoning board to enforce it. The ordinance provided that the board should determine the size and locaton of the parking lot required. Instead, the board had required the applicant to file plans, including a suggested parking area. It had rejected these plans without itself designating any alternative.

This was the principal ground for reversal. The court said: [148:495] "It is the duty of [the congregation] only to suggest and indicate a possible parking area while it remains the duty of the board to actually determine where the parking area should be located and what size it should be. The [congregation] did present to the board  suggested parking areas, and the board attempted either to ignore its duty or to shift the duty of final determination of such area to the [congregation], and upon doing so, disapproved of the areas proposed by the [congregation] and made no determination of its own." Thus the court clearly implied that parking requirements should be enforced. If the applicants had failed or refused to comply, the permit would have had to be denied, directly contrary to the dictum in the Catholic case decided on the same day.

The Charleston, South Carolina, Baptist school case [157] resulted in an order against the Baptists requiring that the number of students be limited to 270. This was based, at least in part, upon considerations of traffic congestion. The court [157:459] said:

> During the passage of the children from the day school on the church premises to the city playgrounds, and their return therefrom, as well as during the period when the school is opened and closed, a serious traffic jam is created, increasing the hazard of fire and [to] the general safety and welfare of those residents immediately adjacent to the premises in question.

More thoroughly than any earlier one, the case of the Bethel Borough, Pennsylvania, Jehovah's Witnesses [159] vindicates traffic control as a justification for church zoning. The ordinance required (a) seventeen parking spaces and (b) a quarter mile of distance between the church and the nearest other place of assembly. The Witnesses failed to comply with either requirement. The court said: [159:242]

> The board of adjustment and the court below found that [the congregation's] land is located at the intersection of Bethel Church Road and Fort Couch Road, which intersection is heavily travelled and is further complicated by the presence of traffic islands in the intersection; that the erection of [the congregation's] church at this intersection would substantially increase traffic dangers and congestion. . . . [The Witnesses] concede that traffic regulation is a proper exercise of the police powers, but they argue that these powers may not be exercised against a church.

The court cited a previous Pennsylvania Supreme Court case in which the opinion had said:

> Those attacking the constitutionality of such a law . . . obviously labor under the mistaken notion that its purpose is merely

to cater to the convenience of the owners and operators of motor vehicles; . . . [I]t's real purpose is to promote the larger and more general good of the community by freeing the streets from the impediments and perils arising from dangerous and often intolerable conditions of traffic congestion. And since the act is concerned with the regulation of the transportation of persons and property along the highways of the municipality, and since the evils it seeks to remedy vitally affect conditions for the transaction of business, the prevention of accidents, the effective operations of fire and police forces, and, in general, the enjoyment of many phases of city life and activities, its justification stems directly from the exercise of the police power, which is the supreme power of government.

On the basis of the evidence above mentioned as to traffic conditions in the area, the court in the Bethel case said:

We are of the opinion that there is ample evidence to justify the findings below to the effect that both regulations here involved bear a reasonable relation to the safety of the public.

In support of this conclusion, the court quoted at length from the Decatur, Indiana, Jehovah's Witnesses case [104] which I have discussed on pages 125-8. It quoted not from the majority opinion but from the minority. (Regrettably, it neglected to mention that the views it quoted were those of the minority.)

In the case of the Wenatchee, Washington, Jehovah's Witnesses,[165] the court decided in favor of the church because of the vagueness of the testimony on traffic conditions. It said: "Apparently no systematic traffic check, certainly no accurate or detailed traffic survey of the area, was made by the [city]. There is no evidence in the record (a) as to the occurrence, time, duration or extent of any periods of heavy traffic in the area, and (b) no evidence that the time of any such periods of heavy traffic would overlap or coincide with the time of any regular church activities."

Another decision which relied on the view of the minority in the Decatur, Indiana, Jehovah's Witnesses case [104] was the decision against the Witnesses and in favor of the city of Milwaukie, Oregon.[184] The court sustained the exclusion of the Kingdom Hall on the grounds of "traffic congestion hazard, and the discomforts arising from noise, fumes, and lights." It held [184:8] that each of these "is a subject bearing a [sufficiently?] substantial relation to, or reasonably necessary for, the protection of the public health, safety, morals and general welfare to warrant regulation through the exercise of the police power." Regarding the general subject, the court said:

"Traffic congestion" is a phrase comprehending many facets. As used in a matter of this kind, it implies all the nuisances, inconveniences and hazards to which the public generally, and those residing in the zoned area, may be exposed. Off-street parking would, no doubt, in some places tend to minimize some of the disadvantages of such congestion, but it cannot be expected to avoid all its resulting annoyances and potential dangers.

The incidents of traffic congestion include, among other things, noise, fumes, the intrusion of automobile lights, the blocking of private driveways by parked cars, and delays in normal travel for those using the highway. But most important are the increased dangers of injury to person and property. We do not mean to infer that the church-going public is less diligent than others in their respect for traffic laws. However, even the worthy and cautious persons of that class and their children are too often the victims of the careless. . . .

The test of whether or not the building of a church in a given zone will produce traffic congestion or augment existing traffic conditions to a point of hazard cannot be made solely in terms of what a given number of church members might produce with their probable use of a certain number of automobiles. If a church is, perchance, in an area where few people live or travel, then it might be relatively easy for a zoning board to determine, in the absence of other circumstances, that the building of a place of worship at such a given site, within the restricted zone, would not create traffic problems.

If so, it would be unreasonable to deny such a religious organization an opportunity to erect its building at that point. On the other hand, if traffic congestion is already a real or threatening problem near the site where a congregation desires to build, and the church would bring to that community enough additional vehicles to definitely establish congestion at that point, then the council would be reasonably warranted, if not duty bound, to deny a permit for its erection. In the absence of [the Witnesses'] evidence to the contrary, it must be presumed that the council gave consideration to and balanced all these factors.

The Oregon court then referred to the case of *Cox v. New Hampshire*,[39] from which I have previously quoted at pages 121-2, and said:[184:19] "We can see no difference in principle between the control of traffic congestion by direct legislation to the subject, as in the Cox case, . . . and the supplementation of such control under the police power by a less direct method of avoidance, when necessary, through the avenue of the zoning ordinance." Note that in the Milwaukie case the "supplementation" was not through off-street parking requirements but through the exclusion of the church. Citing the "substantial relation" of traffic to general welfare,[184:20] the court held that "there is no merit in [the congregation's] claim that it has been deprived of the use of its property without due process of law."

In the Allendale, New Jersey, Jehovah's Witnesses case,[205] the court sustained refusal of a permit for failure to comply with offstreet parking requirements. At the time of the application the ordinance required only "sufficient" space for that purpose. After the permit was denied, while it was on appeal to the board of appeals, the requirements were made more specific, requiring one space for each three seats. This requirement was clearly not complied with by the Witnesses. The court said [205:571] that the Witnesses had not availed themselves of an opportunity to show that the one-for-three requirement was unreasonable and that "on the record before us we are not at all at liberty to say that the requirements have not been imposed in good faith and for the public interest or that they are unnecessary or excessive or that they are not substantially related to the promotion of the public safety and general welfare." The Witnesses seem to have withheld their evidence as to unreasonableness in the hope they could invalidate the ordinance on its face. The Allendale decision was refused review in the United States Supreme Court [219] for "want of a substantial federal question."

While the courts were slow explicitly to recognize it, there is now little doubt that the control of traffic is a sufficiently substantial public purpose to justify the regulation of the religious use of land and, in proper cases, even the exclusion of churches from residential areas. This conclusion is not necessarily in conflict with the basic ideals of those early judges who held that it was traffic, not the churches, that ought to be regulated or "slowed down." It is instructive to compare them with the censures of Lewis Mumford in his great book, *The City in History*,[226] or with the criticisms of the premier of the Soviet Union who came, almost like a man from another planet, to view the traffic jams around Los Angeles.

Without forsaking the gains of modernity, our political leaders, with the help of city planners, should try to restore some of the advantages of the day when people walked to church. But that is a task for them, not for the courts.

# CHAPTER 11.

## DISCRIMINATION IN GENERAL

As appears in Chapter 2, there are three constitutional lines of defense for churches which wish to resist public regulation of their use of land. One is the due process clause. Under it the church may show that the purpose invoked to justify the regulation is not sufficiently substantial. The second line of defense is the equal protection clause. Under it the church may allege that it is being unfairly treated as compared to either (a) other churches or (b) secular enterprises. In Chapters 4 to 10, I have discussed the first line of defense at length, assessing the sufficiency of various justifications that are advanced to support regulation of church land. In this chapter and the three which follow I will study various phases of discrimination, then in Chapter 15 take up the third line of defense, religious liberty.

The rights of churches under the equal protection clause have a bearing on the alleged rule of absolute exclusion discussed in Chapter 3. Some proponents apply this rule to forbid exclusion of any church from any residential zone in any municipality. Others apply it in a more limited way to prevent only the exclusion of churches from an entire municipality or "practically" an entire municipality. In either case, the alleged rule is based on due process. It is contended under the due process clause that, as compared with the social importance of churches, no public purpose can be sufficiently substantial to justify the exclusion.

I disagree with the broader version of the absolute anti-exclusion rule (protecting churches against exclusion from any area). In many cases I would agree with the narrower version (protecting churches against exclusion from entire towns). However, my reason would be different from that of its principal proponents. I would rely less on due process than on equal protection.

It would seem very difficult to exclude churches from an entire municipality without violating their rights under the equal protection clause. Of all the cases studied, I find only one, namely the Sands Point, New York, Jewish case,[148] in which the city was without commercial establishments. There was no attempt in that case at "flat" exclusion of the church. If such an attempt were made, I suppose the New York Court of Appeals would find some ground for rejecting it. But in a supreme court less hostile to religious land use regulation such a total exclusion might have survived on the same grounds as in Porterville,[67] where the California court sustained flat exclusion of churches from a single exclusively residential zone. However, few if any municipalities are so exclusively residential as to justify the banning of churches on a municipality-wide basis.

This point is also illuminated to some extent by comparing the Porterville, California, Mormon decision [67] with the Plandome, New York, Unitarian decision.[87] (See pages 38-9.) The analogy is not complete because in Porterville the exclusion was not from an entire municipality. The New York court in the Plandome case distinguished Plandome from Porterville on the ground that the residential district from which churches were excluded was 100% residential in Porterville while in Plandome the area from which churches were excluded (the entire village) included lands zoned for purposes other than residences, including private clubs.

There were three other cases in which the absolute anti-exclusion rule was invoked in the limited sense. These were the Orchard Lake, Michigan, Catholic church and school case,[94] the Piedmont, California, Catholic school case,[125] and the Bayside, Wisconsin, Baptist church case.[231] In any of these, the courts might have considered invalidating the exclusion of churches, not for lack of adequate public purpose but on the basis of discrimination between religious and secular institutions. In Bayside, for instance, the ordinance permitted "any business."

But very few church zoning cases concern attempts at blanket exclusion of churches from entire towns. In the majority churches are excluded only if they fail to meet standards or conditions specified in the ordinance. In such cases, also, the factor of equal protection has received insufficient attention from the courts. This chapter will discuss cases where discrimination existed and might have formed the basis of a decision although in most of them the issue was avoided. Chapter 12 will discuss the question whether in some cases a desire to protect churches can result in "reverse discrimination" against others. Chapter 13 will discuss the special problem of discrimination between public and parochial or private schools. Chapter 14 will set forth some observations on the subject of prejudice.

Prior to 1945, there were four church zoning cases that mentioned discrimination but their mention of it was only incidental and superficial. The first of these was the Evanston, Illinois, Episcopal seminary case of 1927.[19.23] The principal basis of the decision was the fact that the college relied on an ordinance in effect when it acquired the land, along with the "sudden and unexplained" way in which an amendment was adopted barring schools "not possessing the power of condemnation."

"It may be worthy of note," the Illinois court added,[19:782] though perhaps it may not control the construction of the ordinance, that at the time the ordinance was passed there were two institutions of learning in the [same] residence district not possessing the power of condemnation. . . ." While not relying on it, the court thus obviously was influenced by the discrimination between the Episcopalian institution and the two previously existing schools.

In the Beckley, West Virginia, Church of God case of 1930,[25] although the decision hinged on other grounds, the court considered the city's allegation that the proposed church would interfere with traffic. It brushed this contention aside with the remark that "there are also on this same street a large hospital, church, and several places of business." Without actually saying so, the court suggested that denial of a permit to the Church of God would be unfair discrimination.

In the Reno, Nevada, Roman Catholic church case,[35] the court considered the alleged depressiveness of church funerals insufficient to justify exclusion of the particular church from the residential section. The court made a comparison between church funerals and home funerals (which were permitted) and held them equally "depressive." This was also an implied recognition of the importance of equal protection.

In the Sherman, Texas, Church of God case of 1944,[48,49] the court pointed out [48:101] that "a number of churches are in the residential district of Sherman, in the main erected before zoning; however, . . . since passage of the ordinance, a permit has been issued to the Assembly of God for a church building; also for a Baptist church to rebuild after a fire, both locations in residential areas." In this case the invalidity of the zoning ordinance was admitted, so that these additional observations became irrelevant; but this and the preceding three cases indicate that, from the earliest days of church zoning litigation, the factor of discrimination was in the minds of the judges.

This leads to the Mesa, Arizona, Catholic church case of 1945 [53] which is the first decision based squarely on discrimination. The Mesa ordinance excluded churches entirely from the city's residential zone. However, the zone was residential only in a nominal sense. Also authorized to be built in that zone [53:243] were: schools, colleges, public libraries, public museums, art galleries, parks, swimming pools (municipal or private), athletic fields, polo fields, golf courses, farms, truck gardens, and greenhouses. The court said that the question to be determined was: "May a zoning ordinance constitutionally exclude churches and may it prohibit churches in a zoning district where there is permitted the matters hereinbefore referred to?" The city contended that "churches cause extraordinary conditions different from those caused by any of the uses permitted in such districts." However, the court seems not to have been convinced by the evidence on this point.

"Before the quotation of any case," the decision stated,[53:244] "it affirmatively appears the restriction is purely arbitrary and unreasonable. . . . Under this zoning ordinance an owner of property within the district involved may maintain horses, cows, and swine on his premises and store fertilizer, as long as it is not 'stored within fifty feet of the lot line of any adjoining owner.' For the foregoing reason, we hold that the ordinance . . . is unconstitutional and discriminatory, insofar as it excludes the building of churches within [the] residential district." Against this the city officials argued that:

The inclusion of farming is an obvious necessity. The best zoning practice is to fix the residential zones as far as possible ahead of the influx of population so that business and other uses will not become established and create blighted areas in what otherwise would naturally become residential districts. This results in the taking in of farm lands before they are ready for subdivision. Obviously the owner must be permitted to make some use of his land and logically that use will be the one that he was making of it at the time that the zoning went into effect.

While this argument was overruled in the Mesa case its appeal is obvious. Other church zoning cases have authorized discrimination between religious and agricultural uses, for example the Azusa, California, Jehovah's Witnesses case.[186] An article in the *Harvard Law Review* for July 1957 [164] has a good short statement about discrimination. The article says:

A number of state courts have held zoning ordinances unconstitutional on the ground that the exclusion of churches was arbitrary and unreasonable when considered in relation to other uses permitted in the area. These courts do not indicate whether they consider this to be a deprivation of due process or a denial of equal protection, but it would seem more appropriate to characterize the issue raised as one of equal protection.

When the undeniable characteristics of an excluded use closely parallel those of the use which is permitted, invalidation of a zoning law on equal protection grounds would seem proper. However, permitting a particular type of public building to be erected in a residential area should not necessarily open it to all institutional buildings. The courts must examine closely the specific effect of each type of prohibited use in order to determine whether it can be distinguished from uses which are permitted.

In the Porterville, California, Mormon temple case [67] the problem of discrimination was solved by treating all nonresidential uses with complete impartiality—that is, by excluding them completely. The Mormon bishop could not even raise the issue of equal protection. Churches are sufficiently different from homes so that their separate classification is not unfair. However, the difference between the effect of a church and the effect of a business upon a community is less often a proper ground for discrimination.

The Village of Plandome, New York, tried to defend itself in the Unitarian church case [87] on the basis of the Porterville precedent, but the New York court could reply:

> This ordinance is arbitrary and discriminatory [referring to the Plandome ordinance] in that it excludes churches and places of public worship although permitting uses, including village and municipal buildings, railroad stations, public schools and clubhouses which would entail in an equal or greater degree the harmful or undesirable results which, defendants argue, may flow from the use of plaintiff's property for the erection of a church. For that reason, the case upon which the defendants principally rely [the Porterville case] is not persuasive authority herein. In that case an ordinance was upheld which excluded places of worship from a residence area wherein the sole permitted use was single-family dwellings although, in other areas of the municipality, churches were permitted.

Possibly the ruling in the Plandome case was too broad. As will be shown in Chapter 13, a proper distinction can be made between public and private enterprises that would justify their separate classification for zoning purposes. However, the Plandome decision was on firm ground respecting clubhouses. It is unfair to allow places of assembly for ordinary social purposes and to forbid places of assembly for religious purposes. (Incidentally, in Chapter 12, I will inquire whether the converse of this proposition is also tenable.)

Of all the cases discussed thus far only the Mesa case [53] and the Plandome case [87] specified unfair discrimination as a ground for decision. Such explicitness is rare. Most of the decisions display extreme reticence on the subject. An example is the Beachwood, Ohio, Jewish synagogue case of 1953.[101] The court observed that the ordinance authorized special use permits and that "a number of such permits have heretofore been granted by the council for golf ranges, schools, churches and the like." It seems to me that in this fact the court might well have found a justification for requiring issuance of the permit to the congregation. Instead, it worked out a complex theory under the due process clause. (See pages 61-2.) Some of this hesitancy to put the judicial finger on religious discrimination may be ascribable to the national policy I have mentioned in Chapter 1 of concealing rather than exposing and curing religious antagonisms.

The Decatur, Indiana, Jehovah's Witnesses decision of 1954,[104] invalidating the city's parking requirements as against the Kingdom Hall, was based upon the discredited absolute anti-exclusion theory. Seemingly in order to bolster its opinion, the court also said that "five other churches, within a radius of five blocks, although built prior to the enactment of the zoning ordinance, used the streets for parking. Those in the same block as the proposed location used both Monroe and Ninth Streets for parking."

Obviously there was discrimination here in favor of the other denominations and against the Witnesses. These facts create a special situation, involving "prior nonconforming use." The courts have generally sustained such discrimination as justified, finding a basis for it in the mere fact that the one use is commenced before the ordinance and the other thereafter. To carry the "prior non-conforming use" theory to its logical conclusion, however, could lead to the "establishment" of the old churches and the "disestablishment" of the new. The court might well have examined the question whether in the light of constitutional separation of church and state such discrimination against churches should be permitted. Instead, it dismissed the question with a mere passing remark.

The decision in the case of the Catholic seminary at Morris Township, New Jersey,[128] seems unnecessarily harsh on the sisters. If the court had given greater attention to the factor of discrimination, it might have resulted in granting of the permit. The minority opinion [128:141] said that "Villa Walsh is an attractive Catholic school located amidst the rolling hills of Morris Township and operated under the supervision of the State Department of Education. It is ideally situated on an elevated 100 acre tract and its cluster of buildings is hardly visible from the distant homes of the townspeople." The seminary had been located there for many years.

The sisters contended that reasonable expansion was the only alternative to abandonment of the premises. The zoning commission had granted a variance for an additional building but neighbors took the matter to court. The court overruled the decision. "The majority opinion," said the dissenting

judges, "suggests that the Sunday traffic to Villa Walsh will
be augmented but that consideration is hardly significant in
view of the evidence in the record indicating that the surrounding roads are heavily travelled by persons visiting other
nearby places, including Jockey Hollow Park which had
427,507 visitors during a stated period of one year."

The preceding quotations are from a dissenting opinion
endorsed by Justice William J. Brennan, then a member of the
New Jersey court, now a member of the U. S. Supreme Court.
There was a second dissenting opinion which said among other
things [128;152] that "in the immediate vicinity of the Villa there is
a large armory and the Tufts Dog Kennel." In ruling against
the sisters the majority seems not to have taken these other
uses into account. Neither did they make any analysis of them,
as suggested in the *Harvard Law Review* article [164] quoted at
page 139, to determine whether their "undeniable characteristics" closely paralleled those of the use proposed by the
sisters and whether, therefore, refusal of a permit to the
sisters might have been discriminatory. The dissenting opinion
also queried whether the majority would feel equally compelled
to refuse a permit "if it became necessary to enable reasonable
modernization or enlargement of the university buildings
operated in a residential zone by Princeton, Rutgers, Seton
Hall or other established university in the state."

Quite a different attitude was displayed by the same court
in two subsequent Roman Catholic cases. The first was the
Ocean Township, New Jersey, case.[180,206] It was another application by nuns, for a convent and parochial school to be located
in an old mansion called Ivy Hedge, in a Class A residential
district. Parochial schools were not generally authorized in the
zone but the commission granted a variance under the state
law which authorized them "for special reasons" where they
could be granted "without substantial detriment to the public
good" and where they would not "substantially impair the
intent and purpose of the zoning plan and ordinance." *

Among the grounds mentioned by the New Jersey Supreme

---

* The lower court [180] sustained the decision of the zoning board on the
theory that refusal of the permit would constitute discrimination in favor of
public schools. This reason for its decision was repudiated by the supreme
court as will be shown at pages 180-82. The decision was upheld, but on other
grounds, as indicated above.

Court in sustaining the ruling was a statement that nearby was a residence district "containing a subdivision development, a women's club, a community day school. . . ." The court added [206:582] that "the ordinance contemplates uses other than one family homes. . . . [A]part from houses, garden apartments, apartment hotels, hotels, [and?] boarding houses, churches, public schools, and public playgrounds are authorized upon prior application to the board of adjustment. Hence the use here permitted is not dramatically different from those envisioned in the zoning plan." The New Jersey court was hesitant to suggest that unconstitutional discrimination might exist if the school were excluded, but the facts of discrimination were carefully recited and must have influenced the decision of the court.

There were some differences between the Montclair, New Jersey, Catholic day school case [228] and the two preceding Catholic cases. But in the Montclair decision, the court took pains to point out [228:392] that the authority of the Morris Township Catholic seminary case [128] was "nullified by more recent opinions." There, as in the Ocean Township case,[180] the Catholics had the advantage of favorable decisions of the zoning officials. A variance had been granted enabling construction of a new school building. One of the reasons, as I have previously mentioned (pages 116-17), was the danger of fire at the old building.

The permit was affirmed by both the lower court and the supreme court. The supreme court pointed to the difference in treatment of similar uses that would result from denial of the permit. It said that [228:393] "although the general area in question was residential, it was already populated by several schools." The court added that "the permitted uses within the zone include . . . schools, libraries and museums operated by the town of Montclair, churches, privately conducted schools for less than 13 pupils, and accessory uses customarily incidental to the permitted uses. . . . Several other schools are located within a block or two of Lacordaire; these include Mt. Hebron, a public school through junior high school, St. Cassian's, a parochial school, and a small nursery school on Park Street."

For reasons that I will detail in Chapter 13, I do not believe that the discrimination between public and private schools was necessarily a violation of the equal protection clause, but there seems to have been actionable discrimination between the proposed new school and the other parochial school, the nursery school, and perhaps also the churches. The court did not rely on this feature of the case, but it might have done so.

In the Sands Point, New York, Jewish synagogue case [148] there was also evidence of discrimination. Again it was given superficial treatment by the various courts that considered the case. The zoning board had required that the congregation provide a full set of plans before the application was passed upon. The building was an ancient one and the original plans had been lost. Several previous nonresidential occupants, it seems, had not been required to produce the plans. The minority of the appellate division pointed out [129:206] that it was "unreasonable to require [the] production [of the plans] and to refuse to determine the question of safety on the basis of expert testimony especially in the light of the quasi-public use of the premises permitted in recent years. It seems [148:490] that "French sailors used the property as a place of recreation . . . during 1941 . . . [and that] from the end of 1943 until 1946 the United States Merchant Marine used the property as a rehabilitation and rest center [and that] from 1946 until 1955 the Unied States Navy used the premises as an officers' club." There was obviously discrimination here in favor of other users of the building and against the religious applicant. The court did not call this by its proper name, discrimination, but found other grounds on which to overturn the board's action.

In the case of Jehovah's Witnesses at Haltom City, Texas,[136:703] the city's value witness, a real estate dealer who had formerly been mayor, said that the Kingdom Hall would cause depreciation "in a measure." But the court called attention to his further testimony that "two other churches in the same district depreciated the value of residential property but that permits were granted to said churches while he was mayor and a member of the zoning board of adjustment." The implication was clear that refusal of a permit to the Witnesses would be discriminatory. Again, however, the decision for the Witnesses was on other grounds.

On pages 85-6, I have quoted with approval the justification of the Pennsylvania court of the "proximity requirements" imposed on Jehovah's Witnesses in the Bethel Borough case.[159] But there was another feature of the case to which the court gave inadequate attention. Its dictum seems to impede the invocation of the equal protection clause.

In the Bethel Borough case, the Witnesses alleged [159:244] that "there are churches in the very same neighborhood that have been permitted to operate within the quarter mile area without objection." To this the court answered that "there is no basis for charging the board with discrimination. . . . The only evidence of another church located within a quarter mile of a similar building is the St. Thomas More Roman Catholic Church. The evidence further showed this to be a temporary structure which never came before the board of adjustment. If other public assembly buildings exist contrary to the terms of the ordinance, they are . . . either violations or variances (if not pre-existing non-conforming uses). It has been held quite uniformly that permitting some persons to violate a zoning ordinance does not preclude its enforcement against another. . . . The circumstances in each case might well have been substantially different. Evidence of other variances is clearly inadmissible."

Again it is impossible to quarrel with the actual result of the case. Final decisions always hinge on facts which were before the court and are not fully before this writer. But I disagree with the final sentence of the above excerpt. The fact that the circumstances of other variances could have been different is not a sound reason for banning evidence about them. Without evidence the court cannot know whether they were different. Where the equal protection clause is invoked, evidence as to other variances should be admitted along with evidence as to differing circumstances, if any.

In the Azusa, California, case of 1958,[186] the Witnesses' attorney also argued "unreasonable classification." He contended [186:262] that "a church as such is entitled to come within the . . . zone if libraries, museums, playgrounds or public schools and other buildings owned or controlled by the city or school district are included." He added [186:262] that the "ordinance is discriminatory upon its face because churches are excluded from [a zone] which is open not only to single-family residences but also to agriculture, horticulture, flower and vegetable gardening, nurseries and greenhouses used only for purposes of propagation and not for sale at retail, also libraries, museums, parks, playgrounds, public schools and community buildings owned and controlled by the municipality or school district."

The attorney for the Witnesses may have laid too much emphasis on the eternal verities and too little on the facts of the case. His reference to the rights of the "church as such," and his charge that the ordinance was discriminatory "on its face," indicate that he failed to examine closely the specific effect of his proposed use of the land to "determine whether it can be distinguished from uses that are permitted" in the manner recommended by the *Harvard Law Review* article [164] quoted on page 139.

The result was an adverse decision not because the defense was unsound but because it had not been proved. The court said that there was no proof of the discrimination "on the merits." It said that the church "stands with respect to this claim of unreasonable classification or discrimination on the face of the ordinance in the same position as any other litigant who raises that issue. In other words, proposed use of property for religious purposes does not give *per se* a title to any particular zone; a church, like any other property owner, is to be considered on its merits as fitting into the general scheme of comprehensive zoning, entitled to no preference and subject to no adverse discrimination." If proof had been submitted showing that the adverse effects of the proposed church on the area would be no worse than those flowing from permitted uses, the result in the Azusa case might well have been different.

The result was different in the Menlo Park, California, Jehovah's Witnesses case [194] of the following year. The Witnesses showed that they had complied with the bare terms of the ordinance and the court held in their favor. As a make-weight the court invoked also the concept of discrimination. It referred to the "pertinent fact" that "there are other churches in the same or similar residential districts in Menlo Park built under use permits similar to the one herein sought. . . ." The court said [194:202] that "it is difficult to make an argument that one church that complies with the ordinance assists the public welfare while another that likewise complies is inimical thereto."

Thus the California court sustained the principle that discrimination "between church and church" is an excellent defense. In the Garden Grove Jehovah's Witnesses case,[217] it considered discrimination between a church and secular enterprises. The court indicated that the Azusa case had not closed the door on this basis of attack.

The Garden Grove congregation argued discrimination on the basis not only of the presence of other churches but also of the presence in the immediate vicinity of a school and athletic field. The court found fault with the procedure followed by the Witnesses and for that reason dismissed their appeal. But it advised them to make a technically correct approach and then to "attack the validity of the ordinance as unreasonable or discriminatory by an independent action for that purpose."

The necessity for a strong factual presentation was emphasized by the 1962 case of the Jehovah's Witnesses of Modesto, Stanislaus County, California. They argued [245:916] that "there are two churches in the same restricted zone, the implication being that the Planning Commission and the Board of Supervisors issued use permits to the other churches and therefore discriminated against [Jehovah's Witnesses]." The court said: "We are bound by the record before us and nothing therein indicates that the two churches were granted use permits under circumstances similar to those presented here."

There are two cases in which discrimination was in issue of which the churches unsuccessfully sought review in the Supreme Court of the United States. One of these was the case of the Jehovah's Witnesses of Milwaukie, Oregon,[184,200] and the other the case of the Catholic archbishop and the City of San Marino, California.[223,224] Both decisions were against the church. However, both courts made clear that, in a proper case, the right to equal protection would be enforced.

The application of the Milwaukie Witnesses was rejected by the zoning commission. They filed suit alleging unconstitutional discrimination. The court refused relief, not upon the ground that the objection was invalid, but upon the ground that the necessary facts had not been proved. Indeed, in denying relief, the court stressed the importance of discrimination as a defense against religious land use regulation. The decision emphasizes the importance of evidence on the subject and even suggests how it should be presented—in this respect following, in general, the suggestions of the *Harvard Law Review* article [164] quoted on page 139.

The Witnesses' charge of discrimination was "predicated on the proposition that there are two other churches in the area." To this the court replied that "the record here tells us nothing more concerning the existence of 'two other churches' than is comprehended in . . . two short answers [of witnesses]. . . . We do not know that either of such churches are in the same zone where [the congregation's] property is located or whether in an unzoned portion of the city. . . . We do not know when either of the other churches was built in Milwaukie, that is before . . . the effective date of the zoning ordinance or after that date."

"On the other hand," the court continued, "from a reading of the ordinance, we do know that if 'other churches' were built before that date, and in the same, but later-zoned area, then such churches are classified as 'non-conforming property' untouched by the operation of the ordinance. . . . If, however, the other churches were granted building permits after [adoption of the ordinance] we know not when or where, or whether the same conditions of traffic congestion and hazard which militated against [the Witnesses] were existent at the time of the construction of the 'other churches' or to the same degree. The time of the building of the 'other churches,' their location, and when permits, if any, for their erection were issued are matters of proof which should have been in easy reach of the [attorney for the Witnesses]. We have not even been supplied with the boundaries of the various zones."

Thus the court showed that evidence about unfair discrimination is relevant and important. It rejected the theory of the Bethel Borough, Pennsylvania, case [159] that such evidence is inadmissible. It opened the way for the introduction of such evidence, at least in Oregon. The same rule doubtless applies in California and in many other states. However, no church zoning case has yet appeared in the published reports in which such evidence was fully developed.

In the San Marino, California, Roman Catholic church parking lot case,[223,224] the archbishop also unsuccessfully pleaded discrimination, and for a similar reason. He claimed [223:558] that "several variances have been granted by the city to other churches and business establishments in the immediate neighborhood." His brief argued that "this fact highlights the inequity of the present ruling of the city council. In weighing whether or not the variance to [the church] should be granted, the authorities must afford the [archbishop] at least the same dignity and treatment as to shopping structures and business structures, and the authorities should not be permitted to grant variances to one religious establishment while withholding, in an obviously critical situation, a variance to [the Catholics]."

The court overruled the archbishop's contentions, saying that "the fact that variances may have been granted to some owners and denied to others . . . does not establish unreasonable discrimination. The granting or denial of variances rests largely in the discretion of the body designated by the zoning ordinance for that purpose, and a denial of a variance will not be disturbed in the absence of a clear showing of abuse of discretion."

Obviously even if it were possible the archbishop had not made such a "clear showing." Instead he had stood on his "dignity." In this respect, he made the same mistake as did the Witnesses in the Azusa case,[186] described on pages 145-6. Dignity was irrelevant. The question was whether the uses previously permitted were just as adverse to the public interest as the use which was denied to the Catholics. Failing or refusing to deal with this question, the Catholics properly were overruled. They assumed an "absolutist" approach instead of dealing with actual facts of the case.

In the Meridian Hills, Indiana, case,[229] also involving the application of a Catholic church, the decision said: "At the time the church's petition was pending before the board, it was shown that were two other churches in the town of Meridian Hills, a Congregational church . . . and a Hebrew temple (erected after the overruling of an adverse zoning board decision by the Marion Superior Court) ; and a third church (the Second Presbyterian Church) was under construction on property immediately contiguous to and adjoining the property owned by the [archbishop]. The [archbishop] claims that there has been an arbitrary and discriminatory decision by the Board of Zoning Appeals excluding the Catholic church and school from the community."

Here the Indiana Supreme Court may have had a firm basis for requiring issuance of the permit. Instead, it disregarded the archbishop's charge of unfair discrimination and ruled in his favor on the basis of the discredited absolute anti-exclusion rule. There may have been a reason for avoiding the issue of discrimination. It is just possible that the adverse effects on the community arising from the construction of a Catholic church-school-convent-rectory combination are more severe than those arising from construction of either (a) a Congregational church or (b) a Presbyterian church or (c) a Jewish synagogue. Catholic churches often draw much larger crowds and are used much more intensively than churches of the other denominations mentioned. Maybe the archbishop was not in a position to support his charge of discrimination. At any rate it is easy to see why courts are reluctant to enter into a discussion of these differences between denominations.

Perhaps because I am franker than the judges, lawyers, and other commentators, I have called attention to this distinction with reference to the denominations affected. But I am not the first to recognize its existence. Thus, in the 1942 Upper Arlington, Ohio, church case [40] the court observed that the "small suburban church" (which happened to be Lutheran, would present "a minimum of objections." The Chicago case of 1952 [93] repeated the same observation with regard to an Episcopal church. The *Harvard Law Review* article [164] quoted on page 139 says further: "Although a particular church, especially a smaller one, used only as a place of worship, may not produce these results, it is obvious that a large church, which is to be a center of activity or which is to be accompanied by a parochial school, may have serious adverse effects on the neighborhood."

In the Bayside, Wisconsin, Baptist Church case,[231] the opinion of the court (see pages 46-7) also relied on the absolute anti-exclusion rule when it could have invoked the equal protection clause. The three justices signing it pointed out [231:289] that there were "three filling stations, one retail garden store, five establishments maintaining bars, two municipal buildings and a public school." Under the prior ordinance (which was the one that the court held to be unconstitutional) the potential discrimination was even greater. It had provision [231:290] for "any retail business." Obviously it was discriminatory to exclude churches from the entire town and to permit the other uses mentioned above.

The 1962 case of the Columbus Park, Chicago, Congregation of Jehovah's Witnesses [246] demonstrates that the courts of Illinois, like those of Oregon and California, are influenced by comparisons between excluded church activities and included activities of other kinds. The application was for use of a "storefront" building in a commercial area. The administrative bodies and the lower court all ruled against the Witnesses.

The ground of their decision was the interruption to the continuity of business enterprises in the block. The supreme court reversed the decision, saying among other things that [246:726] "such business continuity would likewise be interrupted by a dance hall, crematory, mausoleum, or trade school, all uses permitted in this . . . district. We are unable to see how the use as a church is more harmful than the aforementioned uses."

The lower court case of Clarkstown, New York, [195] involved the Catholic Franciscan Missionaries of Mary. The decision was affirmed without opinion by the court of appeals. [210, 213] It was almost a duplicate of the decision in the very early Catholic church case at Mesa, Arizona. [53] The permit was sought for a "shelter for normal children in a residential-agricultural use district." The lower court said, very simply and briefly, that "in the light of the circumstances, particularly the rural nature of the community and the conforming uses permitted within the district, including the raising of cattle, sheep and goats and maintenance of schools, it was capricious to deny the application to rear children of tender age on the parcel."

This chapter maintains that the equal protection clause is a defense against religious land use regulation that has been neglected both by litigants and by judges. In the last case mentioned, the permit was not for a church, not for a religious school, but for a children's religious nursery. What would have been the decision if a private nonreligious nonprofit nursery had been involved? This is an inkling of the problem that arises where churches engage in the same secular activity as nonclerical groups. The next chapter will consider whether, in protecting rights of religious groups, we may not sometimes discriminate against other churches or against secular enterprises.

# CHAPTER 12.

## Spot Zoning and Religious Discrimination in Reverse

Spot zoning is defined by Rathkopf [132:369] as:

> An ordinance or amendment thereof which singles out a lot or area and grants such property privileges which are not granted or extended to other land in the vicinity in the same use district [and] adversely affects the proper and orderly development of the district or vicinity where the property is located, and the community as a whole.

This practice is condemned not only by planning and zoning officials but also by legal writers. Yokley [96§90] describes it as a "most vicious practice that has expanded almost to a point where it has become a cancerous growth on the body politic in many, many, municipalities of the land. . . ."

In an early case filed in 1934 by the Methodist Episcopal Church of Linden, New Jersey,[30] an injunction was granted against operation of a bar near the church edifice. A generation later we find that the rule against spot zoning is invoked not to protect churches from saloons but to protect home neighborhoods from church institutions. In 1955, the Supreme Court of New Jersey said: [128:145]

> The spirit of the law is to restrict nonconforming uses. Their position in the zoning scheme is not encouraged because of the tendency to subvert rather than support sound planning. Such uses possess a contagious character which works to infect the neighborhood of their location, . . . and their presence is adverse to the zoning objective of reasonable conformity.

The contagious use referred to by the New Jersey court was a seminary for Roman Catholic nuns at Morris Township.

Spot zoning will be discussed briefly in connection with the more general problem whether by enforcing the rights of churches we may not also at times impinge upon the constitutional right to conduct other enterprises. This is important not only as respects the nonecclesiastical rights, with which we are

153

not now concerned, but also as respects the interests of the public and of the churches themselves.

The reason Yokley refers to "spot zoning" as "cancerous" is that, once a spot of nonconformity is allowed, there is a tendency for it to grow like a physical malignancy. Once a place of assembly is permitted in a residential zone, the board is brought under pressure to permit other places of assembly or other nonresidential uses. The character of the neighborhood may change rapidly and the proper and orderly development of the community may be seriously impeded.

Therefore, in a particular case the question arises not only whether the zoning board is willing to admit a church but also whether it is willing to tolerate other uses that will naturally follow that first exception. The question is not only whether the effects of a particular church upon the neighborhood are sufficiently unfavorable to justify its exclusion but also whether it will lead to other nonconforming uses with additional adverse effects. The board has to consider, not the single apple, but the entire barrel.

The Methodist church case at Linden, New Jersey,[30] is useful as a horrible example of spot zoning. In 1934 the term was not used, had not yet become current, but spot zoning certainly was the subject to which the case related. It formed an important precedent for later decisions on this legal topic. The church was located at Wood Avenue and Knopf Street in a residential district. Exactly 119 feet away from the church edifice was a property, 400 Helen Street, the owner of which happened to be a member of the city council.

He filed an application for a liquor license which was denied because the zoning ordinance forbade nonresidential use of the property except for churches. He went to the board of adjustment and asked for a permit for business use in spite of the ordinance. The board denied it but obliged the alderman by sending a recommendation to the city council for an amendment. The amendment was adopted with record speed. It provided that the property should "be . . . reclassified so that said land and property will come within section 5 (D), business district, of the ordinance. . . ." This would make the lot a commercial island in a sea of homes. The council then itself granted the saloon permit. The church sued to set aside the whole proceeding.

In its decision invalidating the council's action, the court pointed out that the applicant himself was a member of the council. It said that "although he did not vote, his membership on the council seems to have had its influence on the passage of the ordinance. At the meeting, one of the councilmen expressed himself to the effect that the owner 'had served the city faithfully for six years and really deserved something.' The first reading of the ordinance was given in such haste that, not only had the recited resolution not been received, but the ordinance itself had not been prepared; it was read partly from a writing and partly from the body of another ordinance. In other words, no ordinance had actually been introduced."

However, the court did not rely on these procedural improprieties. Instead, it stated a general rule against spot zoning which has since become classic. Among other things, the opinion-writer said that "an attempt to wrench a single small lot from its environment and give it a new rating that disturbs the tenor of the neighborhood should receive the closest scrutiny of the courts lest the zoning enactments . . . be diverted from their true objective. I conclude that the ordinance is not a reasonable exercise of municipal power." It certainly was not. It is easy to understand how disturbed were the neighbors, including the Methodist minister, at the intrusion of this proposed social institution in the midst of a neighborhood occupied by residences.

Resentment was also expressed against "spot zoning" in an Indianapolis, Indiana, case of 1946,[57] where the applicant sought to establish, among other things, a parking lot, gymnasium, recreation building, and outside amphitheater in the midst of a residential zone. In that case, the objections were overruled. The court said that the neighboring property owners "contend further that 'spot zoning' was attempted, which is not permissible in the absence of a unique situation of the property in question, creating 'practical difficulties' or 'unnecessary hardships.' We do not agree with [this] contention and we hold that the question of 'spot zoning' is not involved in this appeal." The Indiana court did not state any reason for its ruling. However, a salient difference between the Linden case and the Indianapolis case was that in Linden the applicant was a saloonkeeper, the objector being a Methodist minister; in the Indianapolis case, the applicant was a Methodist church.

My juxtaposing of these two Methodist cases should not be construed as meaning that they were identical. Spot zoning is not always illegal. It can be justified in particular cases where the service to the public welfare is obvious. There is a difference between spot zoning for a church and spot zoning for a saloon. This point was well put in the Reno, Nevada, Catholic church case,[35:239] when the court said that "cases involving livery stables, garages, gasoline stations, funeral parlors, billboards, two-family residences, morgues, laundries, etc., afford us little aid in the instant case. The law distinguishes between such cases and those relating to churches."

In the Reno case, as shown on pages 112-13, the court overruled objections to the church permit. The decision treated principally of the alleged depressive effect of church funerals. The court compared them in this respect to funerals conducted in homes. The ruling was in favor of the church but was carefully limited so as to prevent the "spot" created by its construction from spreading. The court made clear that it was only authorizing a particular church.

The question arises whether this decision did not engender discrimination against the owners of other property who might want to use their land for, say, a funeral parlor. Are funerals conducted out of funeral parlors any more depressive than funerals conducted out of (a) churches or (b) homes? For this purpose, are not funeral "chapels" and churches almost completely comparable? Is there any real difference except that the undertaker has not received holy orders? And is this a sufficient basis for the discrimination? I don't try to answer these questions nor have any courts tried to do so. But at some time they will have to consider whether such discrimination does not violate our traditional separation of church and state. (See page 22.)

The question of spot zoning was again raised in the Chicago Episcopalian case.[93] There the objector contended that "to allow construction of a church at this point would be 'spot'

zoning." The court in its opinion felt called upon to explain the
meaning of the term. It said: [93:921]

> By "spot zoning" he means that a particular piece of property is
> specially zoned to suit the individual purpose of the owner of that
> property. This is not the case here. Under our interpretation of
> the ordinance, all landowners . . . are entitled to present their
> plans . . . for acceptance as church sites. The city council could
> not arbitrarily refuse . . . in a situation where such refusal was
> not reasonably required for the protection of the public health,
> safety, welfare and morals. All persons similarly situated are thus
> treated alike, in our interpretation.

What the court should have said was that all persons
identically situated (i.e. persons desiring to build churches)
were treated alike. But would such logic have applied in the
Linden case? [30] Would the action of the council have been any
more acceptable if, instead of granting a single liquor permit,
it had opened the entire neighborhood to saloons?

This would not have cured the discrimination against other
landowners who did not want to open saloons. To cure it the
council would have had to provide permits not only for saloons
but also for livery stables, garages, gasoline stations, funeral
parlors, billboards, two family residences, morgues, laundries,
parking lots, gymnasiums, recreation buildings, playgrounds
and outside amphitheaters. The adverse effect of such institutions would be no greater than the adverse effects arising from
the saloon.

In the Chicago case,[93] in order to cure the discrimination
alleged to have been created by the spot zoning of a church,
was it not necessary to do more than permit other owners to
build churches? Would they not also have to be permitted to
build other kinds of assembly places, perhaps including club
and lodge houses, etc.? Readers will understand that I am not
here advocating this sort of destruction of the zone plan but
only pointing out that the granting of one nonconforming use
causes pressure for the granting of others. This is true at
least in kind if not in degree whether the new nonconforming
use is religious or bibulous.

A number of courts have recognized that churches need not
be put in a class by themselves but may be classified with other

institutions. For instance, in the Euclid, Ohio, case,[18] the United States Supreme Court classified churches along with "schools, libraries, and other public and semipublic buildings." That is also the spirit of the dictum in the Upper Arlington, Ohio, Lutheran church decision. It said that [40:522] "the Village of Euclid case, while deciding that commercial and industrial structures may, consistently with the 14th Amendment, be excluded from residential districts, decides nothing with regard to the exclusion of humanitarian, public and semipublic uses like churches, schools and libraries."

The Ohio court broadened the classification suggested by the Euclid case to include "humanitarian" uses. This raises the question whether activities of people like doctors and dentists are not just as humanitarian as the activities of clergymen. For instance, at University Park, Texas,[38] a dentist sought a permit for an office in his home. He contended that various other permitted uses, including churches, made it discriminatory to reject his application. His contention was overruled, the court saying that churches were "more fitting." It may be said that doctors and dentists collect money in connection with their work; but this is also true at times of clergymen. When a church is admitted to an otherwise residential neighborhood, how far must the authorities go in admitting nonecclesiastical enterprises of a "humanitarian" or semipublic character in order to avoid religious discrimination in reverse? This question should be considered before, not after, the church permit is granted.

This question was raised by the minority in the Piedmont, California, Catholic school case,[125] where the court refused to permit the exclusion of a parochial school from substantially the entire area of the city. The dissenting justice said: [125:447]

> If the city is compelled to admit [the church's] contemplated private school, then it would seem that it will be equally compelled to admit other private schools in its single-family residential zone. That is, it must permit all private schools to enter equally unless this court is prepared to examine and censor or itself prescribe the projected curriculum or other basis of classification of each private school which proposes to construct a building and playground and proposes to commence business in Piedmont's Zone A. A list of the various private schools taken from the classified section of the San

Francisco Bay Area telephone directory shows at least 176 private schools, including, among others, schools affiliated with various religious groups, . . . driving schools, language schools, astrology schools, divinity schools, nursery schools, furniture-finishing schools, radio schools, labor schools, beauty-culture schools, secretarial schools, television schools, success schools, engineering schools, fencing schools, dancing schools, sewing schools, charm schools, dramatic schools, and finishing schools, to name but a few.

If the City of Piedmont is obliged by this court to permit [the church] to devote its property to private school purposes, in violation of the city's zoning ordinance, then the conclusion appears indubitably to follow that the city's doors must likewise be opened, upon demand of any other interested property owner, to any or all other private schools, which in the manner of their operation are no more obnoxious to the public peace or quiet, or inherently unlawful, than the school herein authorized, all to the substantial, if not utter, subversion of the planned residential character of Zone A. Zoning ordinances permitting parochial or church schools but prohibiting other private schools in residential districts have been held arbitrary, capricious and invalid. . . . Certainly this court cannot discriminate either in favor of or against a private school because of the religious affiliation, nor can this court properly undertake to censor or prescribe the curriculum of any lawfully conducted school, whether public or private.

This dissenting opinion is quoted at length not necessarily to endorse its conclusions but because it states so dramatically the possible effect of admitting to an area the secular activities of religious institutions. It can lead to destruction of the entire residential character of the area.

The Piedmont decision relied heavily on the *Society of Sisters* case.[17] This case also lends indirect support to the minority opinion that the court "cannot discriminate either in favor of or against a private school because of religious affiliation." It sustained the right of parents to send their children to private schools. It did not refer to religious schools as such. The plaintiffs in the *Sisters* case included not only the sisters, but also a private (military) school. Presumably, then, the admission of parochial schools could also lead to the admission of military schools—and what else?

An article in the *Notre Dame Lawyer* for May 1960 [222]

suggests the possibility that in New York religious discrimination-in-reverse is favored by the courts. It says: [222:410]
"New York courts consistently permit an exception when the
applicant is a religious institution, but have ruled otherwise
when the institution is privately owned and operated." (The
contraposition of "religious" and "private" also seems to
indicate the author's tendency to equate church sovereignty
with that of the state.) In support of this statement, the *Notre
Dame Lawyer* cites the case of Merrick Woods School, a
non-sectarian institution at Hempstead, Long Island, New
York, decided in a trial court in 1958.[181]

There the ordinance forbade operation of day camps in
residential districts. The owners contended that they had a
"constitutional" right to locate there. They based their contention on the broad terms of the Brighton Catholic church and
school case.[149] The supreme court, Nassau County, disagreed,
replying that "as for the [Brighton] and similar cases, the
accessory uses mentioned therein are different from the day
camp situation in this case. The accessory uses mentioned
therein pertain to the year-round accessory uses, to the primary religious activities in those edifices and on those
lands."

If the article in the *Notre Dame Lawyer* [222] is correct,
the New York court has established a certain limit upon the
"malignancy" of the spot zoning authorized in its Brighton
decision. The article makes it appear that the court's support
of such "cancers" is limited to church cases. But there are
rulings that indicate otherwise. For instance, in the case of
*Incorporated Village of Lloyd Harbor v. Town of Huntington,*
decided in 1958,[175] the court of appeals itself said that "a
village ordinance which professes wholly to exclude public
parks and bathing beaches bears no more 'substantial relation'
to zoning purposes than does a regulation which entirely
prohibits the erection of colleges . . . or religious edifices and
schools."

There is a tendency even to extend the growth of such a
"spot" to include purely private enterprises. Thus in the case
of *Tinder v. Clarke,*[176] Justice Arch N. Bobbitt of the Supreme
Court of Indiana dissented from a decision sustaining a
Sunday law regulation as applied to automobile sales lots.

Bobbitt had written the decision in the Decatur, Indiana, Jehovah's Witnesses case,[104] in which the Witnesses had been exempted from the traffic-control provisions of the zoning ordinance. Justice Bobbitt said that "no reasonable person can say that it is a crime in any greater degree for automobile dealers to add to the traffic congestion on Sunday than it is for any other business or sport to do so." He made special mention of churches, citing his previous opinion in the Decatur case.

The reasoning in the Columbus Park, Chicago, Jehovah's Witnesses case of 1962 [246:726] also seems applicable in reverse. (See page 151.) If a Kingdom Hall must be permitted because of the admission of dance halls, crematoriums, mausoleums and trade schools, then must the latter be admitted because of the admission of a church?

There is another case in which the problem is presented in dramatic form although neither the parties nor the court seem to have been conscious of it. This is a case involving the Grange at Mt. Lebanon, Pennsylvania.[208] The court refused to permit the use of an old church for lodge meetings. In Chapter 19, I will describe how the court sustained refusal of a new use permit, when the Beadling Presbyterian Church was sold to the local Grange, because the national Grange "nowhere makes any claim . . . that one of the objects of the Grange is . . . religious worship." Yet the use by the Grange was substantially similar to the use by the Presbyterians. In Chicago a church was using a tract of land for a parking lot. They sold it to a parking lot operator who was refused a permit. In *Rosenfeld v. Zoning Board of Appeals*,[187] the appellate court upheld the decision.

The admission of religious institutions to an area tends to require the admission also of comparable secular institutions. When any court permits the inclusion in residential areas of the secular activities of churches it puts before zoning boards a dilemma. They must either (a) permit the "cancerous" growth of the "spot" thus created or (b) practice religious discrimination-in-reverse.

When land prices boom, so does the business of title abstracters and courts. Before zoning boards also, the evils of spot zoning are accentuated. Miami Beach, Florida, is an island, the southern half of which is crowded neck by jowl with neon-lighted hotels. This gay red-white-and-blue way comes to an end at the Fontainebleu Hotel at 58th Street. From that point north to the island's tip, zoning regulations restrict construction to residential purposes, although some tourist homes and apartments have crept in.

The people on the northern end of the island, who want to preserve the residential character of their houses, live in fear of any change in the zoning regulations. They oppose not so much the particular change as the tendency to change, lest it lead to complete commercialization and hotel-ization of the area. These homelovers are supported, strangely enough, by the hotel owners on the south end of the island. The latter oppose the opening up of the north end because it would mean more competition. (On the other hand, there are also some home owners on the north end who favor rezoning so that they may be able to sell out to hotel operators at fancy prices.)

This complex situation did not exist in Tampa where the court decided in favor of Jehovah's Witnesses.[83] Nor was it mentioned in the decision of the United Lutheran church case at Miami Beach.[124] But it is easy to see why a Florida court would be more conscious of the malignant effect of spot zoning than, for instance, the Illinois court which admitted an Episcopal church to the outskirts of Chicago [93] or the Indiana court which admitted a Methodist church, gymnasium, etc., to a residential area of Indianapolis.[57] I mention this background to help explain why the Florida court in the Lutheran case took a position diametrically opposed to the preceding decisions.

This Miami Beach Lutheran church was a comparatively small one, without gymnasium and without parochial school, which was to be built on Collins Avenue, onto which already pours the bumper-to-bumper traffic from the string of hotels and motels above mentioned. Yet the court held that the church would "create a genuine traffic problem which would result from funeral services, wedding ceremonies and other gatherings where large numbers of persons congregate about the same time and disperse about the same time, not to mention the noise that comes from people congregating in large numbers."

The court said that [124:881] "an expert witness, whom the

chancellor must have believed, testifying for the [city], said that the construction of a church building on the lot would probably result in rezoning the surrounding property to [a] . . . multiple-family classification." It was further held that "the result would be spot zoning, described by an expert witness as the worst thing that can happen to a city . . . in what is a high class residential area." In the later case of the Miami Beach Hebrew academy,[189:52] the same court reiterated this view.

The question whether inclusion of a church in a residential area is spot zoning has seldom been ruled on and the decisions are divided. As with most questions on this subject, there is no rule of universal application. The admission of a church, like the admission of any nonresidential use, raises questions of discrimination-in-reverse. To what extent must other uses also be allowed?

The answer to this question hinges on the answer to another, "What is a church?" discussed in Chapter 19. If the definition includes billiard rooms, then church construction may lead to the intrusion of pool halls. If the church includes a parish hall, used for dances and bingo, then it may lead to the intrusion of other such halls; and so on. Once church-controlled enterprises are admitted, other similar enterprises may not properly be excluded *merely* because they are not church-controlled.

When churches seek to extend their special privilege to more and more functions, they may eventually cause the loss of the original special standing. If the purely residential character of districts is diluted by exceptions granted to churches, perhaps for secular activities, then steps can and will be taken to stop the spread of this "cancer." The patient may even have to be operated on.

Houses of worship are normally consistent with home neighborhoods. So are certain other types of assembly buildings. It is proper for both to be admitted while other enterprises are excluded. However, it is also proper, if necessary in the judgment of the lawmakers, to make an area strictly residential. This will occur more often as the secular activities of churches increase and with them the "contagiousness" of the "spots" they create.

# CHAPTER 13.

## DISCRIMINATION BETWEEN RELIGIOUS AND PUBLIC SCHOOLS

Chapter 3 has considered at length the "absolutist" theory that churches cannot constitutionally be excluded from any residential zone. Another theory has been advanced, that no religious or private school may be excluded from any zone in which public schools are permitted. The grounds of the second theory are that in such circumstances refusal of a permit to a religious or other private school is unfair discrimination and violates the equal protection clause of the constitution. For instance, even the *Harvard Law Review* article,[164] previously cited with approval, says: "Courts are virtually unanimous in holding that a zoning law cannot forbid the erection of a parochial school if it permits new public schools in the same area." There are a number of other articles on this subject which are mentioned in the footnote.*

This dogmatic approach to the question of religious schools seems as untenable as the same approach to the question of permits for construction of churches. Each case should be decided instead on its own merits in accordance with the answers to certain general constitutional questions. These questions include whether the attempted regulation serves a valid and sustantial public purpose, whether any actual undue discrimination exists, and whether there is undue interference with any basic personal rights such as religious liberty. This approach is more rational than any absolute non-exclusion rule and serves the purposes not only of zoning

---

* Oregon Law Review, February 1933; [29] Mississippi Law Journal, May 1951; [84] American Law Reports (Annotation to Orange New Jersey, Protestant seminary case of January 26, 1953) ;[100] Michigan Law Review, March 1955; [116] Marquette Law Review, Spring 1955; [119] University of Detroit Law Journal, May 1955; [121] Notre Dame Lawyer, December 1955; [127] University of Cincinnati Law Review, Winter 1955; [130] UCLA Law Review, April 1956; [141] Minnesota Law Review, June 1956; [144] Stanford University Law Review, July 1956; [146] Catholic Lawyer, July 1956; [147] Miami Law Quarterly, Fall 1956; [151] California Law Review, October 1956; [152] Notre Dame Lawyer, July 1957; [166] New York Law Journal, February 26, 27, 1962; [242] Catholic Lawyer, Spring 1962.[244]

boards but also of religious organization better than a flat rule.

The rule flatly condemning exclusion of parochial schools from areas where public schools exist or are permitted is also supposed to be supported by a majority of the courts. Some writers say the rule is "unanimous" except for one or two decisions to the contrary. Actually, there is about as much judicial authority on one side of this question as on the other, and neither side has received the thorough consideration it deserves. The better decisions indicate that discrimination between public and private schools is not, as such, unconstitutional.

The absolute anti-exclusion rule as to schools is extremely important, as a practical matter, for the Catholic Church. It is a part of that church's fixed policy, established by the Third Plenary Council (of bishops) at Baltimore in 1884, that "near every church where it does not yet exist, a parochial school is to be erected . . . and is to be maintained *in perpetuum* unless the bishop, on account of grave difficulties, judge that a postponement be allowed. . . . All Catholic parents are bound to send their children to the parochial schools unless, either at home or in other Catholic schools, they may sufficiently and evidently provide for the Christian education of their children, or unless it be lawful to send them to other schools on account of a sufficient cause, approved by the bishop, and with opportune cautions and remedies." *

The term "lawful" here refers to diocesan, not to state or municipal law. Since many Catholic children now attend public schools, the existence of this strict rule may come as a surprise. Attendance of Catholic children at parochial schools is still considered an absolute rule in the absence of special circumstances. The "special circumstance" usually is that the church is unable to build enough schools or maintain enough qualified teachers to educate all Catholic children. This, the church fervently hopes, is a temporary situation.

Without the church-controlled public schools that exist in other countries, the parochial school is an essential part of the

---

* Quoted by Pfeffer in *Church, State and Freedom* [97:427] from J. A. Burns, *The Growth and Development of the Catholic School System in the U. S.*, Benziger, N. Y. 1912, p. 195.

"perfect society" which, under its dogma, the Catholic Church seeks to constitute separate from the civil government. The church must be near the school. If the school is excluded then, as a practical matter, so is the church. If there were a general move to exclude parochial schools from residential areas, the church might seek establishment of separate, predominantly Catholic, communities where its schools would be more welcome.

This approach created no special problem, of course, during the early years when it was permissible to establish almost any enterprise in almost any neighborhood. The advent of zoning gives more effective expression to community objections. Such objections are more apt to arise with respect to Catholic schools than with regard to Sunday schools or other religious education activities of the other churches. The Catholic school is large, purports to have a complete curriculum like the public school, and usually is much more crowded. Aside from the great good it does, it also involves many adverse effects on any neighborhood where it exists. These adverse effects are similar whether a school is parochial or public. But when a school is established for the benefit of the entire community, that community bears the ill effects more patiently than when the school is set up to serve a single denomination.

The absolute rule against discrimination between public and private schools would be a solution of the problem of the Catholic Church so far as zoning is concerned. Under our tradition, there are public schools in every neighborhood. Under the absolute rule a parochial school would also have to be permitted in every neighborhood. That is what the church devoutly desires. Once a parochial school is built, the construction of a church follows as a matter of course. The rule proposed by the "absolutist" writers gives the Catholic bishops what amounts to a *carte blanche* with respect to both church and school location.

Singling out of the Catholic Church may make some readers suspect me of bias. But it would be worse to conceal the most important aspect of the problem—the identity of the interested parties. The Catholic Church has an interest in this problem so much deeper than any other church that it can be said to be the *only* denomination vitally affected.

The basic justification for the rule forbidding discrimination between public and private schools is not without appeal. It is comparable to the justification of the bishops for their insistence on tax support. If money is spent for education of public school children, it is discriminatory, they say, not to spend it for educating parochial school children. Likewise, the church has insisted, sometimes successfully, that refusal of parochial permits in places where public schools are permitted is unconstitutional under the equal protection clause.

I do not agree that the parochial schools have the same right as public schools to exist in any neighborhood. That is not to say, however, that the existence of a public school is irrelevant to the consideration of Catholic applications. If a public school already exists, the neighborhood may be more appropriate for another school than one which is not yet disturbed by such an institution. Facts such as these should be given careful consideration both in drafting ordinances and in hearing permit applications. But I challenge any rule which removes discretion from sovereign authorities and requires that parochial schools be permitted unless public schools are also excluded.

Theoretically, the problem is not one that affects only Catholic schools. A number of cases involve non-Catholic schools. This treatment will include all of the religious school cases, regardless of denomination, but will omit all nonreligious school cases. Those who want to read the secular school cases can find their citations in the various articles and decisions referred to in this chapter. There are also many cases, treated in other chapters of this treatise, in which school permits have been approved or rejected (perhaps as part of a general church plant) and where the question of discrimination between public and private schools did not arise.

In Chapter 3 a long list of articles espousing the theory of absolute anti-exclusion as it regards churches was studied, showing how cavalierly the precedents have been handled. The manhandling of precedent on the present subject is just about as bad as on the other. A few examples will be mentioned.

The case of the Episcopalian seminary at Evanston, Illinois,[19,23] was cited in an article in the *Nebraska Law Review* [109] as part of an alleged "weight of authority" pursuant to which the courts condemn as unfair any discrimination between private and public schools. Actually, the Episcopalian case supports no such rule. By implication, at least, it supports a contrary principle. The court held the Evanston ordinance invalid because, as compared to very serious injury done to the Episcopalians, the public purpose served by the ordinance was insufficiently substantial to justify it. The fact was cited that the seminary had raised funds in reliance on an ordinance previously in effect. No doubt this ordinance was discriminatory between public and private schools but the court declined an opportunity to find this discrimination unconstitutional. If it had done so, it would have declared the ordinance invalid as to all private schools. Instead, the court made clear [19:783] that its ruling was effective only "so far as the property which the [seminary] acquired is concerned." There was no general condemnation, such as the article suggests, of the public-private discrimination.

The Portland Catholic school case of 1932 [27] is described as late as 1957 by the *Notre Dame Lawyer* [166:629] as having held that "a zoning ordinance may not discriminate in favor of public schools and against private schools in the matter of their location in a residential zone." This reference is also inaccurate. The ordinance in the Portland case was held invalid for another reason, namely for its unconstitutional attempt to delegate to the bishop's neighbors control over the granting or withholding of his permit. The court specifically rejected consideration of discrimination. It said: "There is much said in the briefs of counsel for either party regarding what the action of the city council has been respecting other applications for schools. . . . These matters are beside the issue. . . ."

The Winnetka Catholic school case of 1939 [34] was the first in which a court actually condemned discrimination between public and parochial schools. The Winnetka decision cited the Portland and Evanston cases but not in the inaccurate manner of the *Nebraska Law Review* article. The Evanston decision [19,23] was cited for the proposition that the police power "is not unlimited but must bear a substantial relationship to the preservation of public health, safety, morals and general welfare." This was not a contested issue in the case. The Portland case [27] was cited as one wherein the exclusion of a parochial school was held "unconstitutional and void as being destructive of certain inherent rights of the property owners," without specifying the nature of those rights. The court may have been trying to give the impression that the two prior decisions supported the ruling it was about to make, but it was careful not to say so.

The meat of the Winnetka decision is in the court's statement that "we fail to perceive to what degree a Catholic school of this type will be more detrimental or dangerous to the public health than a public school. It is not pointed out to us just how the pupils in attendance at the parochial school are any more likely to jeopardize the public safety than the public school pupils. Nor can we arbitrarily conclude that prospective students of the new school will seriously undermine the general welfare. As a matter of fact such a school, conducted in accordance with the educational requirements established by state educational authorities, is promotive of the public welfare."

The Illinois court cited a Florida decision, *City of Miami Beach v. State*,[33] which had invalidated the exclusion of a nonreligious private school where public schools were permitted. The Miami decision had opined that "the prohibited classification finds no foundation or base in reason or experience that has been brought to our attention." The Illinois court said that the Florida reasoning "is applicable here."

However, the Illinois court still seemed hesitant to identify the public-private classification as a violation of the equal protection clause. In the end, it held only that "the ordinance before us bears no substantial relationship to the promotion of the public health, safety, morals or welfare." This is "due process language," not "equal protection language." It refers more to the purposelessness of the exclusion than to the alleged unfairness of the discrimination. Note also the court's statement that it "fails to perceive" any differences between private and public schools, that said differences, if any, are not "pointed out." This is quite different from saying that no such differences exist.

However, an article in the *Notre Dame Lawyer* of December 1955 [127:114] says: "Although no efforts were made to point out what differences, if any, do exist between a public and private school, the court [in the Winnetka case] indicated that none actually did exist." The article reiterates that the Illinois court "held that no dissimilarity exists between private and public schools." The court held no such thing. The Winnetka case held only (in effect) that the burden of proof is on the city rather than on the church. (See page 251.)

The question of discrimination between public and private schools was skirted in the Cleveland Heights, Ohio, case excluding a Jewish school. The dissenting justice [59:245] accused the planning commission of acting "in a discriminatory manner in denying [the congregation] the use of its property . . . for a parochial school of moderate size, especially in the face of the fact that schools had been allowed in other zones of the municipality of the same classification as the one herein involved." The majority of the justices disregarded this contention and sustained the refusal of the permit. It is not clear from the decision whether the "other schools" permitted in other zones were public, private or both.

The Wauwatosa, Wisconsin,[106] decision sustaining discrimination between public and private schools was not issued until 15 years after the Winnetka decision [34] had condemned such discrimination. It would be interesting to know how many zoning boards during this period assumed, under various misinterpretations of the Winnetka decision, that they could not regulate the use of land by church schools.

The Wauwatosa case involved an application for a permit by the Wisconsin Lutheran High School Conference. The city's ordinance set up an "A" district in which nonresidence construction was forbidden, with certain exceptions. One of the exceptions was for public schools and "private elementary schools." Private high schools were by implication excluded. The zoning board turned down the application under the clear terms of the ordinance. In the lower court the zoning board was overruled and issuance of the permit was ordered. But the supreme court overruled the lower court and reinstated the board's action.

The Lutherans relied heavily on the Winnetka decision.[34]

The Wisconsin Supreme Court, like the writer in the *Notre Dame Lawyer*, misread that opinion. It assumed that the Illinois court had condemned such discrimination as the Wauwatosa ordinance embodied. This (nonexistent) ruling, the Wisconsin court accepted as contrary to the city's position.But it refused to follow the precedent. It said that the Winnetka decision's "authority is persuasive only, and it does not persuade."

The Wauwatosa case was comparable to the Winnetka case [34] so far as the evidence was concerned. The city showed that the new school would bring congestion, noise, night lights, loss of tax revenue, lowering of real estate values, etc. But the Lutherans contended that "there is no difference in the effect on the community between the permitted public high school and the prohibited private one, and hence the ordinance's discrimination between them is unreasonable, not founded on a difference in fact material to the object sought to be attained by building ordinances, and is a measure which denies to [the Lutherans] the equal protection of the laws. . . .

As to the evidence, the court agreed with the Lutherans. In addition to the various adverse effects alleged by the city, the court said that "other detriments are easily thought of" but that "each such discordant feature attends the presence of a public school to an equal degree." This would have required a decision in favor of the Lutherans. But the court did not stop there. Instead, it did something that the Illinois court had refused to do. It took judicial notice of some differences between public and private schools which the city presumably had not shown.

For one thing, the court called attention to a fundamental difference between public and private activities. It said: [106:46] "The subject of public education and the establishment and operation of public schools is a governmental function of this state. . . . In the performance of other governmental functions, we do not restrict the behavior of persons or the use of property to the same extent that we do when only private interests are pursued and the fact that standards are different commonly raises no suspicion that an illegal discrimination is thereby imposed or that the difference between municipality and citizen is insufficient to support separate classifications."

"For example," the court continued, "who considers that he has the right to ignore speed laws because they need not be observed by the fire department responding to a call? Nor is the state controlled by a building requirement which an individual must observe. . . . It may be that the essential differences between government and governed are so great that the two are in different classes *per se* at any time when governmental functions are involved, and no ordinance is void, by reason of discrimination alone, merely because it gives a preference to the government, acting in its governmental capacity, which it withholds from private corporations or individuals."

This is the gist of the problem. It is an excellent statement of the proper prerogatives of government as distinguished from those of private persons including churches. Such a distinction is essential to the preservation of the majesty of government which is the principal sanction of its laws. No church can insist on equal treatment with the government unless, as in some other countries, it shares the government's sovereignty. For the government to concede equality and sovereignty to the churches would involve its abdication. To put church and state on a par under the law would fragmentize power and authority, especially here in America where we have not one but hundreds of churches over which the government—properly—has no control.

In support of this basic distinction between private and public activities, the Wisconsin court cited a number of cases where zoning ordinances forbade privately owned beaches but allowed public beaches; where private driving ranges were forbidden but public golf courses were allowed; and where other nonresidential uses were forbidden but firehouses and public utilities were allowed.

This part of the decision may be endorsed but should not be overrated. Actually it was not the basis of the court's ruling. The court said only that "it may be" that government and governed are in different classes *per se*. After having justified the principle so well, the court then put it aside and decided on other grounds, which I will now describe. It was in the later Orange County, California, Catholic case that the distinction above described was relied upon more directly. (See pages 179-80.)

The Wisconsin court said: [106:47] "We decide the present appeal on the narrower ground that tangible differences material to the classification of the ordinance can be readily pointed out which sustain the distinction made by the ordinance between schools." Thus, the court retreated to a narrower ground which I consider less sound. Its final decision was based more on a distinction between religious and nonsectarian than on a distinction between public and private schools. The court justified the city's discrimination against the Lutherans on the ground that they themselves were practising discrimination.

"The public school," said the court, "has the same features objectionable to the surrounding area as a private one, but it has, also, a virtue which the other lacks, namely that it is located to serve and does serve the area without discrimination. Whether the private school is sectarian or commercial, though it now complains of discrimination, in its services it discriminates and the public school does not. Any one in the district of fit age and educational qualifications may attend the public high school. It is his right. He has no comparable right to attend a private school. To go there, he must meet additional standards over which the public neither has nor should have control."

"The private school," the court continued, "imposes on the community all the disadvantages of the public school but does not compensate the community in the same manner or to the same extent. If the private school does not make the same contribution to the public welfare this difference may be taken into consideration by the legislative body in framing its ordinance. If education offered by a school to the residents of an area without discrimination is considered by the council to compensate for the admitted drawbacks of its presence there, that school may be permitted a location which is denied to another school which does not match the offer, and we cannot say that such a discrimination is arbitrary or unreasonable or that such discrimination between the two schools lacks foundation in a difference which bears a 'fair, substantial, reasonable and just relation' to the promotion of the general welfare of the community."

So the court shifted from the ground involving invidious comparison between the majesty of government and the lesser majesty of churches. Perhaps it was trying to be kind. If so, it failed. While the court did not mention specifically what the "standards" were to which religious school pupils must conform, one obvious reference was to the requirement for religious conformity. In other words, very properly and legally, the Lutherans discriminate against non-Lutherans. The court held the discrimination sufficient to justify the counter-discrimination by the zoning board.

In a sense, this makes the Wauwatosa, Wisconsin, Lutheran case comparable to the so-called restrictive covenant case of *Shelley v. Kraemer*,[64] decided in 1948. There the court held that a covenant excluding Negroes and Jews from a residential area was legal, like the Lutheran discrimination, yet refused to enforce it. The decision was based on grounds of public policy. Was the religious "segregation" practiced by the Lutherans comparable to the anti-Semitic and anti-Negro discrimination challenged in the *Kraemer* case? It is not surprising that the feelings of those who sponsor and support private religious schools were seriously hurt. One resentful article appeared in the *Marquette Law Review*[119] and another, written by the dean of that law school, was published by the *Miami Law Quarterly*.[151] Possibly the proponents of religious schools would prefer reflections cast on their churches' majesty to having their practices compared with racial segregation.

Some of the articles about the Wauwatosa decision were favorable. An article in the *Nebraska Law Review*[109] said: "Further support for the court's argument is found in the fact that a public school cannot constitutionally teach religious education; so it must follow that a school which does teach religious subjects is different. . . . The difference between the two types of schools seems to be a very important one which has been neglected in past cases dealing with the subject. This difference would justify a city council's careful consideration when drafting zoning ordinances for the promotion of the general welfare of the community."

I do not question the logic either of the court or of the article last mentioned. Yet it seems unwise to base land use regulation of private schools on religious grounds when other and stronger grounds are available. The distinction should be between public and private rather than between discriminatory (i.e. religious) schools and nondiscriminatory (i.e. nonreligious) schools. The article's proposal smacks of governmental regulation of educational content. It might seem to transform the shield of religious liberty into a sword.

The result would be different and more favorable treatment for the private schools of atheists, which practice no religious discrimination, than for those of Christians and Jews, which do practice such discrimination. Most people abhor religious division, especially among children. But this division, it seems to me, is a necessary concomitant of religious liberty and the "pluralism" which it fosters. If we want to keep that precious liberty, we will have to live with its disadvantages.

A *Michigan Law Review* article [116] said that "both the reasoning and the conclusion of the court . . . are certainly open to doubt." I agree as to the reasoning, not as to the conclusion. The writer adds: "As a given school satisfies the requirements of the state in the performance of its educational function, what can it matter that it admits students on a restricted basis?" Put so baldly, this question may shock those readers who are distressed by racial and religious discriminations. But it seems that such religious discrimination is essential to the existence of the separate religions. So long as it is not government supported, there is nothing in the constitution to prevent it.

The article in the *Marquette Law Review* of Spring 1955, said: [119:277] "The grave danger of the philosophy of the [Wauwatosa] case is that it could be used by communities to zone out private schools completely from all residential areas." This is correct. But the article goes on to say: "This is contrary to the well-considered and unanimous authority of other jurisdictions." So far as I can determine it was contrary to the authority of only one religious zoning case, that of the Winnetka Catholic school. [34] That decision was unanimous, but it was very equivocal, too.

"If schools are forced into business and industrial areas,"

the article continues, "or outside the city limits, these schools become less accessible and desirable. The state is then an active party to unwarranted limitation upon the right of all parents to educate their young as they see fit. The Wisconsin Supreme Court should have seriously pondered the clear language of the United States Supreme Court in [the *Society of Sisters* case [17]]."

That case involved an attempt by the State of Oregon to require attendance by all children at its public schools. The Supreme Court of the United States construed this as an attempt to bar private schools from the entire state. The court held this attempt invalid, saying that "the fundamental theory of liberty on which all governments of the Union repose excludes any general power of the state to standardize its children by forcing them to accept instruction from public teachers only. The child is not the mere creature of the state. Those who nurture him and direct his destiny have the right, coupled with the high duty, to prepare him for additional obligations."

It did not take the courts long to recognize the importance of this point. Before the article was published, presumably while it was being written, a court of appeals in California in the Piedmont Catholic school case [115] had invoked the selfsame *Society of Sisters* case [17] and had decided against exclusion of parochial schools from 98.7% of the area of that municipality. The decision was affirmed in the Supreme Court of California.[125] Some of the language in both decisions is inconsistent with the logic of the Wauwatosa case.[106] However, the result is not, because in the Wisconsin city only a single district, presumably a small segment of the city, was involved, while in Piedmont the exclusion was from practically the entire municipality.

In Piedmont, not only private high schools but also private grammar schools were excluded, but this difference seems not to have been important. Public schools were permitted and there were in fact three elementary schools, one junior high school and one high school in the residential zone. The decision in the court of appeals closely follows the Winnetka decision [34] as interpreted by the *Notre Dame Lawyer*.[127·114] The court states the single "narrow" question before it as "May . . .

Piedmont permit public elementary schools in [a zone] and at the same time constitutionally prohibit the conduct of all other elementary schools in the same area?" The answer was negative and the "rationale" stated by the court was that "no reasonable basis of classification exists between, or among, schools furnishing the same type of education to the same class of students." This was the same rationale that the *Notre Dame Lawyer* had attributed to the Illinois court in the Winnetka case. The court of appeals decision did not mention the Wauwatosa case. The judges seem not to have been acquainted with it. But they clearly took a contrary position.

When the Piedmont case came to the California Supreme Court,[125] the interference with personal liberties of parents was dealt with more thoroughly, but the decision is full of confusion. The supreme court first refused to hear the case at all, then a month later reversed itself and granted a hearing. Then its decision was by a court divided 4-3. As will be shown in Chapter 20, many "friends of the court" appeared, representing very influential religious organizations. A *Catholic Lawyer* [147] article said (see page 307) that this shows what can be achieved by the united action of all denominations. I doubt, however, that the participation of so many cooks improved the stew.

The California Supreme Court decision leaves a great deal of doubt whether it is based on the same grounds as the court of appeals decision or on other grounds. This appears by reference to two excerpts from the opinion. At one point [125:439] the majority says:

> *There is only one question involved,* whether . . . Piedmont may, by ordinance, constitutionally prevent the construction of a building to be used for private school purposes in an area where public schools are located. (My italics.)

This is a nice, clear, statement of the issue under the equal protection clause. It disregards the "practically total" nature of the exclusion, which might give rise to another question. It repeats, in almost identical language, the "narrow" question decided by the court of appeals. If the court had proceeded to decide this "only one" question, we could say with confidence that the Supreme Court of California, like the court of appeals, stands on the other side from the Wisconsin court. If it had stood firm on this statement of the issue, the precedent would prevent parochial school exclusion not only from 98.7% of a city but also from 9.87% or from .000987%. Any exclusion from any area where public schools were permitted would be illegal.

However, the court did not stand firm on its original statement of the "only one question." Three pages later the selfsame decision says: [125:442]

> *The only question before us* is whether a city may constitutionally by legislation exclude all private schools from 98.7% of its total area, which, when the character of the remaining area is taken into consideration, constitutes an effective exclusion of private schools from the entire city. (My italics.)

This is an excellent statement of the issue, not under the equal protection clause but under the due process or the religious liberty clause. It challenges not the discriminatory character of the regulation but its "total exclusion from substantially an entire municipality," a subject discussed fully in Chapter 3. If the case were decided on this basis, it would not overrule the Wauwatosa rationale.

If one reads the Piedmont decision [125] often enough, he is bound to gain the impression that the four men who signed it were originally divided among themselves, perhaps two and two; that each of these minorities within the majority wrote its own separate opinion, one based on the factor of discrimination and the other on undue oppression of Catholic parents; that, being unable otherwise to agree, they assigned the two opinions to a secretary, gave her scissors and a pot of paste and told her to put them together without omitting anything; and that the two decisions thus combined into one were signed by all four majority justices while blindfolded.

The Piedmont decision has also been commented on by learned writers, but most of their efforts have been devoted to determining what the judges actually said. Stanton G. Ware, in his *California Law Review* article of July 1956 [152] makes a very practical observation. He says: "It is possible, of course, that [the Piedmont decision] will be considered in future cases to have rested solely on the *Pierce* rationale." In other words, it will be treated not as a discrimination case but as a total exclusion case. Thus, Mr. Ware makes a choice between the two "only" questions. If his choice is correct, and I believe it is, the California Supreme Court decision in the Piedmont case is less relevant to this part of my treatise than to Chapter 3 where it has already been discussed. (See pages 41-2.) The reason I believe his choice is correct will appear in my discussion below of the Orange County, California, Catholic church and school case.[193,202] The three-man minority in the Piedmont case also made some sage observations about the sovereignties of church and state but I will not detail them here.

The distinction between public and private activities was the foundation of the decision in the Orange County case. It was heard in the court of appeals and decided against the church; it was heard again in the court of appeals and again decided against the church. It was then taken to the supreme court where hearing was denied.

On the rehearing before the court of appeals, the archbishop raised the issue whether "the zoning ordinance is unconstitutional because it discriminates against private schools." He cited the Piedmont decision and claimed that such discrimination was "an unconstitutional denial of equal protection of the laws if applied to private schools." The court rejected this contention, saying: [202]

> The argument is untenable in that it assumes that due process and equal protection of the law are synonymous with equal treatment of private citizens and the sovereign. [The church's] argument is that since the state may not be regulated in this particular field of activity, neither can the same activity of a private individual or corporation be so regulated. If this theory of equal protection were valid, it would necessarily apply to all activities of the state, not just public schools. . . . The list of state activities which are not subject to local zoning is long and varied and the law does not prohibit the regulation of the counterpart of each of these activities in private ownership. Equal protection of the law does not require the equating of private rights with those of the sovereign.

Thus the California Court of Appeals came to the same conclusion as the Wisconsin court in the Wauwatosa case [106] but based its decision on much firmer ground. If the Piedmont case [125] is treated as a case of discrimination, then the Orange County decision directly contradicts it. The archbishop seems to have thought so, too, for he appealed to the supreme court. But that court refused to hear the case. Thereby, it seems, at least by implication, to have approved treatment of the Piedmont case as suggested by Mr. Ware,[152] not as an equal protection case but as a due process case.

In 1958, the issue was again raised in New Jersey. The case involved a Catholic parochial school at Ocean Township. The lower court [180] practically identified the church with government and firmly forbade any discrimination between public and private schools. The supreme court of the state also ruled in favor of the church [206] but repudiated the grounds invoked by the lower court.

The township zoning ordinance allowed public schools in the residential zone; it further authorized the zoning board to grant variances where this could be done "without substantial detriment to the public good." The board granted the permit. The neighbors appealed. The lower court sustained the decision. In effect, the judge construed the words "public schools" as including parochial schools. The judge said: [180:263] "While the ordinance is silent in reference to parochial schools, under the equal protection clause, legislation cannot be unequal, partial or discriminatory. It cannot treat members of the same class differently. [The church] could have sought a permit under p-1 of the ordinance instead of asking for a variance."

Section "p-1" was the provision authorizing construction of public schools. The court read the word "public" as if parochial schools were as "public" as those operated by the school board. This would certainly have been the answer to the prayers of all the good sisters who operate parochial schools. A year earlier, at a meeting of the American Society of Planning Officials, Rev. Joseph Fichter of the Department of Sociology of Notre Dame University had been discussing [155:29,34] "parochial schools (which are semipublic) and private schools (which are not parochial)." He said that "in other words there are three kinds of elementary schools in this country: public, parochial and private schools." Father Fichter did not refer directly to the principle stated by the New Jersey judge, but he did suggest that "teachers hired by the city should be sent to teach in parochial schools."

In equating public and parochial schools, the judge did not mention the Winnetka [34] and the Piedmont [125] Catholic school cases. Instead, he relied on a mistaken interpretation of a passage in the New Jersey Supreme Court's decision in the Orange, New Jersey, Protestant case.[99] In the Orange, New Jersey, Protestant case, the court had mentioned that parochial schools "are in the same category as public schools for zoning purposes and are so grouped in the ordinance." From this the judge in the Ocean Township case [180] inferred that the supreme court considered such "grouping" constitutionally necessary. In this, he was mistaken.

The Ocean Township case was then taken to the supreme court of the state.[206] There the permit was again sustained, but the court shifted the grounds. It said: "Before the trial court, defendants, or one of them, apparently injected a claim, not within the pleadings, that constitutionally the treatment of public and parochial schools must be identical. The trial court apparently read [the Orange, New Jersey, Protestant decision [99]] to support the view that [the church] could have sought a permit under the terms of the ordinance itself upon an equation of a parochial school with a public school."

"We express no view," the Supreme Court of New Jersey continued, "of the constitutional issue, since it is not necessarily involved. No doubt a municipality may legislatively determine to include public and private schools in a single category for zoning purposes, and [the Orange, New Jersey, Protestant case [99]] approves that course. But there are differences which may well support another approach. In weighing its obligation to provide public education against some ensuing hurt to residential property, a municipality may decide to accept some detriment in order to furnish such education with reasonable convenience to the several areas of the community."

"It may, however, be proper," the court concluded, "to strike a different balance when weighing a detriment to a residential district against the need for a private school which draws its students from the entire community or from beyond its borders. Moreover, the governmental unit is politically responsible to the public for its selection of a school site and hence is alert to the various facets of public interest involved in this decision. If need be, it may resort to eminent domain to secure the appropriate location. On the other hand, a private school may not have had an equivalent sense of obligation to consider the interests of others and in any event is limited to parcels available to it by voluntary sale. We need not, and hence do not, express an opinion upon the question."

Thus the Supreme Court of New Jersey reversed a decision requiring equal treatment of parochial and public schools. However, on January 10, 1962, the legislature in effect reversed the supreme court by adopting a statute providing that: "No planning or zoning ordinance heretofore or hereafter enacted by any municipality governing the use of land by, or for, schools, shall by any of its terms or provisions or by any rule or regulation adopted in accordance therewith, discriminate between public and private day schools, not operated for profit, of elementary or high school grade." This statute is comparable to the Massachusetts law described at page 37.

Since public schools are not subject to zoning laws, this statute required a decision in favor of the Morris Plains Borough, New Jersey, Lutheran school [241] and in favor of a Catholic parochial school at Montclair.[248] In the latter case, the court refused to enforce a provision requiring a fixed amount of playground space depending on the number of children in attendance. The city defended on the ground that the statute was an unconstitutional discrimination against schools operated for private profit. This contention was also overruled in the superior court, but the issue has not at this writing been decided by the supreme court of the state.

The constitution may permit but it does not require such a policy as New Jersey has adopted. This was held during 1962 by the Supreme Court of Errors of Connecticut in the Darien Catholic school case.[247] This was an advisory opinion as to the validity of a requirement that a parochial school obtain a building permit. The court said that [247:48] "the public school . . . is a creature of statute." It described various legal controls exercised over it and said that "none of them apply to parochial or private schools." It added that:

All of these requirements tend to assure that those objectives which are the fundamental purpose of a zoning ordinance will be safeguarded. None of them apply to parochial or private schools. Therefore the establishment and the use of the physical plant of a parochial or private school, unless controlled in some manner such as is attempted in the present regulations, would enjoy an immunity not accorded to the public school.

The court held that "these factors clearly justify the treatment of the parochial and private school as a class separate and distinct from the public school." It also made clear that the other course amounts to establishment of a private "immunity."

It may be that the New Jersey law can be set aside as an unconstitutional discrimination against schools operated on a profit basis. If so, the New Jersey legislature may very possibly extend the immunity also to such schools, without correcting the discrimination against public schools or the abdication of its sovereign right to control land uses. The equal protection clause is intended to protect citizens and private corporations from mistreatment by their governments. I am doubtful that it contains anything to prevent a government from mistreating its own institutions in this way.

For the present it seems unnecessary for church schools in New York State to seek such legislative immunity as has been granted in New Jersey and Massachusetts although the judicial policy is rather confused. It is based on a dictum of the court of appeals that is self-contradictory, and upon the attempts of lower courts (generally taking a hair-shirt approach) to interpret that dictum. In 1955, a trial court in Nassau County had ruled on the application of the Great Neck Community (nonsectarian) School case. It said: [117:223]

> The public school is controlled and operated by the state through boards of education or trustees in each school district. . . . Private schools are different. They are aiding, under state supervision, in the necessary and important function of education but they are not the state in action. They do not, for example, possess the power of eminent domain. Nor are they empowered to cause a tax to be voted upon the people. They are not managed by persons selected in elections by citizens of the state.

In short, private schools are something less in prerogatives than public schools. There is thus a valid basis for denying to a village the power to control by zoning regulation the state school system but granting to the village the power to set aside areas by zoning regulations in which private schools are not permitted. The ordinance here is not invalid because of the treatment accorded to private schools as distinguished from public schools.

In the Brighton Roman Catholic church and school case of 1956,[149:834] the court of appeals said that "any ordinance will also be stricken if it attempts to exclude private or parochial schools from any residential area where public schools are permitted." This was one of a number of passing remarks included in this decision over and above the argument on which the ruling was based. The case was decided on grounds other than discrimination. In fact, the court said [149:833] that no discrimination was even alleged.

This statement of the court of appeals was at best dictum. The Nassau County trial court could have disregarded it. It did not do so. In 1959, it was called on again to consider the issue, this time upon an application of the Brandeis Jewish School of Lawrence.[191] Citing the Brighton case, the same justice who had decided the Great Neck case said: [191:697]

> This court has heretofore expressed the view that in respect to the exercise of the zoning power, a distinction can validly be made between public and private schools. Those views were expressed before the Court of Appeals in [the Brighton case] announced its view to the contrary. Therefore the court finds that the ordinance in question discriminates against private schools.

It is not asserted that the courts "unanimously" or "by overwhelming weight of authority" have sustained my view that, on proper occasion, religious schools can be subjected to land use regulation from which public schools are exempt. However, I would certainly challenge any assertion that there is a weight of authority to the contrary. The view is based upon what I consider the best opinion of those few courts that have actually passed upon the issue.

Municipalities have the power, without violating the equal protection clause, to admit public schools and at the same time to exclude private schools. The question whether such regulation would violate the due process or religious liberty clauses of the constitution depends, as I have said elsewhere, upon how wide is the area from which private schools are excluded and how inaccessible are alternative available sites.

While cities are free thus to regulate land use by religious schools, I would not necessarily recommend that this power be exercised to its utmost. Municipalities should consider the vital importance of the private school system to the Catholic Church. If the power to exclude or regulate such schools is exerted too severely, the church might seek establishment of exclusively or predominantly Catholic suburbs (comparable to Jewish "ghettos") where the Catholic institutions would be treated less harshly. Such a development, in my opinion, would be very undesirable.

It would seem wise for the states and their municipal instrumentalities to practise restraint in the exercise of their tremendous governmental power over religious land use. At the same time they should avoid such practical abdications of sovereignty as are involved in the Massachusetts and New Jersey laws. These statutes amount to the granting of an immunity to church authorities from the land use regulations that govern the rest of the population.

# CHAPTER 14.

## SUSPICIONS OF PREJUDICE

John Robinson, pastor of the Pilgrims, is supposed to have said that "Protestants living in the countries of papists commonly plead for toleration of religions; so do papists that live where Protestants bear sway; though few of either, especially the clergy, . . . would have the other tolerated where the world goes on their side." *

Most readers of church zoning cases get the impression that this is all changed. From what the judges say, it would appear that the bigotry, intolerance, prejudice and bias mentioned by Robinson has been dissipated from this land of the free. This gives even so careful a student of church-state relations as Paul Blanshard the impression, expressed in his *God and Man in Washington* [214] that: "No decent citizen would condone [exclusion of churches] if it happened to be based on anti-Semitism, anti-Catholicism or any other form of religious discrimination." There is respectable opinion, however, that prejudice exists, expressed in an article entitled "Zoning Can Be Anti-Religious" published in *Columbia Magazine*, official organ of the Knights of Columbus for November 1956.[153] Reading the cases very thoroughly, I have concluded that such prejudices continue to exist and that they have an important effect on the outcome of cases. They are not immediately apparent but this is only because the judges conceal them.

A judge might object that my views are based on suspicions, that he could not act on them but must have facts to support any decision. It has been suggested that views based only on suspicion have no place in a law book; but this is more than a law book. To many the omission of this factor would give the treatise an appearance of unreality. Since I am neither judge nor advocate, I am free to express views based on suspicions,

---

* Quoted by Leo Pfeffer in *Church, State and Freedom* [97:20,65] from Bates: *Religious Liberty; an Inquiry* (International Missionary Council, New York and London, 1945).

186

which I will now proceed to do. I believe my suspicions are sound.

This is the most personal part of the book and I don't ask my reader to share my suspicions. In evaluating them, he should remember that they are based only on the facts stated in the courts' decisions. Courts sometimes fail to state facts—or arguments—with complete accuracy. In a particular case, the suspicion of intolerance might disappear if certain facts unknown to me were revealed. In the cases described below the decision itself reveals one or more of the following elements:

A. A sharp difference in the treatment of two denominations under comparable circumstances.

B. Procedural harassment of an applicant.

C. Sudden changes in requirements, imposed when a particular church application is about to be filed or just after it is filed.

D. Harsh language or other indication of a hostile attitude.

E. Absence of a rational basis for a decision against a church.

F. Truculence on the part of the church-applicant that would try the patience of angels.

G. Adverse action against a church or racial group which is notoriously the victim of widespread intolerance.

The earliest of the church cases discussed herein, that of the Grace Missionary Church of Zion, Illinois,[13] is perhaps the best example of bigotry in action. It involved not only the Grace Missionary Church but also the "Dowie Church" which had founded, and to all practical purposes controlled, the city of Zion. John Alexander Dowie's story is told briefly in Anson Phelps Stokes' *Church and State in the United States*.[75] During the Chicago World's Fair of 1893, Dowie, a Presbyterian minister from Australia, had created a popular sensation by his preaching. Soon his following grew to a point where he controlled a vast and rich organization known variously as the Christian Catholic Apostolic Church in Zion, the Theocratic Party, and the Zion Land and Investment Association.

Dowie controlled, among other things, several large office buildings near Chicago's Loop.

Ideas founded on faith are usually more tenaciously and belligerently held than those founded on reason alone. Dowie challenged the foundations of other religious faiths, so it was to be expected that prejudice would arise against him. He claimed direct personal divine inspiration for his doctrines. This was a challenge to the priesthoods of other churches as well as to the "priesthood of all believers." Dowie claimed that he was the "Messenger of the Covenant" and that he had the right to rule not only his own followers but also the followers of other Christian clergymen.

Dowie incurred the special wrath of the medical profession by claiming divine power to heal. Chicago became so intolerant of him that he decided to move his entire flock elsewhere. He decided that they should all go to a place where, like the followers of John Robinson, they would be free of oppression directed against them and able to oppress the members of other religions.

One morning the *Chicago Tribune* startled the city with the news that overnight, in secrecy, Dowie and his people had left town and set themselves up in tents on a farm north of the city. The farm was the site of the new Zion. Plans included the location of Dowie's temple at the center. This was to be a theocracy under the clergyman's control.

Zion got a charter under ordinary man-made laws and adopted ordinances in the usual form. It was obvious, though, that Dowie, pursuant to his alleged divine authorization, dictated all of the settlement's affairs. The extent of his control was demonstrated by the fact, among others, that in one presidential election every single vote in the town was cast for one candidate, who happened to be Theodore Roosevelt.

Eventually Dowie got into financial and personal difficulties. He had to be removed in 1906. The church was split into a number of fragments, three or four of which survive to this day, in addition to the main body. One of these fragments was called the Grace Missionary Church. After Dowie's departure, Grace Missionary sought and obtained a construction permit for its edifice. The new congregation lacked money to complete the building, so after finishing the basement they roofed it over and for a decade continued to use it for their services.

The number of adherents of Dowie's church had shrunk to a point where they represented only about half of the population. Dowie had been replaced by another formidable character, Wilbur Glenn Voliva. Voliva made a great name for himself as a radio preacher. He enforced a ban on the use of tobacco anywhere in the city. He was famous especially for his predictions of the imminent end of the world, as well as for his agility in explaining why the predicted catastrophe did not occur on schedule.

Voliva established a number of economic enterprises under church auspices which were highly successful. At one point he claimed he was "the biggest manufacturer of fig bars in the world," having shipped 26 million of them in one year. He controlled, according to his boast, 26 industries and institutions, in addition to schools, colleges, publishing houses, and "what not." He also seemed to have full control of the mayor of Zion, W. Hurd Clendennin, who in private life was a personal employee of Voliva.

By 1921 the Grace Missionary people had accumulated enough money to finish construction of their church and to add a gymnasium. The old permit had expired, so they applied for a new one. The ordinance was still the same as when enacted in 1902. It did not specifically forbid new churches nor, for that matter, any other type of structure. It merely required that permits for new buildings be obtained from the mayor. It contained 35 sections with respect to materials, methods of construction, setback and height limitations, etc. It authorized the mayor to issue additional rules and regulations, although no such regulations had ever been issued.

One section of the ordinance provided that [13:269] "until fire limits are established, frame buildings not exceeding 35 feet in height to the highest point of the roof may be constructed. If the basement is of brick or stone, the height may be extended to 45." In 1913 fire limits had been established, so that presumably this provision was no longer in effect. The Grace Missionary application was for a building 50.2 feet high. When the city clerk received it, he said that "the only objection that the city might raise as to the plans submitted was in respect to the height of the church." He told the church officials to go ahead with the work while the application was under consideration. For twenty days, the work proceeded. Then the mayor asked for new plans and specifications which were submitted. The mayor refused to issue a permit and ordered the work stopped.

According to the decision of the Illinois Supreme Court,[13:269] "ten workmen were arrested and, having been released on bail, returned to their work, when they were again arrested and lodged in jail until evening." The Grace Missionary people then asked the mayor "whether a permit would be granted if the height . . . was lowered to 45 feet so as to comply with section 13?" The mayor replied that "it does not matter; that is not the point. Those fellows think they can do as they please and we will show them different." Meanwhile, Voliva announced that he would drive from the city of Zion all persons who were not members of his church and announced from his pulpit in the city that he had stopped the building of the church and would keep it stopped.

Obviously, this case was decided by the city without respect to any rational or relevant theory. It came within the legal definition of prejudice, being decided "for some reason other than its justice." The court might very properly have pointed out this fact and condemned both Voliva and his puppet, the mayor. Instead, as in subsequent cases, the judges were silent about prejudice. The court decided the case against the Grace Missionary Church on technical grounds not here relevant. At the same time, however, it said: [13:270] "If it was a fact that the refusal of a permit was due to the unlawful and malicious action or interference of any person for the purpose of preventing the erection of any church building, the [new church] would not thereby be deprived of its remedy by mandamus." Thus the court invited the church to file a new suit in proper form. The warning that such a suit would be successful seems to have been sufficient, without further court action. The permit was later granted and the "heretical" church is now thriving in the city of the two theocrats, Dowie and Voliva.

Another aspect of the case should be noted because it

characterizes cases of religious prejudice. After the church's workmen were jailed,[13:270] a great deal of building material left out in the open was destroyed by the weather. The court refused to remedy this injury and, so far as I know, it was never compensated for. This illustrates how, within the law, prejudiced officials can give special treatment to certain chosen people in the form of procedural harassments, regardless of the merits of the case, and even regardless of its final outcome in the courts.

Few of the later cases provide such clear evidence of bias as the Zion case. Writing in the July 1957 issue of *Commentary Magazine*,[163] William Schack says that "where bias does exist, it is not written large for all to see." He quotes Charles Abrams, an anti-discrimination official of the city of New York, who says that "administrative chicanery is highly difficult to detect. . . . Those in control are not prone to make a record of their discriminatory policies, or to give the minority evidence on which their oppression can be tested. The civil rights lawyer is no longer afforded the luxury of a clear test on the admitted facts."

This was true of the Sherman, Texas, Church of God case of 1944.[48,49] There was no testimony, as there had been in the Zion case, from which the motives of the city officials could be directly deduced. Yet there was so little basis in reason, law or fact for the city's decision that it could only have been based on prejudice. The court decided for the church, but was unwilling to express any suspicion of bigotry. The case was decided on other grounds.

In the Sherman case, from the beginning, the city admitted the invalidity of its ordinance restricting churches to business and manufacturing districts. Whether the ordinance was actually void or not, it is important that the city officials thought it was and acted accordingly until the Church of God application was filed.

Previous to the filing of that application, permits for construction had been issued in spite of the ordinance to one Baptist church and to one church of the Assembly of God. A Church of God asked permission, not to construct a new building, but to use an old one for congregational purposes. The ordinance not only—in terms—forbade churches in the zone (said provision being deemed invalid) but also provided that "no building . . . shall be changed in use until a certificate of occupancy and compliance shall have been issued by the building inspector stating that such change of use complies with all the building, fire, sanitary and health laws and ordinances."

The church had been using the building without a permit and had violated some of the safety requirements. However, in its application it expressed willingness to comply and stated: [48:101] "We understand that should the said Church of God . . . be used and occupied . . . in violation of the provisions of any building, fire, sanitary, health or zoning laws, that we shall be subjected to a fine of not more than a hundred dollars per day so long as such violation exists."

The minister of the church had not always been so submissive to man-made laws. When previously charged with violating safety regulations, he had told an inspector [48:101] that he "didn't recognize any law but God's. These others didn't make any difference." It was only natural for the city officials to react in a hostile way. However, his past violations were legally irrelevant to his new application. If the officials had acted rationally, they could have fined him for past violations, then issued the new permit with safeguards against future violations.

Instead, the permit was denied altogether and upon the ground that "the proposed use of the [building] does not comply with the zoning ordinance . . . as this would be a nonconforming use of the property in a residential district." The building commissioner relied entirely upon the section of the ordinance which the city had itself condemned as void and which it had declined to enforce against other churches.

The city then also sued the Church of God for an injunction against further use of the building. The trial court might properly have enjoined further violation of the law. Instead, it followed the same bullheaded procedure as the city officials. It [48:102] "perpetually enjoined and forbade [the church's] use of the described property except for residential purposes." Again, the court invoked the provision which the city had admitted was void.

This situation was not remedied until the case reached the

court of appeals. The court said [48:103] that the city had admitted the invalidity of the ordinance excluding churches. It then ordered that "the church be permitted to comply with [such safety, etc. regulations] as may be necessary and appropriate to the use of the described property for church premises, being thereby entitled to the permit requested." In the event of noncompliance, the court indicated that a new injunction against violation could be obtained.

In view of its admissions, it is hard to see how the city could have hoped for a more favorable decision in any respect. However, the city was not yet satisfied. It took the case to the supreme court of the state. There it was reviewed again [49:415] on the "question of the authority of the city to exclude churches from residential districts and relegate them to business and industrial districts."

Since the city had waived this point there seemed to be no rational basis for its having ever been discussed (a) by the building commissioner, (b) by the lower court which issued the injunction, (c) by the court of appeals which dissolved the injunction and directed issuance of the permit, or (d) by the supreme court which affirmed that decision. The mere fact that the issue was raised indicated that there was prejudice at the first two levels and, at the higher levels, a blind refusal to recognize it. The supreme court added some glittering language about the rights of churches, affirmed the uncontested point that the law was invalid, and confirmed the permit. It did not so much as mention the prejudicial conduct of the commissioner. Meanwhile, I presume, the church had been deprived of the use of its property for almost two years, without hope of compensation.

In the Pentecostal Holiness church case of 1946 at Montgomery, Alabama,[56] the purpose to discriminate against a minority religion was made more explicit. Among other allegations of objecting property owners was one [56:562] that the applicant "is not an established church but that it represents a commercial enterprise by the so-called pastor of such organization who is directly interested in the financial return thereof . . . , that such church did not have a creed of worship in the usual sense of the word but that their services consist of appeals to passion and emotion and in an attempt to inculcate emotional frenzy resulting in manifestations of disorderly and sacrilegious nature." Here the court had a wonderful opportunity to strike a blow for tolerance by dismissing and condemning all allegations as to doctrine. It did not take advantage of this opportunity.

A similar bit of evidence of bigotry in this case [56:562] was that the permit was first granted, then, after complaints by the neighbors, retroactively cancelled. Retroactive action is not usually unconstitutional in civil cases, but it provides valid ground for suspicion that prejudice exists. In 1960, a Pennsylvania court in the Philadelphia Baptist church case said: [216] "As nothing can be more unjust in criminal law than an *ex post facto* law, so nothing is more frowned upon in civil law than a procedure which has the effect of making illegal what the law has already recognized as legal. No lover of American sports would approve of changing ground rules to favor one side or the other after the game had begun."

The court ruled in favor of the Pentecostals but in doing so, intentionally or not, it actually fed the fires of prejudice by implying that the allegations concerning doctrine would, if proved, have made a difference in the outcome. The court said that the objectors had proved "only the fact that the method of offering prayer in this church permitted all members to pray at the same time." It added that the "proof failed to show that the doctrine and practices of this church were in anywise such as would bar it from the claim that it was a protestant church and entitled to the ordinary considerations as such." Presumably, if the Pentecostals had not qualified as "protestant," the treatment accorded them by the court might have been different.

Another religious group that, as the court saw it, was very noisy was the Full Salvation Union which operated a camp meeting near Portage, Michigan, until its removal was ordered, with the approval of the Supreme Court of Michigan.[60,63,65] No doubt the operation disturbed some neighbors; no doubt it violated sanitary regulations; it might have been quite proper for the court to enjoin such violations. But if the court had been more tolerant it might have ordered issuance of a new permit. It might have conditioned a new permit on compliance with such regulations, as was done in the Sherman, Texas, case.[48,49] Instead, the Michigan court ordered the whole enterprise removed from the township.

This decision was supported on the theory, similar to the one unsuccessfully advanced in the Pentecostal Holiness case at Montgomery, Alabama,[56] that the enterprise was not truly a church at all. The court invoked a dictionary definition of "church" which describes it as a "building, etc." and said that this would not include the open-air activities or the temporary living quarters involved in the camp meeting. Neither would they be included in the term "accessories of" a church.

The ecclesiastical corporation then contended that if the ordinance was to be interpreted as excluding their religious activities it would be unconstitutional. The court overruled this contention. It is not possible from this distance to disagree conclusively with the court's decision, either as to the definition of the words, or as to the constitutional problem. The objection goes rather to the attitude displayed by the court toward this minority sect, especially as compared with the attitude assumed five years later by the same court in the Orchard Lake, Michigan, case.[94] That case involved, not a minor sect, but the largest denomination. The following are quotations from the court's discussions of one issue, namely the burden of proof. The quotations are placed opposite each other to facilitate comparison.

| FULL SALVATION CASE, 1947 [60:301] | CATHOLIC CASE, 1952 [94:310] |
|---|---|
| . . . That the ordinance must stand the test of reasonableness is not disputed. However, the presumption is in favor of validity. Courts may not properly invalidate a statute or ordinance unless the constitutional objections urged against it are supported by competent evidence or appear on the face of the measure in question. In [a previous case] it was said: "The generally accepted rule is that a presumption prevails in favor of the reasonableness and | . . . [W]e are confronted with an enactment showing on its face that which, combined with the competent evidence in the case, obviates the necessity for resort to the presumption of reasonableness and validity and raises a question for judicial determination. The ordinance of 1787 for the governing of the Great Northwest Territory, of which Michigan is a part, pronounced a conviction and purpose, reiterated in the Michigan Constitution of 1908, . . . which formed the cornerstone of |

validity in all particulars of a municipal ordinance, unless the contrary is shown by competent evidence or appears on the face of the enactment." In [another case], the general rule was stated as follows: "It is elementary that every intendment is in favor of the constitutionality of an ordinance and plaintiff has the burden of showing that it has no real or substantial relation to the public health, morals, safety, or general welfare."

the governmental structures of the territories and of the states subsequently carved therefrom, in these exalted terms: "Religion, morality and knowledge being necessary to good government and the happiness of mankind, schools and the means of education shall forever be encouraged." Hardly compatible with this is a presumption that exclusion of school and church from an entire municipality is conducive to public safety, health, morals or the general welfare, a presumption which we decline to indulge.

There might have been factual differences between the two cases that would justify the difference in the court's treatment of them. It is not impossible that for some reason undisclosed by the court the camp meeting was much more disturbing to the rural area where it was located than the archbishop's enterprise would have been to the urban area where it was to be constructed. There may have been some other basis of distinction. There is no way to know whether these differences existed because the court in the Orchard Lake case made no attempt to differentiate the two situations.*

The important aspect of the decision in the Orchard Lake case was this failure or refusal to explain its inconsistency. The city officials cited the Portage case in their brief. The court declined to discuss it. This gives the Orchard Lake decision, read in conjunction with the Portage decision, an air of irrationality and raises a suspicion of prejudice in favor of large denominations and against small ones. In judges such prejudices are inexcusable.

---

* As indicated on page 254, there had been an earlier church zoning case in the state, the Grand Rapids Lutheran church case.[28] Although the zoning board declined even to state the reasons for its action, the court upheld it, saying that its "decision was final in the absence of fraud or bad faith. . . ." However, this case was different from either the Portage or the Orchard Lake case in that the action of the board was favorable to the church.

An article in *St. John's Law Review* of December of the same year, 1952,[95] in reviewing the Orchard Lake decision, sees bigotry in another sense. It says [95:102] that any zoning law is "bigoted" which "prohibits or limits the use of land for any church or other religious purpose or . . . prohibits or limits the use of land for any religious, sectarian, or denominational educational purpose." It advocates the adoption in all states of legislation like that of Massachusetts which completely outlaws such action.

This article seems to use the term "bigoted" more for invective than for description. There is bigotry in church zoning cases; but it is usually not to be found in the original ordinances as such. Usually, it arises during the course of administration from the attempts of majority denominations or their adherents to exclude the new, the different, or the strange religions that arise occasionally in this country.

The *St. John's Law Review* proposal for giving churches *carte blanche* is extreme. On the other hand, the Michigan court in the Portage case should have found a way to eliminate the disturbance without eliminating the religious activity. Likewise, the courts should find a way to eliminate the bias in zoning cases without eliminating zoning. If churches were given free and unrestricted use of any land for such purposes as they might desire, they would be able to destroy the integrity of every neighborhood.

The decision in the Beachwood, Ohio, Jewish case of 1953 [101] also shows how loath are the courts to point their fingers at prejudice. The decision favored the congregation but without mentioning the existence of bias against it. The membership of the proposed synagogue was 1801 not including women or children. The congregation wanted to take 31½ acres off of the tax rolls and use it for tax-exempt religious purposes, at the same time increasing the budget of the town by the cost of additional policing, etc. Of the membership of the synagogue, only 20 lived in the village. As surely as night follows day this must have given rise to prejudice against the Jews or intensified prior existing bigotry. Yet the court was oblivious of it.

The fears of the community were to some extent reflected in a statement by the city's attorney that "a large institution of nonresidents, comprising a membership over three times the size of the community in which it was located, would soon dominate its social and political life." If there was no bias against such a prospect, then I would have to admit that John Robinson was wrong. It is a human reaction, especially among Christians. What disturbs me is the fact that the court never mentioned this element. The case was decided as if the judges were living in a dream world where the hearts of all men are pure. The court disregarded the argument of the Jewish group as disclosed in Mr. Schack's discussion of the case: [163]

> Mr. Morris Berick [attorney for the Jewish congregation] . . . openly charged that the council acted from bias in turning down the temple's application. Before the court of appeals, he declared that "the method of refuting the possible charge that the discrimination against the temple was based on racial and religious grounds is hardly persuasive. [The city's] counsel asked the village officials whether anyone at the council meeting expressed opposition to the temple on the grounds that it was Jewish. We are sure that he did not expect a 'Yes' answer. Neither did we, and that is why we did not bother to put the question. Indeed, we were surprised when the president of the council did not immediately answer with a positive 'No' but gave the qualified answer, 'Not to my recollection.' "
>
> In order to show that the council was free of religious bias, its attorneys in their first brief pointed out that there were already a Presbyterian church and Catholic church and parochial school in the community and that "in all probability a pending application for a small Jewish temple . . . will be granted." But why, asked Mr. Berick, later, was a permit given to one church (Catholic) without a public hearing? Why did the notice of public hearing for the other (Presbyterian) expressly advise the neighbors that the zoning commission had recommended the issuance of the permit? Why did the council in the Temple case act without any recommendation, favorable or adverse, by the zoning commission?
>
> Why were not petitions circulated to obtain the views of the entire village population in connection with the other (church) applications or with the applications for the golf range and the schools, which were also granted? If the village population of 1950 was 1057, it was undoubtedly about 700 or 800 in 1948. It is very unlikely that any Christian denomination or any one of three Jewish denominations then had enough residents at Beachwood to

support a church. Why was the question of the nonresidence of the members not a factor in the 1948 application (of the Catholic church)?

The court did not take cognizance of the issue of discrimination. They did not have to. The case was won upon the court's determination that failure to issue a permit (to the Jews) was an abuse of discretion in the administration of the zoning ordinance. What we should like to know is how the council came to commit this abuse—innocently, in mistaken judgment, or deliberately from bias?

At pages 61-2, I have praised the result in the Beachwood case. I here criticize only this covering up of the existence of religious prejudice. It is comparable to a sore that will not heal until lanced by the knife of judicial publicity and subjected to the antibiotic of full discussion.

In the case of the Protestant evangelical center at Dallas, Texas,[102] the applicant was again a group so small that it seemed almost an individual enterprise. Jack Coe was famous, not to say infamous, as a radio and television preacher and faith healer. No doubt his practices evoked the displeasure of numerous highly respected citizens including both the clergy and the judiciary. But this displeasure should have been set aside for purposes of the decision which should have been based on reason and law alone. Here again the court defeated a minority institution by invoking the theory that it was not a church at all. The grounds for the ruling are summarized below, along with my comments on each:

(a) That only one fifth of the building was devoted to the "auditorium or church proper." The balance, however, was given over to "healing and prayer rooms." (The function of "healing and prayer" is no less religious than that of an "auditorium proper." Does the Texas court intend to supervise the distribution of church space by religious denominations?)

(b) That only an estimated three to fourteen per cent of the members were expected to attend services regularly. (The application of any test based on percentage of attendance would probably disqualify most churches. It is irrelevant.)

(c) The practice of healing. (This has been a part of

the ministry since the days of Jesus, and long before. Practically all clergymen still insist that prayer has power to heal. It may be that Coe was a charlatan; but the courts cannot take upon themselves the impossible task of determining which ministers of religion are charlatans and which are not.)

(d) The use by Coe of "loudspeakers, a Hammond organ, and tent services." (These facilities are not uncommon in church activities.)

(e) That Coe's organization was incorporated. (Since the Dartmouth College case,[4] our courts have given protection to the rights of corporations. Most churches are incorporated.)

As in other cases there may have been facts undisclosed by the decision to justify the court's conclusions. But it was only on the basis of the facts above summarized that the court in the Coe case held that "the building, not being a church, there is no question of the council's authority to refuse the permit under the building ordinance." Not only is this palpably wrong. It is also based on such insubstantial reasoning that it argues the existence of prejudice in the court of civil appeals against the Coe corporation.

An opposite side of the coin of religious bigotry should not be overlooked. This is the tendency of some persons interested in church zoning cases to disadvantage their opponents by ascribing bigotry where it does not actually exist. This tendency has been noted previously in the article from *St. John's Law Review* [95:102] which called all church zoning actions "bigoted." The lower court of Pennsylvania that decided the Cheltenham Township Jewish case [105] dealt with a similar manifestation of "reverse bigotry" in an intriguing way.

The decision was in two parts, one written after the original hearing and the other after rehearing. In the latter part, the judge said that he had "received a number of letters praising the opinion as a victory over bigotry." If the anti-bigotry bigots were so bold as to write letters to the judge, presumably they were active at the earlier stages of the case as well. There is no indication that they had any influence on any public official. The court said that "the interested parties who appeared for and against the special exceptions were all of the

Hebrew faith and some, at least, were members of long standing in the Congregation Adath Jeshurun. Obviously, there was no contention between persons of different faiths in the present case. Possibly, instead of a zoning question, this may be a family controversy between members of the same congregation."

At least two writers, one in a Catholic periodical and one in a Jewish periodical, see evidence of prejudice in the mere fact that so many church zoning cases arise in smaller, less cosmopolitan communities. In his article in *Commentary*,[163] William Schack says: "Suspicion of anti-Semitism was nourished by the further circumstance that all the congregations encountering difficulties were located in the suburbs to which they were newcomers from the large cities where they had been relatively immune to the gross problems of discrimination practiced against Jews as a group."

An article in the August 1957 *Notre Dame Lawyer* [166:640] advances a similar theory. It says that "a common denominator in many zoning cases is their suburban origin. One sixth of today's 170 million Americans reside in the suburbs and the rights of minorities frequently clash with the local public opinion of the majority in these areas. Scores of suburbs are merely collections of houses thrown up since World War II, having no corporate existence. They are largely subject to county zoning laws and seldom does local bigotry and prejudice prevail at the county level. However, many of these new communities are being incorporated as villages, towns, and cities. As these communities incorporate, they adopt their own local zoning laws, such laws frequently reflect bigotry and (as in Piedmont, Sands Point, Wauwatosa and Brighton) they eventually may clash with the constitutional guaranties of the First and Fourteenth Amendments." *

I agree with both comments, at least in general. As to the Brighton, New York, case,[149] the opinion expressed in the *Notre Dame Lawyer* clashes with that of a "spokesman of the building commission of the archdiocese of New York." This

---

* This refers, presumably, to the Wauwatosa, Wisconsin, Lutheran high school case,[106] the Piedmont, California, Catholic school case,[125] the Sands Point, New York, Jewish synagogue case [148] and the Brighton, New York, Catholic church and school case.[149]

priest wrote to Mr. Schack, saying that "to my knowledge we have never felt that there was any bias or anti-Catholic opposition. Whenever we have had difficulty, it was in the technical language of an ordinance and in its interpretation." However, I am more inclined to agree with the article than with the chancery office of the church. Further, I say that interreligious prejudice, nay hatred, exists in most communities. Zoning board hearings give people an opportunity to vent their feelings in this respect. Everything possible should be done to prevent cases from being decided on so base a motive.

The difference that the *Catholic Lawyer* mentions between prejudice at the county level and prejudice at the village level is easy to explain. In New York State, for example, there are many Catholic and Jewish citizens. Yet it is still possible to find, a "WASP" (white Anglo-Saxon Protestant) enclave in a particular suburb or village. There are few counties, however, where the minority of Jews and Catholics is not sufficiently large for self-defense. This does not mean that irrational anti-Catholicism and anti-Judaism is at an end. It means merely that it is counteracted by a contrary prejudice that is sometimes no healthier than the one it counteracts.

The attitude of the clergy is sometimes sufficiently belligerent actually to provoke hostility. I have already mentioned how Mr. Sims in the Sherman, Texas, Church of God case [48] refused to respect "any law but God's." In the San Marino, California, Catholic parking lot case [223,224] the archbishop seems to have acted in similar fashion. In direct contravention of the law, he had maintained a parking lot next to his church. The village officials for years neglected to stop him. Then, when the archbishop was ready to build a new rectory, he insisted on building it in the area where a special permit was required, although he had additional land immediately adjacent where a rectory could be built without special approval.

In the case of Jehovah's Witnesses at Haltom City, Texas,[136] a similarly defiant attitude was displayed by the Witnesses. An individual member took out a permit for the construction of a residence. He then proceeded, instead, to build a Kingdom Hall. The authorities knew nothing of this until construction was almost complete. Then the commissioner stopped the work. Only after this did the congregation take title to the premises and, with great protestations of innocence, seek a church permit.

An emotional reaction to this line of conduct was quite predictable. The city refused the permit, giving a number of reasons but notably omitting to mention the personal hostility that they must have felt. The court overruled all the stated objections for reasons that have been discussed elsewhere. It also took cognizance of prejudice when it quoted one witness who said that "his principal objection was that they took it out (the residence permit) and told them it was a residence. They took out a permit as a residence and then they turned it out as a church."

Whether or not the Witnesses were parties to this deceit, it was strictly irrelevant in the proceedings on the new application. The individual presumably could have been punished for his misdeeds, but they should not have been taken into consideration in the proceedings for a permit. The court should not only have mentioned such prejudice but should have condemned it.

The South Euclid, Ohio, Jewish synagogue case,[140] also contained some of the elements mentioned at the beginning of this chapter as indicating possible prejudice. Suddenly, when the synagogue application was filed, requirements for parking space were increased from one to each ten seats to one to each four seats. The negotiations for the permit extended over a period of two years. It was denied in face of the fact that, across the street,[140:175] there was a large apartment house development and nearby was a Masonic temple and golf course. Also almost directly across the road was a junior high school. The court of appeals made no mention of the possibility of prejudice but decided the case on other grounds.

The Creve Coeur, Missouri, Jewish temple case[192] also contains several of the factors that I have recited on page 187 as giving rise to a suspicion of prejudice. Temple Israel had bought the property while it was still zoned to permit churches. Immediately thereafter the property was rezoned to permit churches in residential areas only by special permit. There followed a long delay after which the Temple Israel application was denied. These facts were all disregarded by the court in its final decision. While that decision was favorable to the temple, it was based on an extremely shaky statutory interpretation, one which will have a tendency to disrupt city plans throughout the state. If the court had overcome its timidity and dug into the issue of prejudice, it might very well have found a firmer ground for deciding the particular case in favor of the Jews without establishing a difficult precedent that will surely embarrass it in the future.

It has been suggested that the decision in the Protestant evangelical center case at Dallas [102] was so lacking in rational foundation as on its face to appear biased. In his *Commentary* article, Mr. Schack expresses a similar reaction to the zoning board decision in the Garden City Jewish case, a decision that was overruled by the trial court.[150,154] The permit was denied in the first instance on the theory that the space was too small to allow for future expansion of the synagogue. Schack says: [163]

> So patently indefensible an objection argued the desperate case. What really seemed to be troubling the board came out openly in its further findings that the synagogue would "alter the character of the neighborhood." This is a broad statement of the kind usually made in cases of this sort. In Garden City, it had a more precise meaning. As the *New York Times* reported the case, "until about five years ago, Garden City was, in effect, a restricted community with few Jewish families living there. But in the last few years, the Jewish population has increased, with the center now numbering 200 members, representing 68 families."

Mr. Schack continues: "Among the Center's members, the belief that they were faced with discrimination was very strong, even if they were unable to point to any more overt evidence of bias than the extreme bitterness of the opposition. Fortunately, the attorney for the Center, C. Walter Randall, did not have to grapple with this shadowy issue to make his case; he based it entirely upon the right of any sect to establish a church in Garden City."

For once, I cannot agree with Mr. Schack's approach, nor with that of Mr. Randall. It may be that the factual ruling (i.e. that 1.38 acres was insufficient for future expansion of a 68-family synagogue) was so preposterous that it bespeaks prejudice. If so, then the court knew it; it made a personal inspection of the premises with the consent of the parties. If the ruling was clearly prejudicial, then the court should have so held. I disagree with Mr. Schack that it was "fortunate" not to "grapple with this shadowy issue."

The grounds chosen by the court as a basis for its decision have been discussed below at page 234. In effect the court held that the zoning board had power to "plan" only for the present and not for the future! Instead of making good law on the subject of bias, the court made very bad law on another phase of church zoning. It might better have followed the example that Jesus provided when on the mountaintop He "wrestled with" the Power of Darkness.

At the beginning of this chapter I have outlined elements in zoning cases that give rise to suspicions of prejudice. The last mentioned is "adverse action against a church or racial group which is notoriously the victim of widespread intolerance." In this connection we should not forget the Negroes, although from reading the cases it would appear that the courts have done so. Not a single one of the cases mentions that it involves a Negro church. By a little personal investigation I have been able to discover that three of them do. There may be many more.

One of these was the Baptist church case at Modesto, California.[167] The zoning board granted the permit, whereupon nearby property owners, all white, filed a petition for mandamus in the superior court. The court dismissed the petition without even hearing evidence. The court of appeals sustained the decision. There may have been some sound ground for the filing of the petition but if so it does not appear in the decision of the court of appeals. The court summarily overruled the objectors but did not mention the fact that they were all white and the church members were all Negroes.

Another Negro case involved a Baptist church at Atlanta, Georgia.[55] The zoning officials tried to cancel the permit without even serving notice on the permit holders. It might have been easier to understand the arbitrariness of the officials if the court had mentioned in its decision that the members of the church were colored people.

The third Negro case is that of the Believers of Islam in Chicago,[188] who were denied a hearing on appeal on strictly technical grounds.

As previously mentioned at pages 147-8, the Milwaukie,

Oregon, Jehovah's Witnesses decision [184] held the proof of discrimination insufficient but invited a better showing in future cases. The court held that the charge of bias was "an unwarranted and unjust conclusion unsupported by the evidence." This may well have been true. However, several questions arise. Is it really possible to prove the base motives of a public official where they exist? Is not the condition of a man's conscience a matter very peculiarly within his own knowledge? If so, would it not be appropriate for courts to put the burden on him of showing nonexistence of prejudice instead of the contrary?

In the Milwaukie case, the attorneys charged prejudice. The charge rebounded and they were severely criticized by the court. The same thing occurred in the case of Azusa, California, decided a few days later.[186,199] In that case, there was slightly more direct evidence of prejudice. A witness for the city blurted out [186:267] the facts in this respect. The transcript of the evidence reads in part as follows:

> Stemrich: I am not prejudiced, but if people know that there is a Witness church in the neighborhood, they would just as soon move out.
> Hawkins: Would any other church do it?
> Stemrich: As far as I am concerned all religions are the same, but there are some people that have different outlooks.

The court held this evidence insufficient to show prejudice. Instead of criticizing the city it criticized the Witnesses. It said that "the inference from the hearing record seems plain that the [congregation] sought to ride through the hearing upon the emotional issue of prejudice against Jehovah's Witnesses."

The Witnesses were thus charged with the kind of anti-bigotry bigotry I have mentioned above. This inference was not without foundation. The court described one petition filed by the Witnesses [186:268] as "breathing defiance of the zoning authorities." The court said of this particular document:

> It does pay formal obeisance to the constituted authority, saying . . . "I am making this application for a variance so as to render 'unto Caesar that which belongs to Caesar' for the purpose of orderliness and complying with the regulations and ordinance

of the city of Azusa." It seems unfortunate that the other precept of the Master was not kept in mind: "And whosoever shall compel thee to go a mile, go with him twain."

The reference was to Matthew 5:41, about impressment of Caesar's soldiers.

No one can blame the court for impatience with defiance of law. However, it could have inquired whether the "people" who would "just as soon move out" included the members of the council. If they did not personally hold such views, then might they not have been influenced by their constituents who did? In this case the court might have thrown the burden of showing purity of motives upon the city officials. In many towns it is true that people would just as soon move out as live near a Kingdom Hall. This is prejudice. Why should courts close their eyes to it?

A possible cure is suggested by Justice Currie of the Supreme Court of Wisconsin in his dissenting opinion in the Bayside Baptist case.[231:303] First he quotes, as a general rule, a textbook passage [66:332] which says: "Neither the motives of the members of a municipal legislative body nor the influences under which they act can be shown to nullify an ordinance duly passed in legal form within the scope of their powers." The judge then proposes an exception. He says: "Because of the possibility of zoning ordinances being used to discriminate against minority religious groups, an exception to the above rule probably ought to be invoked to ascertain if the enactment of a particular ordinance had such a motivation."

The courts should be much more open-minded on the subject of prejudice. They should not only inquire as to the motives for enactment of ordinances but should also probe the prejudices of administrative officials and even of the objectors who show up at board hearings. It is true that they might not uncover the state of each man's mind, but they would uncover a great deal.

As previously mentioned, the "suspicions of prejudice" mentioned herein are based only on an examination of the court decisions. Examination of a few transcripts of board hearings indicates that they sometimes provide a field day for bigots. If such persons were convinced in advance that manifestations of irrational hate would be examined and condemned in the decisions of the highest courts, they might learn, if not virtue, at least discretion.

Church zoning decisions often have the ring of sermons. Quotations from the Bible abound, expressing an urge to exert moral leadership. The purpose is sound, but these judicial efforts usually come to nothing. As a matter of strict propriety, judges should be careful not to impose a personal moral code in the guise of law. This subject will be discussed as part of the chapter which follows. But equality is a sort of national moral ideal, firmly based in our constitution and laws. It is the kind of morality that every judge is authorized to preach. The Currie proposal for a judicial attack on unequal treatment under law suggests one way that judicial moral leadership can be exercised.

# CHAPTER 15.

## RELIGION AS A PERSONAL RIGHT AND AS A PUBLIC SERVICE

Viewing religious activities and institutions, the courts see them in two different lights. In one they see the right of churches and their members to worship, to preach and to pray—and to build churches for those purposes. In the other they see a sort of public service that is rendered by the churches from which the public—and the government itself—may benefit, and in exchange for which special consideration should be given to religious organizations.

The personal right to worship is one of our most highly prized. The courts have accorded it, along with the rights of free speech, press and assembly, a preferred position as compared to purely economic rights. Thus, in the Catholic retreat house case at Pittsburgh, Pennsylvania,[81:183] the court cited the case of *Marsh v. Alabama*,[54] where the Supreme Court of the United States said:

> When we balance the constitutional rights of owners of property against those of the people to enjoy freedom of press and religion . . . we must remain mindful of the fact that the latter occupy a preferred position. As we have stated before, the right to exercise the liberties guaranteed by the First Amendment "lies at the foundation of free government by free men" and we must in all cases "weigh the circumstances and . . . appraise the reasons . . . in support of the regulation . . . of the rights."

In the Chicago Jehovah's Witnesses case of 1962,[246:725] the Illinois Supreme Court said:

> While there is no doubt that the location of churches can be regulated in a proper case, . . . the right of freedom of religion and other First Amendment freedoms rise above mere property rights. . . . As the United States Supreme Court stated in a case involving the door to door activity of Jehovah's Witnesses: "Freedom of religion has a higher dignity under the Constitution than municipal or personal convenience." (Citing *Martin v. Struthers*.[43])

209

Mr. Rathkopf says: [132:19-4] "Curiously enough, while the constitutional guaranties of freedom of religious worship and of public assembly were raised in several of the . . . cases and referred to in the opinions, no court has based its decision with respect to the invalidity of [zoning] ordinances directly on this ground."

Courts seem to be groping for a way to give expression in zoning cases to the preference expressed in the *Marsh* decision. The first difficulty is that the conflicting right in zoning cases is not the "constitutional right of owners" to which the *Marsh* case refers, but the general welfare of the public. The second difficulty arises because, in most cases where churches are excluded, the interference with religious liberty is too slight to be the basis for decision. Certainly this is true in cases where alternative sites are available.

The third and greatest difficulty in the way of granting special preference to religious liberty in church zoning cases arises from the fact that preference to a church would also require preference to other forms of public assembly. The *Marsh* case creates a preference not for religious rights alone but for all First Amendment freedoms. If a church is given preference, then similar preference must be given to lodge halls, political clubs, and other forms of public assembly. The courts, it seems, are not so ready to give the same right to these groups as to religious groups. This is illustrated by cases like that of the Mt. Lebanon, Pennsylvania, Grange [208] in which the court refused a permit for continued use by the Grange of a building that had been used for Presbyterian services for many years.

So preference is seldom given in zoning cases to church activities viewed in the first light above mentioned, namely as exercises of personal freedom. Few if any decisions are based on the First Amendment. Instead, the court views such activities in the second light mentioned, namely as a service to the public. Thus it is possible to balance the advantages to the public from religious activities against the benefits accruing from the proposed regulation (as described in Chapter 4).

The theory that special consideration is due a church because of public service rendered or to be rendered can be invoked in almost any case. Because of its general character this concept is capable of considerable expansion, depending on the proclivities of the judge, including his desire to stand on the side of God. The services rendered by religion can often seem much more substantial than any public purpose served by the regulation, so that the zoning board's purpose becomes by comparison insubstantial and insufficient.

The concessions granted in church zoning cases in exchange for religious public service sometimes even take on the aspect of sovereign rights, just as privately owned public utilities are granted the sovereign power of condemnation. An example is the equal treatment accorded in some cases to public and religious schools. In our discussion of "what Is a church," we will see in Chapter 19 that churches are sometimes permitted to define the term themselves and thus to determine whether or not they are covered by a law.

Regarding religious liberties as such, it is well to begin with an often-quoted passage from the decision of the United States Supreme Court in the case of *Cantwell v. Connecticut*[37] in which the court sustained regulation of religious street meetings. The court said:

> The First Amendment embraces two concepts—freedom to believe and freedom to act. The first is absolute but, in the nature of things, the second cannot be. Conduct remains subject to regulation for the protection of society. The freedom to act must have appropriate definition to preserve the enforcement of that protection. In every case, the power to regulate must be so exercised as not, in attaining a permissible end, unduly to infringe the protected freedom.
>
> No one will contest the proposition that a state may not, by statute, wholly deny the right to preach, or to disseminate religious views. Plainly such a previous and absolute restraint would violate the terms of the guaranty. It is equally clear that a state may by general and nondiscriminatory legislation regulate the times, the places, and the manner of soliciting on its streets and of holding meetings thereon; and may, in other aspects, safeguard the peace, good order and comfort of the community, without unconstitutionally invading the liberties protected by the Fourteenth Amendment.

Paraphrasing, it may also be said that a "state or municipality may by general and nondiscriminatory legislation regulate the places where churches may be built." This is true as long as the area from which they are excluded is not so great that they are deprived of reasonably accessible alternative sites. Such deprivation would "unduly infringe the protected freedom."

Those writers whom I have called "absolutist" deny the right of municipalities to exclude churches from any area. Their view must be based not so much on constitutional religious liberty as it is upon the second consideration above mentioned, namely the special concessions due to churches for the public service they render. While this concept has an age-old tradition, it is not based on our constitution.

If the treatment of churches as public service institutions is covered at all in the federal constitution, it is in a negative sense. Our constitution not only protects the members of each church in their religious freedom. It also protects members of other churches—and unbelievers—by its principle of separation of church and state. It may well be that churches have less right than, say, public utilities to ask special consideration from the courts in exchange for public service rendered.

Yet this concept is an ancient one. It is inherent in the history of cities described by Lewis Mumford [226] and mentioned herein at page 6. The pagan villages, progenitors of cities, were presided over by the priests in charge of the shrines. When walled cities developed, the ecclesiastical and military leaders shared political power. As the city developed its true function, that of a reservoir of labor, supplies and public services, the military and religious powers were gradually subordinated to civil powers, but never quite entirely. In the Acropolis, the priests had their exclusive "zone." After Christianity, churches also held a central position, being treated as governmental or quasi-governmental institutions. Nor did the final victory of democracy eliminate the reliance of public authorities upon the support of the church, or their reciprocation of that support.

In a sense, it may have intensified this mutual reliance. It was the theory of de Tocqueville [5] that democracy, above all other forms of government, depends for its viability on religion. The restraints imposed on the people by democracy were so light, he felt, that without the moral restraints of religion society would be destroyed by the natural mischievous tendencies of men. A similar thought was expressed by George Washington. It was incorporated into the Northwest Ordinance and some state constitutions. A manual prepared for the American Institute of Planners' Workshop of Church Planning of 1955 asked: [126:4] "Can church strategy combine forces with city planning to bring truly a 'New Jerusalem in this green and pleasant land?'"

It may be that government is now able to exercise greater restraints on citizens than it did in de Tocqueville's day. It may be that men are now less mischievous. However, the concept of religion as a public service, one that should be encouraged and sustained, is by no means dead. The Euclid, Ohio, case [18] mentions churches only incidentally. But they are described under the classification "public and semipublic buildings."

The tendency of the courts to treat religious liberty, not in isolation, but in association with other First Amendment freedoms is illustrated by two early United States Supreme Court cases which in recent years have become relevant to church zoning. In 1923, in *Meyer v. Nebraska*,[16] in invalidating a statute which forbade teaching of foreign languages in schools, the court had referred to the "liberty" guaranteed by the Fourteenth Amendment against state infringement. It said (emphasis added): "Without doubt, it denotes not merely freedom from bodily restraint but also the right of the individual to contract, to engage in any of the common occupations of life, to acquire useful knowledge, to marry, establish a home, *and bring up children, to worship God according to all the dictates of his own conscience* and generally to enjoy those privileges long recognized at common law as essential to the orderly pursuit of happiness by free men."

The *Meyer* case was followed two years later by the decision in the *Society of Sisters* case,[17] invalidating an Oregon law which in effect "outlawed" private schools. There the court said that: "Under the doctrine of *Meyer v. Nebraska*, we think it entirely plain that the Act . . . unreasonably interferes with the liberty of parents and guardians to direct the upbringing and the education of children under their control. The fundamental theory of liberty upon which all governments in the union repose excludes any general power of the state to standardize its children by forcing them to accept instruction from public teachers only. The child is not the mere creature of the state; those who nurture him and direct his destiny have the right, coupled with the high duty, to recognize, and prepare him for, additional obligations."

Thus, the court held unconstitutional a law which, by requiring attendance at public schools, in effect and as admitted by the state, practically excluded private schools from an entire state. The law would also have been held unconstitutional if this purpose had been accomplished by zoning all the land in Oregon in such a way as to forbid construction of such schools.

How much farther can the logical implications of this case be carried? In other fields, they have been carried quite far. As shown by Pfeffer,[97:328] it has been contended that the principle of the *Society of Sisters* case requires the provision of official school time for religious instruction. "Under this decision," the argument (as restated by Pfeffer) goes, "parents have the right to send their children to private or parochial schools rather than to public schools. Financial considerations make it impossible for many parents to avail themselves of this right—particularly since the states refuse to support the parochial schools as they support the public schools. But if the states were to refuse to release a child for religious education in the church centers for one hour a week, it would be abridging his religious liberty to an extent differing only in degree from its refusal to allow him to attend parochial schools at will."

A similar argument is advanced, very prominently in recent times, in support of government subsidies for parochial schools. It is contended that such are necessary in order to "implement" the rights guaranteed in the *Society of Sisters* case. The case is much more relevant to church and school zoning cases than it is to "released time" and "aid to education." It seems a little surprising that it was not invoked in zoning cases until 1955.

When it was tried, it proved successful. In the Piedmont Catholic school case,[125] the California court refused to sanction the exclusion of private schools from "practically" the entire city of Piedmont. This action was the same in kind but quite different in degree from the action of the Supreme Court of the United States invalidating the practical exclusion of private elementary schools from an entire state. The language of the California case went even farther "in degree." It said [125:441] that "parents have the right to send their children to private schools, rather than public ones, which are located in their immediate locality or general neighborhood."

If the California expansion of the theory of the *Society of Sisters* case were carried to its logical extreme, of course, it would prevent exclusion of private schools—or the exclusion of churches—from any "locality or neighborhood." Charles R. Currey, writing in the *U.C.L.A. Law Review*,[141] makes the sound comment that "religious rights should receive protection on a par with those concerning education."

But in the Piedmont decision the California court expressly renounced any desire to reverse the Porterville Mormon temple decision [67] which had excluded all churches from a residential zone. Later, it refused to review the Orange County Catholic church and school case [202] in which private schools were excluded from a residential zone.

It seems to me that in most cases exclusion of churches or religious schools from large towns would be an undue infringement since it would deprive them of reasonably accessible alternative sites. But I question whether the same rule would apply to each "locality or neighborhood." By its subsequent actions, the California court seems to have nullified this particular dictum. However, it may eventually find greater validity in other circumstances.

It is well to recall a statement of Justice Oliver Wendell Holmes that was quoted in the synagogue zoning case of Philadelphia, Pennsylvania.[51] Justice Holmes said that: "I have heard it suggested that the difference is one of degree. I am the last man in the world to quarrel with a distinction simply because it is one of degree. Most distinctions, in my opinion, are of that sort, and are none the worse for it."

Distinctions of degree are very important in church zoning cases. That is why no "absolutist" approach to the subject is valid. Each case must be decided on the basis of its own facts in the light of general principles. The question is not only whether there is an interference with religious liberty but also whether such interference is "undue."

There is one obvious reason why, for 30 years, the *Society of Sisters* case,[17] was not cited in the church zoning cases; it did not have to be. These cases were decided—almost uniformly in favor of churches—on the basis of the special consideration due to churches in return for public service rendered or to be rendered. This was true although it never became explicit, so far as I can see, until 1942 when the Upper Arlington, Ohio, Lutheran church case [40] was decided.

That decision, it will be recalled, relied principally on the misrepresentations of the zoning officials on the basis of which the church had invested its money in the disputed tract. But as a makeweight for its conclusion, the court said the following:

> How does the case stand with respect to the protection of public morals and the general welfare? The church in our American society has traditionally occupied the role of both teacher and guardian of morals. . . . Fully to accomplish its great religious and social function, the church should be integrated into the home life of the community which it serves. . . . To require that churches be banished to the business district . . . is clearly not to be justified on the score of promoting the general welfare."

The court was probably convinced that there were no other suitable sites available for the church. In the back of the judges' minds there may have been a belief that the liberty of the Lutherans was being unduly restricted. But the decision says nothing about religious liberty. It is based rather on the prerogatives of churches resulting from the benefits they bestow upon the public.

Promptly another court attempted (a) to base this special treatment also on religious liberty grounds and (b) to transform the prerogative into a right. In the Sherman, Texas, Church of God case of 1944,[48,49] the city had already admitted the invalidity of its ordinance so that the court should not have discussed it. It did, however, and held the ordinance invalid again, saying [49:417] that "to exclude churches from residential districts . . . and to relegate them to business and manufacturing districts could conceivably result in imposing a burden upon the free right to worship and, in some instances, in prohibiting altogether the exercise of that right. An ordinance fraught with that danger will not be enforced."

A natural question is "fraught with what danger?" Will an ordinance be invalid because it actually imposes a burden, or merely because such a burden is "conceivable"? Will it be invalidated because it imposes a burden or only if it prohibits worship altogether? Will an ordinance be invalidated if it imposes any burden or only if the burden is "undue"? The court in the Sherman case obviously failed to make those fine distinctions of degree that are important in balancing private against public rights.

The Porterville, California, Mormon temple case of 1949 [67] was the first to rule squarely on the question of religious liberty. The court held valid an ordinance which completely excluded churches from a residential area. It said: "We find no merit in [the bishop's] contention that the application of the ordinance to the [temple] results in an unwarranted restriction of religious worship. The denial of a building permit did not prohibit anyone from religious worship and there is nothing in the record before us to indicate that the church building could not be erected if located in the area zoned for that purpose.*

The Porterville rule seems to be entirely sound except that it should not be applied in any "absolutist" fashion. There are at least hypothetical cases to which it cannot properly apply, either because reasonably accessible alternative sites are not available or because the church is of a kind that causes no inconvenience that the state is properly authorized to abate. The Porterville decision went to the Supreme Court of California where it was refused review and to the Supreme Court of

---

* The California court also said that: "Petitioner is not a congregation but holds his property as a corporation sole, the existence of which depends upon the laws of the state. Having such rights from the state, the enjoyment is subject to reasonable regulations." In this respect, one may find fault with the Porterville decision, and also with the case of the Protestant evangelistic center, at Dallas, Texas,[102] which followed Porterville in this respect. The approach was sounder in the appelate court decision of the Piedmont case [115] which said that "the fact that petitioner is a corporation does not deprive it of asserting its basic constitutional rights. Since the Dartmouth College case,[4] corporations have always been afforded the protection of basic constitutional provisions."

the United States [71,76] where the same thing occurred, "for lack of a substantial federal question."

The Porterville case was disposed of in the supreme court in a one-line decision. But later, in the case of *American Communications Association v. Douds*, decided in 1950,[80] the court referred to it as having a "relatively small" effect on religious liberty. See pages 331-2.

The religious issue was brought before an intermediate federal court in the Atlanta, Georgia, Jehovah's Witnesses case of 1951.[91] The Georgia courts had sustained the action of the zoning board in excluding a Kingdom Hall from one area of the city because it would create a serious traffic problem.[78] So the Witnesses moved to another site and set up operations without a permit. The city threatened prosecution of one Galfas, the owner of the building. The Witnesses sued in the federal court under the Civil Rights Act. They contended [91:933] that the provisions of law were "void on their face because an abridgment of [their] right to freedom of assembly and freedom of worship. The broad basis of this claim is that the city can place no restriction upon the location of a place of religious worship."

The federal circuit court of appeals refused to pass on the case, invoking the "rule of abstention" usually followed where a state court has not yet decided the issue. It also said: "The [district court] found that the plaintiffs other than Galfas were not threatened with criminal prosecution. This is not challenged here. The petition admitted, and the court found, that the plaintiffs continued to use the premises in question for assembly and religious meetings. Upon its examination of the local law, the court found that the challenged ordinance gave no power to interrupt religious services and that the [city] had neither threatened nor intended to do so; that the only provision for criminal or quasi-criminal sanctions was prosecution of Galfas, the title holder of the property. . . ."

This decision implied that the circuit court of appeals would not be inclined to act unless it found actual interruption of religious services. During the same year, the Pittsburgh lower court decided in the Catholic retreat house case [81] that it would require a zoning board to issue a permit for the operation of a lodging house by a religious order in a high class residential neighborhood. It took a view of religious liberty diametrically opposed to that of the federal judges who decided the Atlanta Jehovah's Witnesses case.

There are two possible approaches to the relations between church and state. A commonly used one is that the state may enact and enforce such laws as it sees fit, except when they unduly infringe religious liberty. The position adopted by the Pittsburgh court was the converse: that the church may follow such practices as it pleases, without regard to man-made laws unless and until such practices constitute a "real threat" to the community. The vast difference between these two approaches is obvious.

The Pittsburgh ordinance forbade use of the particular property except for residences, plus a few other enumerated purposes (including churches and "uses customarily accessory thereto"), for which special permits were required. As will be shown on pages 279-80, the court held that the proposed sleeping quarters for retreatants were an "accessory to a church" under the ordinance. The reason for this ruling, simply stated, was that the Franciscan Order had so decided. The court decision went even farther and held that, if the city had forbidden such "accessories" as the Franciscan friars deemed proper then it would have violated the religious liberty of the Order. The court said: [81:178]

> The religious freedom guaranteed by our federal and state constitutions is the freedom to worship Almighty God according to the dictates of one's own conscience and, in exercising such worship, to adopt such practices as one sees fit or deems appropriate. Neither the state nor the federal government are permitted to dictate or influence religious doctrines, concepts or practices. Religious freedom means freedom to follow, not only one's own beliefs, but one's own practices and procedures, unhampered and uninfluenced by majority practices or by customary rules or regulations made by others, whoever they may be.
>
> As far as this court is concerned, and as far as the City of Pittsburgh and the State of Pennsylvania are concerned, the Third Order of St. Francis may pursue any religious practice that, in its sole discretion and judgment, it sees fit or decides to pursue, unless such practice substantially interferes with rules laid down for the protection of society; rules, moreover, which, as we have already stated, are subject to severe limitations.

The judge in the Pittsburgh case did not assert the superior sovereignty of the church group. However, he came as close to doing so as have any of the decisions covered in this treatise. The conferring of special privileges on churches "to the degree" that it was done in the Pittsburgh Catholic case is manifestly unsound.

In the Tampa, Florida, Jehovah's Witnesses case,[83] the court gave the church special consideration but fell short of conferring sovereignty on the sect. The principal basis of the decision was that the ordinance required only parking space and that the Witnesses had complied "substantially" with this requirement. As additional support for its action, however, the court said: [83:79]

> The Church is not bound by some of the regulations imposed on other institutions. In American life, the family is the foundation on which democratic institutions are reared. The church and the school are but auxiliaries to the family. The school, private, public, and college, is the offspring of the church. Different species of democracy have existed for more than 2,000 years, but democracy as we know it has never existed among the unchurched. A people unschooled about the sovereignty of God, the Ten Commandments and the ethics of Jesus, could never have evolved the Bill of Rights, the Declaration of Independence and the Constitution. There is not one solitary fundamental principle of our democratic polity that did not stem directly from the basic moral concepts as embodied in the Decalogue and the ethics of Jesus. None knew this better than the Founding Fathers. Hence, we say that when the church enters the picture, different considerations actuate any and all spheres of regulation. . . .

This decision is vague where it refers to "some regulations" by which the church is not bound. It does not specify the "different considerations" that actuate regulation when a church is involved. Therefore, it is difficult to quarrel with the conclusion above stated. Regarding the nonexistence of democracy among "the unchurched," the judge who wrote this opinion seems not to have read Pfeffer's opinion [97:85] which is that "in respect to the population of the total country, the best estimate is that church affiliation at the founding of the republic was limited to 4% of the population." The principles of the American Revolution were evidently based more on French rationalism than on the Decalogue.

The Florida court itself did not take the little sermon above quoted with sufficient seriousness to prevent it from enforcing zoning regulations against a Lutheran church in Miami Beach,[124] Jewish school at the same place,[189,198] and an Advent Christian church in Tampa itself.[160] In none of the cases last cited did the court bother to mention the Tampa Jehovah's Witnesses case.

There could be church zoning cases in which the "preferred status" accorded to religious activities by the *Marsh* case, as quoted in the beginning of this chapter, could be given full force and effect. This is why I have said that the rule stated in the Porterville case [67] cannot be enforced in any "absolute" way. Chapter 19 will show the contrast between the "maximum" type of church and the "minimum" type. The maximum type includes community centers, parish halls, schools, recreation facilities, residences for the clergy, faculty, etc., in addition to a place for common worship. But the term church can also include a minimum type which is described by St. Matthew as "any two or three gathered together in My Name". It is doubtful that the Porterville rule, permitting absolute exclusion of churches from residential areas, could be enforced against churches of this minimum type, which have no adverse effects with which the state ought properly to concern itself.

This question was skirted in the case of the First Baptist Church of Chico, California,[88] which I have already discussed on page 36, where one of the defendants sought unsuccessfully to prove that he was being forced to take out a permit merely to "sing, pray, and worship God." The question of licenses for such basic religious functions is discussed by Mr. Pfeffer in his *Church, State and Freedom*.[97:600] He says that the "United States Supreme Court has split sharply on the issue and . . . the same justices have reached a different conclusion at different times. . . ." In *Murdock v. Pennsylvania*,[44] the court invalidated a requirement for a license for the handdistribution of religious tracts, a requirement that remained enforcible against commercial handbills. It may well be that the court would take a similar view regarding the strictly religious functions performed by a few friends in a private house.

The Jewish people also seem to have a type of synagogue that if small enough might never be barred from a residential area. I refer to the kind of service that is described in the South Euclid, Ohio, Jewish case of 1956.[140:176] People of the orthodox persuasion are "prohibited from performing any manner of labor on Saturday and holidays and using any form of transportation, except walking to the place where the religious services are held on those days. . . . Because they adhere to this faith, their places of worship must be within walking distance of their home." It seems that a house of worship entirely devoted to such purposes by the traditional ten Jewish men might be difficult to exclude from a residential zone. City councils seem to be conscious that ordinances like that of Porterville, unconditionally excluding churches from particular districts, cannot be universally enforced. This may be why so few such ordinances have appeared in church zoning litigation. The typical ordinance leaves the way open for exceptions. The purpose may be to provide for those cases in which enforcement would be unconstitutional.

There are many variations "of degree." For instance, there is the Newark, New Jersey, Jewish case [89:838] involving a *mikvah* or ritualarium bath used by Orthodox Jewish women as part of their wedding ceremony. The attorneys for the congregation contended that "under the New Jersey Constitution of 1947, every person is given the privilege of worshiping Almighty God in a manner agreeable to the dictates of his own conscience and that a denial by the city authorities of the right to construct and operate a ritualarium or a *mikvah* in the property . . . would violate the section of our constitution above cited. And counsel for [the congregation] further cite the First and Fourteenth Amendments to the United States Constitution as a guaranty of their right to religious freedom in the respect mentioned."

Attorneys for the Jews cited the Pittsburgh Catholic retreat house case,[81] discussed a few pages back, in which the lower court vindicated the "religious freedom" of the Franciscan Order to maintain a kind of boarding house in a swank residential area. But the New Jersey Superior Court said that "to adopt that view would in substance deny to a city the right to restrict or regulate by zoning ordinance the construction and operation of an edifice where any religious rites are performed in a church or elsewhere. It is not necessary to freedom of worship or freedom of religion that a *mikvah* or religious mission or a parish house or a kosher abbatoir be permitted to exist or operate in a first class residential neighborhood."

"There are numerous other neighborhoods," the court continued, "in which such institutions may legally operate without violation of the zoning ordinance and without interference with the constitutional provisions of religious freedom and the privilege of worshiping in a manner agreeable to the dictates of the worshiper's own conscience." The decision was affirmed by the appellate division in 1952. It was never carried to the Supreme Court of New Jersey. However, it was cited by that court with approval in 1959 in the case of the Allendale Jehovah's Witnesses.[205] (See page 237.)

The decision of the Michigan Supreme Court in the Orchard Lake Catholic church and school [94] falls in another category. It is not based on religious freedom. Instead, it is one of those decisions that recognize the quasi-governmental status of religion, its status as an auxiliary of government, and the special considerations which flow therefrom. The exclusion of the Catholic church and school was from so large an area of the city that the court deemed the exclusion practically total. For that reason, when the city attorneys cited the Porterville, California, Mormon temple case,[67] the court refused to follow it. The court said it was "not insensitive to the persuasiveness of some of the reasoning" in that decision but refused to apply it because, as to Porterville, "there is nothing in the record before us to indicate that the church building could not be erected if located in the area zoned for that purpose."

The court still did not invoke "religious liberty." It asked: "Does exclusion of church and school from the entire village bear a real and substantial relationship to public health, safety, morals or the general welfare and thus constitute a reasonable and legitimate exercise of the police power? The [attorneys for the city] say that a presumption prevails in favor of the reasonableness and validity of the ordinance unless the contrary is shown." The court cited the Michigan constitutional provision, quoted above at pages 195-6, which decreed that "religion, morality and knowledge are necessary to good government and that the means of education should be forever encouraged." The court held that the constitutionality of the ordinance "will not be accepted by way of presumption, nor at all in the absence of competent evidence establishing a real and substantial relationship between the attempted exclusion and public health, safety, morals or the general welfare."

The court's purpose was not to protect the religious rights of the archbishop as such. Its purpose was to enforce the pro-religious public policy of the state for the benefit of its citizens. In this sense the case differs from the decision in the Piedmont, California, case [115,125] which is based on the civil right of parents to educate their children. Because of our constitutional church-state separation, it might have been wiser to base the Michigan decision on religious liberty. The Michigan constitution held necessary to good government (a) religion, (b) knowledge and (c) morality. However, it decreed the governmental "encouragement" not of all three of them but only of "education."

The Michigan decision seems to have inspired the writing of the article in *St. John's Law Review* of December 1952. That article [95:99] praised the Orchard Lake decision and condemned the Porterville decision. It said: "The view that exclusion of churches from residential neighborhoods will promote the American home is a philosophy alien to the United States since our constitution is based on the fundamental principles of Natural Law." This is a generality like the "fundamental principles of our democratic polity" mentioned in the Tampa Jehovah's Witnesses case [83] quoted on page 220 above.

Former Attorney General Francis Biddle has written a profound little book on *Justice Holmes, Natural Law and the Supreme Court*. "Natural Law," he says,[225:32] "is spoken of as that body of moral behavior practiced in the community by men of good will over a long period of years, so that it has come to be universally accepted as a broad canon of decency on which most men agree. . . . [T]he kind of Natural Law espoused by the Roman Catholic Church claims that its precepts are universal and eternal."

"Only Catholic law schools," Mr. Biddle continues, "teach that Natural Law has a higher and more august sanction than human law, that laws in contravention of Natural Law are invalid; and that any statute or decision conflicting with Natural Law is inherently vitiated. In other schools, 'law' is not taught as being eternal; it could not be, for the modern lawyer, pragmatic and scientific as far as possible in his approach, has learned to keep his law and religion apart. It is to this separation that the Catholic teachers object. The Catholic doctrine, fundamentally inconsistent with separation of church and state, goes much further than the concept that, in determining whether he should resist a particular law, thought to be evil, a man should abide by the dictates of his conscience, since it insists that he must obey the dictates of his church irrespective of the expressed will of his sovereign. To the Catholic, Natural Law is what the Church says it is."

The article in *St. John's Law Review* insists that our constitution is based on "natural law." To the writer of that article, I am sure that the natural law is not "what the judges say it is" but what the Church says it is. The article does not insist directly that in case of conflict with such natural (or canon) law, our constitution must be disregarded. Neither has such a contention been made in any church zoning cases. Neither have any judges explicitly so held. Any reader who wants to study the Catholic concept of church sovereignty may consult the books mentioned in the footnote.*

If the natural law is "what the Catholic Church says it is," then, of course it would have little application to our "pluralistic" society. I doubt that Catholic canon law would uphold the superior sovereignty of the Jewish congregation at Beachwood, Ohio.[101] Yet that case was decided, not under the ordinance, not under the state law, not under the state constitution, not under the federal constitution, but under something just as vague as natural law, namely the "fundamental

---

* Rev. John Denis Davis, The Moral Obligations of Catholic Civil Judges;[98] Joseph Le Cler, S. J., The Two Sovereigns;[90] Charles E. Marshall, The Roman Catholic Church and the Modern State.[26]

principles of democracy," the "brotherhood of man," and "historical truth."

From the discussion of the Beachwood case on pages 61-2 my reader may recall that the result hinged upon the insistence of the court that the "public welfare" required to be observed in administration of the ordinance included not only the public welfare of the residents of the village but also the public welfare of the entire metropolitan area. This is a sound view. I do not criticize the final results of the case. However, it is important to point out what the court said on the issue of religious prerogatives here under discussion: [101:69]

> How it is possible to hold that a religious institution [will not serve the public welfare] which has for one hundred years been one of the outstanding centers of religious education in Greater Cleveland, devoting its services not only to the devotional and religious needs of its members but in a broad sense contributing to the welfare of all the people of the community through its interdenominational activities, is hard to understand. Every religious institution contributes to the common good or general welfare of the whole community, even though it be attended by a particular group or is denominational in character. A democratic society where every man must unselfishly devote some part of his energy in the interest of good government cannot succeed without the moral and spiritual influence of the church.
>
> The place of the church is to be found in that part of the community where the people live. It is to be associated with the home, its influence is concerned with family life. It is an institution to which we look for leadership in furtherance of the brotherhood of man, in moulding the moral progress of our children and sustaining and giving strength to purity of our family life. To hold that a church is detrimental to the welfare of the people is in direct contradiction of historical truth and evidence of failure to recognize basic fundamentals of a democratic society.

Bear in mind that the village officials were thinking of *local* public welfare and that only 20 of the 1800 members of the congregation were townsmen! It was this court's kind of thinking that Justice Holmes criticized when he wrote to Harold Laski in 1926 that: [225:40]

> There is a tendency to think of judges as if they were independent mouthpieces of the infinite, and not simply directors of a force

that comes from the source that gives them their authority. I think our court has fallen into the error at times and it is that that I have aimed at when I said that the Common Law is not a brooding omnipresence in the sky and that the U. S. is not subject to some mystic overlaw that it is bound to obey.

"To Holmes," says Biddle, "there was no such thing as the Common Law *in abstracto* and that is precisely how he thought of Natural Law. A mystic overlaw, not law in any true sense, theology or morals if you like, but not law. The demand for the superlative that we find in all men was at the bottom of the philosopher's effort to prove that truth was absolute and of the jurist's search for criteria of universal validity which he collects under the head of Natural Law. That is why the jurists who believe in Natural Law seem to him to be 'in that naive state of mind that accepts what has been familiar and accepted by them and their neighbors as something that must be accepted by all men everywhere.' To a Jesuit priest, reared in Natural Law, Holmes' view that it was a product of wishful thinking must have seemed blasphemous."

Certainly Biddle did not mean to suggest that Catholics have a monopoly on the citation of moral principles in lieu of legal precedents. One is reminded of Mr. Jack Collins of Bayside, Wisconsin, where the recent Baptist Church dispute [231] took place. About him the *Milwaukee Journal* * reports:

> Bitter opposition and some approval for the rezoning of a tract in the south end of Bayside, which would allow a church to be built there, was voiced Thursday night. . . .
>
> Apparently seeking to keep heads as cool as possible, Jack Collins, Village President and Chairman of the [Plan] Commission asked at the outset that everyone "refrain from quoting the Bible." The issue, he said, was "whether there is a logical plan or not."

When judges attempt to apply religious "mystical overlaw" at the grassroots of America, with its 300,000 or more local churches and almost 300 religious bodies, [238] then the even more stringent demands of consistency sometimes discover a sort of

---

* Quoted in American Society of Planning Officials: Churches and Planning Controls. [172]

sovereignty in unexpected places. Thus, in the Decatur, Indiana, case,[104] the court not only recognized that prerogatives should be conferred on Jehovah's Witnesses, presumably for public services to be rendered, but also identified these prerogatives as constitutional rights. Further, the court gave recognition to the right of the Witnesses to determine whether the law of the land should apply to them.

The court refused to enforce a parking lot requirement because "under the facts in the case, [it] would prohibit the building of the proposed church." Note especially the use of the word "proposed." This precluded the possibility that the Witnesses might be required to change their proposals to conform to the plans of the public agency. The proposals of the public, as incorporated in the city plan, were subordinated to the proposals (read canon law) of the Watchtower Bible and Tract Society. Fortunately the decision is inconsistent. The court did give full force and effect to the setback requirements although, like the off-street parking rule, they also conflicted with the plans of the Witnesses.

As reported on pages 175-6 the Wauwatosa, Wisconsin, decision, by which a Lutheran high school was excluded from an entire residential district, provided an occasion for the exhumation of the *Society of Sisters* case,[17] for use in church zoning disputes. This is a wholesome development. The *Society of Sisters* case is based not on the prerogatives of churches but on the rights of people. It may eventually draw the attention of the courts away from considerations of the fundamental principles of democracy, the natural law, and the brotherhood of man and into a discussion of express constitutional rights. While the Piedmont Catholic school decisions,[115,125] went too far in insisting that facilities for schools (and by implication for churches) must be "in the same neighborhood" as citizens using them, the judges were clearly on the right track. The principal constitutional right is that of people to have facilities reasonably available.

The Piedmont case was decided in 1955. In 1956, the Court of Appeals of the State of New York took up its first church zoning cases. It failed to follow the lead of California along the course of individual civil liberty. It enunciated a rule based on the social values of churches and parochial schools.

The cases were the Brighton Roman Catholic church and school case,[123,131,138,149] and the Jewish synagogue case at Sands Point.[129,148]

In sustaining refusal of the permit to the Catholics, the trial court had said: [123:490]

> Petitioners seem to contend that since the increased denominational population requires additional churches and facilities in Brighton, the board should, *ipso facto*, grant the necessary permits. To concur with this theory would be to give the churches of all denominations priority over the state, regardless of rights of citizens generally. . . . Despite the urgency of the expansion of petitioner's physical equipment in Brighton, it does not follow that the plan and purpose of zoning provisions must be automatically subordinated or eliminated to permit churches and schools in zoned areas.

Various phases of the Brighton decision in the court of appeals have been touched on in this volume but its net effect is well summarized in the *Catholic Lawyer* article of Summer 1959 [204] which says that it "recognizes that churches, like other places of assembly, produce noise, congestion and traffic hazards but regard these as offset by the social and moral values inherent to religious institutions."

Like the Decatur, Indiana, Jehovah's Witnesses case,[104] the Brighton decision contains certain inconsistencies. It espouses,[149:834] then it repudiates [149:836] what I have called the absolute anti-exclusion rule. Then it takes up *seriatim* the various justifications advanced by the board for refusing the application. Aside from mentioning lack of authority in the ordinance, the court had the following observations:

(a) Regarding alleged loss of tax revenue, the court cited the religious tax exemption law of the state and said that "the paramount authority of this state has declared a policy that churches and schools are more important than local taxes." (See pages 89-90.)

(b) Regarding alleged "decreased enjoyment of neighboring property" the court merely said that "noise and other inconvenience have been held to be insufficient grounds on which to deny a permit to a church." (See page 111.)

(c) Regarding the contention that the area was "completely built up" and that previous churches had built "in areas where future residential development could accommodate itself to a church and school," the court repeated a dictum pronounced in the Chicago Episcopal case [93] that: "Wherever the souls of men are found, there the House of God belongs."

(d) As to the adverse effect of the church on adjacent property values, the court said that "in view of the high purposes and the moral values of these institutions, mere pecuniary loss to a few persons should not bar their erection and use." (See page 99.)

Note in each of these an affirmation of the superiority of ecclesiastical over civil purposes. It was only in dealing with justification (e) on the subject of traffic hazards, that the court veered from this insistence. The court's objection to this last justification had as its basis only that "no such policy or standard was declared in the statute." This is important. Traffic hazards form the principal justification for regulating the use of church land. The court's attitude on this issue may provide a basis for a future change in judicial policy when an ordinance, properly drafted, is before it. But clearly the burden of the Brighton decision is the social value of church activities.

In the Sands Point Jewish synagogue case, decided on the same day, [148] there was only an incidental reference to religious rights. After having decided the case on the basis of other issues, the court said: [148:496] "The position of the village . . . is that [it] should have the power to deny an application for the location of a church at a 'precise spot.' This would not, of course, *prohibit* the use, erection, alteration or improvement of buildings or structures for churches and synagogues, in municipalities such as [this], but would limit it. While many may be tempted to think that the solution offered by [the village] is excellent, when one thinks it through one realizes that if the municipality has the unfettered power to say that the 'precise spot' selected is not the right one, the municipality has the power to say eventually which *is* the proper 'precise spot.' " (Italics in original.)

The opinion writer seems to have misunderstood what the village had said. Certainly it did not claim "unfettered" power but only the power to reject any application that did not conform to the public interest. On this inflated assumption about the village's claims, the court then went on to confer "unfettered" power not on the village but on the religious institution:

> That we can all see is the wrong solution. The men and women who left Scrooby for Leyden and eventually came to Plymouth in order to worship God where they wished and in their own way must have thought they had terminated the interference of public authority with free and unhandicapped exercise of religion. We think that we should accept the fact that we are successors of "We, the People," of the preamble of the United States Constitution and that a court may not permit a municipal ordinance to be so construed that it would appear in any manner to interfere with the "free exercise and enjoyment of religious profession and worship."

The justice neglected to mention that the men and women who left Scrooby eventually established their own religious tyrannies in the New World. But this is not important. What is important is the generality of the rule that this dictum pronounces. It might properly be called the Caesar's Wife Rule of church zoning. It not only condemns undue interference with religious worship, which is what the constitution condemns. It also condemns any law which interferes "in any manner" with religious practices. It goes further and condemns laws which "would appear" in any manner to interfere with them. Thus, presumably, a traffic law which forbids a pastor to exceed speed limits in order to get to his church on time would be void as "appearing in some manner" to interfere with a religious practice. If anyone in the Sands Point case failed to "think through," it was the judge who wrote the opinion. We should not assume that the statement above quoted, which was irrelevant to the result, is the law of New York State.

The New York court in the Brighton case relied on the Tampa, Florida, decision of 1950.[83] It failed to mention a Florida decision to the contrary which was entered prior to the Brighton case. This was the decision against the United Lutheran Church at Miami Beach.[124] The church was much smaller than the Catholic church-school-convent-rectory combination at Brighton. The court found nevertheless that a traffic problem would arise, "not to mention the noise that comes from people congregating." The court recognized the social value of religious institutions but clearly distinguished between this factor and the religious liberty guaranteed in the constitution. The court said: [124:882]

> It is commonly known that generally the activities of the present day churches are wide and varied, as, indeed, they should be. The use of church buildings and facilities is not confined to worship periods on Sunday and midweekly prayer meetings. They are often used as places of instruction and entertainment.
>
> We do not frown on these activities. On the contrary, we think that they should be promoted and encouraged. But we do not agree that because of the merits of these activities it can be said that an infringement of the constitutional rights of the owner results if it is not allowed use of the property for such purposes in the midst of a section of the city which has been restricted and which [the congregation] knew had been restricted primarily to homes occupied by individual families.

The court also noted that "sites for churches were available in other parts of the city" and affirmed the action of the zoning board denying the permit.

The public service rendered by religious education also formed part of the argument advanced by the Catholic nuns' seminary at Morris Township, New Jersey,[128] during the same year. There the church met a rebuff. From the discussion of this case on pages 141-2 it will be recalled that the sisters had occupied the property long before the ordinance had been enacted designating the area as residential. They sought a variance so that they might expand their plant to care for increased needs.

In his brief,[128:146] the attorney for the sisters said that "eleemosynary institutions are saturated with and serve vital public purposes in our society." The sisters further "argued that 'we have numerous special reasons required by the statute, . . . the furtherance of the general welfare and the advancement of numerous public purposes . . . which this section of the statute was intended to foster. . . . There is competent authority that uses of property designed for public convenience and welfare, such as educational and religious uses, can be made the subject of proper exceptions to zoning regulations.'"

The court recognized the potency of this argument. It said [128:144] that "the factual situation and circumstances present an appealing case. The salutary motive of Villa Walsh in seeking to increase its facilities and thus to train more teachers to meet the educational needs of the parochial schools and children of this state is commendable." In spite of these kind words, the court decided against the seminary. It said that "such uses possess a contagious character which works to infect the neighborhood of their location."

The Haltom City, Texas, Jehovah's Witnesses case [136] decided in February of 1956 also used "religious liberty" language to support its adherence to the rule of absolute anti-exclusion. It said that "the maintenance of churches is such a valuable right that their existence will not be denied because of mere inconvenience to the neighbors" and that "under the facts in this case, to deny the permit because of traffic conditions would not only prevent the use of the church but would restrict the right of freedom of worship and assembly to an extent that outweighs any benefit to the safety, health, morals and general welfare of the public." The reference to the "facts in this case" indicates, however, that the court relied on the almost complete compliance of the Witnesses with the ordinance.

During March 1956 the Connecticut court decided another case (against the West Hartford Methodist Church) [139] which the New York court, in its decision of July of that year,[149] did not see fit to mention. The court sustained denial of the permit mainly because of noise and traffic. It made only passing reference to the social value of religious activity. This mention had a reverse twist which is of some interest: "The denial of the exception in the case at bar is not to be taken as a determination that a church is detrimental to the welfare of the community." The court then cited a passage from the recent United States Supreme Court decision in *Berman v. Parker:* [111] "The concept of the public welfare is broad and inclusive. The values it represents are spiritual as well as physical, aesthetic as well as monetary."

"Ordinarily," the court then said, "a church adds incalculably to public convenience and welfare and, for the purposes of the case at bar, it can be conceded that that statement is applicable." The statement quoted by the court was taken from a case that did not concern churches at all. Its reference was not to church activity but to public activities of officials of the government of the District of Columbia for the betterment of the nation's capital by renewal of rundown neighborhoods. The Connecticut court seemed to be hinting that the state, like the church, has spiritual functions.

In Connecticut and Florida, then, the courts are inclined to place state purposes on a plane higher than church purposes; but in New York, after the Brighton decision, the trend has been in the opposite direction. Within a few days after it was issued, a trial court of Nassau County decided the Garden City Jewish center case.[150] Under an ordinance requiring adequate parking facilities the zoning board had refused a permit. It alleged that the parking area was not large enough to take care of future needs of the congregation. The court held that, under the Brighton decision future needs could not even be considered by the zoning board.

"As to the future," the court said, "the board may not require excess parking facilities now to take care of all future growth. It is [the synagogue's] responsibility to consider whether such growth in the foreseeable future will make these facilities inadequate and will prevent the effective use of its property and will compel the acquisition of a larger and more suitable site. To hold now that provision for the unforeseeable future must be made would restrict the freedom of worship by denying the right to establish a church not because the facilities are presently inadequate or unsuitable but because they may become so with the passage of time." This passage in the decision comes close to tarnsferring public functions out of the hands of public officials and into the hands of a religious body.

The religious freedom argument was again rejected in the Bethel, Pennsylvania, case of 1957,[159] where the Kingdom Hall was excluded because its location was too close to other places of assembly. The Witnesses claimed violation of their First Amendment rights. The court cited the cases previously mentioned in this chapter and said that "certainly freedom of worship does not mean that churches are exempt from reasonable police regulation. The concepts of religious freedom,

freedom of speech and the press, which are embodied in the First Amendment, have never been construed as absolute rights and beyond the power of reasonable regulation under the police power."

The danger inherent in the policy of giving *carte blanche* to churches is well described in an article by Ralph W. Crolly in the April 1957 issue of the *Brooklyn Law Review*.[161] It said that: "To hold that a church may as of right be constructed at any place in such a district would be to hold that a municipality is virtually helpless to protect its zoning plan and the characteristics of the district. The interests of private citizens who have expended substantial sums of money and constructed homes in the area in the hope of enjoying the comforts, satisfaction, peace and quiet of that area would be at the mercy of private bodies and groups who may have no interest in the area other than a desire to erect and maintain a church therein."

The case most roundly rejecting the First Amendment as a bar to zoning action was the Milwaukie, Oregon, Jehovah's Witnesses case of 1958.[184] The opinion devotes six pages to a discussion of the claimed violation of religious freedom. It is a learned statement of the law on the question, meriting full perusal. In closing, the court said: [184:28] "The denial of a building permit to [the congregation] did not prohibit any one of its members from religious worship. Moreover, there is nothing in the record before us to indicate that alternative opportunities to locate do not exist. We do know that a church building could be erected without a permit in one of the other zoned areas; indeed it is possible a permit might be issued on proper application as to another site in the same residential zone where traffic congestion would be less likely, or in an unzoned area of Milwaukie if it exists. We are not persuaded by [the congregation's] argument that the denial of its application to erect a church in the zone reserved for single dwelling residences works a trespass on its religious liberties as protected by the federal or Oregon constitutions."

The Azusa, California, Jehovah's Witnesses case [186:257] also contains a learned discussion of religious freedom. It was not really relevant to the case, since the Witnesses had admitted that "churches are subject to zoning regulations so long as the

same are not discriminatory on their face or in their administration." But, like the Milwaukie case, it is worth reading in
detail. The Azusa case is also interesting in that it affirmed the
principles of the Porterville decision [67] which some felt had
been weakened by the Piedmont case.[115,125] The Modesto, California, Jehovah's Witnesses decision of 1962 [245:916] said that the
California decisions "have settled beyond cavil that zoning
laws as such do not abridge the constitutional right of freedom
of worship."

The Creve Coeur Jewish case of 1959,[192] which was decided
in favor of the congregation, is cited in a *Notre Dame Lawyer*
article of May 1960 [222] as "one of the few decisions resting on
the First Amendment freedom of religion ground." This is not
correct. The decision rests rather upon an interpretation of
the statute. This case presented the same issue that came up in
the old cases of the Church of God at Beckley, West Virginia,[25]
and the Pentecostal Holiness church at Montgomery, Alabama.[56] In the Beckley case, the question was whether a church
could be excluded by an ordinance zoning out any "public
garage, filling station, store or other industry of any other
kind or character." In the Montgomery case, the question was
whether it was excluded by an ordinance barring any "store,
filling station, automobile laundry, garage, or any other type
of building to be used for commercial purposes."

In the Creve Coeur case, the statute authorized the zoning
only of "the location and use of buildings, structures and land
for trade, commerce, industry, residence and other purposes."

The Missouri court had to decide only whether churches
were included in the designation "and other purposes" in a
statute wherein churches as such were not mentioned at all.
This was a simple decision, nothing on which anyone should
make a great constitutional case. It is true, however, that the
Supreme Court of Missouri mentioned freedom of religion.
After deciding the issues under the enabling act, the court
added another justification. It said: [192:454] "Freedom of religion is one of the fundamental freedoms protected by the bill
of rights, of both our federal and state constitutions. . . .
[I]n view of its absolute prohibition, we do not believe our
legislature, in using the language it did, had any intention of

granting authority to municipalities to restrict locations and uses of buildings and land for churches."

It was obvious nevertheless that the court had no desire to hold the exclusion of a church unconstitutional under the religious liberty clause. It said [192:456] that "if it is believed to be necessary to regulate the location of churches, this is a matter for the legislature to provide, with proper safeguards for the fundamental liberty of the free exercise of religion protected by the constitution."

In the Allendale, New Jersey, Jehovah's Witnesses case of 1959,[205,219] the court had before it facts and contentions almost identical with those in the Decatur, Indiana, case.[104] It came to an opposite conclusion. The decision in the New Jersey case says [205:571] that "the [congregation's] real contention is that the off-street parking requirements . . . are invalid on their face and as applied because they abridge 'freedom of assembly and worship contrary to the state and federal constitutions.' We consider this contention to be without merit."

"The off-street parking requirements," continued the New Jersey court, ". . . do not restrict the plaintiff's freedom of worship and assembly at its present quarters or at any suitable quarters in the AA residential zone or in any of the other zones in the borough or even at the [congregation's] relatively small lot on Hillside Avenue, if its plans are altered to reduce its proposed seating capacity and increase its proposed off-street parking facilities so as to comply with the terms of the . . . ordinance. [The requirements] appear to come well within the principle expressed in cases which have heretofore held that property used for church purposes, along with property used for other purposes, may be lawfully subjected to reasonable zoning restrictions."

In the Garden Grove, California, Jehovah's Witnesses case of 1959,[217:69] the court again considered the traditional quasi-governmental status of churches. This court refused to go into the question at all, insisting that this was the function of the zoning board. The court said that "[The congregation] urges upon the court the fact that churches and establishments for religious worship are favored by the law and that they are not to be considered as objectionable. This court is entirely in accord with those principles. They are, however, factors that should be, and presumably were, taken into consideration by the planning commission and the city council in passing upon whether the proposed amendment was compatible with the overall scheme of zoning and planning of the city. . . . [T]hese considerations . . . are not before us."

The Meridian Hills, Indiana, Catholic church and school case of 1961 [229] was decided in favor of the church for reasons described on pages 103-104. Its factual basis was lack of substantial public purpose and its legal basis was the due process clause. However, the court also relied on the public functions of religion and education. Regarding them it said that "the education morally and spiritually of children is a matter of great public concern and private interests, although important, should not outweigh such general public welfare." This case is also distinctive in that it followed the *Notre Dame* (Indiana) *Lawyer* article [222:407] in misusing the Creve Coeur, Missouri, precedent.[192] It even found fault with counsel for not misinterpreting the Missouri decision as the *Notre Dame Lawyer* had done.

Referring to the Creve Coeur case, the court said that "it is there held, in view of the state and federal constitutional provision of freedom of worship and the encouragement of education, that an enabling act authorizing a city to zone should not be interpreted as granting to the zoning board the authority to restrict or exclude churches or schools in residence districts." Not one word did the Indiana court say about the omission in the Missouri law of any mention of schools or churches. This passage, in my opinion, is a gross misinterpretation of the Missouri case. Any lawyer who made such misuse of precedent should be reprimanded by the court. In Indiana, lawyers are criticized for not doing so!

In the majority opinion in the Bayside, Wisconsin, Baptist case of 1961,[231] (see pages 46-7) First Amendment grounds were also mentioned. The mention was only incidental, and possibly irrelevant, but the court's statement on the subject [231:295] is sound enough to bear repeating. It said:

> A church . . . is not to be viewed merely as the owner of property complaining against the restriction on its use. It may also challenge an ordinance as an unwarranted burden upon, or inter-

ference with, the freedom of the adherents of the church to worship after the manner of their faith. . . .

The test is whether a regulation is an *undue infringement*. Any restriction upon the opportunity to build a house of worship is at least a potential burden upon the freedom of those who would like to worship there. Whether the burden is slight or substantial will depend upon circumstances. In a community where adequate and accessible building sites are available in all districts, it might be a negligible burden to exclude churches from some of them. There must be many circumstances under which a religious group could demonstrate that an exclusion from a particular area would be a substantial burden. (Italics in original.)

The court then went on to say that no such demonstration had been made with respect to the subsisting ordinance in Bayside. For other reasons, the court held that the ordinance should not be applied to the particular case. This does not, in my opinion, detract from its soundness as a general rule. This passage, in my opinion, points the way for church organizations which seek to defend themselves on grounds of the First Amendment; this is true although I might be less sanguine than the court in predicting the success of such an approach.

If this treatment of religious rights seems a bit foggy, it is because of a very foggy legal situation. Summarizing, it may be said that a number of cases have granted special treatment to churches on the basis of the special public service that they render. Such action has no real foundation in the First Amendment. It is even apt to conflict with separation of church and state.

Meanwhile, as first stated, the courts have groped for a way to give preference to churches under the religious liberty clause. They have not met with much success. Although the decision in the Piedmont, California, Catholic school case [115,125] may have made a faulty application of the principles announced by the Supreme Court of the United States in the *Society of Sisters* case,[17] it may point the way for future decisions based on individual rights more than on alleged prerogatives of churches.

As indicated on page 70, the churches are being advised to lay less emphasis on property rights under the due process clause and more on religious liberty under the First Amendment. This is sound advice, subject to qualifications. The first is that the religious liberty clause is ordinarily available only when the area of exclusion is so large (perhaps from an entire large town) that the church is deprived of reasonably accessible alternative sites. The second qualification is that the church can properly demand no better treatment under the First Amendment than is given to other forms of public assembly.

This may be a discouraging conclusion. It may seem a hard choice whether:

(a) to invoke the due process clause, trying to show that the purpose of the regulation is insubstantial, or

(b) to invoke the equal protection clause and attempt to show that there has been unfair discrimination, or

(c) to invoke the religious liberty clause, seeking to demonstrate that there has been substantial and undue interference with worship or with religious expression.

It is fortunate that this hard choice does not have to be made. The churches may invoke all three principles and, as in the past, will continue to do so. It is to be hoped that without having to rely on any "absolutist" rules they will win all the cases in which justice is on their side.

# CHAPTER 16.

## THE ROLE OF PRECEDENT

Our most universal rule of judicial decision is based upon the Latin phrase *stare decisis et non quieta movere.* The "rule of *stare decisis*" requires, once a point of law has been settled, that it shall form a precedent not to be "lightly overruled." The common law system gives judges tremendous power over our affairs but it imposes upon them this restraint which is supposed to impart consistency to their rulings and stability to the legal principles which so directly affect our lives.

This is important to us all especially when we enter into contracts or buy or sell property. These dealings consist of the disposition of legal rights and their value depends entirely upon the nature of those rights. This is determined by the law on the subject. The parties know the law on the basis of legal opinions which are in reality just predictions of how the subject will be treated in possible future litigation. If judges were free to decide without regard to previous decisions such predictions would be impossible. Without this restraint our law would be deprived of that comparative certainty which is its most admirable aspect.

This characteristic is unique to, our system. Thus, Alexis de Tocqueville, who visited America in 1820 and wrote the classical book, *Democracy in America,*[5] found the law of precedents, as here administered, rather strange and distasteful. He wrote:

> The English and Americans have retained the law of precedents; that is to say, they continue to found their legal opinions and the decisions of their courts upon the opinions and decisions of their predecessors. . . . The English and American lawyer investigates what has been done. The French advocate inquires what should have been done. The former produce precedents, the latter reasons.
>
> A French observer is surprised to hear how often an English or American lawyer quotes the opinions of others and how little he al-

ludes to his own, while the reverse occurs in France. There the most trifling litigation is never conducted without the introduction of an entire system of ideas peculiar to the counsel employed; and the fundamental principles of law are invoked in order to obtain a rod of land by the decision of the courts.

De Tocqueville, then a recent law school graduate, preferred the French system. He referred to the American lawyer's "abnegation of his own opinion," to his "deference to the opinion of his forefathers," which, he said, amounted to "servitude of thought." This is no place to quarrel with the great French critic about the relative merits of the French and American legal professions or about the comparative advantages of the common law and the Napoleonic code system.

De Tocqueville is quoted mainly to help explain to nonlawyer readers how the system of precedents works. My opinion, like his, is based on personal predilections, my own having been developed in a lifetime of American legal practice. The details of legal principles can be worked out more accurately by the courts on the facts of cases as they arise than they can by legislators who seek to propound in advance detailed rules that shall govern each future case. The Napoleonic code was a work of genius. But its approach was less scientific than that of our own courts, which develop theories and rules in the "laboratory" of the courtroom.

De Tocqueville refers to the introduction into each French case of "an entire system of ideas peculiar to the counsel employed." This seems an overstatement. Yet it highlights the advantages of our own arrangement with its comparative stability and predictability. The "servitude of thought" which he criticizes does exist here. Our lawyers are less prone to flights of logic than those of the French bar, but essentially there is nothing to prevent them. The application of the human intelligence to a mass of preceding cases requires as much skill as its application to the "fundamental principles" enunciated in the French code or commentaries.

De Tocqueville errs in this criticism to the extent that judges and lawyers properly and skillfully apply the law of precedent. He is justified to the extent that it is applied in a wooden way. Judges and lawyers often forget the true purport of the rule which is: If a case arises that is similar in all its details (as lawyers say, "on all fours") to a case previously decided in the same court or one superior to it, the decision in the new litigation should be the same as in the earlier case unless the earlier decision is patently wrong. The same process is applied to a lesser extent when the circumstances are not entirely similar but in certain respects can properly be compared. The rule applies not only to the final decision of the case as such but also to the decision of incidental and preliminary issues arising therein.

The rule of *stare decisis* requires no more deference to the opinions of our ancestors than the deference that de Tocqueville and his colleagues pay to the opinions of those who wrote the code or commented on it. Indeed it requires perhaps a closer and more critical analysis. The analysis of any precedent should determine two questions: (1) whether and to what extent the case at bar is similar in fact and circumstance to the case cited as precedent; and (2) whether the case cited as precedent is so wrong that it should be reversed.

In church zoning cases the principle has been grossly misapplied. The judges seem not to "found their legal opinions upon the opinions of their predecessors" but rather upon fragments of those opinions. They take casual passages out of context, without analysis, and apply them as if they were applying a passage out of a code of law. How this occurs can be learned by tracing very briefly the "ancestry" of a single legal principle enunciated in 1956 by the highest court of New York State.

The principle happens to be the same one discussed in Chapter 3, the absolute anti-exclusion doctrine. I have previously criticized the doctrine itself and shown that the New York court contradicted itself. Here I will only criticize the manner in which the court derived its conclusion from the previous cases. The purpose is to show how the rule of precedent, when misapplied, can lead to almost ludicrous results.

In the Brighton, New York, Roman Catholic case,[149:834] the court said:

> It is well established in this country that a zoning ordinance may not wholly exclude a church or synagogue from any residential district. Such a provision is stricken on the grounds that it

bears no substantial relation to the public health, safety, morals, peace or general welfare of the community.

Let us bear the above text carefully in mind as we trace its genealogy in previous decisions. As de Tocqueville [5] suggested, the New York court does not produce reasons—it only produces precedents—in support of this conclusion. A list of them is appended, by page and volume number, immediately following the statement quoted. Let us next take a look at the latest of the precedents there listed, then in turn examine the latest precedent on which the next preceding case was based and so on back to the beginning, which happens to be fourteen years and five cases earlier.

The latest of the cases cited by the New York court was the South Euclid, Ohio, Jewish decision issued earlier in the same year.[140] It is true that the South Euclid ordinance contained a provision excluding churches from residential districts. It is true that the Ohio decision quoted a statement to the same effect as that of the New York Court of Appeals. But the provision was not "stricken" as the New York court seems to have thought. To the contrary the Ohio court left it in full force and effect as to subsequent cases, requiring only that an exception be made as authorized by the ordinance in favor of the particular applicant. The statement of the absolute anti-exclusion rule appeared in the Ohio decision as pure dictum, not in any sense necessary to the decision of the case and therefore possessing no status as precedent in cases to follow. The Ohio court did not itself abide by the rule.

Now look at the background of the Ohio dictum. The latest of the cases cited in the South Euclid decision was the Jehovah's Witnesses case at Decatur, Indiana.[104] There, as will be recalled, the court required issuance of a permit, but only on condition that the congregation comply with the setback line prescribed by the zoning board.

The Indiana decision was properly described in 1958 by a justice of the Oregon Supreme Court who said: [184:21]

> Some seize upon statements like the following of the Indiana Supreme Court . . . : "The law is well settled that the building of a church may not be prohibited in any residential district" as a dogmatic and immutable injunction against denial of any church's application to build in a zoned area. This, of course, is not true. . . .

It was not even so intended by the Indiana court, which, elsewhere in the same opinion, correctly says, "The building of churches is subject to such reasonable regulation as may be necessary to promote public health, safety, or general welfare."

The Indiana court's statement first above quoted was not only unnecessary to the final decision of the case. It was actually in conflict with that decision. We don't know from the opinion whether the Kingdom Hall was not itself by the very decision "prohibited in a residential area." Whether it was or not depends on whether the Witnesses changed their plans in accordance with the decision. Certain it is that the church as originally planned was prohibited by the very decision which affirmed the illegality of such prohibition.

The dictum in the Indiana case was, in turn, based upon a citation of the Plandome, New York, Unitarian church case of 1951.[87] There the exclusion of a church was actually condemned. But the exclusion attempted was not from a single district; it was from an entire village. The Plandome facts are obviously distinct from the Brighton situation covered by the New York Court of Appeals' conclusion.

The appearance of the Plandome decision in this line of precedents is also interesting because it was issued by a trial court. The court of appeals in the Brighton decision proudly displays the Plandome case at the head of the list of precedents supposedly supporting the conclusion above stated. But there is nothing in the law of precedents requiring or justifying reliance by courts of appeal on the decisions of trial courts. Such a practice seems quite inconsistent with the purpose and function of courts of review, which is to correct erroneous decisions of subordinate tribunals.

The Plandome decision in turn relied upon the Sherman, Texas, Church of God case of 1944.[48,49] Like the other decisions, it supplies not a shred of support for the conclusion drawn from it. In the Sherman case the attorneys for the city waived the point and refused to argue in support of the ordinance. The rule does not require courts to conform to precedents which are established without argument of counsel.

This brings us back to the true origin of the doctrine which the New York Court of Appeals said has been "firmly established in this country." The Sherman case relied upon the

Upper Arlington, Ohio, Lutheran church case of 1942,[40] specifically the passage where the court said that "we seriously question the constitutionality of any enactment that seeks flatly to prohibit the erection of churches in a residential district." No cases were cited to support this statement. It would have been inappropriate as the court was expressing not a conclusion but merely a doubt or "question." In the sentence following the one quoted immediately above, the court said: "We believe that this question does not arise."

Thus we find that the conclusion of the New York Court of Appeals quoted on pages 243-4 was based on a series of inapplicable precedents. In the long run it stood not upon the decision of any other court but upon a "question" raised 14 years earlier by the Ohio court and by it left unanswered.

The construction of legal principles under the rule of precedents can be compared either to the construction done by children at play with their building blocks or to the more scientific methods of engineers on large buildings. The child at play merely places block on block, as the unskilled or inattentive lawyer puts one case on top of the other to support the principle for which he contends. The skilled engineer follows a similar procedure; but he joins the various tiers of his structure together with steel girders. This holds the parts together so that the 52nd story is not 100% dependent upon the stability of the first.

This process is comparable to the proper use of precedent in which the prior decisions should be joined each to the other with the girders of statutory and constitutional principles and of factual analysis. The handling of precedents in the series of cases above mentioned is more comparable to child's play than to skyscraper construction. The worst of it is that these practices are common in church zoning cases. When the lowest block, in this case the Ohio court's "question," is removed, the structure collapses.

There is a special aspect of church zoning cases which tends properly to lessen the authority of previous decisions as precedents. The United States Supreme Court has never dealt directly with church zoning. The cases have been decided in 25 different states, few cases being decided in any one state. This means that most precedents available for citation in any case come from "foreign" jurisdictions, that is from states other than the one in which the case at bar is being argued. Precedents established in one state are not binding on the courts of other states. They are merely "persuasive," which leaves any court free to decide that it will not be persuaded.

Another such limitation is the policy of the courts which applies the rule of *stare decisis* less strictly in cases involving the sovereign police power than in cases involving property or contracts. This is partly because historically the rule was intended to protect the stability of business affairs. But it also stems from a reluctance on the part of the courts to interfere with the other branches of government or to fix by court decision the boundaries within which the state may exercise a power so necessary to its very existence.

Perhaps the most stringent limitation is the stress properly laid by judges in zoning cases on consideration of the particular facts and circumstances of each case as it arises. This test applies not only to the immediate situation but to general conditions in the community, state and nation at the time when a particular land use regulation is attempted. A decision issued in the "horse and buggy days" may have comparatively little relevancy to the era of the automobile and the high speed freeway.

The "question" raised by the Ohio court in the Upper Arlington Lutheran church case [40] was not without validity in an earlier day. The judges there seem to have been thinking in terms of their childhood when people used to walk to church and the parishioners all came from the same neighborhood. The same logic would have quite a different application in a day when Sunday morning at church very possibly means clogging the streets and annoying the neighbors with thousands of persons and hundreds of cars congregated from miles around.

The Ohio court in 1942 was perhaps not as ready to think in modern terms as was the "ultraconservative" United States Supreme Court in 1923. If the judges in Washington, D. C., had been as tradition-bound as those in Columbus, Ohio, the basic theory of zoning as such would not have passed its first test of constitutionality. The Euclid, Ohio, decision,[18] which first upheld such laws, contains the following passage:

Building zone laws are of modern origin. They began in this country about 25 years ago. Until recent years urban life was comparatively simple; but with the great increase in concentration of population, problems have developed and constantly are developing, which require, and will continue to require, additional restrictions with respect to use and occupancy of private land in urban communities.

Regulations, the wisdom, necessity and validity of which, as applied to existing conditions, are so apparent that they are now uniformly sustained, a century ago, or even half a century ago, probably would have been rejected as arbitrary and oppressive. . . . And in this there is no inconsistency, for, while the meaning of constitutional guaranties never varies, the scope of their application must expand or contract to meet the new and different conditions which are constantly coming within the field of their operation.

In a changing world, it is impossible that it should be otherwise. But although a degree of elasticity is thus imparted—not to the meaning but to the application of constitutional principles— statutes and ordinances which, after giving due weight to the new conditions, are found clearly not to conform to the constitution, of course, must fall.

This passage has not been taken out of context in the manner criticized above. The "changing world" concept seems to have been essential to the decision in the Euclid, Ohio, case. If the court had not adopted this view as to the force of precedent, it would have come to an opposite conclusion and nullified the whole concept of comprehensive land use regulation in its modern sense.

The law of precedent is applicable to church zoning cases. In them lawyers should pay due deference to the opinions of their legal "forefathers." They should not introduce into each case an entire system of ideas "peculiar to the counsel employed." Neither should present day legal opinion be abandoned or withheld. It should be applied more thoroughly than it is to the careful analysis of any previous decision relied upon. Above all things, the judges should follow the example of the United States Supreme Court in "giving due weight to new conditions" of a general or social nature.

# CHAPTER 17.

## PRESUMPTION OF LEGALITY AND BURDEN OF PROOF

An important factor in the outcome of any lawsuit may be the judicial presumptions that are entertained in behalf of one party or the other. To the nonlawyer the most familiar of these is the one which holds that a person charged with crime is presumed innocent until proved guilty.

Where a presumption exists in favor of one party, the other party (in the criminal case mentioned, it would be the state) is required to assume the burden of proof. In zoning cases, the most important presumption is a firmly established one which is the opposite of that ruling criminal cases. It is a presumption of the validity and propriety of official actions. In most church zoning cases, the courts continue to recognize this presumption but in a few it has been reversed.

In all litigation these are important technical considerations. The presumption—and the burden of proof corollary to it—involve corresponding practical advantages and disadvantages. Let us assume for illustration that the court recognizes the presumption of the validity of the city's action regulating the use of church land. This imposes on the church the burden of proof. Only when the church's lawyer has presented enough evidence to overcome the presumption (to "make a prima facie case") is the city required to present any proof at all. Then the city may bring forward evidence sufficient to balance the church's evidence, whereupon the "burden of going forward with the evidence" shifts back to the church. And so, back and forth, the obligation shifts from one party to the other until the efforts of each are exhausted.

This burden of going forward with the evidence, upon whomever it may fall, is only temporary. It is more important that the party upon whom the overall burden of proof originally falls must continue to bear it throughout the case. He must present a "preponderance of the evidence" or lose the case. Of course, this burden is not as heavy in civil as in criminal cases, where the proof must be "beyond a reasonable doubt." However, it is a substantial burden. If the evidence and arguments on each side are equally convincing, if in other words they are "in equipoise," then that party upon whom the burden of proof originally fell will lose. Under the general presumption of validity of official action, this party would be the church.

This is important in church zoning cases for another reason. Because of the expense and effort involved, the cases actually taken to court do not generally include those in which the evidence and arguments on one side very clearly outweigh the evidence and arguments on the other. It is the hard cases, the ones in which the evidence is almost "in equipoise," that the judges are called upon to decide, not usually those in which one side is clearly right and the other clearly wrong. Every judge from day to day faces a series of quandaries like the father of a family called upon to decide an argument between two of his children, each equally beloved. Like other citizens the judge may be loath to decide such arguments directly on the merits. He may hesitate to tell either side that they are wrong, and prefer to tell them that they lost the case because of technical reasons.

This is especially true because the outcome of a case often depends upon the credibility of the witnesses and the willingness of the court to accept their views as to the facts. Is the court going to reject the evidence of the city officials or the evidence of the clergyman and his flock? The church in a sense seems to represent the voice of God. The city in a similar sense seems to represent the voice of the people. It may be that because the quarrel involves religion it also involves a certain amount of acrimony. This kind of case is different from one in which the conflict is between a policeman and an alleged pickpocket. The church zoning case pits against each other two groups of antagonists, both of whom are among the respectable elements in the community.

In church zoning cases the judge will be especially anxious to avoid repudiating either side. The alternative is to invoke seemingly technical rules as to presumptions and burden of proof. These rules are supposedly established, not by the judge in the particular case, but by previous judges in different cases. The rules are supposed to be immutable. So the judge may be inclined to say to the losing party, not "you are wrong," but "you may be right but the unchangeable legal presumptions are against you."

The usual presumptions favor the validity of any official action. The burden of proof is upon any party who challenges such action. This rule applies first with respect to the action of the state legislature in adopting a zoning enabling act under which the city proceeds. It also applies with respect to the action of the city or county in adopting an ordinance which incorporates the city plan. It applies again with respect to the action of a zoning board or building inspector who turns down the church's application. It also applies to the refusal of a board of appeals to overturn this ruling.

Innumerable courts have said about such administrative decisions that they are "regarded as presumptively fair, reasonable and correct so that the burden is upon one complaining thereof to show that the action is improper." This general rule was enunciated with respect to zoning cases in general in the Euclid, Ohio, decision of 1926 [18] which first upheld the validity of such laws. The Supreme Court of the United States said that no judge should set aside a determination made by a public officer in a zoning case unless it is clear that the action "had no foundation in reason and is a mere arbitrary or irrational exercise of power having no substantial relation to public health, the public morals, the public welfare in a proper sense."

This is a strong reaffirmation of the general rule. It makes no exception in favor of churches. However, the reluctance of state courts to follow the rule becomes apparent even in decisions where it is not openly repudiated. In the Winnetka, Illinois, parochial school decision of 1939,[34] the Illinois court (by clear implication) cast the burden of proof upon the city rather than upon the church. It reversed the city's refusal of a permit. The writer of the opinion said [34:594] that he "failed to perceive to what degree a Catholic school of the particular type would be more detrimental than a public school." He added that this distinction was "not pointed out," and that therefore he "could not arbitrarily recognize its existence." In other words, the court found fault with the city for not carrying the burden of proof in this respect. A similar attitude was assumed in the Reno, Nevada, Catholic Church case [35:22] where the court said that it was "unable to perceive" a substantial difference between home funerals and the church funerals complained of by the city.

The first church zoning case expressly challenging the accepted presumption of validity was the Upper Arlington Lutheran church case of 1942.[40] There the court said that "in determining whether [the city's] administrative acts and policies may be upheld, it should be observed that the usual presumption of the validity of the acts of public boards and officials does not apply to acts involving the forfeiture of an individual's rights or the depriving him of the free use of his property. . . . Applying this exception to a case like the one at bar, where the public officials seek under a zoning ordinance to deny a landowner a particular use of his property, the highest court of Maryland has held that the board of zoning appeals has the burden of showing reasons sufficient to support its authority in refusing a building permit."

This passage has been cited in some church zoning cases as establishing a special exception in favor of churches. This is not its true intent. The reference was not to churches but to "landowners." The Maryland case cited was *Applestein v. Mayor* [24] which was only in a limited sense "like the one at bar." The Ohio decision was in a church case, but the Maryland case concerned a mercantile establishment. However, the Ohio court was invoking an exception, not in behalf of churches, but in behalf of any landowner faced with use regulation.

This exception has little support in general zoning law. The standard texts all certify to the survival of the general rule supporting validity. For instance, the article in *American Jurisprudence* on "Zoning" [32,§256] reaffirms it, saying that "Decisions of zoning boards of appeals, review or adjustment as to exceptions or variations in the application of zoning regulations are regarded as presumptively fair, reasonable and correct, so that the burden is upon one complaining thereof to show that the board acted improperly."

In support of this established rule this encyclopedia refers to a large number of cases. It goes on to say that there is a contrary view. "There is authority," it says, "involving a zoning law provision that the usual presumption of validity does not apply." The only authority to which direct reference is made is the Upper Arlington Lutheran church case.[40]

The Upper Arlington theory was adopted in the Sherman, Texas, Church of God case,[48] the court of appeals saying [48:102] that "the assumption of validity usually ascribed to zoning legislation . . . does not extend to the proscription of churches *en masse* from residence districts. If the exclusion of the church promoted substantial public purposes, the burden was upon the . . . city to establish it." This made the rule specifically applicable to churches.

However, the Upper Arlington theory did not survive in the Ohio Supreme Court itself. Only three years later, in the Cleveland Heights Jewish case,[59] this attitude was reversed. In sustaining the exclusion of a Jewish school, the court said that "in the absence of evidence of abuse of discretion, a writ of mandamus will not be issued . . . unless in the judgment of the commission the public convenience and welfare and the appropriate use of neighboring property will not be substantially and permanently injured thereby."

The factual "judgment" on which the court said it would rely was not its own judgment but that "of the commission." In other words, this court presumed the validity of the commission's decision, contrary to its previous ruling in the Upper Arlington case. If the courts view the Upper Arlington decision in its proper scope, as revoking the presumption altogether, I doubt that it will be followed any oftener than the Omaha, Nebraska, Presbyterian case [14] which invalidated setback requirements.

The Supreme Court of Michigan shifted the burden of proof in the Orchard Lake Catholic case.[94] Its conclusion was buttressed by "other evidence in the case," which the court's decision does not detail, and by a distinctive provision of Michigan's constitution. The court said that: "We are confronted with an act showing on its face that which, combined with the competent evidence in the case, obviates the necessity for resort to the presumption of reasonableness and validity." Michigan's constitution recognized "religion, morality and knowledge" as being "necessary to good government and the happiness of mankind." The court said: "Hardly compatible is this with a presumption that exclusion of church and school from an entire municipality is conducive to public health, safety, morals or the general welfare, a presumption which we decline to indulge."

The attitude of the Michigan court on the subject we are now discussing is not made consistently clear. What was the "other competent evidence in the case" to which the court referred? Was it introduced by the church? If so, was the court really shifting the burden or proof, or merely accepting the church's *prima facie* case and shifting the "burden of going forward"? In spite of this ambiguity, the emphatic verbal repudiation of the presumption should not be disregarded.

This contrasts with the harsh treatment accorded to the smaller denomination in the Portage Full Salvation Union case.[60] (See pages 195-6.) It also contrasts with the treatment accorded objecting property owners in the Grand Rapids, Michigan, Evangelical Lutheran case.[28:181] There the zoning board had granted the church a special permit allowing violation of setback lines, etc., under an ordinance which authorized them on showing of "practical difficulties." When the case came to the Supreme Court, the property owners pointed out that the city had not even stated the nature of the "practical difficulties" allegedly justifying its action. The court said: "The reasons and grounds of these findings we have no means of knowing and the board of appeals is not required to state them, for no review is contemplated. Under the statute and the ordinance, the discretion is that of the board, not of the courts, and the decision is final, in the absence of fraud or bad faith, which is not here alleged."

The burden-of-proof issue was also raised by Jehovah's Witnesses in the Milwaukie, Oregon, case.[184] They relied on the *Applestein* case,[24] above mentioned, the Upper Arlington, Ohio, Lutheran church case [40] and the opinion of the lower court in the Decatur, Indiana, Jehovah's Witnesses case.[104] The Oregon court overruled the Witnesses' contention, saying: [184:10]

> [The congregation] represents that, when a church seeks a permit, the burden is upon the Council to show the reasons for denying the application. . . .
> We find no merit in this contention. We find nothing in the cases cited that would justify its representation that a special rule

exists exonerating a church from assuming the burden of proof necessary to overcome the presumption of regularity of action on the part of an administrative agency. The Maryland case . . . did not involve church property. In the Indiana case, the Supreme Court makes no reference to the burden-of-proof rule one way or the other.

It is true that the Decatur, Indiana, decision did not mention the issue. But the Oregon court might also have pointed out that in the earlier church zoning case involving a Methodist edifice at Indianapolis [57] the Indiana court had strongly supported the presumption of validity of administrative action. There the objectors had contended that the evidence supporting the board's grant of the permit was "so proportionately meager . . . compared to the evidence opposing" that reversal was justified. The court said [57:616] that it "would not weigh the conflicting evidence" because "these matters are the peculiar responsibility of the hearing agency."

The Indianapolis, Indiana, Methodist case,[57] like the Grand Rapids, Michigan, Lutheran case,[28] had been decided by the zoning board in favor of the church. No one seriously contends that the usual rule should be reversed in such cases, but only in those where the board decision is against the church. The New York courts, at least theoretically, sustain the usual rule even where the board decides against the church. In the Brighton, New York, case,[149] the court said that: "It is well settled that a court may not substitute its judgment for that of the board or body it reviews unless the decision under review is arbitrary and unreasonable and constitutes an abuse of discretion." Thus it affirmed the rule in favor of the presumption of validity. The case is cited over and over again in other cases in support of that rule. Yet the zoning officials took what might be described as a very severe beating. In Indiana, they take such beatings in every case. In church zoning cases the acceptance by courts of the presumption of validity of governmental action is sometimes nominal rather than real.

In this respect, church zoning cases are not peculiar. In his standard work, *Statutory Construction*,[42§4509] J. G. Sutherland says that "it is constantly asserted by the courts that every presumption favors the validity of an act of the legislature and that all doubts must be resolved in support of the act. . . . Nevertheless this presumption, though frequently reiterated, has little operative effect in the determination of a particular case. The presumption is asserted as frequently when the statute is declared unconstitutional as it is when constitutional attack is denied. The 'presumption' is obviously not conclusive and has, apparently, little effect upon the actual decision of cases."

Sutherland obviously believes that presumptions and burdens of proof are not important. Nor do I want to magnify the actual importance of these technical problems. However, there is much discussion about them in the church zoning cases. And for the reason I have described above they may have a greater actual effect on the decision of these cases than on the decision of others. If this is so, it is important to know whether the particular jurisdiction stands firmly upon the usually accepted doctrine or rejects it.

Should the presumption of validity be enforced or not? This question is important not only in cases involving religious liberty but also in those which concern any interference with free speech, press or assembly. Most state courts entertain doubts on the subject which they do not resolve, yet permit such doubts to influence their decisions. Thus in the 1962 case of Jehovah's Witnesses at Chicago, Illinois,[246:725] the supreme court of that state said: "It has been strongly doubted since Justice Stone's famous footnote in [*United States v. Carolene* [33A:152]] that legislation regulating First Amendment freedoms has the normal strong presumption of validity. See [*Thomas v. Collins* [52:529]]".

It may be that the courts should make a finer distinction based on the type of issue raised. In some cases, the issue is due process; the church alleges that the public purpose served by the regulation is insufficient to uphold it, as compared to the damage inflicted. The church says that the social effect of constructing the church is not sufficiently adverse to justify its regulation or exclusion. Who, then, is to "go forward with the evidence" about the adverse effects of the church? It could be argued that the city ought to be "first up" in this regard. This can be supported on the ground, often invoked, that the burden shifts when one party has peculiar knowledge of the facts.

The situation may be different where the issue involves equal protection. There the church alleges that there is discrimination against it and in favor of some other church or nonecclesiastical enterprise. It would seem appropriate for the church, not the city, to bring forth evidence of the alleged discrimination. The same would be true if the church alleges an undue restriction upon its religious liberty. The party to prove such a restriction is the one who claims he is oppressed.

At the same time, when all the evidence is in it is the private party, not the state, that should be required to show a "preponderance." Perhaps this view is based on personal predilections which place popular sovereignty upon a plane higher than individual or corporation rights, including the rights of churches. Citizens, lawyers, or judges with contrary predilections might come to contrary conclusions.

# CHAPTER 18.

## THE REGULATIONS AND THEIR INTERPRETATION

The central problem in church zoning cases is constitutional. However, the results in a great many of the cases depend, not upon the federal constitution, but upon the judicial interpretation of some ruling or regulation of a board, some city ordinance, some state enabling act, or, more rarely, some state constitution. This fact should not be neglected in the midst of extended discussion of federal constitutional issues. If a particular case was, or could have been, decided on the basis of other considerations, the incidental discussion of constitutional principles is probably irrelevant. This is true of many church zoning cases.

The numerical preponderance of nonconstitutional problems is inevitable. The total wordage of board regulations and decisions, city ordinances, state enabling acts, etc., involved in the cases is vastly greater than the brief provisions of the federal constitution which the courts must consider. Many decisions contain page after page filled with verbatim transcripts of such provisions. There are reasons for the verbosity of zoning laws. One is the rule against undue delegation of legislative power. Churches are usually permitted under discretionary authority of administrative officials and under conditions and standards which are specified at length.

### Standards

State constitutions forbid the delegation of power to subordinate officials whether by the legislature to the city council, by the city council to the zoning board, or by the zoning board to its subordinate officers, without fixing appropriate standards governing and limiting its exercise. In the Portland, Oregon, Catholic school case,[27] the ordinance was invalidated for the reason, among others, that it contained no standards whatsoever. However, if standards are set forth, the courts are not inclined to find fault with them.

This has been especially true with respect to the standards

258

for special permits, the procedure usually involved in church cases. In the Orange County, California, Catholic church and school case, the statute said only [202:919] that the board could authorize church permits "under conditions which will preserve the integrity and character of the district, the utility and value of adjacent property and the general welfare of the neighborhood." This was more or less a restatement of the abstract public purposes that the courts infer from the due process clause as described on pages 20-21.

The archbishop contended that the ordinance was so indefinite as to be unconstitutional. The court rejected this contention, saying: "To devise standards to cover all possible situations that could be exceptions, that is, which would warrant the granting of a conditional use permit or a variance permit, would be a formidable task and one that would tax the imagination. If a legislative draftsman blessed with such omniscience were available and he could draft standards to govern the likely as well as the possible contingencies which a conditional use permit or variance is designed to relieve, there would be no need for a conditional use or a variance. . . . All of which goes to point up our belief that, if the purposes of zoning are to be accomplished, the master zoning restrictions must be definite while the provisions pertaining to a conditional use or a variance designed to relieve against certain eventualities must of necessity be broad and permit an exercise of discretion."

In the Porterville, California, Mormon temple case,[67] the court sustained an ordinance which completely and unconditionally excluded churches from a particular residential zone. This decision was refused review in the United States Supreme Court.[71,76] At page 221, I have expressed doubt that the ruling in Porterville could be applied to all types of churches. Legislatures and city councils seem to share this doubt, with the result, as the cases indicate, that few have enacted such blanket ordinances.

Instead the ordinances usually provide for the erection of churches under variances or conditional permits issued in pursuance of prescribed standards. One obvious, if unexpressed, purpose of this policy is to provide for cases in which strict application of a blanket law would be unconstitutional.

By putting churches under such provisions rather than excluding them, it is made possible for them to obtain relief if they can show zoning boards that they have no adverse effect on the community and that their exclusion therefore would be unconstitutional.

In the Azusa, California, Jehovah's Witnesses case when the standards set out in the ordinance were attacked as too vague, the court said: [186:270] "It is manifestly impracticable if not impossible to enumerate in the ordinance itself the varied factual situations in which the ordinance is not applicable because of *constitutional objections* or other special considerations. Consequently almost every zoning ordinance, including the one under consideration, contains provisions whereby an owner may apply to an administrative body for permission to put his land to a nonconforming use. The statutory rule of 'unnecessary hardship' as a guide for variances has been generally upheld as adequate." (My italics.)

The "hardship" provision mentioned by the California court is also contained in the New Jersey enabling act and has led to much difficulty of interpretation. This will be recalled from my discussions of the Morris Township Catholic seminary case.[128] In the Cleveland Heights, Ohio, Jewish school case,[59] nonconforming buildings, including churches, were permitted under the ordinance but only "on a lot determined by the city planning and zoning commision, after public notice and hearing, to be so located that such building will, in the judgment of the city planning and zoning commission, substantially serve the public convenience and welfare and will not substantially and permanently injure the appropriate use of neighboring property." Similar provisions were interpreted in the Beachwood, Ohio, Jewish case[101] and in the Haltom City, Texas, Jehovah's Witnesses case.[136] In the first Kansas City, Missouri, Catholic case,[156:886] the exception was to be granted only subject to such conditions as would "protect the appropriate use of neighboring property in harmony with the general intent of [the] regulations."

The statute involved in the Haltom City, Texas, Jehovah's Witnesses case provided [136:703] that churches would be permitted in the residence district:

(a) on a lot already devoted to the use for which the building permit is requested;

(b) on a lot having a side line common to a public park, playground or cemetery, or directly across a street from any one or combination of said uses;

(c) on a corner lot having a minimum of 100 . . . foot frontage;

(d) on a lot three sides of which will adjoin streets;

(e) on a lot approved by the board of zoning adjustment, subject to final approval by the city council, following public hearing, as being a location where such building will not materially injure neighboring property for residential use.

Most of the ordinances seem to be in general terms like those quoted above. However, drafters of some zoning ordinances try to exercise that omniscience which the court in the Orange County, California, case [193,202] said was unavailable. The ordinance in the Bethel Borough, Pennsylvania, Jehovah's Witnesses case [159] was so specific as to forbid granting special use permits to any "places of worship" located within a quarter mile of another place of assembly. The Wenatchee, Washington, ordinance under which the court required issuance of a permit to the Witnesses [165:196] provided that the board should investigate with respect to "present land utilization pattern and density of buildings within the neighborhood of appellant's land; conditions existing or predating this ordinance concerning topography, traffic, automobile parking and utilities and such other information as is set forth in official maps, development plans, reports and findings of the planning commission." The Witnesses in that case were successful because the zoning board's investigations regarding traffic were insufficiently profound to satisfy the court.

The Menlo Park, California, ordinance, also litigated by Jehovah's Witnesses, stated [194:197] certain general purposes, including: "ease of access as between land use areas; designation, regulation and restriction of parking; the lessening of street congestion; the preservation and extension of the inherent residential character of the city and the promotion of health, safety, comfort, convenience and the general welfare of the city." Nonresidential uses, including churches, were permitted in residential sections upon special permit, in the issuance of which the board was instructed to "take into consideration the location and provision for adequate off-street parking, . . . architectural control review, . . . such review to be concerned particularly with trees, shrubs, planting and landscape treatment to preserve the beauty and charm of the city and the residential character of the land use district in which said use is located."

The ordinance in the Milwaukie, Oregon, Jehovah's Witnesses case [184:9] permitted nonresidential use permits in residence zones after the commission "had been satisfied as to the propriety of such use." It stated the general purposes of zoning in the usual way, then said that its provisions "shall be deemed to be the minimum requirements to encourage the most appropriate use of land; to conserve and stabilize the value of property; to provide adequate open spaces for light and air; to prevent undue concentration of population; to lessen the congestion in the streets; to facilitate adequate provisions for community utilities and facilities such as transportation, water, sewage, schools, parks and other public requirements, and to promote the public safety, health, convenience, comfort, prosperity and general welfare of the people." These standards leave considerable leeway to the boards in administering the provisions allowing churches and other nonresidential uses.

The ordinance interpreted in the Azusa, California, Jehovah's Witnesses case,[186:264] however, seemed to encourage a policy against admission of such uses except in extreme circumstances. It provided: "When practical difficulties, unnecessary hardships or results inconsistent with the general purposes of this ordinance occur through a strict interpretation of its provisions, the commission . . . may . . . in specific cases initiate proceedings for the granting of a variance . . . under such conditions as may be necessary to assure that the spirit and purpose of this ordinance will be served, public safety and welfare secured and substantial justice done." The statute further provided that "before any variance may be granted, it shall be affirmatively shown: (a) that there are special circumstances attached to the property . . . which do not apply generally to other property in the same district; (b) that the granting of such variance is necessary to do subtsantial justice, and to avoid practical difficulties, unnecessary hardship, or results inconsistent with the general purposes of this ordinance; (c) that the granting of the variance will not result in material damage or prejudice to other property in the vicinity, nor be detrimental to the public health, safety, or general welfare."

*Conditions.*

In addition to the standards of judgment which boards must follow in granting variances, exceptions, and special use permits, most ordinances also explicitly authorize the imposition of conditions upon the granting of such permits. These are sometimes "conditions precedent," which must be met before the permit is issued, or they may be "conditions subsequent" which must be agreed to in advance (sometimes by way of a recorded deed) and which must be complied with as long as the permitted use continues. Violation of such conditions subsequent can be enforced either by injunction or by cancellation of the permit.

The most universal condition precedent to the building of a church or other structure is, of course, the requirement for a building permit. Yokley says that this requirement is universally valid.[96§296] It was objected to in the Chico, California, Baptist church case [88] and in the Darien, Connecticut, Catholic school case [247] and the challenge to it was overruled. Another very common condition is compliance by the permitee with fire, health, and sanitary regulations, whether contained in the zoning ordinance or in the general city code. This requirement was sustained in the Sherman, Texas, Church of God case.[48] Another is the requirement that the church or other structure shall provide adequate off-street parking facilities (see Chapter 10). Churches are also subject to the usual setback or percentage-of-lot-occupancy provisions (see Chapter 6).

In the Dayton, Ohio, Christian Science case [122:574] the proposed parking lot was approved but it was made subject to "conditions laid down by the Plan Board with relation to blacktopping, landscaping, setbacks, bumper blocks, one entrance and exit, restricted use, gate to be closed when not in use," etc. In the South Euclid, Ohio, Jewish case,[140:176] the court noted that "suitable landscaping is to be provided as appears in the plans and specifications, with shrubbery on the side and rear lines separating the area from neighboring property."

In the Garden City, New York, Jewish case,[154:436] the court specified that "the use of the premises by the petitioner as a church or synagogue or temple for its religious purposes shall be confined to the first or ground floor of said building. . . . At no time shall any portion of the premises be used for public gatherings of any nature other than those embraced within the purposes of its religion; . . . no parking of vehicles by members of the petitioner congregation along the easterly boundaries . . . shall be permitted at any time." In addition, the zoning board provided in the permit that "no recreational, social, educational, or other group activities other than the conduct of religious services or Sunday school or similar school should be conducted on the premises."

Several religious school cases contain examples of rather stringent conditions upon issuance of the permit. In the Charleston, South Carolina, Baptist school case [157:459] the permit limited the attendance at the school to 270 pupils. The Baptists challenged this provision but the challenge was overruled. In the Ocean Township, New Jersey, Catholic case,[180:263] the following conditions were imposed:

1. That the exterior of the existing building not be changed or altered.

2. That the property east of the building, known as the front yard, shall be maintained in its present state of landscaping.

3. That the main entrance and exit for school purposes shall be limited to the extreme westerly portion of the property, known as the rear.

4. That any public area, playgrounds, athletic field, etc., shall be established to the rear of the existing building.

5. That St. Mary's parish would accept the children of Ocean Township who are now attending other parochial schools.

6. That St. Mary's parish install at its own cost and expense a sanitary sewer line to connect with existing school systems according to the specifications as determined by the township engineer.

7. That the convent and parochial school shall be limited to the existing main building.

Similar detailed conditions were imposed in the Montclair, New Jersey, Catholic school case [228:390] and in addition a limitation on the total attendance at the school. There was also a provision that "the auditorium-gymnasium be not used for public or private functions except Lacordaire [school] functions directly connected with and limited solely to its educational and cultural program, and . . . that Lacordaire by acceptance of the conditions shall be deemed to have agreed to abide by them so long as its premises are in a residential zone under a zoning ordinance having substantially the same limitations as are now in effect."

*Interpretation.*

When a church complains that its land is being improperly regulated, the court does not start by studying the Constitution of the United States. Instead, it must first determine whether the order complained of has the effect on the church that is charged. In the case of the Baptist church of Chico, California,[88] the plaintiff alleged violation of religious liberty because he was being restrained from "conducting church services or church functions, singing, praying, preaching or worshiping God on the premises described." The court refused to consider this constitutional question because it took a different view of the effect of the lower court's ruling. It said that the order "in no sense enjoined or restrained appellant individually from singing, praying, or worshiping God as and where he pleases." Whether or not this interpretation was correct, it determined the outcome of the case without regard to constitutional principles.

After analysis of the judicial or administrative decision complained of, the court studies the ordinance under which it is supposed to be authorized. The question is whether the city intended that the board should be permitted to exclude the church or to regulate it in the manner complained of. The court may have to consider "what is a church" under an ordinance (see Chapter 19). It may have to determine whether the conditions and standards have been complied with. A good example is the Indianapolis, Indiana, Catholic case of 1948.[62] The zoning ordinance forbade construction of any "school with living quarters maintained." In face of this prohibition the zoning board granted a permit for construction of a church plant including school and convent. The neighbors sued but the court upheld the board. By a process of reasoning that might not appeal universally (see pages 275-8) the court held that the quoted provision did not forbid the convent permit. Again, the case was decided without regard to constitutional principles.

The case of the Jewish temple at Creve Coeur, Missouri,[192] necessitated interpretation of the state enabling act. That act authorized zoning with respect to the "location and use of buildings, structures, and land, for trade, industry, residence or other purposes." Churches were not mentioned and the court refused to interpret "other purposes" as including them. In the Orchard Lake, Michigan, Catholic church and school case [94] the controlling factor was a provision in the state constitution with respect to the social value of religion. In neither of these cases was the federal constitution controlling.

It appears that in states like New York and Indiana, where it is so difficult to regulate the religious use of land, the ban on such regulation is enforced not on constitutional but on statutory grounds. Statutory interpretations are usually final at the state level while constitutional interpretations are subject to review in the federal courts. Under the "doctrine of abstention" the federal courts refrain from even passing on the constitutionality of a law until the state court has had the opportunity to do so itself. The rule was enforced by the Circuit Court of Appeals, Fifth Circuit, in the Atlanta, Georgia, Jehovah's Witnesses case.[91] By deciding on statutory grounds the state courts avoid review of their decisions by the federal judiciary.

The fact of fifty separate state judiciaries, each supreme in its field, can lead to results that to a layman seem incongruous. In the Creve Coeur, Missouri, Jewish case,[192] above mentioned, the court refused to permit regulation of churches under a statute authorizing the zoning of "buildings, structures and land for trade, industry, residence and other purposes." The rule of law is that where an enumeration of specific items is followed by a generalization like "other purposes," the generality refers only to things that are of the same kind or character (*ejusdem generis*) as those enumerated. Are churches of the same kind or character as residences? It is so contended in cases where they seek admission to residential zones. But where the result would have been to exclude them, the Missouri court found no likeness between churches and homes.

In this respect, the enabling act of Wisconsin reads exactly as did the enabling act of Missouri. Less than two years later, however, in the Bayside, Wisconsin, Baptist church case,[231] the court specifically refused to ground its action on the theory espoused by the Missouri court. Neither of these cases went to the Supreme Court of the United States. But if they had, both of the two varying interpretations of the statute might have been sustained by the high court. Although the two states have a common language, an identical statute means one thing in Wisconsin and the opposite in Missouri.

*Liberal vs. Strict Interpretation.*

The basic purpose of any court in interpreting a written document is to discover the true intent of its authors, be they the people of the state who adopted a constitution, the legislators who adopted an enabling act, the city councilmen who adopted an ordinance, or the administrative officials who entered an order. In the course of such interpretations most of the legal argument centers upon the wording of the document and whether it should be construed strictly or liberally. Thus, in the Creve Coeur case,[192] the court interpreted the word "other" strictly. In the Bayside, Wisconsin, case,[231] the court interpreted the word liberally.

The legal principles applicable to this issue are numerous and the church zoning cases are inconclusive. The same is true of legal textbooks and encyclopedias. It is held that a statute should be construed:

liberally where necessary to effectuate the actual intention of the legislature;

liberally or strictly depending on which is necessary to avoid holding the law unconstitutional;

liberally if the statute is remedial in nature;

liberally if enacted for the purpose of advancing the public welfare; but

strictly if in derogation of property or personal rights, especially the latter.

The regulation of religious land use is remedial; it is

enacted for the public welfare; it is also in derogation to greater or lesser extent of property and personal rights. While the courts in general avoid theoretical discussions of this point, it seems that in most cases they make liberal or strict interpretations depending on which approach is more apt to favor the church.

The reasoning behind this policy appears in the Creve Coeur, Missouri, decision.[192] In holding that a church was not an "other purpose," the court said that "freedom of religion is one of the fundamental freedoms protected by the bill of rights of both our federal and state constitutions." Referring to the First Amendment, the court said: "In view of its absolute prohibition, we do not believe our legislature, in using the language it did, . . . had any intention of granting authority to municipalities to restrict location and use of buildings and land for churches. . . . It certainly has not specifically stated any such authority, as there is no mention of religious or church purposes either in the act or in its title. Therefore the phrase, 'other purposes,' as used in this context, should not be broadened by construction to include use of property for religious purposes by religious organizations whose rights to free exercise of religion are protected by such constitutional guaranties."

This leaning over backward to interpret statutes favorably to churches is very common. Perhaps the most flagrant example is the case of the Catholic regional high school at Cheltenham Township, Pennsylvania, decided in 1957.[162] The court was called on to determine the meaning of an ordinance which provided, among other things, that "in interpreting and applying the provisions of this ordinance, *they* shall be held to *be* the minimum requirements for the protection of the health, safety, morals and general welfare of the township." (My italics.) The court said that the ordinance should be strictly construed and [162:594] that "it is this section which provides sufficient appropriate conditions and safeguards controlling the board's discretion." In other words, the court interpreted this section as contracting rather than expanding the discretion of the board. It seems that to do so it had to disregard entirely the word "be" italicized in the above quotation. It also had to interpret the word "they" as if it referred to administrative authorities rather than to the provisions of the ordinance. Otherwise this clause would be interpreted as broadening, not narrowing, the power of the board.

The Pennsylvania court treated the clause as a kind of manacle on the wrists of the administrators. This interpretation colored the entire decision and governed the result. One of the grounds given for excluding the proposed school was the expected increase in traffic problems. The court said [162:598] that "the discretion of the board could be constitutionally exercised only within the standards provided in the ordinance," and that the justification of traffic control failed "by reason of the fact that the evidence is insufficient to show a high degree of probability that the anticipated increase in traffic will adversely affect the health or safety of the community."

Thus in Cheltenham Township a regional high school was permitted, to accommodate 2,000 students, together with a faculty house, three convents, etc. In the Milwaukie, Oregon, decision of the following year [184] an almost exactly similar ordinance was interpreted "liberally." The court sustained exclusion of a Jehovah's Witness Kingdom Hall. Congregations of Jehovah's Witnesses are uniformly held down to about 200 people.

*Severability.*

Another phase of statutory interpretation which sometimes assumes importance is called, variously, the problem of severability, separability, or divisibility of the various parts and applications of a law. Oftentimes, for example, churches invoke, not the general provisions of the law, but an exception. If an exception is held unconstitutional, the question arises: Is the general clause to which it is attached also void? The importance of this issue is shown in the discussion of the Portland, Oregon, Catholic school case,[27] the Bronxville, New York, Lutheran college case,[82] and the Orange, New Jersey, seminary case [92,99] in Chapter 20. The general purpose, again, is to determine the intention of the framers. What must be decided is, if they knew that the one clause would fail, whether they would have wanted the other to remain in effect.

The same principle is important when a law is voided with

respect to its application to a particular situation or set of facts. The courts may read into the law an exception covering those situations that the legislature is constitutionally power-less to govern, leaving the statute in effect to the extent it is valid. In church zoning cases judges sometimes neglect to indicate clearly whether they are holding a provision generally void or only as it relates to the case before the court. This has led to considerable confusion. However, in New York and Indiana, the two courts most unfriendly to religious land use regulation have carefully indicated that the factual situations covered by their decisions are separable from other factual situations that may arise in future cases. At page 126 I have shown how carefully the Indiana court in the Decatur Jeho-vah's Witnesses case [104] specified that its decision was appli-cable only to the case at bar. The same can be said of the decision of the New York Court of Appeals in the Brighton case [149] where it said that "an ordinance constitutional on its face (or deemed so) may be construed and applied in an unconstitutional manner. If the construction of an ordinance as applied to a particular piece of property and a particular set of facts is arbitrary and unreasonable and results in invasion of property rights, the act of the zoning board thereunder will be invalidated." The converse is probably also true, namely that an ordinance invalidated with respect to the Brighton situation could be treated as valid in the circum-stances of some future case.

In his standard work on zoning law, Yokley says it is important that the zoning power be "exercised pursuant to the zoning enabling statute." [96§184] He adds that "any municipal-ity attempting to deviate and depart from this fixed rule is heading for the same trouble the master of a ship invites were he to deliberately ground his vessel on a rocky reef." Thus he dramatizes the importance of interpretation of documents and statutes other than the Constitution of the United States. Likewise, in the consideration of precedents, a careful distinc-tion should be made between those cases that are based on the interpretation of the United States Constitution and those that are based on the interpretation of orders, ordinances, laws, or state constitutions.

# CHAPTER 19.

## WHAT IS A CHURCH?

Definitions are always important in litigation based on statutes. The question "what is a church?" is an important and embarassing one for the courts. The American principle of separation of church and state forbids official recognition of any religion. Judges also seem a little hesitant and clumsy in defining religious terms as that becomes necessary from time to time in connection with the interpretation of zoning laws.

Many of the states and communities have provided in zoning laws for special or separate rights and privileges for religious activity. It is mainly in this connection that the terms, "church", "religious", etc. must be defined by the courts. In addition the question becomes important in those courts which have adopted the constitutional anti-exclusion rule discussed in Chapter 3, whether in its absolute form which prevents the exclusion of churches from any residential zone, or in its less absolute form which forbids their exclusion from an entire city or "practically" an entire city.

A review of the various courts' answers to this question provides a view of the fascinating spectrum of judicial opinion that can radiate from a single simple legal issue. Usually, the term to be defined is "church" but the courts have also discussed the meaning of terms like: parish house, parochial school, parsonage, place of worship, convent, priests' mansion, "protestant church," rectory, religious and educational buildings, religious use, sisters' home, and "strictly religious use." One statute authorized a "community center" attached to a church, and the courts have passed on such questions as whether churches are included in "commercial" or "industrial" purposes, etc. They also have had to interpret ordinances which authorized uses prescribed by "the disciplines, rules and usages" of particular denominations.

Facilities sought to be included within the scope of religious exemptions were not only churches, but also synagogues, convents or sisters' homes, parsonages or priests' mansions,

271

parochial or Sunday schools, and parking lots. They included Boy Scout and Girl Scout and youth group facilities, recreational buildings, small games areas and hard top play areas, playgrounds, facilities for corporate meetings and meetings of sisterhood and men's groups, dormitories (including overnight sleeping quarters for retreatants) a conference center, community services, group activities, Red Cross work, camp meetings, tent services, an outdoor amphitheater, gymnasiums and swimming pools, healing rooms, a *mikvah* or ritualarium for ceremonial bathing, cemeteries, and a Grange hall. One court saw fit to caution that while much would be conceded, the religious institution proposed in the particular case could not be turned into a place of entertainment "such as a country club."

Webster's Dictionary [190] defines a "church" as: "1. A building for public worship, esp. Christian worship. 2. Church service, divine worship. 3. The organization of Christianity, as in a nation; esp. ecclesiastical power or government. 4. The clerical profession. 5. The collective body of Christians. 6. A body of Christian believers having the same creed, rites, etc.; a denomination, as the Presbyterian Church. 7. Any body of worshippers; a religious society."

The same dictionary defines "religion" as: "1. The service or adoration of God, or a god, expressed in forms of worship. 2. One of the systems of faith and worship. 3. The profession or practice of religious believers, religious observances collectively; pl. rites. 4. Devotion or fidelity, conscientiousness. 5. An awareness or conviction of the existence of a supreme being, arousing reverence, love, gratitude, the will to obey and serve, and the like; as man, only, is capable of religion."

One of the earliest of the zoning cases mentioned in this volume, the 1927 Evanston, Illinois, Episcopal seminary case,[19] has occasionally been cited as helping to define the scope of religious exemptions both statutory and constitutional. It is true that a question arose there whether the term "school and college buildings," as used in a zoning ordinance, was broad enough to include proposed "dormitories." The court held that it was. This ruling is used in an article in *St. John's Law Review* [95:99] to support the theory that "the parish house, school and convent accompany the church as a matter of right." The ruling referred not to a church, nor even to a church college, but to colleges in general.

A 1930 case skirted the issue more closely. This was the Church of God case at Beckley, West Virginia.[25] The pastor wanted to build a church but was refused a permit because his lot was in a residential zone and because the ordinance forbade any "public garage, filling station, store or other industry of any kind or character." The court decided—as would now seem obvious—that a church is not properly included under such a classification and that the board had no authority to exclude this church.

Fifteen years later, in a Philadelphia, Pennsylvania, synagogue case [51] another attempt was made to delineate the legal characteristics of a church for zoning purposes. The decision had only a limited effect, namely, that the use of the building by the rabbi as both home and synagogue did not take it out of the classification of "churches" as authorized by the ordinance. The objectors to the permit said that the ordinance authorized fourteen types of uses, including both home and synagogue, but insisted that each use must be separate, not in combination with one of the others. If the authorized uses were allowed to be combined, the neighbors insisted, then "all 14 types of use might take place simultaneously in the same building."

The court held that under the law the uses might be combined as long as they were not incongruous. The opinion said that "there is obvious incongruity in 14 different types of uses in one building, or in having a residence over a railroad passenger station, or over a public museum or over a public utility. But there is no such incongruity in having a dwelling over a church or attached to a church in any way." Mention was made of those "well-known religious sects which erect no churches as such but conduct divine service in the homes of their communicants." The maintenance of the home and synagogue in the same building not being incongruous, the rabbi obtained his permit. There had been an earlier case at Pittsburgh [46] which also concerned a combination synagogue and residence but the result there depended upon the interpretation of different terms of the ordinance.

The Beckley case [25] had distinguished between religion and industry. The difference between religious and commercial uses was touched on in the Montgomery, Alabama, Pentecostal Holiness church case of 1946.[56] The ordinance excluded from the residential district "any store, filling station, automobile laundry, garage, or any other type of building to be used for commercial purposes." The objecting neighbors tried to bring the church within this definition by distinguishing between "established" churches and those of some other unspecified type, presumably those operated for private profit.

They contended that the Pentecostal church was "not an established church," but that it represented a "commercial enterprise by the so-called pastor of such organization who is directly interested in the financial return thereof." They added that "such church does not have a creed of worship in the usual sense of the word, but that their services consist of appeals to passion and emotion and in an attempt to inculcate emotional frenzy resulting in manifestations of a disorderly and sacrilegious nature."

The justices were reluctant to get into this kind of argument. The neighbors, said the opinion, had "attempted to inject into the case the difference in the doctrine between this church and other churches, and proved only the fact that the method of offering prayer in this church permitted all members to pray at the same time if they desired." The proof failed, said the court, "to show that the doctrine and practices of this church were in anywise such as would bar it from the claim that it was a protestant church and entitled to the ordinary considerations as such." As shown at pages 193-4 the implication that a "protestant" church is entitled, as the neighbors had contended, to classification separate from other churches for zoning purposes seems improper.

In the Creve Coeur, Missouri, Jewish temple case,[192] the court held that a church was not included in the classification of "trade, industry, residence or other purposes." However, it indicated that a parochial school might be included thereunder. And in the Bayside, Wisconsin, Baptist church case,[231] the supreme court of that state rejected the reasoning of the Missouri court and included both church and school thereunder. These two cases have been discussed at length at pages 266-7.

The cases above cited help to define the word "church" by

comparing churches with other things. They show a certain similarity or congruity between churches and homes, and a certain dissimilarity or incongruity between churches and business institutions. Much more important, however, are the cases which define the concept by expanding or limiting the scope of church activities intended to be covered by the law. No one doubts that the term includes the basic religious activities of prayer and preaching and worship. The controversies usually arise when attempts are made to include such things as recreation, fellowship, and education. These are the fields in which the churches sometimes compete with secular agencies, private and public.

The first case concerning this problem was the Indianapolis, Indiana, Methodist church case [57] decided in 1946. The ordinance authorized permits to churches in residential zones in accordance with certain standards. The Fifty-First Street Methodist Church and the Meridian Street Methodist Church were seeking to merge and build a new "large" Methodist church on a block-square tract. Included in their plan were not only a church building but also a parking lot, gymnasium, recreation building, playground and outside amphitheater. The board of zoning appeals granted a permit but the neighbors took the case as far as the appellate court.

The court sustained the permit, saying that "the right to erect and use a modern church building may, in a proper case, such as the one before us, include a parking lot for the use of members in attending church services and any meetings held by the church and all such rooms and facilities under one roof as ordinarily form and constitute a part of the building, equipment, and are deemed necessary, or useful, in connection with a modern church of the particular denomination involved."

Note the use of the word "deemed." The opinion did not specify who was to "deem" the additional uses "necessary or useful." But later cases made it clear that the church itself was to have this authority. Justice Hamilton, who wrote the opinion above quoted, also wrote the opinion in the Indianapolis Catholic case of 1948. There the applicant was the Catholic archbishop. He wanted [62:598] a "combination unit" consisting of "Catholic church, priests' mansion, a convent or sisters' home, school, and off-street parking facility" on a vacant lot at 301-59 East 57th Street. The school and church were directly authorized under separate sections of the ordinance. However, it provided that any school should be "without living quarters maintained."

The neighboring property owners objected only to the convent. The zoning board overruled the objection and granted the permit in full as requested. The lower court overruled the board, but the appellate court reinstated the permit. Justice Hamilton got around the clause forbidding living quarters by insisting that the convent was included under the term "church."

The court [62:600] delved into the history of the Catholic Church in America in some detail. The decision explained the Catholic "plan . . . to take care of the needs of both body and soul of individuals." Since early times, the opinion said, "when a Catholic church was established, a school was also established as soon as possible. . . . Wherever there was a church, there was also a school." The court concluded that a "sisters' home" must be considered an "integral part of any Roman Catholic church project, which is composed of four component parts, viz: church, priests' mansion, a 'sisters' home' and school." *

I do not mean to suggest that it was either proper or improper for the council to have excluded "living quarters" in connection with schools. But I question the correctness of the decision which, without raising this question, nullified the provision only insofar as it concerned Catholic parochial schools. The court relied on the history and practices of the Catholic Church. In a sense, the court was being nonsectarian, having made the same mistake in a Methodist case a year or so earlier.[57]

The same issue came to the Supreme Court of Indiana in 1961 in the Meridian Hills Catholic church and school case.[229] The Meridian Hills ordinance had authorized both churches and schools and had mentioned nothing about "living quar-

---

* Priests' residences are not always considered to be religious institutions. There are a number of cases, for instance *Missionaries v. Whitefish Bay*,[110] where a residence for a number of priests having no family relation to each other was treated as a "one-family" residence. See also References Nos. 45 and 145.

ters." The board of zoning appeals denied the application of Archbishop Paul C. Schulte on various grounds. Whether the whole "combination" came under the definitions of the ordinance seems not to have been principally in issue.

The court went out of its way, however, to say [229:42] that "in this state it has been decided that facilities that go with the church of the particular denomination may not be excluded if the church is admittable. For example, a recreation building and playground in connection with the Meridian Street Methodist Church . . . and a sisters' home for the teachers in a Catholic church-school. . . ." A concurring opinion added that "activities or building which are, by tradition and custom, integral or component parts of a particular church or house of worship may not be excluded."

The Indiana Supreme Court had gone a step farther than did the two appellate court decisions. It held that if the ordinance allowed churches it could not exclude the other items. The appellate court decisions had held only that the council did not intend to exclude them. But note in each case the reference to the "particular denomination involved." In other words, in the Methodist case, the law would be one thing or another depending on what was to be found in the Methodist Discipline. In a Catholic case, the law would depend on what might be found in the official Canon Law, the pronouncements of the bishops, etc.

It seems that the customs of all religions are entitled to consideration when courts determine what the legislature or city council means by the word "church." But once its meaning is established, the regulation should apply equally to all churches. There should be no legally enforced difference between the Methodists and the Catholics. Under the Indiana rule, presumably, the Methodists would not be allowed, for instance, to set up a parochial school because it has not been their custom in the past.

For the law to be applicable denomination by denomination, depending on the denomination's own "law," is an improper delegation of law-making power to ecclesiastical authorities. It violates our traditional separation of church and state. It also leads the court into peculiar byways. For instance, I wonder on what page of the Methodist Discipline the judge in the 1946 case [57] found the requirement that all (Methodist) facilities be "under one roof." And how did he manage to get that outdoor amphitheater under the roof?

In 1947 the Supreme Court of Michigan [60] had to pass on whether the activities of an ecclesiastical corporation called the "Full Salvation Union" came within the statutory definition of a "church" or of "uses accessory to a church." In fixing the meaning of those words, no consideration was given to the rules, regulations and customs of the "particular denomination."

The ordinance of the Township of Portage [60:299] authorized churches in its rural residential area, as well as schools, farming and truck gardening, nurseries and greenhouses, golf courses and other enterprises, together with "uses accessory to those expressly enumerated." The Full Salvation Union owned a sizable piece of land on which it had constructed a tabernacle under a duly granted permit. A caretaker's home was also built, though it is not clear whether the permit for it was as a residence or as an adjunct to the tabernacle. The Union constructed a number of buildings which the township authorities called "shacks" for temporary use by worshipers during camp meetings. It also set up tents for the same purpose. The small buildings and tents did not comply with the sanitary regulations.

The township brought suit for an injunction requiring their removal and the order was issued. The Union took the case to the Supreme Court of Michigan but the injunction was affirmed. The Union contended that the small buildings and tents were accessory to the tabernacle. Considering this contention separately from the violation of sanitary regulations, the court held that the ordinance authorizing churches was not intended to authorize camp meetings.

The customs, traditions and "canon law," if any, of the Full Salvation Union are unfamiliar to me. I assume, however, that the camp meeting was a regular practice of the Union. It is part of the historic tradition of Christianity, weather permitting, throughout this country. And similar meetings were held in the first century. At one of the most famous of these, the miracle of the loaves and fishes is reported to have occurred.

These traditions and customs were disregarded by the

Michigan court. Instead,[60:300] it quoted a strictly secular source, Webster's Dictionary. It disregarded the secondary meanings [190] listed above on page 272 and defined a church as "a building set apart for worship, esp. Christian worship." The injunction requiring removal of the buildings was affirmed.

However, the Michigan court receded a long way from the single building concept in the Orchard Lake Catholic church and school case [94] decided five years later. There, a permit was granted to the archbishop for the usual combination of separate buildings. The contrast between the Portage and Orchard Lake cases has been discussed at pages 194-7.

In 1950 a trial court in Pittsburgh, Pennsylvania, decided the case of a retreat house of the Catholic Third Order of St. Francis.[81] It relied not on a definition made by the church but upon a definition adopted by the particular order within the church. This case goes as far as any in delegating to a religious body the power to determine what activities it may conduct on restricted land. Its whole theory was later repudiated by the supreme court of the same state, so it is of comparatively little real use as precedent. However it is cited by other writers on church zoning. I will discuss it briefly here.

The ordinance of Pittsburgh [81:186] provided in this particular district for (1) one-family dwellings; (2) churches; (3) libraries and museums; (4) greenhouses (as accessory buildings); and (5) accessory uses customarily incident to the specified uses. The Order acquired property on Beechwood Boulevard between Reynolds Street and Hastings Street. It contained a large house and building that formerly had been used as a stable and servants' sleeping quarters. It was located among "other expensive single family dwellings."

The grantor of the property first applied for a permit to use it as a "church, chapel, and retreat house." This was clearly not authorized, so the application was refused. Thereupon a new application was filed, which was granted, for use of the main building as a church. This church, it seems, was unrelated to the parish in which it was located and did not serve the people of that parish. The reason for locating it there did not appear until six years later when the Order filed a new application asking for a permit to use the rear building as a "dormitory for retreatants during closed spiritual retreats."

The Order was seeking to obtain, in the form of two permits, what had been refused in the form of one. The new permit was granted.

Objecting neighbors took the case to court. They contended that retreatants' sleeping quarters were not customary as accessories to churches under Catholic or any other tradition. The court held that "the evidence abundantly supports that position." [81:186] However, the court sustained the permit, holding that "the term 'church' properly construed in the light of the constitutional guaranties of freedom of religion requires the issuance of the permit."

The Pittsburgh court had gone farther than any of the Indiana decisions above discussed. It rejected the Webster definition. It even rejected the Catholic Canon Law definition.[81:180] Instead, it said that "it is a matter solely for the decision and judgment of the Order itself and not a matter of practice, or custom, of other religions, or even of groups or sects or orders within the same religion." The court added [81:187] that "the principle of freedom of religion . . . does not vest the authority in any public body to determine definitely what is or is not a church. Any building in which a religious group or sect worships Almighty God according to its own practice is a church."

Churches should be free to define for purposes of their own internal government what activity comes within their proper scope. But the definition in the Pittsburgh zoning ordinance was not for that purpose. It was intended to fix the type of ativities that could be conducted on restricted land. On this subject, the decision in the Pittsburgh Catholic case made the Franciscan Order a "law into itself." The opinion is carefully written. It covers 25 pages. It is full of quotable passages. But it is a weak precedent because its basic concepts were later rejected by the supreme court of the same state in the Russian Orthodox cemetery case of 1959.[207]

The Jewish religion was again involved before the courts of New Jersey in the Newark ritualarium case of 1951. The decision was written by a trial court [89] but it was adopted in full by the appellate division during the following year.[94A] Again the court took a restrictive view of the meaning of the term, church. It considered the traditions of the Jewish faith, but did not permit them to control the final result.

The ordinance of Newark authorized the construction of churches in residential zones, and "accessory uses customarily incident thereto." It provided that an "accessory use" had to be one that was conducted on the same lot as the use to which it is accessory." The congregation wanted a permit to alter a one-family residence at 130 Renner Avenue and install a *mikvah* or ritualarium in the basement. The *mikvah* is a ceremonial bath used by Jewish ladies for purposes of spiritual purification before marriage. Although, both before and since, various secular bathing facilities have been permitted as accessories to churches and religious centers, the New Jersey court rejected this particular type of religious rite.

The building inspector had issued the permit treating the *mikvah* not as an accessory but as a church. The neighboring owners asked for an injunction against the work. The court consulted a booklet issued by the Union of Orthodox Jewish Congregations of America. It quoted the Jewish religious law which provides that when a community has insufficient means to provide both a *mikvah* and synagogue, the *mikvah* must take precedence. The ritualarium thus has at least as high standing in orthodox Jewish practice as has the parochial school among American Catholics. The rite is called Tevilah, a "religious experience giving the woman the seal of sacredness and respect."

The booklet said that "a Jewess who does not perform Tevilah in a proper mikvah cannot be called a true Jewish wife." The applicants contended that "where an edifice is devoted wholly to the observance of a religious rite, worship of the Deity is being performed, and that therefore a church exists." To the contrary, the neighbors contended that "one could as well argue that an abbatoir wherein animals and poultry are slaughtered in accordance with certain rites of the Jewish religion is a church."

The court referred to Webster's lexicographic bible and to some previous New Jersey decisions on the subject. It considered the opinions in the Pittsburgh Catholic retreat house case [81] and in the Indianapolis Catholic church and school case [62] and attempted to distinguish them. It sustained the injunction on the basis of the points made by the objectors.

Another comparatively obscure religious corporation, called Jack Coe, Inc., was refused a permit for a Protestant evangelistic center in Dallas, Texas,[102] on the theory that its proposed building was not a "church." The court considered that if the institution was a church, the permit must be granted. It does not make clear in its decision whether this determination was based on some statutory provision or on constitutional grounds. The parties seem to have agreed that churches must be permitted. The ruling is discussed at pages 199-200. On the question of whether the institution was a church, the court's exact words were:

> The facts . . . showed some 2400 square feet devoted to healing rooms or prayer rooms and only 600 square feet for the auditorium or church proper. Although [Coe] testified that there would be only thirty to a hundred people at services, still he claimed a membership of from 700 to 1100. His own testimony showed a history and practice of healing and tent services with loud speakers and Hammond organ.
>
> He admitted parking his five or six big trailers on the premises. Appellant here is a corporation composed of Rev. Coe, his wife, and his sister as the incorporators, and including de Cordova, described as a business manager. We feel therefore that the city council was within its authority in finding that this proposed building was not a church and that the trial court had ample grounds for finding to the same effect. The building not being a church, there was no question of the council's authority to refuse the permit under the zoning ordinance.

I have previously said in another connection that the opinion does not supply a reasonable basis for the decision. The factors mentioned are not sufficient to disqualify the institution as a church.

The importance of definitions, both legislative and judicial, was demonstrated by three New York cases all of which were pending in various courts at the same time between 1955 and 1957. These were the Brighton Catholic case,[123,131,138,149] the Sands Point Jewish case,[129,148] and the Garden City Jewish case.[150,154]

In the Brighton case, the ordinance provided [149:829] for "educational or religious buildings." In the Sands Point case, the ordinance provided [148:491] for:

> A church for public worship and other strictly religious uses *and* in accordance with the discipline, rules and usages of the religious corporation which will own, support, and maintain it. (Italics mine.)

The Garden City ordinance [150:526] defined a permissible church as:

> A structure used for public worship and other strictly religious uses in accordance with the discipline, rules and usages of a religious corporation which owns, supports and maintains the same and of the ecclesiastical governing body, if any, to which such corporation is subject.

Note the omission of the word "and" from the Garden City ordinance and its use (italicized) in the Sands Point regulation. This became important in the decisions of the cases.

The application of the Catholic diocese in the Brighton case [149:827] was for a "church; school; meeting room; kindergarten; small games, open field and hardtop play areas; and parking lot, which would accommodate 144 cars." The application was considered not only in the administrative agencies but in four different court decisions. The objectors alleged [149:832] that the proposed playground, parking lot and "other combined uses" were not authorized by the ordinance.

The court observed that "the accessory uses proposed by the diocese, which are allowed by the ordinance, are within the scope of a church's activities." In support of this conclusion the court cited passages from its own Sands Point decision of the same day,[148] also passages from the Indianapolis, Indiana, Catholic case [62] and from the Indianapolis, Indiana, Methodist case.[57] Unlike the Indiana court, it showed no inclination to base the definition of "church" on the private laws of the church itself.

In New York, the delegation of lawmaking power to religious groups seems to have been effectuated by the municipal councils, not by the courts. In the Sands Point ordinance the italicized word "and," if given any meaning at all, clearly indicates that the church may conduct activities on restricted land over and above the "public worship and other strictly religious uses" expressly authorized. The nature of these additional activities is to be determined, it seems, not by the council but by the church.

The absence of the word "and" in the Garden City ordinance at that particular place gives the passage an opposite twist. It means that petitioning churches may obtain permits only for activities which are sanctioned by their own rules, and which also come within the statutory discription. Both these approaches seem inconsistent with separation of church and state, but especially the Sands Point provision which gives the religious denominations the last word on what kinds of activities will be permitted in the restricted area.

The Sands Point Community Synagogue had acquired a large tract of land in that swank suburb. It asked permission to use it for a "church for public worship and other strictly religious uses and in accordance with the discipline, rules, and usages of the religious corporation which owns, supports, and maintains such church and of the ecclesiastical governing body to which that corporation is subject, together with a church or Sunday school to be conducted by said religious corporation and in accordance with the following statement of principles. . . ." The terms used are exactly the same as the ordinance, including that key word "and."

The certificate of incorporation of the synagogue was attached. One interesting clause provided for "education, social welfare activities and such other means as shall serve to convey the teachings of Judaism." A statement of principles was also filed which, among other things, stated that the synagogue was a "place of fellowship and friendship among its adherents, wherein there is present a men's group, a sisterhood (women's group) and a junior high school age group, and that the synagogue is also a place where services for the community are performed, such as Red Cross work, Boy Scout work, and the work of other such organizations." [148:492]

The contention of the zoning officials of Sands Point was that these statements demonstrated an intention to use the premises for purposes other than those authorized in the ordinance. The court of appeals quoted the ordinance and italicized, as I have, the word "and." The court said that it could not agree with the board's stand, adding [148:493] that:

> A church is more than merely an edifice affording people the opportunity to worship God. Strictly religious uses and activities are more than prayer and sacrifice. All churches recognize that the area of their responsibility is broader than leading the congregation in prayer. Churches have always developed social groups for adults and youth where the fellowship of the congregation is strengthened with the result that the parent church is strengthened.
>
> We find evidence of this in the Old Testament. When a member of a congregation cements a friendship with other members of the congregation, the church benefits and becomes stronger. It is a religious activity for the church to provide a place for these social groups to meet since the church by doing so is developing into a stronger and closer knit religious unit. To limit a church to being merely a house of prayer and sacrifice would, in a large degree, be depriving the church of the opportunity for enlarging, perpetuating, and strengthening itself and the congregation.

Under the ordinance as worded, this reasoning is basically sound. However, the purpose of a zoning ordinance is not to "limit the area of responsibility" of a church. Neither is it to "limit a church to being merely a house of prayer and sacrifice." Its purpose is merely to regulate the uses to which particular areas of land may be devoted.

The court of appeals may have had misgivings about the effect of its decision as precedent in future cases for it added:

> It is true that the religious aim of strengthening the congregation through fellowship may not be permitted to be perverted into a justification for establishing a place of entertainment, such as a country club, but the facts clearly show that there is no such attempt here, and each case ultimately rests upon its own facts.

The Garden City case [150,154] was decided in the trial court and never considered in the court of appeals. This zoning board seemed also to be slightly suspicious that the congregation was planning to conduct other than "strictly religious" activities as described in the ordinance. However, its rejection of the proposed center was based on various grounds not connected with that suspicion. The court found these grounds insufficient and overturned the board's decision. The case was returned to the board "for the purpose of the issuance of the use permit upon such administrative conditions as the board deems reasonable and necessary." At this point the board seems to have acted on the basis of its suspicions. It issued the permit subject to a proviso that "no recreational, social, educational, or other group activities other than conduct of religious services or Sunday school or similar school should be conducted on the premises."

The congregation appealed again—perhaps thereby confirming the neighbors' suspicions—and insisted that the clause above quoted should be stricken out. The court gave the religious group only partial satisfaction. It refused to change the board's decision but issued a statement for the guidance of enforcement officials. It quoted passages from the Sands Point decision [148] and said:

> The court may not assume that the municipal authorities will disregard the pronouncement of our highest court and give to the Board's decision a construction which would prevent the petitioner from holding corporate meetings, meetings of the congregation's sisterhood and men's club, or meetings of the boy and girl scouts composed of children of the congregation.

This ruling is notable as much for what it omits as for what it says. It must have been considered a mixed blessing by the congregation. It mentioned the "congregation's" sisterhood and men's club, also the Boy and Girl Scout groups "composed of children of the congregation," thereby presumably excluding outsiders. Whether or not the zoning board intended to limit the use made of the property, certainly the court did so. It omitted all reference to "social welfare work," to "work for the benefit of the community," to Red Cross work, etc., etc.

Temple Israel of Lawrence, New York, induced another trial judge [173] to permit a gymnasium and swimming pool for the use of the congregation in connection with a religious school. The decision contains some interesting additional observations, but it was overturned by the appellate division. [195]

Two cases involved the question of whether a sign is a proper adjunct of a church erected in a residential area. The

Believers of Islam of Chicago [188] were denied by zoning authorities a permit to erect a certain type of sign. The case was carried to the Apellate Court of Illinois, which refused to pass on the issue because of failure of the "Black Moslems" to file their papers on time. A few months later, the Supreme Court of Colorado considered a similar question in the case of the Parkview Baptist Church of Pueblo.[196] The court held that an ordinance authorizing construction of churches and "any use customarily incidental thereto" authorized by implication the erection of an identifying sign. The quarrel seems to have arisen not so much from the sign as such but from the fact that it was neon-lighted, 27 square feet in size, and placed a considerable distance from the church. The court forbade the city council or zoning board to interfere with the sign.

In the case of the Wartburg Theological Seminary at Dubuque, Iowa,[197] the American Lutheran Church sought to establish a "dormitory" for married students and their families under an ordinance which permitted "educational, religious, or philanthropic use, excluding business school and college or correctional institutions." The ordinance also authorized "accessory use on the same lot with and customarily incident to any of the above permitted uses." With this and a few other exceptions, the area was restricted to single family residences. Apartment houses were consigned to a separate area.

The proposed dormitory was on the same campus with the college, but a property owner objected that otherwise it was no different from an apartment house. The objector had recently built a $100,000 house nearby. The proposed building of the Lutherans was one of a series of such "dormitories" planned by the Church.

The Lutherans contended that "the wording of the ordinance is plainly directed to the use to be made of the land and buildings. . . . The plain words provide for the use not the particular type of building. It follows that a building that may be used as an apartment house . . . is not so used when in fact it is being used as a married students' dormitory." The court sustained the Lutherans' position, properly relying on the Episcopal seminary case at Evanston, Illinois,[19,23] cited herein at pages 272-3.

A similar line of reasoning was invoked to justify the use of a large estate including a fine lakefront at Cazenovia, New York, for a Protestant Episcopal project which the municipal officials called [218:941] a "conference center" but which the Episcopalians called a "religious education center for adults and selected teenage youths, including a series of programs of supervised study, seminars, contemplation and training, with emphasis on Christian living and service." The ordinance authorized use of land in the district for single-family homes and, in addition, any "church or similar place of worship, parish house, public school, parochial school, etc." It also authorized a "rectory" and "convent".

The Episcopal diocese contended that "all zoning ordinances, including the one here under attack, are drawn to control functions and activities and not merely to regulate the form that stone and mortar and wood should take." A trial court sustained this position stated, saying: [218:944]

> Naked dictionary meaning of separate words should not be allowed to distort intent. Verbiage should convey—not dominate—meaning. The uses proposed certainly come within the true intent of the ordinance, i. e. to permit places of worship, schools, and to allow buildings for community living for the purpose of religious study, education, fellowship and contemplation. It cannot be denied that even under a strict and literal interpretation of the applicable ordinance, "Thornfield" could be used as an edifice for worship (a church), or as a place of instruction maintained by a religious body (a parochial school), or as a center for social life of members of a religious faith (a parish house), or as an abode for persons devoted to particular religious life (a convent or monastery). The Diocese should not be denied the right to use "Thornfield" for these various purposes, even though the proposed programs do not exactly coincide with dictionary definitions of the uses enumerated by the zoning ordinance.

The Cazenovia ordinance seems to have been couched in terms of Roman Catholic practices. The court merely applied the same to Episcopal practices which it considered different only in form. The decision was sustained without opinion by the appellate division [234] and leave to appeal to the court of appeals was denied.[236]

On the question of definitions, some additional Pennsylvania cases are also of interest. Already discussed is the decision in the Pittsburgh Catholic case [81] which approved conversion of a stable, located in a high class residential area, into sleeping quarters for retreatants. This decision practically permitted the religious order to determine the meaning of the word, "church," as used in the law. This position was utterly rejected by the supreme court of the same state in the case of the Russian Orthodox church at Rochester Township, [207] where the church sought use of the land as a cemetery.

A distinction can be made between the temporary sleeping quarters for which a permit was granted in the Pittsburgh case and the quarters for more permanent sleep for which a permit was refused the Russian Orthodox in Rochester Township. However, the decision was based on profounder issues. The arguments of the majority and minority judges highlight the difference between those who would give conclusive weight to the "precepts of the church" and those who believe that they are only incidental to more secular considerations. The ordinance authorized any "educational, religious, philanthropic use and hospital." The church insisted that the proposed cemetery was a "religious use."

Historically graveyards were attached to churches. But times have changed, as well as our ideas about sanitation. No church would now seek to establish a graveyard in a center of population. That is not what the Orthodox sought. The area was a rural district. Nevertheless, since it was "rural—residential," the court decided against the proposed use.

The majority said [207:400] that the word, "religious" is one of "nebulous bounds" and "depends for its definition, if construed in the abstract, upon the subjective criteria used by the definer." The court refused to adopt such subjective criteria as the laws of a particular church. Instead, it took a "look at the general purpose of zoning and the zoning ordinance itself." It pointed out that if a business corporation had purchased the 88 acres for use as a cemetery, it would no doubt be excluded. The Russian Orthodox church argued that "the place of burial and burial rites are important elements within the dogma of its religion."

If this were accepted, the court indicated, a slaughterhouse owned by a business would not be permitted while the same slaughterhouse owned by a religious sect requiring that animals be slaughtered in a certain way would be permitted. Thus, without mentioning it, the court recalled the reasoning of the Newark, New Jersey, ritualarium case [89] discussed at pages 222-3. The court in the Russian Orthodox case said: [207:491]

> We believe that a cemetery is basically a secular use of land. . . . We do not believe that the fact that the land will be owned by a religious institution alters the basic secular use to be made thereof, and we would be most reluctant to construe the ordinance so as to make a distinction not found therein based upon the nature of the owners of the land rather than the nature of the use to be made of the land. Any secular use, under [the Church's] contention, can be capable of a religious characterization if a particular sect ascribes religious implications thereto.

Justice McBride filed a well written dissenting opinion emphasizing the precepts of the Russian Orthodox Church which require that burial be in consecrated or sacred ground. He said that there is a religious rite for the burial of the dead required by the ecclesiastical laws and canons of the church and that "a church cemetery is a religious use of land in the opinion of the clergymen of the church."

The ordinary citizen's attitude on this fine point was expressed by one of the witnesses and by a member of the zoning board, both quoted in McBride's opinion. The witness was asked [207:492] if he believed that burying the dead was a religious use. He answered that "I think I would be an awful heathen if I didn't." One of the zoning commissioners said that "a cemetery can be considered a religious function . . . because it does state in the Bible to bury the dead; but I cannot possibly believe that the men who drew up this zoning ordinance meant that a beautiful home should have a cemetery next door as a religious purpose. If they would have believed that a cemetery should be in a residential area, they would have said so." The majority of the court agreed with this simple reasoning. By applying secular, as distinguished from ecclesiastical, standards, it upheld the action of the board.

The decision in the Mt. Lebanon, Pennsylvania, Grange case [208] was written by the same Justice McBride who dissented in the Orthodox case. All justices concurred. The ordinance authorized any "church and additions thereto, including parish house, parsonage, sisterhouse, and the like, when adjoining and under auspices of the church" and any "community center when operated by and within, adjoining or attached to, a church or school." It seems that the Grange bought the old church on the assumption that it could be used for lodge meetings. The organization told the court that it would face a serious financial loss if it could not be so used. However, the court sustained the refusal of the zoning board to issue a permit for the new use.

The lodge contended [208] that their "use of the building was substantially similar to the use of the building as a church." But Justice McBride's opinion held that such use "would be a new and decidedly different nonconforming use and certainly one of a lower classification under the zoning ordinance." He said that the National Grange "nowhere makes any claim or assertion that one of the objects of the Grange is a meeting together of the members for the purpose of religious worship." He added that "the use of the property by the Grange is not similar to the use of it by the Beadling Presbyterian Church and is certainly one of a lower classification under the zoning ordinance."

The interpretation of the ordinance seems correct. However, here is another example of a legislative body making a distinction between secular activities conducted by a church and those conducted by a nonreligious organization. As has been indicated at page 161, this may represent "discrimination in reverse."

Having attended many meetings of rural people and organizations, I find that they often include profound discussions of moral principles. The meetings of some churches, especially urban ones, involve discussion of secular matters almost as extensively as of those having moral content. Religious organizations and groups like the Grange should make common cause. If those seeking to vindicate the religious rights of corporate religious bodies would place emphasis not only on the religious liberty clause, not only on the due process clause, not only on the equal protection clause, but also on the clauses guaranteeing freedom of speech and assembly, it would tend to eliminate the embarrassment that arises from the gauche attempts of courts to define such nebulous terms as "church," "religion," etc.

There is a general trend toward minimizing the distinction between secular eleemosynary organizations and those more truly religious. This takes the form, not of abolishing religious special privilege, but of extending such privilege also to secular groups. The famous decision of the United States Supreme Court in the *Society of Sisters* case [17] asserted the right of parents to send their children not only to a religious but to any private school. The nonsupernaturalist Ethical Societies now obtain tax exemption as churches.

Religion is coming more and more to be defined, not as prayer and the worship of God, but as a conviction deeply felt, or as Webster [190] puts it "devotion or fidelity, conscientiousness." Even the "established" churches, or some of them, have to a certain extent de-emphasized their supernaturalist doctrines. In the future churches may become less distinguishable from secular groups having a moral purpose. If so, it will become less necessary for the courts to decide "what is a church." For the courts, and the public respect they need, this will be a gain, for it will help them to avoid looking a little ridiculous. The question "what is a church" is a sticky one.

# CHAPTER 20.

## PRIVATE OPINION

It should be obvious to anyone how improper it would be for neighboring property owners to decide whether or not a church might be built on a particular tract. Yet this is substantially the arrangement provided in some of the earliest church zoning cases. In Omaha when the Westminster Presbyterian Church applied for a building permit, the granting or denial of the permit was made contingent on whether a certain percentage of the neighbors agreed to it. The Nebraska court [14] rejected this ruling and the courts have rejected similar arrangements time and again. Yet councils and zoning officials continue to enact them. As late as 1958, the Supreme Court of Missouri [192] had such an ordinance before it.

This problem is analogous to that of extra-legal pressure on judicial, legislative, and administrative bodies. In his standard work on zoning,[132:19-10] Mr. Rathkopf discusses the reasons why churches are usually governed by special exception procedures, administered by local bards, rather than by self-operative provisions of law. One reason he mentions is a realization by the legislature of the "impact which such a church could bring to bear upon a district and those who control it."

Legislators are also conscious of the impact of such organizations upon themselves. They tend to shift responsibility to the city council. The council shifts it to the planning board; the planning board may transfer it to a city engineer or inspector. If possible it may be transferred farther down—to ordinary citizens or property owners near the site. This shifting of power often takes the form of a provision, obviously void, under which church permits may be sought only by petitions signed or approved by some fixed percentage of property owners in a prescribed area surrounding the proposed location.

The following eight pages will be devoted to a discussion of the consent-of-neighbors clause and will be of special interest to lawyers faced with such problems. Readers with a more general interest in the subject will perhaps be more interested in the discussion of extra-legal private pressures which begins on page 301.

It is fortunate for the churches that consent-of-neighbors clauses are invalid. The opposition to church construction seems to increase in direct proportion to the proximity of the opponent to the construction. Neighbors object strenuously. When the issue comes to court it is handled by officials who do not live in the neighborhood. These people are much more favorable to religious building. Most favorable of all are the writers of articles and books such as the "absolutist" writers mentioned in Chapter 3. These people usually live much farther from the proposed site than even the judges and lawyers. If they live far enough away their enthusiasm for the proposed new church may become almost lyrical.

Naturally the most enthusiastic are church organizations. They are also distinguished by their unanimity. This is perhaps the one public issue on which the denominations are nondenominational. It is "all for one and one for all." They all agree in their opposition to any interference with the building programs of any one of them. More on this later.

In the case of the Westminster Presbyterian Church at Omaha, Nebraska,[14] the Presbyterians applied, not merely for a permit, which was conceded to them, but for exemption from the building line prescribed universally for all landowners. The legislature, as described at page 52, had authorized zoning regulations for the avowed purpose of advancing "safety from fire and other damages" and "the public health, safety and welfare." For the area including the church site, the council had provided that no building should occupy more than 25% of its lot. In other areas, 40% occupancy was permitted. When the Westminster Presbyterian Church asked for an exception, the city planning commission adopted a motion providing in effect that if a majority of the property owners within 300 feet of the proposed church would consent the commission would recommend that the church lot be transferred to the 40% district.

The church people were unable to obtain majority consent and asked the court to order the permit without it. The court nullified the requirement for consent. It seems that it served no public purpose. The evils of the overcrowding of land are not lessened by the fact that particular landowners agree to it. The court said that the consent of adjoining owners would not advance any purpose of the law, such as safety from fire, "nor do we find the pretended authority in the statute, nor does the ordinance pretend to empower the planning commission to delegate the power conferred upon it to a majority of the property owners. . . ."

The court held the delegation of power to property owners to be void. It handled the case on the assumption that the attempted delegation did not exist and treated the action of the planning commission as an unconditional recommendation for the granting of the permit. It based its final decision on this recommendation, and on other factors that I have discussed earlier.

In the Portland, Oregon, Catholic school case of 1932,[27] the ordinance prohibited all uses and occupancies except residences, their gardens, garages, etc. However,[27:391] it authorized buildings for "educational, religious, philanthropic, fraternal and other institutional use" pursuant to a prescribed procedure. This procedure could be commenced in either of two ways. The first method was initiation at the uncontrolled option of the city council or planning board, no standards being prescribed for exercise of that option. The other was by petition signed by a percentage of neighboring property owners (in certain circumstances by 50% and in other circumstances by 100%).

The archbishop failed to get the required number. To the contrary, when he personally requested the council to initiate a proceeding, 73.8% of the adjoining owners filed a petition against it. The council refused to act. The court held invalid the provisions for initiation by the council because no adequate standards were prescribed. (This issue is treated in Chapter 18.) The provision for initiation by landowners was also invalidated. The court said that the consent clause left the archbishop "at the will or caprice" of the neighboring owners.

The court not only invalidated the subordinate clauses of the ordinance, which created the exceptions, but also refused to permit enforcement against the archbishop of the principal clause forbidding construction of churches, etc. In other words, the two clauses were held inseparable from each other. At pages 269-70 I have discussed the principles applicable to this problem.

The Reno, Nevada, Catholic church case [35] concerned an ordinance substantially similar to the one invalidated in the Portland case. But the court avoided this issue. There may have been an ulterior motive for the refusal of the Nevada court to consider the question. It was in the form of an exception to a clause which was in negative form and forbade, not only eleemosynary institutions, but all nonresidential construction. If the court had invalidated the consent clause, it might also have felt obliged to invalidate the principal clause. This would have meant complete destruction of the planning scheme. By finding another ground for decision the court gave the particular bishop what he wanted without at the same time obstructing planners generally. To justify this happy result, the judge had to discuss a number of glittering generalities including the comparative virtues of funerals at home and funerals at church. This discussion would have been completely irrelevant if the judge had faced up to the nullity of the consent proviso.

The ordinance of the City of Montgomery, Alabama, challenged by the Pentecostal Holiness church [56] prohibited not only the erection of churches, philanthropic institutions, and other nonresidential buildings, but also the erection of any "building of substantially different type or size from the existing buildings in the immediate vicinity." An exception was provided as in the Portland and Reno cases but the consent of neighboring owners was required to be unanimous.

The Montgomery city fathers must have had some premonition that legalized blackmail could result. Under such provisions the granting of consent was entirely voluntary, subject to no conditions or public controls. There was no evidence in the particular case that this had occurred but an individual owner could hold out for payment of money or other considerations. Under a valid law this would have been solicitation of a bribe but under the provisions mentioned it would have been permissible.

Presumably sensing this possibility, the council went on to

provide that "in cases where the property owners . . . fail
. . . to state . . . their objections or should . . . their objections seem trivial . . . or if it appears that such . . .
owners are merely holding up the improvement for the purpose
of selling . . . their property, then the City Commission
reserves the right . . . to issue a permit."

The preparation of this ordinance was given careful
thought—but not enough. The court held the consent provision
invalid even in light of the qualification. The decision cited a
previous Alabama case, as follows (with the court's own
interpolation) :

> Ordinances which invest the city council, or a board of trustees
> or officers (and we may here interpolate, adjoining property
> owners) with a discretion which is purely arbitrary and which
> may be exercised in the interests of a favored few are unreasonable
> and invalid.

Instead of invalidating the exception only, the court held the
entire clause invalid. The Pentecostal Holiness church was
given its permit conditioned only on compliance with sanitary
and police regulations. The result was destruction of the
entire plan, which seems justified.

Perhaps the most conclusive church zoning decision dealing
with a requirement for consent of neighbors was the 1950 case
of Concordia College of Bronxville, New York, in the court of
appeals of that state.[82,82A] This college was a Lutheran institution long established in that city. In 1938 the village passed
an ordinance dividing its area into business and residential
zones. Ninety seven percent was made residential and the
balance, down by the railroad tracks, was made commercial.

As originally enacted, the ordinance allowed any "educational or religious building" in residential districts. In 1941
an amendment was passed [82:633] repealing this provision and
replacing it with a clause which authorized variances. These
might be granted to "permit in any residence district the
erection of . . . a building for educational, religious or eleemosynary purposes . . . provided the petitioner files the con-
sents, duly acknowledged, of 80% of the owners of property on
the streets enclosed in the block within which lies the property
intended for such use."

As the court said, this would obstruct construction of college buildings as well as churches almost anywhere in the village. At the same time, the ordinance authorized boarding houses, multi-family houses, hospitals and hotels in the residence areas without the consent of neighbors. This was discriminatory. However, the court did not dwell on this discrimination.

Instead, the decision rested on the contentions of the attorney for the Lutherans, obviously a very competent one. He said: [82:634] "The provision requiring consent from 80% of the adjoining owners before the Board of Appeals is even empowered to consider an application imposes a restriction on an inoffensive and legitimate use of property, not by a legislative body, but by other property owners, and that such delegation of power is repugnant to the due process clause." The court agreed. It cited [82:635] a United States Supreme Court case in which a somewhat similar ordinance was condemned, and in which that court said:

> One set of owners determines not only the extent of use but the kind of use which another set of owners may make of their property. In what way is the public safety, convenience or welfare served by conferring such power? The statute and ordinance, while conferring the power on some property holders to virtually control and dispose of the property rights of others, creates no standard by which the power thus given is to be exercised; in other words, the property holders who desire, and have authority, to . . . [so control their neighbors] may do so solely for their own interest or even capriciously.

The court of appeals then noted that its condemnation of such clauses, while applicable to projects of an "inoffensive" nature, as mentioned by the Lutherans' attorney, might not apply to such things as "billboards and garages." This minor exception has no immediate interest for us. Having invalidated the consent clause, there remained the balance of the 1941 amendment to consider.

Here we should note a distinction between the Bronxville ordinance and those of Reno,[35] and Montgomery.[56] In the earlier cases, the consent clause was attached to a provision forbidding construction of churches. In the Bronxville case, the consent clause was attached to a provision which permitted them. If the principal clause and the subordinate consent clause were treated as inseparable, the court would have been required to invalidate both and the college would still have been deprived of its permit. Instead, the court found grounds for treating the two clauses as separable. It said that "the local legislature evinced no desire to bar permits for educational buildings. It recognized that educational use is harmonious with the public interest (and who, indeed, could consider it otherwise?) but made it subject to the consent and approval hereinbefore outlined, which we find invalid. Hence no limitation remains."

The Protestant seminary case at Orange, New Jersey,[99] seems to be the first in which the court held a consent clause invalid and still managed to exclude the church institution. The court ruled favorably to the Seminary as to the consent clause but still justified its exclusion by ruling against it on the question of separability.

The township ordinance permitted "public and parochial schools, municipal playgrounds, parks and recreation buildings, etc." but provided separately that "private schools, clubs, lodgings, social community center and recreation buildings are prohibited unless the written consent of 80% by frontage of the owners of all lots within 200 feet . . . be filed . . . and approved by the board of appeals." The seminary had already been using the Colgate mansion at Orange for classrooms without benefit of any permit. The neighbors sued for an injunction to forbid such use and the city joined in the suit. The lower court held the consent provision invalid.[92] It said [92:456] that it 'is palpably an attempted delegation of a legislative power vested in the municipality and not transferable to the individual citizen or property owner." It also said that "the ordinance provision, even if otherwise unobjectionable, lacks legal vitality for the reason that no standards are fixed for the exercise by the individual property owners of the power attempted to be delegated to them."

With this phase of the ruling the supreme court agreed; [99:485] but it refused to sustain the lower court's order dissolving the injunction. Instead, the higher court went on to consider whether sufficient valid verbiage remained in the ordinance to authorize the permit. It held that no such permit was authorized and affirmed the injunction against the seminary.

In justification the court first found that the college was not a "public or parochial school" as described in the section permitting construction of such institutions without neighborly consent. The court decided that this clause referred only to schools on the elementary and secondary level, not to those on the college level. These latter were covered, said the court, by the separate reference to "private schools." This meant that the council had discriminated between (a) public and parochial elementary and high schools and (b) private colleges. The court held that this discrimination was not improper. Thus the court avoided ruling on the issue discussed in Chapter 13, whether it violates the equal protection clause to discriminate between public and religious schools.

Our interest here is in the court's determination that the entire clause respecting "private schools" etc. was invalid, not just the part which provided for consent of the neighbors. The court said: "There was, in this case, a distinct effort on the part of the municipal governing body . . . to emphasize their determination . . . that uses of the categories listed . . . were opposed to the common good and general welfare of the residential area involved . . . under their comprehensive plan for the municipality and giving reasonable consideration to the character of the neighborhood. . . . The emphasis of the ordinance was to exclude the uses in any event, unless a special 'spot' should be created by action of the neighboring landowers and approval of the [zoning] board of appeals. . . . It follows that the intention must have been to exclude the uses even in the event that the 'spot zoning' provision . . . was declared invalid."

Parenthetically, it should be noted that this Protestant institution was refused relief in a decision which resulted from very close reasoning. Hard cases often make bad law. Three years later, the same court had to decide whether a Catholic nuns' seminary at Morris Township, New Jersey, should be permitted to expand its buildings.[128] By a divided vote, with Justice Brennan (now of the Supreme Court of the United States) joining another justice in dissent, the court decided against granting the permit.

The issues in the Catholic case were different and I do not necessarily challenge the result. But the court in the Catholic case may have been influenced by a desire to demonstrate intersectarian impartiality. Later, after Justice Brennan had left the court, the reasoning of the Morris Township case was repudiated.

Whether the result is favorable to the churches as in the Portland, Oregon, Catholic case,[27] the Reno, Nevada, Catholic case,[35] the Montgomery, Alabama, Pentecostal Holiness case,[56] and the Bronxville, New York, Lutheran case [82] or unfavorable to the church as in the Orange, New Jersey, Protestant seminary case,[99] the consensus seems to be that it is unconstitutional to require the consent of nearby property owners as a condition to granting a church building permit. However, there is nothing to keep a zoning board from listening to their views. As indicated by a close examination of a few church zoning cases, these views are often expressed and with considerable vehemence. They sometimes influence the decisions not only of boards but of courts as well.

Here is an important distinction between court proceedings and administrative proceedings. No individual citizen may go into court and insist upon expressing an opinion as to how the judge should decide the case. He can testify as to facts, if he possesses them, but private opinions, except those of scientific experts, etc., are inadmissible. Zoning boards are not strictly bound by these rules of evidence, and they have often been known to take a poll of the people in the hearing room and to count noses as an aid to decision.

The courts are also sometimes influenced by the views of neighboring property owners. This is not entirely improper. Certainly, the attitudes of such neighbors, while not controlling, are relevant to such questions as whether a proposed building will "disturb or annoy" them, or whether it will "lessen their enjoyment" of their property. The avoidance of such results is a valid and substantial public purpose which zoning regulations may properly serve.

I will mention here a few examples of how this influence is felt. In the Indianapolis Methodist case,[57] the court, as mentioned at pages 275-7, greatly expanded the definition of the word church. The court said that "a crowd of residents and property owners both for and against the petition were present" at the hearing where the board had granted the permit and that "a large number of interested property owners appeared in person and by attorneys and expressed themselves both in favor [of] and against the granting of the petition." The court also stated that there were 37 "owners and residents" of property on the adjoining streets who filed written requests for granting of the permit. On the other hand, said the court, there were only 28 "property owners" who signed a "petition of remonstrators" against it.

The court obviously wanted to justify its conclusions, not only by reference to the law of the case, but also by reference to the wishes of the neighbors. How many of the "owners and residents" who favored the court's decision were owners and how many were residents? All those opposed were owners. Were any of the court's supporters perhaps mere boarders or roomers at the home of some devout and honest Methodist widow? If so, was not the court's justification comparable to that of the man who advertised "horse and rabbit sandwiches" filled with a mixture composed of one horse and one rabbit?

In the Dayton, Ohio, Christian Science parking lot case,[122] the suit was filed, not by one, two or three, but by 69 nearby property owners. The court held against them on grounds that seem adequate. However, the author of the decision was quite apologetic. "Indeed, it is difficult," he said, "to understand why 69 plaintiff property owners or holders . . . prefer to have more automobiles parked at their curb while defendant church is holding services than to have fewer automobiles as a result of the off-street parking . . . on defendant's lot." The court could not permit itself expressly to observe that perhaps the neighbors wanted not fewer automobiles but fewer Christian Scientists.

In the Catholic school case at Piedmont, California,[125] which was won by the archbishop, a dissenting justice tried to show that his views were popular nearby to the proposed grammar school. He pointed out [125:445] that the zoning provision under which private schools were banned had been approved by a vote of 3408 to 1285 of the electors of the village. He also described a meeting of the St. James' Wood Homes Association, composed of all the owners in an adjacent subdivision, who voted 170-2 against granting the permit. The dissenting justice then said: "It is thus shown that petitioner's land was acquired by it with advance knowledge that such land lies in a single family residential zone and further that the adjacent land within the city of Piedmont is used for single family residential rather than private business purposes." To prove this point, the justice did not have to cite the voting records. He seemed to be supporting his views, not with law, but with private opinion.

In the Catholic seminary case at Morris Township, New Jersey,[128] mentioned just above, the court also said that hearings were attended by "other owners of the property in the immediate area." It added that only one resident favored the variance asked by the sisters. The New Jersey court had a number of sounder reasons for its ruling against the Catholics, but this is the one of interest here.

In the Kansas City, Missouri, Catholic church and school case, the decision gave only an inkling of the passions involved. The court said: [169:322] "There was widespread and energetic opposition to the granting of this building permit. This opposition was demonstrated by the number of witnesses appearing, by the size of the protest petition and by the vigor with which the appeal in all its stages has been prosecuted. The chief complaints voiced by those giving oral testimony included: added traffic hazards, destruction of trees and beauty generally, and the dilution of a pure and exclusive residential area by placing in its midst a public gathering place which these witnesses claimed would lessen all surrounding property values."

The Brighton, New York, Catholic church and school case, rated by many as a very strong one on the "church side" of zoning issues, was decided in the intermediate court [131] against the church, then reversed in the court of appeals.[149] The intermediate court did not go into great detail about the views of residents, but it did mention [131:394] that "at a board hearing practically all the arguments and considerations, pro and con, were aired by both the proponents and the representative group of objectors. Also, both in support of and in opposition to the application, petitions containing a large number of signatures were before the board."

This was rather a pale report of the excitement that must have prevailed at the hearing. It was presumably either the local residents or other supporters of the archbishop who took the matter to the legislature. Perhaps they were joined by Jewish representatives because the Sands Point case [148] had been decided by another branch of the appellate division only ten days earlier.

When the Jewish case was finally argued in the court of appeals, the New York State Catholic Welfare Committee appeared as amicus curiae "in support of the position of" the synagogue [148:489] and may therefore have influenced the final decision written by Justice Conway. When the Catholic case was argued, the American Jewish Congress appeared as amicus curiae "in support of the position of" the Diocese of Rochester [149:828] and may well have helped influence the final decision written by Justice Froesel. Without suggesting any illegality one might suspect that there was mutual back-scratching by the two great faiths. While Froesel and Conway were considering their decisions, the religious proponents of the permits were also active in the legislature.

Some years previously Massachusetts had enacted a law which eliminated church zoning problems by eliminating church zoning. It completely forbade boards to exclude either religious or educational institutions from any neighborhood or to "limit" them in any way. In the Dover, Massachusetts, Catholic case,[85] it had been held effective retroactively. The article in *St. John's Law Review* of Brooklyn, New York,[95:103] had urged enactment of similar laws in all states, in order to eliminate this "bigoted legislation" (zoning churches). As revealed by Ralph W. Crolly in the *Brooklyn Law Review*,[161] bills were introduced in the New York State Assembly session of 1956 seeking to conform New York's law to that of Massachusetts. This session followed immediately after the intermediate court decisions against the synagogue [129] and the archdiocese [131] in December of 1955.

It is a mystery to me how the Massachusetts planners and zoners get around the state law forbidding them to "limit" churches or schools, or whether they do get around it. If not, this is the sort of law which, it seems to me, would wreck any comprehensive zoning plan. The Supreme Judicial Court of Massachusetts itself had recognized the danger of such a carte blanche to religious organizations. In the Beverly, Massachusetts, Jewish cemetery case of 1944, it said [47:695] that "it might well defeat the purpose of the zoning ordinance if religious corporations could locate new cemeteries and enlarge old ones without regard to the zoning ordinance to which all others must conform." The judges in the New York cases must have known about the legislative campaign for a similar law in New York. The decisions issued on July 11, 1956, rendered unnecessary the legislative campaign then in progress.

In the Froesel decision in the Catholic case [149] there is no discussion of the attitude of private opinion respecting the case. But Justice Conway in deciding the Jewish case [148] goes out of his way to mention that "the petitioner called six witnesses to testify in its behalf at the hearing before the board, and the Village of Sands Point called one—the village building inspector. There was no objection by any residents of Sands Point, or, indeed by anyone, except the village board of trustees." Here, again, we catch a judge in the act of counting noses, in order to discredit the action of the board of trustees.

Justice Conway's remarks, like those of the appellate division with respect to the Brighton case, reveal less than the entire picture. The article by William Schack in the May 1957, *Commentary Magazine*,[163] published by the American Jewish Committee, discussed this case at length. It reveals that a half-dozen ministers testified before the board in favor of granting the permit. It also tells about the telegram sent by Governor W. Averell Harriman calling the Sands Point regulation "un-American and undemocratic." Does anyone believe that the appeals court justices were too busy to read about this in the newspapers?

The article quotes the mayor of Sands Point as saying that Harriman's action was merely a gesture toward the Jewish vote, and as insisting that the permit would never be granted. A seeming anomaly—though not really one—is that the mayor himself is of the Jewish faith. It shows that anti-Semitism often has a social or economic rather than a racial or religious foundation.

The mayor is also supposed to have said that it was "not the good old Jewish families of Sands Point, Bernard Baruch, the Guggenheims, and others, but the newcomers who were creating religious problems that they came here to escape," in a town "where there has never been any discrimination and where there are probably the largest number of successful intermarriages in the country." The mayor was referring to marriages between Jewish and non-Jewish people. Schack comments that perhaps the mayor was afraid the presence of a synagogue would "disturb the equanimity of the successfully intermarried." He also mentions that the head of the synagogue group, referred to by the mayor as newcomers, had lived in the town for sixteen years!

Schack also quotes an interview that he conducted with a "realistic rabbi." The clergyman said that "a religious institution, church or synagogue, is a royal pain in the neck in a residential area. Traffic, noise, parking, are all legitimate concerns of the neighbors." Regarding the earlier Beachwood, Ohio, case,[101] Schack says [163:4] that a petition was circulated and a large majority of residents opposed granting of the permit. He adds that "several people objected to the establishment of a temple for the reason that they had moved to a suburb in the first place to escape churches and all such institutions. While no one voiced this objection at the Sands Point hearing, I have heard it many times, from Jews as well as non-Jews, around Sands Point and elsewhere."

Thus there may have been many objections at Sands Point that were unvoiced at the hearing. It may be that the people were not as unanimously behind Justice Conway as he thought. He seems to have closed his ears to this underground rumbling in order to make it seem that the ordinary citizens of Sands Point, millionaires and multimillionaires alike, were on his side of the argument.

Although there are other instances, these are enough to show how zoning boards and courts of law are influenced, like the proverbial Joneses, by the opinions of the neighbors. But there is a more formal kind of private opinion which also influences the courts. I refer to those of attorneys who do not represent the parties to the litigation. Some of them merely meet judges in the street, discuss zoning law with them, and attempt to influence their decisions as suggested by Mr. Purdy in the statement [11] quoted on page 95. Some of them write articles and books, like the articles cited in Chapter 3 and like the present volume. Others, like Bettman in Ohio, Bobbitt in

Indiana and Weintraub in New Jersey may be adjudging in their old age cases like those which in their youth or middle age they handled as attorneys.

Others appear in court representing, not the parties, but outside organizations, and filing their briefs as *amici curiae*. They might better be called *amici ecclesiarum*. I don't mean to suggest that they misrepresent their role. The term "friend of the court" is an ancient one that no longer means what it says. It refers to any public-spirited organization that comes into court, by permission, to grind its own ax. Those who appear under this designation in church zoning cases are usually opposed to the particular public regulation of the religious use of land.

Do I seem to overemphasize the role of these "friends of the court"? Then read the article about the Piedmont case [125] in the *Catholic Lawyer*.[147] It praised the decision highly. The final paragraph is most striking:

> The favorable decision in the Piedmont case illustrates what can be achieved through the united action of all denominations. There, eleven members of the California bar and two members of the New York bar appeared as amici curiae, representing such organizations as the Jewish Welfare League and the Protestant Episcopal Bishop of California.

The article also said that "to prevent a recurrence of the events which took place in Porterville, Piedmont, and Wauwatosa, an active interest should be taken by laymen in the formulation of local zoning ordinances. In addition, strong public opinion should be aroused and brought to bear when such cases are litigated in the courts."

Attached to the article is a sort of "news flash" saying that, as the *Catholic Lawyer* went to press, the New York Court of Appeals had announced its decision in the Sands Point [148] and Brighton [149] cases. The magazine promised early coverage of both cases. This was the July issue of the *Catholic Lawyer*. The court of appeals decisions were actually issued on July 11.

Law review articles and books can have an influential effect on decisions. Judges, like other lawyers, dislike to read law cases. They often cut down on their work by consulting, not the cases themselves, but what writers say about the cases. The standard authors on zoning all take attitudes rather like that of Bassett, who reported that in 1916 church zoning was unthinkable.[36]

Typical is the statement of Mr. Metzenbaum in his otherwise admirable general work on zoning: [113:1458]

> Churches, with their influence for good and for uplift, should be welcome in every community, regardless of their denomination. Upon frequent occasions, there may be sound reasons why a certain location here and there in a municipality might, possibly, be an imprudent choice for a church owing to special congestion already existent or due to unusual traffic and similar conditions. Such singular conditions can readily be determined by sensibly conducted, dispassionate, conferences among the public authorities and church leaders. It is deplorable that any should lead to court controversy.

This amounts to a suggestion that churches should never be zoned out of any quiet residential district, although the decisions of a number of courts find such exclusion justifiable in order to preserve their peace, quiet and other advantages. It is essentially a suggestion that churches should have freedom of choice and not be subjected to the same legal process as any other citizen or corporation.

I also disagree with the description of court proceedings as deplorable. If the churches are disappointed by the action of a zoning board, they should take it to court. The zoning board should there defend its point of view. If the adjoining owners are disappointed, they should also feel free to go to court, without having their action called deplorable.

Court proceedings are also sensible and dispassionate. They are probably more sensible and dispassionate than some conferences, perhaps between an irate clergyman and resentful public officials or property owners. Court proceedings usually preserve peace. They do not destroy it.

Rather more than half of all the articles on church zoning mentioned in this book were published in periodicals issued by colleges owned and operated by a single denomination. Many others may have been inspired by sectarian interests. Many are slanted against zoning boards which have tried to regulate land use by churches.

Such partiality may be wholesome. But it is also a little clumsy. This is indicated by quotations used herein from some such articles. This clumsiness could defeat the very purpose of the authors. It could cause an angry judicial reaction, such as that of the Supreme Court of Oregon: [184:21]

> There is a tendency upon the part of some authors, textbook writers, and a few courts, to cloak petitioning churches with a species of judicial favoritism under the zoning laws which seems to vest them with an immunity beyond the reach and touch of certain zoning provisions. . . .

How many other courts may have reacted similarly to these writers' efforts without incorporating their resentment in published decisions?

It might be better in the long run if the boards and courts themselves studied legal and economic problems more and relied on private opinions less, even where those opinions are held by numerous or important people. Neither preachers nor landowners should be excluded from the board rooms. Both should be heard, without too much formality. However, it might be useful to the cause of justice and to the cause of religion if the courts paid less attention to nose counting. It might also help if legal writers, without necessarily abandoning their partisanship, would not carry it to such a point that they forget to mention the cases which disagree with their views.

Court proceedings, especially in church cases, should retain their ancient dignity. The judicial atmosphere has no place for outside interference. Church zoning cases should not be an occasion for lawyers to urge that "strong public opinion be aroused and brought to bear."

# CHAPTER 21.

## CHURCH ZONING IN STATE COURTS

For the convenience of readers interested in the decisions in particular states, they are all listed below, although all the important cases have been covered previously in much greater detail under the various topics concerned.

*Alabama.*

In 1946, the Alabama Supreme Court [56] ordered issuance by the City of Montgomery of a permit to a Pentecostal Holiness church for a location in the Highland Park area. The ordinance forbade "any store, filling station, automobile laundry, garage, or any other type of building to be used for commercial purposes." The court held that this provision did not cover the church although neighbors contended that it was really a commercial enterprise of its pastor. The ordinance also forbade new buildings of a "substantially different type or size" without the consent of nearby property owners. This provision was held unconstitutional as an undue delegation of uncontrolled public authority to private persons. However, the decision did recognize the validity of regulation of religious land use at least to the extent of requiring compliance with police and safety regulations.

*Arizona.*

The Mesa Catholic church case,[53] decided in the supreme court in 1945, is cited extensively as authority against the exclusion of churches from any residential zone. It was actually limited to a condemnation of discrimination against a particular church. Permitted in the area were various non-residential uses including the raising of pigs. The court invalidated the exclusion of a church. Other state courts have permitted exclusion of churches in residential-agricultural zones.

## California.

This was the first jurisdiction to sustain the express total exclusion of churches from a residential area. This occurred in the Porterville Mormon temple case,[67] decided in the court of appeals, then refused review in both the Supreme Court of California and the Supreme Court of the United States.[71,76] This is the only church zoning decision which sustains total exclusion by express provision although there are many others which have permitted such exclusion upon failure of the church to comply with some condition for issuance of permits. The Porterville decision was a milestone in the development of church zoning law and is discussed at length on various pages of this treatise.

The case of the Baptists at Chico [88] challenged the universality of the Porterville doctrine, but unsuccessfully. In the Piedmont Catholic school case [115,125] the supreme court disavowed any intention to overrule the Porterville doctrine, yet reversed the Piedmont board's refusal of a permit to a parochial school. One distinction was that in Piedmont the exclusion was from 97.3% of the town's area while in Porterville the exclusion was from a more limited district. Another was that other activities, including public schools, were permitted in Piedmont's restricted area while in Porterville the area from which churches were excluded was 100% residential. By its invocation of the *Sisters of Charity* case,[17] the Piedmont case may have pointed the way to future determinations based on religious liberty rather than property rights.

The Azusa Jehovah's Witnesses case [186] affirmed the city's exclusion of a Kingdom Hall from a residential area. An attempt was made to apply the Piedmont rule but it failed because the court found no proof of the charge that the exclusion was from 90% of the city's area. The court also held that a charge of discrimination was not supported by the evidence. The Azusa case was also refused review in the California Supreme Court and in the Supreme Court of the United States.[199]

In the Orange County Catholic church and school case, both were excluded from a residential area within the city.[193,202]

This court of appeals decision was refused review by the state supreme court. The exclusion in both the Azusa and Orange County cases was for failure to comply with conditions, not by way of a blanket provision in the ordinance. These two cases serve to limit and define the scope of the Piedmont decision. It seems that in California religious land use can be fully regulated except if churches or church institutions are excluded from entire municipalities.

Other California cases include the Modesto Baptist case [167] in which the zoning board's grant of a permit to a Negro church was sustained; the Garden Grove Jehovah's Witnesses case [217] in which denial of a permit was sustained; and the San Marino Catholic case [223] in which the board's denial of a permit was sustained and an injunction against violation of zoning regulations was issued. The San Marino case was distinguished by the firm limitations which it imposed on the doctrine of balancing of conveniences. (See Chapter 4.) This case was also refused review in the United States Supreme Court.[224] In the Menlo Park Jehovah's Witnesses case [194] the action of the board in refusing a permit was reversed, having no basis in the ordinance. In the Modesto Jehovah's Witnesses case [245] the court sustained exclusion of a Kingdom Hall.

Of nine California cases only three were decided in favor of the church. Of these only two reversed the action of the administrative agency.

*Colorado.*

There have been two cases the first of which [196] involved a Baptist church at Pueblo. The court held only that the zoning commission could not order removal of a bright neon sign. The court said it was "customary and incidental" to uses authorized by the original church permit. In the second case,[233] respecting an Apostolic Christian church at Englewood, the zoning board's refusal of a permit was overturned. The opinion endorsed the absolute anti-exclusion rule. It is discussed at page 48.

*Connecticut.*

In 1956 the Supreme Court of Errors of Connecticut decided the West Hartford Methodist church case.[139] In a brief but sweeping opinion it sustained the exclusion of a church from a residential zone. The application was for a 400 seat church with 150 parking spaces. It was rejected on the ground [139:642] that it would result in "(1) overintensification of a reasonable use of the land, (2) undue concentration of traffic, (3) substantial depreciation in the value of the surrounding property, and (4) a condition which would not be in the best interests of the surrounding propery owners."

In the Darien, Connecticut, Catholic school case of 1962 [247] the church officials insisted that it was unfair discrimination to require them to obtain a special permit and to comply with other requirements not imposed with regard to public schools. The court held that such requirements did not violate the equal protection clause and that there are reasonable grounds for separate classification of public and parochial schools.

*Florida.*

A 1950 case involving the Tampa Jehovah's Witnesses [83] has been very widely cited against exclusion of churches from residential areas. This is not correct. While the ordinance did provide for exclusion of churches not complying with certain requirements, the court specifically declined to pass on constitutionality. It held only that the Witnesses had "substantially" complied with its requirements and so were entitled to a permit.

In the Miami Beach United Lutheran case of 1955 [124] the same court sustained denial of a permit to the church on broad grounds of protection of property values, prevention of noise and disturbance, avoidance of spot zoning and prevention of traffic hazards. In 1957 the court sustained refusal of a permit to the Frances Avenue Advent Christian Church of Tampa,[160] saying that the issue was "controlled" by the Miami Beach decision. In 1958 the court of appeals affirmed refusal of a permit to the Greater Miami Beach Hebrew Academy.[189] This decision was sustained by the supreme court in 1959.[198]

*Georgia.*

There were two early, unimportant, cases. One was the case of a colored Baptist church in Atlanta [55] in which the court invalidated an attempt to revoke a permit without first giving notice and hearing. The second was that of the Evangelical Lutheran church of Decatur.[70] The court sustained a rezoning of the land to permit erection of the church over an objection that on a previous request the council had refused to take such action. The court held the previous action was not *res adjudicata*.

The most important Georgia case is that of the Atlanta Jehovah's Witnesses [72,78] in which the Supreme Court of Georgia ruled that their Kingdom Hall could properly be excluded from a residential site at Juniper Street, N.E., between 8th and 10th. This was the first case that specifically considered traffic problems. It held that their solution was a proper public purpose to justify religious land use regulation.

The Witnesses later operated at Gordon Street and also at Flat Shoals Avenue without benefit of permits. They were notified that, if they did not discontinue, the city would "proceed as the law directs" including prosecution. The Witnesses filed suit under the Federal Civil Rights Act. Their action was dismissed. The United States Circuit Court of Appeals [91] affirmed the dismissal. It refused to enjoin the city for the reason, among others, that there was no actual attempt to interfere with religious services.

*Illinois.*

In the case of an Episcopal seminary at Evanston [19,23] the supreme court decided in 1927 that the city could not enforce against the church a newly enacted ordinance forbidding construction of colleges not possessing the power of eminent domain after the church had acquired land and raised funds in reliance on an ordinance previously in effect which permitted construction of such institutions.

In the Winnetka Catholic school case of 1939 [34] the same court decided against enforcement of an ordinance forbidding construction of parochial schools in an area where public schools were allowed, the city not having pointed out any basis for distinction between them. In the Chicago Episcopalian case of 1952,[93] under an ordinance requiring that churches be built only on lots surrounded by streets and alleys, the appellate court decided that compliance could be accomplished by dedicating new alleys out of church-owned land on the premises.

In the case of a Jewish school in Chicago [135] the supreme court interpreted an ordinance which permitted schools in a two-family residence district only if "adjoining" a larger apartment building. The court held that the school "adjoined" even though there was an alley between it and the apartment house. The appellate court decided one other case, in 1958, on purely procedural grounds. It refused to review denial of a permit requested for erection of a sign by the Believers of Islam.[188]

In 1962 the supreme court upset [246] refusal of a permit to Jehovah's Witnesses for a storefront location in Chicago upon "speculative fears of traffic congestion" and alleged detrimental effect of the Kingdom Hall on a solid business block. The court said that "the location of churches can be regulated in a proper case" but that the particular house of worship "would be no more harmful than a dance hall, crematory, mausoleum, or trade school," all permitted uses in the area.

*Indiana.*

There are four reported cases in this state, involving Indianapolis Methodists,[57] Indianapolis Catholics,[62] Decatur Jehovah's Witnesses [104] and Meridian Hills Catholics.[229] All were decided in favor of the church involved. In the first two the boards' action in favor of the church was sustained by the appellate court; in the last two, zoning board decisions against the churches were reversed in the supreme court.

The first two cases involved determination of what was meant by the word "church" in an ordinance. The courts gave the term a broad meaning including such things as a gymnasium, an outside amphitheater and a convent (even though the ordinance forbade "schools with living quarters attached"). The items to be included were to be determined, it seems, by the customs or laws of the particular denomination.

Then, in the Meridian Hills case,[229:42] the supreme court expanded the doctrine to mean that the "facilities that go with the church of the particular denomination may not be excluded if the church is admittable." Meanwhile in the Decatur Jehovah's Winesses case the same court had held that "the law is well settled that the building of a church may not be prohibited in a residential district" and that "if the refusal of the zoning board to grant a variance results in the exclusion of a church . . . such action is illegal and must be reversed."

These statements add up to a rule that neither churches nor any facilities that the church itself deems suitable may be excluded and that no conditions may be imposed upon their admission with which the denomination is unwilling or unable to comply. This rule would be ridiculous and the Indiana court itself has made exceptions to it, for instance for the enforcement of setback lines and "reasonable" off-street parking requirements. In spite of inconsistencies, which are discussed in detail elsewhere, the attitude of the Indiana courts is clearly more hostile than that of any other state to public regulation of the religious use of land.

*Iowa.*

A permit issued to a Lutheran theological seminary at Dubuque for the construction of a "dormitory" for married students and their families was challenged by objecting property owners.[197] The supreme court sustained it, holding that the dormitory was authorized under an ordinance permitting "educational, religious, or philanthropic use," etc. This was a rather broad interpretation in favor of the church, since the dormitory seemed like just another apartment house. However, the opinion was well-reasoned. No fundamental questions of church zoning law were discussed.

*Kentucky.*

The only church zoning case concerned Baptists who sought a permit for a location on Brownsboro Road at Olympic Avenue in Louisville.[69] The permit was granted but the court of appeals reversed and remanded on technical grounds. It also made clear that the permit should be conditioned on the elimination of night lighting, the provision of parking facilities, etc. This is an indication that this court will approve reasonable regulation of the religious use of land.

*Massachusetts.*

In this state, the legislature has attempted to take the question of church zoning out of the hands of the courts by giving the churches a carte blanche. The statute forbids any ordinance to "limit the use of land for any church or religious . . . purpose." In the Dover, Massachusetts Catholic case [85] the Supreme Judicial Court held that the law was applicable to ordinances previously adopted. It said, however, that it was not expressing an opinion as to the constitutionality of the measure.

*Michigan.*

The supreme court of this state has had three church zoning cases before it. In one it treated the applicant about as harshly as any church has ever been treated in such a case. In the other two the churches were treated as favorably as was possible. The first case involved a Lutheran church at Grand Rapids; [28] the second concerned the Full Salvation Union and its camp meeting at Portage, [60] and the third the Roman Catholic archbishop and a church plant at Orchard Lake. [94]

In 1933 the Evangelical Lutheran church at Grand Rapids was granted a permit to construct a church which would not comply with area and setback limitations. The board issued the permit on grounds of "practical difficulties and unnecessary hardship." The court sustained the board's decision in spite of its refusal to specify the difficulties and hardships on which its action was based.

In the Portage case, the court held that camp meetings were not authorized under a statute permitting "uses accessory to" churches. The court declared the camp meeting facilities a nuisance and required their destruction or removal. In the Orchard Lake case, the court, over the opposition of the zoning board, required issuance of a permit for a full Catholic church plant, saying that the usual presumption of validity of the board's action would, in such a case, represent "a thesis inconsistent with the spirit and genius of our free institutions and system of government and the traditions of the American people."

In the *Full Salvation Union* case, the court adopted a narrow interpretation of the ordinance. In the Catholic case, it adopted a broad interpretation of the Michigan constitution and of the "spirit, genius, institutions and traditions" mentioned above. (Discussed at pages 194 to 197.)

Apart from this the result of the Orchard Lake case is not

necessarily unsound. In the absence of justification it refused to sustain the total exclusion of churches from about 90% of the area of the village. There seem to be no Michigan cases which prevent (a) the reasonable regulation of religious use of land, or even (b) the exclusion of churches so long as it is not from "practically" an entire municipality. However the attitude of the supreme court seems quite hostile to any such regulation.

*Missouri.*

There have been three decisions in the Kansas City Court of Appeals, none of which is conclusive on constitutional issues. The first,[156] sustained a permit to Visitation Catholic Church for additional parking facilities across from its edifice. The church had a regular Sunday attendance of 2,000 with parking space for only 25 cars. The new facilities applied for would provide for only 25 more. The dispute concerned only interpretation of the ordinance.

The second case [169] in the same court involved a permit for construction of a Catholic church and school. The question was whether the plans complied with off-street parking requirements. By a rather broad interpretation in the church's favor of the computations provided by the ordinance, the court was able to hold that compliance had been made.

The third case [192] was decided in the supreme court. It concerned a Jewish temple at Creve Coeur, a residential suburb of St. Louis. The basis of the decision was that the legislature in its enabling act had not authorized the regulation of the religious use of land. However, the decision is a long one and discusses, with varying degrees of relevancy, a number of phases of church zoning law.

*Nebraska.*

The earliest of the church zoning cases, that of the Westminster Presbyterian Church at Omaha,[14] was decided in the supreme court in 1922. The court held (a) that it was unconstitutional for administrative authorities to make their decisions contingent upon approval of neighboring property owners and (b) that the set-back requirements of the ordinance were void and unconstitutional (as to church and nonchurch property alike). The decision on the first point is correct. On the second, the decision, by modern judicial standards, is wrong.

This decision was typical of those early cases that took a restrictive view of the scope of the police power and compared it to the right of self-defense. In this respect, a much broader view was adopted in the minority opinion of Justice Rose which is quoted at length at pages 54-5. The Omaha court has since indicated a trend toward this view [20] but there are no additional church zoning cases upon which an estimate of this state's judicial policy could be based.

*Nevada.*

In 1939, the supreme court [35] required issuance of a permit to the Catholic bishop for a church in Reno. The only public purpose discussed in the decision was the prevention of the alleged depressive influence of church funerals. The court held this justification for refusing the permit insufficient but clearly limited the scope of its decision to the particular case.

*New Jersey.*

In 1949, the supreme court in the Lodi Township Baptist case [73] held an ordinance applicable prospectively only. There have since been eight reported church zoning cases in New Jersey. In them, a Protestant seminary, a Jewish ritualarium, a Catholic seminary and a Jehovah's Witnesses Kingdom Hall have been denied permits and four religious grade schools have been granted permits.

The Protestant seminary case [86,92,99] arose at Orange when a nondenominational group transformed the old Colgate mansion into a dormitory and classrooms. The area was zoned residential with exceptions allowed for parochial and public schools. There was a separate ban on "private schools." The lower court held that the ordinance was unfairly discriminatory as between public and private schools, but the supreme court reversed this opinion. It construed the word "private" as including only schools of higher learning which it said could be classified separately from both public and private grade and high schools.

In the Newark Jewish case [89,94A] the ordinance authorized

permits for churches. The court sustained denial of a permit for a Jewish ceremonial bath on the ground that it was not a "church."

Displaying a very strict attitude toward variances,[128] the supreme court upheld denial of an addition to a Catholic sisters' seminary at Morris Township. Although the sisters had an "appealing case," and three of the seven judges dissented, the majority upheld the action of the board, saying that such uses "infect the neighborhood of their location."

The strictness of the supreme court with respect to variances was later relaxed. In two cases that involved Catholic grade schools, the court affirmed grants of permits, one at Ocean Township [180,206] and the other at Montclair.[228] In the Ocean case, the court said that, while approving the variance in the particular case, it did not intend to lay down any general rule forbidding discrimination between public and private schools. However in 1962 the legislature adopted a measure forbidding discrimination against nonprofit private grade schools. A trial court then reversed the denial of a permit to a Lutheran school at Morris Plains Borough [241] and the appellate division of the superior court reversed a denial of such a permit to a Catholic school at Montclair.[248] The last-mentioned decision also sustained the validity of the resulting discrimination against private profit schools and in favor of those organized on a nonprofit basis.

In 1959 the court also decided the Allendale Jehovah's Witnesses case [205] in which it upheld refusal of a permit for failure to comply with off-street parking requirements. This decision was refused review in the United States Supreme Court. Apparently the New Jersey court will permit reasonable regulation of religious land use and will usually uphold zoning board decisions except to the extent its decisions are controlled by the law above mentioned.

*New York.*

A total of 13 published church zoning cases have been decided in this state. The jurisdiction is peculiar in that published opinions include not only those of the highest court (the court of appeals) but those of the intermediate court (the appellate division) and also a great many of those of the trial courts located in the various counties, which are called "supreme courts." As a result of this the 13 cases include a total of 25 published opinions. For our purposes, however, only a few are important.

Although the Plandome, New York, Unitarian church case [87] was finally decided in one of the trial courts above mentioned, it has been cited and relied upon by courts of much greater dignity and authority, including even the highest court of New York State. It held that the church could not be excluded completely from a town in which other uses, including clubhouses, were permitted.

The decisions in New York State are adverse to religious land use regulation. The tone is set by the decision in the case of the Brighton Catholic church and school [149] which has been discussed at length in this text. The *Catholic Lawyer* for Summer 1959 [204] says that this case "recognized that churches like other places of assembly produce noise, congestion and traffic but regards these as off-set by the social and moral values inherent in religious institutions." This attitude has also been adopted by the lower courts of the state. The result has been massive reluctance on their part to recognize as substantial any justification advanced for regulation of religious land use.

The Sands Point, New York, Jewish synagogue case,[148] decided on the same day as the Brighton case in the court of appeals, was based mainly on the failure of the board properly to fix the parking requirements. However, in dictum, the court also expressed hostility to religious land use regulation in general.

There is a great deal of language in the Brighton opinion [149] justifying such a policy. However, the purposes invoked by the city to justify its action against the Catholics were not specifically authorized by the local ordinance. The strict policy stated by the *Catholic Lawyer* should not be considered conclusive unless and until a case has gone to the court of appeals which involves an ordinance providing such standards and guides.

Other cases decided in New York State are:

The Bronxville, New York, Lutheran college case [68,74,77,82] in which the court of appeals invalidated a provision requiring that the consent of the neighbors be obtained before the permit could be issued.

The Irondequoit Jewish case of 1954,[107] in which a requirement for parking facilities was invalidated as unauthorized by the ordinance.

The New Hyde Park Jewish school case,[137] in which a trial court refused to invalidate an ordinance permitting parochial schools in residential areas. It rejected the contention of objecting property owners that under the Village Law of the state it had to be adopted unanimously.

The Garden City Jewish center case,[150,154] in which a lower court overruled a zoning board decision and ordered issuance of a permit, but placed severe limitations on the congregation's use of the property.

The Pelham Manor Jewish case,[171,178,179,220] in which, after unsuccessful attempts at all three judicial levels, the congregation finally obtained a judgment of a referee declaring invalid an ordinance which prohibited churches in a residential area. The decision was affirmed by the appellate division but no opinion was published.

The Lawrence, New York, Temple Israel case,[173,182] in which the zoning board denied a permit and was overruled by the trial court which in turn was overruled by the appellate division. The last decision was on procedural grounds.

The Lawrence, New York, Brandeis School case,[191] in which the trial court reversed the action of a zoning board and ordered issuance of a permit.

The Clarkstown Catholic child shelter case,[195,210,213] in which the court required issuance of a permit for a "shelter" in which to "rear children of tender age." The decision was based on the fact that other uses were permitted, including "the raising of cattle, sheep and goats."

The Cazenovia Episcopalian case,[218,234,236] in which the court ordered issuance of a permit for an Episcopalian "conference center." It decided a dispute about the meaning of certain words in the ordinance in favor of the church.

The Long Beach Jewish temple case,[239] in which a trial court sustained a permit to expand in excess of setback provisions. Objectors said the temple had not proved "unnecessary hardship" but the court affirmed in view of the "special status" accorded churches under New York law. Objectors also said the temple was planning to operate a commercial restaurant in a residential zone, but the court said that, if so, it could be stopped by injunction.

## North Carolina.

At Winston Salem,[134] the Catholic bishop had accepted a school permit on condition that it would not be changed or expanded. He later conveyed the legal title to some sisters who sought to have this limitation lifted. The court upheld the city authorities in refusing the change and held that the sisters were bound by the bishop's agreement.

## Ohio.

In 1942, the Supreme Court of Ohio decided the Upper Arlington Lutheran church case.[40] As a thorough and studious exposition of a legal viewpoint this decision is equalled only by that in the Milwaukie, Oregon, Jehovah's Witnesses case [184] which took a contrary position. The Upper Arlington decision discussed most of the problems that arise under the due process clause. In general, it cast the burden of proof upon the city and minimized the justifications advanced, namely elimination of noise, annoyances, and traffic hazards.

However, the Supreme Court of Ohio itself has stated [59] that "reduced to its lowest terms, the decision in [the Upper Arlington case] was based upon the . . . fact that the [synod] had been misled by the zoning and village commission. . . ." There was also a clear indication that the commission had acted in excess of the authority granted in the ordinance. Therefore much of the Upper Arlington opinion should be treated as dictum. This is my view even though the case is cited with approval perhaps more often than any other church zoning case.

In the Cleveland Heights Jewish case [59] the court sustained the permit denial on the grounds that it would help prevent depreciation of nearby property. The court impliedly repudiated its own previous view casting the burden of justification on the city authorities. The case was refused review in the Supreme Court of the United States.[61]

I have characterized the Beachwood Jewish case of 1953 [101] as one in which bias and prejudice actually existed which the court refused to call by its proper name. Instead, the decision was based on a careful balancing of various factors, including a favorable opinion of religion as a public service, a narrow interpretation of the ordinance under which the board acted, and a very unfavorable opinion of the justifications advanced, including the enhancement of the tax base.

In the Dayton Christian Science case of 1955 [122,142] the central question was whether parking lots were "customarily incidental or accessory" to churches. The court held that under modern conditions they are.

In the South Euclid Jewish case of 1956 [140] the court of appeals of Cuyahoga County rejected another attempt to ban a Jewish synagogue from a location on Cedar Road in that city. The synagogue was of the orthodox branch of Judaism which forbids its members to make use of automobiles on the Sabbath.

The four Ohio decisions are inconclusive. There is no indication that its courts will invalidate regulation of the religious use of land if justfied but there is some indication that such justification will be examined with care.

*Oregon.*

The Portland Catholic school case of 1932 [27] and the Milwaukie Jehovah's Witnesses case of 1958 [184] contrast judicial attitudes of the Jet Age with those of earlier eras. The first decision nullified the action of the city denying a permit for a parochial school at 39th and East Glisan, at the intersection of two busy traffic arteries.

The decision was sound in itself, being based on the unconstitutional delegation of power by the city. However, the court discussed many irrelevant problems and cast very serious doubt upon the validity of the justifications advanced such as protection of property values, elimination of noise, inconvenience and traffic dangers, and aesthetic purposes.

In the 1958 case [184] the same supreme court sustained exclusion of a Kingdom Hall from a residence district in a Portland suburb. It wrote what is probably the most learned and thoroughgoing opinion on church zoning. It repudiated the "absolutist" doctrines, declined to give a "cloak of immunity" to churches, and denied that exclusion was an undue interference with religious liberty. It sustained the purposes of regulation which the earlier decision had rejected, saying that the earlier controversy had been "disposed of . . . in terms of facts prevailing at that time (1930)."

*Pennsylvania.*

Writing in the *University of Pittsburgh Law Review* for March 1961,[230] Richard D. Klaber says that "it would be dangerous and difficult, if not impossible, to glean from the Pennsylvania church zoning cases a hard and fast rule of law. . . ." The decisions are as confused and confusing as those in any state of the Union.

In 1943 the supreme court sustained [46] the grant of a permit for a combination home and synagogue in a residential area where churches were also permitted. In 1945, the court had before it two synagogue cases, in one of which it refused a permit [50] and in the other of which it granted one.[51] In refusing the permit in the case first mentioned,[50] the court compared the synagogue to a theatre, and showed readiness to subject churches to the same kind of land use regulations that are enforced against other institutions.

Yet in 1950 a trial court in Pittsburgh decided a case in favor of the Franciscan Brothers [81] requiring issuance of a permit for sleeping quarters for retreatants in a residential area. The decision is probably the strongest judicial statement to be found in support of a special status for churches under zoning laws.

In the Cheltenham Township Jewish case [105] the decision of a trial court was also adverse to the city but it was not appealed.

The Bethel Borough Jehovah's Witnesses case [159] was decided by an intermediate state court in favor of the city, and was refused review in the Supreme Court of Pennsylvania and in the Supreme Court of the United States.[168] It is one of the strongest on record in support of the right of cities to regulate the religious use of land.

Almost simultaneously with its refusal to review the Witnesses' defeat in the Bethel case the Supreme Court of Pennsylvania was deciding the Cheltenham Township regional high school case [162] in favor of the Catholic archbishop. As shown elsewhere, this result was achieved by gross misinterpretation of the ordinance.

A year later, in *Best v. Zoning Board of Adjustment*,[174] it cited with approval the Connecticut case excluding a Methodist church from a residential district in West Hartford.[139] The court said: "We are satisfied that at long last conscientious municipal officials have been sufficiently empowered to adopt reasonable zoning measures designed toward preserving the wholesome and attractive characteristics of their communities and the values of . . . property."

In 1959 in the case of the Russian Orthodox church at Ambridge [207] the court sustained refusal of a permit to use land as a cemetery, holding that it was not a "religious use" under the ordinance. Almost simultaneously, in the Mt. Lebanon Township case,[208] it also refused a use permit to the local Grange for a church which they had purchased from the Presbyterians. The Grange's use was held to be "decidedly different . . . and certainly . . . of a lower classification" than a religious use. Lastly, in 1960, the court decided in favor of the Lettish Baptist Church at Philadelphia, sustaining a permit issued by the zoning board.[216] The result was sound, but in addition the court enunciated some very bad law on the subject of separation of church and state.

In his article Mr. Klaber says that the Pennsylvania decisions "run somewhere near the middle of the stream." I suggest instead that they zig-zag from one side of the stream to the other. The results seem to depend principally on the identity of the judge writing the opinion.

*South Carolina.*

In 1957 the supreme court decided a case [157] involving a proposed expansion of the school attached to the First Baptist Church of Charleston. The board granted the permit subject to a limitation upon enrollment to 270 students. The objecting property owners challenged the issuance of the permit. The church challenged the limitation to 270 students. The supreme court sustained the zoning board in both respects. There is nothing in the decision to indicate any reluctance on the part of this court to sustain reasonable regulation of the religious use of land.

*Texas.*

The Supreme Court of Texas has decided only one church zoning case (in favor of the Church of God at Sherman in 1944 [48,49]). In addition, the El Paso court of civil appeals decided a case in 1953 against a Protestant evangelical center at Dallas; [102] the Fort Worth court of civil appeals decided one in 1956 in favor of the Haltom City Jehovah's Witnesses; [136] and the Austin court of civil appeals decided one in the same year in favor of the Episcopal Seminary of the Southwest at that city.[143]

The Sherman case has been relied on extensively as forbidding the exclusion of churches from residential zones. Actually, it is not a precedent on this point because, during the hearing, counsel for the city—wisely or unwisely—admitted that the ordinance was invalid.

In the Haltom City case the court of appeals held that the Witnesses had complied with the ordinance, so that discussion of constitutional issues became irrelevant. However, the decision includes much dictum favorable to the absolute anti-exclusion rule, relying in turn on the dictum in the Sherman case.

The other two decisions are of no great importance. The evangelistic center was held "not a church" and the seminary's library was held not to be such a "nuisance per se" as would authorize an injunction against its construction once it had obtained a permit in due form.

While, as stated, the Supreme Court of Texas has not ruled definitively, the courts seem generally hostile to the regulation of the religious use of land.

*Washington.*

The only case is that of Jehovah's Witnesses at Wenatchee in 1957.[165] The ordinance authorized permits for churches in residential areas upon approval by the planning board, pursuant to certain standards. The only substantial reason advanced by the board for refusing the permit was that "the proposed use would cause an undue amount of traffic through a primarily residential district."

The court examined the evidence in detail and said: "We do not think there was substantial evidence before the board to support this contention." A mandamus order was entered compelling the issuance of the permit. The court also discussed the absolute anti-exclusion rule and expressed its disapproval of that rule. There was also a strong minority opinion opposing issuance of the permit.

*West Virginia.*

In 1930, the supreme court of appeals granted mandamus against the City of Beckley requiring issuance of a permit for construction of a Church of God.[25] The zoning board action refusing the permit had been based on a statute which banned any "public garage, filling station, store or other industry of any kind or character." The court held that a church was not included under any of these descriptions. Incidentally the court also held that there was inadequate proof of undue interference with traffic by the particular church. This case is often cited in support of the absolute anti-exclusion rule. In my opinion it does not support that rule but is based entirely on an interpretation of the local ordinance.

*Wisconsin.*

The decision of the Supreme Court of Wisconsin in the Wauwatosa Lutheran high school case of 1954[106] was a milestone of church zoning law comparable to the Porterville, California, case of 1949.[67] The Wauwatosa case repudiated the theory that it is necessarily an unconstitutional discrimination to exclude religious or other private schools from an area where public schools are admitted. The case is discussed at length in this text.

On the other hand, in the Bayside Baptist church decision of 1961,[231] the court joined New York, California and Michigan, all of which had disapproved the exclusion of churches from an entire town or from "practically" an entire town. Another opinion, signed by the same number of justices, supported the absolute anti-exclusion rule as applied even to a single residential zone. A seventh justice dissented.

The Wisconsin court decided one other case,[201] in favor of the Evangelical Covenant Mission Church of America. It had requested a permit to restore or replace a building destroyed by fire. The permit was refused by the board, which decision was reversed by the supreme court with instructions to the effect that under the ordinance the church had a right to restore the house. No important issues were settled by this decision.

# CHAPTER 22.

## CHURCH ZONING IN UNITED STATES COURTS

The United States Supreme Court has refused to review a total of ten cases in which state courts have upheld the public regulation of the religious use of land. So far as I can discover, no attempt has ever been made to obtain review in that court of any zoning case decided in favor of a church. However no firm conclusions should be drawn from these statistics. The supreme court exercises very broad discretion in selecting the issues it will decide.

Except in an extreme case, I would not expect the supreme court to follow the example of those state courts which, because of the comparative importance of the public service rendered by religion, have deemed so many justifications for religious land use too insubstantial under the due process clause. However, the court would be prompt to overthrow any undue discrimination against a church. It would also invalidate any regulation that amounts to a substantial interference with religious liberty. I believe that such an interference would be found to exist only if the church or church school were excluded from so large an area that alternative accessible sites were not reasonably available.

This opinion is based in part on the decision in the case of the *Society of Sisters* [17] invalidating an attempted exclusion of parochial and other private schools from the entire state of Oregon. However, I would not expect the high court to follow the California Supreme Court in the Piedmont case [125] in saying that people are entitled to send their children to private schools located in their immediate neighborhoods—and implying that churchgoers are entitled to equally accessible churches.

Pfeffer in his *Church, State and Freedom,* [97] said in 1953 that it was "safe to predict that the United States Supreme Court, if called upon to decide, would invalidate a zoning ordinance that bars churches from an entire municipality." Pfeffer believes, then, that the United States Supreme Court would have affirmed such decisions as were handed down in the cases of the Plandome, New York, Unitarians,[87] the Orchard Lake, Michigan, Catholics,[94] the Piedmont, California, Catholics,[125] and the Bayside, Wisconsin, Baptists.[231] No such cases have been presented to the court. I believe it would rule as Mr. Pfeffer predicts, but only if it were shown that the exclusion actually deprived the church of reasonably accessible alternative sites. It would not adopt so artificial an index of accessibility as the state courts have used, namely the town boundary.

A year after the *Society of Sisters* decision,[17] the supreme court decided the leading case on zoning, the Euclid, Ohio, case.[18] The court made clear that it was not deciding as to the validity of the clause excluding churches from residential zones. However, in 1947, the court refused to review the Cleveland Heights Jewish decision by which the same Ohio court had sustained refusal of a permit for a religious school in a residential area. In 1953 the New Jersey Supreme Court, in the Orange, New Jersey, Protestant seminary case,[99] with Mr. Justice Brennan (now of the United States Supreme Court) concurring, saw fit [99:490] to cite the Euclid, Ohio, case as part of its justification for excluding the seminary.

In 1948, the supreme court refused [63,65] to review the Michigan decision [60] excluding the Full Salvation Union camp meeting from a site in Portage Township, a decision which treated the church institution harshly. In 1950, it refused,[71,76] for want of a substantial federal question, to review the Porterville, California, decision [67] sustaining the total exclusion of churches from a residential area. Pfeffer says [97] that by this refusal the California decision was "in effect sustained" by the United States Supreme Court.

In 1950, the supreme court made its first and only direct statement on church zoning. It appears in the case of *American Communications Association v. Douds*.[80] The court referred back to its Porterville decision [71,76] which had then been only recently issued. It said: [80]

> When the effect of a statute or ordinance upon the exercise of First Amendment freedoms is relatively small and the public interest to be affected is substantial, it is obvious that a rigid test requiring a showing of imminent danger to the security of the

nation is an absurdity. We recently dismissed for want of substantiality an appeal in which a church group contended that its First Amendment rights were violated by a municipal zoning ordinance preventing the building of churches in residential areas.

In January of 1952 a United States circuit court of appeals [91] was asked by Jehovah's Witnesses to enjoin under the Civil Rights Act the enforcement by criminal action of the zoning ordinance of Atlanta, Georgia. The federal appeals court refused to intervene, stating that the challenged ordinance gave "no power to interrupt religious services."

In December of the same year the oft-quoted article in St. John's Law Review [95] made a prediction with respect to the supreme court's attitude which, in view of the circumstances, seems almost incredible. It referred to the Porterville decision as merely a "decision of an intermediate court of California." It disregarded the fact that the Porterville case had gone also to the Supreme Court of California and the Supreme Court of the United States and that both courts had refused further review. It disregarded the action of the United States Supreme Court in the Portage, Michigan, case.[63,65] It disregarded the court's remarks in the Douds case. Regarding the prospects for church zoning in the United States Supreme Court, the St. John's Law Review article said:

> It is submitted that if this [church zoning] legislation were presented to the supreme court, the court would declare it to be inconsistent with American philosophical and social values, to contravene the purpose of zoning, and strike it down as being violative of due process. It would seem that this opinion is not unwarranted in view of the treatment afforded charitable institutions in the supreme and federal courts, the weight of authority by state judicial decision, and the position taken by leading text writers.

The only church zoning decisions cited in support of this statement are a few decided in state courts. Because the author of this article disregarded the previous decisions of the United States Supreme Court in church zoning cases, I do not consider his predictions regarding future policy to be reliable.

In 1955 the court was asked [120] to review a decision, that of the Wauwatosa, Wisconsin, Lutheran case,[106] in which a religious school was excluded from a residential zone. It again refused review, and the *Notre Dame Lawyer* [127] said that "the refusal . . . to hear the appeal . . . for lack of a substantial federal question seems to indicate that the exclusion of the private school from an area where public schools were allowed was not arbitrary or otherwise violative of federal constitutional provisions."

The court has refused review of several other cases of religious land use regulation decided adversely to churches. These include the Bethel Borough, Pennsylvania, Jehovah's Witnesses case [159,168] and the Milwaukie, Oregon, Jehovah's Witnesses case.[184] In the Milwaukie case, the Oregon court [184:27] had relied largely on the Porterville case [67] and its subsequent treatment by the United States Supreme Court.[71,76] It had said that "as was later demonstrated by *American Communications Association v. Douds*,[80] the Porterville exclusion is not an infringement upon the liberties guaranteed by the First Amendment." The high court refused to review the Oregon decision.[200]

In 1959 the court also refused [199] to review the decision of the California court against the Jehovah's Witnesses of Azusa.[186] In 1960 it refused [219] to review the decision against the Allendale Jehovah's Witnesses by the Supreme Court of New Jersey [205] wherein the state court had sustained a three-pews-per-car parking space requirement enacted after the Witnesses had filed their application. It also refused to review [224] the California decision in the San Marino case [223] enjoining the continued use of a Catholic church parking lot and refusing a permit therefor.

The record of the United States Supreme Court is sparse but it indicates that the court will probably not intervene unless and until there is a clear showing of violation of the equal protection clause or of the religious liberty clause. I do not expect the states to commit such violations in the near future, if ever. Indeed the Supreme Court of the United States may never intervene in church zoning cases. If not, the law of church zoning will continue to be written by our 50 different judicial systems. There will be an interesting variety of opinion among these courts, on which I hope my readers will keep informed by reference to the supplements to this volume.

# CHAPTER 23.

## Conclusion

A distinguished New York lawyer who helped me with this book said: "All of the church cases, it seems to me, have been decided on emotional grounds rather than on correct legal principles." As to his own state, this is quite true. In other states emotion is a large element in many cases but other decisions reflect intellectual integrity and careful legal, social and political thought. The difficulty is the universal one that the time of both lawyers and judges is usually budgeted and working hours allotted to a single case are so limited as to preclude profound consideration. I hope this book will make a contribution to the work of presenting and deciding cases and arriving at informed and just decisions.

The early chapters showed how the absolute anti-exclusion rule was developed from the concept of due process of law which forbids interference with private property except for a valid and substantial public purpose. Since no regulation of religious land use can be effective unless backed up with the power to refuse permits, the absolute anti-exclusion rule would really be an absolute anti-regulation rule.

Further investigation of its sources revealed, however, that the absolute anti-exclusion rule had not been adopted by any substantial number of courts to which it had been attributed. There is properly no absolute anti-exclusion rule. Each church zoning case ought to be decided on its own merits after weighing the purpose accomplished and the adverse effect, if any, on private rights. The investigation which led to this conclusion included an examination of various public purposes which the courts have actually recognized as justifications for the regulation of the religious use of land.

Equal protection of the laws was found to be a concept that in one sense has been overemphasized. This occurred in cases holding it necessarily unconstitutional to exclude religious or private schools from zones where public schools are permitted, or to impose upon them zoning regulations different from

334

those imposed on public schools. In another sense, this clause of the constitution has been underemphasized. Churches have neglected it as a defense against regulation which actually does unduly discriminate between them and other churches, or between them and secular enterprises. As property owners, churches may not hope for much better treatment than that accorded other property owners under the due process clause. However, under the equal protection clause, they can certainly insist on being treated no worse. Such discrimination has sometimes occurred and been underemphasized in church zoning cases. Fault is also found with the courts for failure to uncover and condemn irrational prejudice or bias where it exists.

Religious liberty, which is largely an individual right, must be carefully distinguished from the special status that some courts have bestowed on churches in consideration of the great public service they render. True constitutional religious liberty, however, is the final bastion against real oppression in church zoning cases. It can be invoked successfully in any case where zoning regulations actually and substantially interfere with the right to worship. This would occur, for instance, when they exclude church institutions from so large an area as to deprive them of reasonably accessible alternative sites.

As to the future, I recommend consideration of the views expressed in 1955 by Frederick H. Bair, Jr.: [215]

In its new role in residential neighborhoods, the church is becoming an increasingly important social element. It serves all ages, which schools generally do not. As denominational differences are minimized, there is promise of substituting a smaller number of well-supported and well-run churches for myriad starveling branches. This gives the church, as an institution, the promise of serving more people and serving them better.

The Church is evolving into a very desirable kind of non-tax-supported community center at a time when tax money for the support of other kinds of community centers is hard to find.

Churches in residential neighborhoods may create problems of noise, traffic, parking and overcrowding of land. In their traditional role, and in locations near commercial centers or in developed residential areas, churches contributed to these problems for limited times and in places where the church contribution to general confusion was a minor one. In their new roles and their new locations, this is no longer the case. The seven-day-a-week church in a new residential neighborhood may become a major cause of trouble in an otherwise serene environment.

The trend of future restrictive legislation depends on the success of voluntary action. If developers can be induced to provide suitable church sites in new subdivisions, and if church planners and church administrators choose and use sites carefully, with full regard for protection of the public interest, public action will be limited. If voluntary action is lacking or inadequate, there will be increasing pressure for public controls.

The courts are already becoming aware of the need for some public control of location, planning, and operation of churches. If church-created conflicts with the public interest are not reduced voluntarily, there is little doubt that the judiciary will uphold increasing legal restrictions.

# TABLES

---

\* This listing includes only church zoning cases fully analyzed herein.
\*\* This listing includes all cases mentioned herein.

# CHRONOLOGICAL TABLE
## OF REFERENCES
(AND PAGES OF TEXT WHERE CITED)

1. Holy Bible: 96, 120, 205, 206, 208, 221, 227, 278, 285, 290.

2. Magna Charta, 1215 (Sir Edward Coke: The Second Part of the Laws of England, 1642, p. 578) : 21.

3. Thomas More: Utopia, 1516 (Heritage Press, New York, 1959) : 6.

4. Dartmouth College, Trustees of v. Woodward, 4 Wheat (17 United States Supreme Court Reports) 518 (Supreme Court of the United States, February, 1819) : 200, 217.

5. Alexis Charles Henri Maurice Clerel de Tocqueville: Democracy in America, 1830 (A. A. Knopf, New York, 1945) : 212, 241, 244.

6. Ernst Freund: The Police Power, Public Policy and Constitutional Rights (Callaghan and Company, Chicago, 1904) : 18.

7. Noble State Bank v. Haskell, 219, United States Supreme Court Reports 104, 31 Supreme Court Reporter 186, 55 Lawyers' Edition, United States Supreme Court Reports 112, 32 Lawyers' Reports Annotated, New Series, 1062, American Annotated Cases, 1912-A, p. 487, Supreme Court of the United States, January 3, 1911: 18.

8. Proceedings of the Fourth National Conference on City Planning, Boston, Massachusetts, 1912 (University Press, Cambridge) : 8, 17, 52, 71, 79.

9. William B. Patterson: The Religious Value of Proper Housing, The Annals, January, 1914, Housing and Town Planning (American Academy of Political and Social Sciences, Philadelphia) : 7, 17, 51, 73, 79.

10. Proceedings of the Ninth Annual Conference on City Planning, Kansas City, Missouri, 1917 (University Press, Cambridge) : 17, 52, 88.

11. Proceedings of the Tenth Annual Conference on City Planning, St. Louis, Missouri, 1918 (University Press, Cambridge) : 95, 306.

12. Catholic Bishop v. Village of Palos Park, 121 North Eastern Reporter 561, 286 Illinois Supreme Court Reports 400, Supreme Court of Illinois, December 18, 1918: 77.

13. Grace Missionary Church v. Zion, 133 North Eastern Reporter 268, 300 Illinois Supreme Court Reports 513, Supreme Court of Illinois, December 22, 1921 (Zion, Illinois, Grace Missionary church case): 6, 187, 189, 190, 191.

14. State ex rel. Westminster Presbyterian Church of Omaha, Nebraska v. Edgcomb, Engineer, etc., 189 North Western Reporter 617, Second Case, 108 Nebraska Reports 859, 27 American

Law Reports 437, Supreme Court of Nebraska, June 28, 1922 (Omaha, Nebraska, Presbyterian church case): xi, 27, 30, 52, 53, 54, 56, 71, 73, 79, 80, 84, 127, 253, 293, 294, 318.

15. T. Harold Hughes: Towns and Town Planning (The Clarendon Press, Oxford, 1923): 6.

16. Meyer v. State of Nebraska, 262 United States Supreme Court Reports 390, 43 Supreme Court Reporter 625, 67 Lawyers' Edition, United States Supreme Court Reports 1042, 29 American Law Reports 1446, Supreme Court of the United States, June 4, 1923: 213.

17. Pierce, Governor of Oregon, et al. v. Society of Sisters of Charity of the Holy Names of Jesus and Mary and Hill Military Academy, 268 United States Supreme Court Reports 510, 45 Supreme Court Reporter 571, 69 Lawyers' Edition, United States Supreme Court Reports 1070, 39 American Law Reports 468, Supreme Court of the United States, June 1, 1925: 41, 159, 176, 213, 216, 228, 239, 292, 311, 330, 331.

18. Village of Euclid v. Ambler Realty Co., 272 United States Supreme Court Reports 365, 47 Supreme Court Reporter 114, 71 Lawyers' Edition, United States Supreme Court Reports 303, 54 American Law Reports 1016, Supreme Court of the United States, November 22, 1926: 26, 29, 43, 55, 58, 71, 95, 103, 119, 158, 213, 247, 251, 331.

19. Western Theological Seminary v. Evanston, 156 North Eastern Reporter 778, 325 Illinois Supreme Court Reports 511, Supreme Court of Illinois, April 20, 1927 (Evanston, Illinois, Episcopal seminary case) (Same case as Reference No. 23): xi, 27, 30, 31, 68, 137, 168, 272, 287, 314.

20. Pettis v. Alpha Alpha Chapter, Phi Beta Pi, 213 North Western Reporter 835, 115 Nebraska Reports 525, Supreme Court of Nebraska, April 26, 1927: 319.

22. Nectow v. Cambridge, 277 United States Supreme Court Reports 183, 48 Supreme Court Reporter 447, 72 Lawyers' Edition, United States Supreme Court Reports 842, Supreme Court of the United States, May 14, 1928: 21, 58, 61, 65, 66.

23. Western Theological Seminary v. Evanston, 162 North Eastern Reporter 863, 331 Illinois Reports 257, Supreme Court of Illinois, June 23, 1928, (Evanston, Illinois, Episcopal seminary case) (Same case as Reference No. 19): xi, 30, 137, 168, 287, 314.

24. Applestein v. Osborne, 143 Atlantic Reporter 666, 156 Maryland Reports 40, Court of Appeals of Maryland, November 16, 1928: 252, 254.

25. State ex rel. Howell v. Meador, 154 South Eastern Reporter 876, 109 West Virginia Reports 368, Supreme Court of Appeals of West Virginia, September 16, 1930 (Beckley, West Virginia, Church of God case): xi, 27, 31, 35, 46, 119, 121, 137, 236, 273, 328.

**26.** Charles Clinton Marshall: The Roman Catholic Church in the Modern State (Dodd, Mead and Company, New York, 1931) : 225.

**27.** Roman Catholic Archbishop of Oregon v. Baker, 15 Pacific Reporter, Second Series 391, 140 Oregon Reports 600, Supreme Court of Oregon, October 18, 1932 (Portland, Oregon, Catholic school case) : xi, 10, 27, 31, 72, 73, 96, 106, 111, 115, 119, 120, 124, 127, 168, 169, 258, 269, 295, 301, 324.

**28.** Beardsley v. Evangelical Lutheran Bethlehem Church, 246 North Western Reporter 180, 261 Michigan Reports 458, Supreme Court of Michigan, January 3, 1933 (Grand Rapids, Michigan, Lutheran church case) : xi, 196, 254, 255, 317.

**29.** Otto J. Frohnmayer: Municipal Corporations—Zoning— Constitutionality, Oregon Law Review, 12:136, February, 1933: 164.

**30.** Linden M.E. Church v. City of Linden, 173 Atlantic Reporter 593, 113 New Jersey Law Reports 188, Supreme Court of New Jersey, July 13, 1934: 153, 154, 157.

**31.** Corpus Juris Secundum (American Law Book Company, Brooklyn, New York, 1936 with annual supplements) (Article on Zoning) : 29.

**32.** American Jurisprudence (Bancroft Whitney Co., San Francisco, and Lawyers' Cooperative Publishing Company, Rochester, 1936 with annual supplements) (Article on Zoning) : 29, 39, 45, 252.

**33.** City of Miami Beach v. State ex rel. Lear, 175 Southern Reporter 537, 128 Florida Reports 750, Supreme Court of Florida, June 30, 1937: 169.

**33-A.** United States v. Carolene Products Co., 304 United States Supreme Court Reports 144, 82 Lawyers' Edition, United States Supreme Court Reports 1234, 58 Supreme Court Reporter 778, Supreme Court of the United States, April 25, 1938: 256.

**34.** Catholic Bishop of Chicago v. Kingery, 20 North Eastern Reporter, Second Series 583, 371 Illinois Supreme Court Reports 58, Supreme Court of Illinois, April 14, 1939 (Winnetka, Illinois, Catholic school case) : xi, xv, 10, 14, 27, 31, 168, 170, 171, 175, 176, 181, 251, 314.

**35.** State ex rel. Roman Catholic Bishop of Reno v. Hill, 90 Pacific Reporter, Second Series 217, 59 Nevada Reports 231, Supreme Court of Nevada, May 8, 1939 (Reno, Nevada, Catholic church case) : xi, 10, 14, 27, 31, 32, 96, 106, 112, 113, 137, 156, 252, 296, 298, 301, 319.

**36.** Edward Murray Bassett: Zoning: The Laws, Administration, and Court Decisions during the First Twenty Years (Russell Sage Foundation, New York, 1940) (Quoted by permission) : 8, 11, 26, 72, 119, 308.

**37.** Cantwell v. State of Connecticut, 310 United States Supreme Court Reports 296, 60 Supreme Court Reporter 900, 84

Lawyers' Edition, United States Supreme Court Reports 1213, 128 American Law Reports 1352, Supreme Court of the United States, May 20, 1940: 211.

38. Connor v. University Park, 142 South Western Reporter, Second Series 706, Court of Civil Appeals of Texas, June 8, 1940: 158.

39. Cox v. State of New Hampshire, 312 United States Supreme Court Reports 569, 61 Supreme Court Reporter 762, 85 Lawyers' Edition, United States Supreme Court Reports 1049, 133 American Law Reports 1396, Supreme Court of the United States, March 31, 1941: 121, 128, 133.

40. State ex rel. Synod of Ohio of United Lutheran Church in America v. Joseph, 39 North Eastern Reporter, Second Series 515, 139 Ohio State Reports 229, Supreme Court of Ohio, January 28, 1942 (Upper Arlington, Ohio, Lutheran church case): xii, 10, 11, 12, 17, 19, 27, 30, 32, 36, 39, 67, 72, 79, 97, 100, 106, 107, 109, 110, 111, 120, 150, 158, 216, 246, 247, 252, 253, 254, 323.

41. Same case, with annotation: Zoning Regulations as Affecting Churches, 138 American Law Reports 1274: 32, 36.

42. Jabez Gridley Sutherland: Statutes and Statutory Construction, Third Edition by Frank E. Horack (Callaghan and Co., Chicago, 1943 with supplements): 255.

43. Martin v. City of Struthers, 319 United States Supreme Court Reports 141, 63 Supreme Court Reporter 862, 87 Lawyers' Edition, United States Supreme Court Reports 1313, Supreme Court of the United States, May 3, 1943: 209.

44. Murdock v. Commonwealth of Pennsylvania, 319 United States Supreme Court Reports 105, 63 Supreme Court Reporter 870, 87 Lawyers' Edition, United States Supreme Court Reports 1292, 146 American Law Reports 81, Supreme Court of the United States, May 3, 1943: 221.

45. Annotation: What Constitutes a "Family" within the Meaning of a Zoning Regulation or Restrictive Covenant, 172 American Law Reports 1172 (following the report of a case decided September 7, 1943): 276.

46. Appeal of Floersheim, et al., 34 Atlantic Reporter, Second Series 62, 348 Pennsylvania State Reports 98, Supreme Court of Pennsylvania, October 15, 1943 (Pittsburgh, Pennsylvania, Jewish synagogue case): xii, 273, 325.

47. Foster v. Beverley, 53 North Eastern Reporter, Second Series 693, 315 Massachusetts Reports 567, Supreme Judicial Court of Massachusetts, February 29, 1944: 305.

47-A. Same case, with annotation: Zoning Regulations in Relation to Cemeteries, 151 American Law Reports 742: 77.

48. Simms v. City of Sherman, 181 South Western Reporter, Second Series 100, Court of Civil Appeals of Texas, April 28, 1944 (Sherman, Texas, Church of God case) (Same case as Reference No. 49): xii, 27, 33, 34, 97, 115, 116, 138, 191, 192, 193, 195, 202, 216, 245, 253, 263, 327.

**49.** City of Sherman v. Simms, 183 South Western Reporter, Second Series 415, 143 Texas Supreme Court Reports 115, Supreme Court of Texas, November 15, 1944 (Sherman, Texas, Church of God case) (Same case as Reference No. 48) : xii, 11, 27, 33, 97, 138, 191, 193, 195, 216, 245, 327.

**50.** Kurman v. Zoning Board of Adjustment of City of Philadelphia, 40 Atlantic Reporter, Second Series 381, 351 Pennsylvania State Reports 247, Supreme Court of Pennsylvania, January 2, 1945 (Philadelphia, Pennsylvania, Jewish synagogue case) : xii, 79, 80, 86, 325.

**51.** Overbrook Farms Club v. Zoning Board of Adjustment of City of Philadelphia, 40 Atlantic Reporter, Second Series 423, 351 Pennsylvania State Reports 77, Supreme Court of Pennsylvania, January 2, 1945 (Philadelphia, Pennsylvania, Jewish synagogue case) : xii, 215, 273, 325.

**52.** Thomas v. Collins, 323 United States Supreme Court Reports 516, 65 Supreme Court Reporter 315, 89 Lawyers' Edition, United States Supreme Court Reports 430, Supreme Court of the United States, January 8, 1945 : 256.

**53.** Ellsworth v. Gercke; 156 Pacific Reporter, Second Series 242, 62 Arizona Reports 198, Supreme Court of Arizona, February 24, 1945 (Mesa, Arizona, Catholic church case) : xii, 11, 27, 34, 138, 140, 151, 310.

**54.** Marsh v. Alabama, 326 United States Supreme Court Reports 501, 66 Supreme Court Reporter 276, 90 Lawyers' Edition, United States Supreme Court Reports 265, Supreme Court of the United States, January 8, 1945 : 209.

**55.** New Mission Baptist Church v. City of Atlanta, 37 South Eastern Reporter, Second Series 377, 200 Georgia Reports 518, Supreme Court of Georgia, February 21, 1946 (Atlanta, Georgia, Baptist church case) : xii, 205, 313.

**56.** Pentecostal Holiness Church of Montgomery v. Dunn, 27 Southern Reporter, Second Series 561, 248 Alabama Supreme Court Reports 314, Supreme Court of Alabama, June 20, 1946 (Montgomery, Alabama, Pentecostal Holiness church case) : xii, 27, 35, 46, 116, 193, 194, 195, 236, 274, 296, 298, 301, 310.

**57.** Keeling v. Board of Zoning Appeals of City of Indianapolis, 69 North Eastern Reporter, Second Series 613, 117 Indiana Appellate Court Reports 314, Appellate Court of Indiana, November 21, 1946 (Indianapolis, Indiana, Methodist church plant case) : xii, 12, 72, 97, 155, 162, 255, 275, 276, 277, 283, 301, 315.

**58.** People ex rel. Everson v. Board of Education, 330 United States Supreme Court Reports 1, 67 Supreme Court Reporter 504, 91 Lawyers' Edition, United States Supreme Court Reports 711, 168 American Law Reports 1392, Supreme Court of the United States, February 10, 1947 : 22.

**59.** State ex rel. Hacharedi v. Baxter, 74 North Eastern Reporter, Second Series 242, 148 Ohio State Reports 221, Supreme Court of Ohio, July 2, 1947 (Cleveland Heights, Ohio, Jewish school case) (Same case as Reference No. 61) : xii, 11, 12, 27, 33, 67, 100, 107, 170, 253, 260, 323.

**60.** Portage Township v. Full Salvation Union, 29 North Western Reporter, Second Series 297, 318 Michigan Reports 693, Supreme Court of Michigan, October 13, 1947 (Portage Township, Michigan, nondenominational Protestant camp meeting case) (Same case as Reference Nos. 63 and 65): xii, 4, 27, 35, 107, 108, 110, 116, 194, 195, 254, 278, 279, 317, 331.

**61.** Ohio ex rel. Vaad Hachinuch Hacharedi (Traditional Education Council) v. Baxter, 332 United States Supreme Court Reports 827 No. 426, 68 Supreme Court Reporter 209, 92 Lawyers' Edition, United States Supreme Court Reports 402, United States Supreme Court, November 24, 1947, (Cleveland Heights, Ohio, Jewish school case) (Same case as Reference No. 59) : xii, 12, 324.

**62.** Board of Zoning Appeals of City of Indianapolis v. Wheaton, 76 North Eastern Reporter, Second Series 597, 118 Indiana Appellate Court Reports 38, Appellate Court of Indiana, January 9, 1948 (Indianapolis, Indiana, Catholic combination unit case) : xiii, 27, 35, 265, 275, 276, 282, 283, 315.

**63.** Full Salvation Union v. Portage Township, Kalamazoo County, Michigan, 333 United States Supreme Court Reports 851 No. 609, 68 Supreme Court Reporter 735, 92 Lawyers' Edition, United States Supreme Court Reports 1133, Supreme Court of the United States, March 15, 1948 (Portage Township, Michigan, nondenominational Protestant camp meeting case) (Same cases as Reference Nos. 60 and 65): xii, 4, 194, 331, 332.

**64.** Shelley v. Kraemer, 334 United States Supreme Court Reports 1, 68 Supreme Court Reporter 836, 92 Lawyers' Edition, United States Supreme Court Reports 1161, 3 American Law Reports, Second Series 441, Supreme Court of the United States, May 3, 1948: 174.

**65.** Full Salvation Union v. Portage Township, 334 United States Supreme Court Reports 830 No. 609, 68 Supreme Court Reporter 1336, 92 Lawyers' Edition, United States Supreme Court Reports 1757, Supreme Court of the United States, May 24, 1948 (Portage Township, Michigan, nondenominational Protestant camp meeting case) (Same case as Reference Nos. 60 and 63) : xii, 4, 194, 331, 332.

**66.** Eugene McQuillin: The Law of Municipal Corporations (Callaghan and Company, Chicago, 1949, Third Edition with supplements) : 65, 207.

**67.** Corporation of Presiding Bishop of Church of Jesus Christ of Latter Day Saints v. City of Porterville, 203 Pacific Reporter, Second Series 823, 90 California Appellate Reports, Second Series 656, District Court of Appeals of California, Fourth District, March 17, 1949 (Hearing denied by Supreme Court of California, May 12, 1949) (Porterville, California, Mormom temple case) (Same case as Reference Nos. 71 and 76) : xiii, xv, 9, 12, 14, 35,

38, 42, 100, 114, 122, 124, 136, 139, 215, 217, 221, 223, 236, 259, 311, 328, 331, 333.

**68.** Concordia Collegiate Institute v. Miller, 88 New York Supplement, Second Series 825, Supreme Court of New York, Westchester County, April 4, 1949 (Bronxville, New York, Lutheran college case) (Same case as Reference Nos. 74, 77 and 82) : xiii, 321.

**69.** Hill v. Kesselring, 220 South Western Reporter, Second Series 850, 310 Kentucky Reports 332, Court of Appeals of Kentucky, April 22, 1949 (Louisville, Kentucky, Baptist church case) : xiii, 114, 122, 316.

**70.** Johnson v. Evangelical Lutheran Church of the Messiah, 54 South Eastern Reporter, Second Series 722, 79 Georgia Appeals Reports 604, Court of Appeals of Georgia, July 15, 1949 (Decatur, Georgia, Lutheran church case) : xiii, 314.

**71.** Corporation of the Presiding Bishop of the Church of Jesus Christ of Latter-Day Saints v. City of Porterville, 338 United States Supreme Court Reports 805 No. 245, 70 Supreme Court Reporter 78, 94 Lawyers' Edition, United States Supreme Court Reports 487, Supreme Court of the United States, October 10, 1949 (Porterville, California, Mormon temple case) (Same case as Reference Nos. 67 and 76) : xiii, 9, 12, 100, 218, 259, 311, 331, 333.

**72.** Galfas v. Ailor, 55 South Eastern Reporter, Second Series 582, 206 Georgia Reports 76, Supreme Court of Georgia, October 12, 1949 (Atlanta, Georgia, Jehovah's Witnesses' Kingdom Hall case) (Same or related cases under Reference Nos. 78 and 91) : xiii, 122, 123, 314.

**73.** Mt. Zion Baptist Church of Lodi Township v. Melillo, 68 Atlantic Reporter, Second Series 741, 3 New Jersey Reports 61, Supreme Court of New Jersey, October 24, 1949 (Lodi Township, New Jersey, Baptist church case) : xiii, 319.

**74.** Concordia Collegiate Institute v. Miller, 93 New York Supplement, Second Series 922 Case No. 1, 276 New York Supreme Court Appellate Division Reports 872, Supreme Court of New York, Appellate Division, Second Department, December 27, 1949 (Bronxville, New York, Lutheran college case) (Same case as Reference Nos. 68, 77 and 82) : xiii, 321.

**75.** Anson Phelps Stokes: Church and State in the United States (Harper, New York, 1950) : 3, 187.

**76.** Corporation of the Presiding Bishop of the Church of Jesus Christ of Latter-Day Saints, 338 United States Supreme Court Reports 939 No. 245, 70 Supreme Court Reporter 342, 94 Lawyers' Edition, United States Supreme Court Reports 579, Supreme Court of the United States, January 9, 1950 (Porterville, California, Mormon temple case) (Same cases as Reference Nos. 67 and 71) : xiii, 9, 12, 100, 218, 259, 311, 331, 333.

**77.** Concordia Collegiate Institute v. Miller, 94 New York Supplement, Second Series 829, 276 New York Supreme Court

Appellate Division Reports 922, Supreme Court of New York, Appellate Division, Second Department, January 23, 1950 (Bronxville, New York, Lutheran college case) : (Same case as Reference Nos. 68, 74 and 82) : xiii, 321.

78. Galfas v. Ailor, 57 South Eastern Reporter, Second Series 834, 81 Georgia Appeals Reports 13, Court of Appeals of Georgia, Division 1, February 17, 1950 (Atlanta, Georgia, Jehovah's Witnesses' Kingdom Hall case) (Same or related cases under Reference Nos. 72 and 91) : xiii, 122, 123, 218, 314.

79. O. Boldt: Pennsylvania Court Rules on Snob Zoning, American City, 65:129, April, 1950: 72.

80. American Communication Association, CIO v. Douds, 339 United States Supreme Court Reports 382, 70 Supreme Court Reporter 674, 94 Lawyers' Edition, United States Supreme Court Reports 925, Supreme Court of the United States, May 8, 1950: 218, 331, 333.

81. Stark, Appeal of, 72 Pennsylvania District and County Reports 168, 98 Pennsylvania Law Journal 361, Court of Common Pleas of Allegheny County, Pennsylvania, June 26, 1950 (Pittsburgh, Pennsylvania, Catholic retreat house case) : xiii, 27, 36, 98, 107, 108, 111, 209, 218, 219, 222, 279, 280, 281, 289, 325.

82. Concordia Collegiate Institute v. Miller, 93 North Eastern Reporter, Second Series 632, 301 New York Court of Appeals Reports 189, Court of Appeals of New York, July 11, 1950 (Bronxville, New York, Lutheran college case) (Same case as Reference Nos. 68, 74 and 77) : xiii. 269, 297, 298, 301, 321.

82-A. Same case, with annotation: Validity of Zoning Ordinance or Similar Public Regulation Requiring Consent of Neighboring Property Owners to Permit or Sanction Specified Uses or Construction of Buildings (G. H. Fischer), 21 American Law Reports, Second Series 551: xiii, 297.

83. State ex rel. Tampa, Florida, Company of Jehovah's Witnesses, North Unit, v. City of Tampa, 48 Southern Reporter, Second Series 78, Supreme Court of Florida, October 6, 1950, (Tampa, Florida, Jehovah's Witnesses' Kingdom Hall case) : xiii, xv, 27, 37, 60, 61, 115, 123, 124, 126, 127, 162, 220, 224, 231, 313.

84. George E. Gleason: Zoning—Consent as Prerequisite to Building for Educational or Eleemosynary Purposes, Mississippi Law Journal, 22:257, May, 1951: 27, 164.

85. Attorney General v. Inhabitants of Town of Dover, 100 North Eastern Reporter, Second Series 1, 327 Massachusetts Reports 601, Supreme Judicial Court of Massachusetts, Suffolk, July 3, 1951 (Dover, Massachusetts, Catholic school case) : xiv, 27, 37, 304, 317.

86. Yanow v. Seven Oaks Park, 83 Atlantic Reporter, Second Series 28, 15 New Jersey Superior Court Reports 73, Superior Court of New Jersey, Chancery Division, July 20, 1951 (Orange,

New Jersey, Protestant seminary case) (Same case as Reference Nos. 92 and 99) : xiv, 4, 319.

**87.** North Shore Unitarian Society v. Village of Plandome, 109 New York Supplement, Second Series 803, 200 New York Miscellaneous Reports 524, Supreme Court of New York, Special Term, Nassau County, Part II, October 31, 1951 (Plandome, New York, Unitarian church case) : xiv, 27, 38, 42, 47, 136, 140, 245, 321, 331.

**88.** City of Chico v. First Baptist Church of Chico, 238 Pacific Reporter, Second Series 587, 108 California Appellate Reports, Second Series 297, District Court of Appeals of California, Third District, December 20, 1951 (Chico, California, Baptist church case) : xiv, 36, 221, 263, 265, 311.

**89.** Sexton v. Bates, 85 Atlantic Reporter, Second Series 833, 17 New Jersey Superior Court Reports 246, Superior Court of New Jersey, Law Division, December 31, 1951 (Newark, New Jersey, Jewish ritualarium case) (Same case as Reference No. 94-A) : xiv, 222, 280, 290, 319.

**90.** Joseph LeCler, S.J.: The Two Sovereigns (Burns and Oates, London, 1952) : 225.

**91.** Galfas v. City, 193 Federal Reporter, Second Series 931, United States Court of Appeals, Fifth Circuit, January 31, 1952 (Atlanta, Georgia Jehovah's Witnesses' Kingdom Hall case) (Related cases under Reference Nos. 72 and 78) : xiii, 218, 266, 314, 332.

**92.** Yanow v. Seven Oaks Park, 87 Atlantic Reporter, Second Series 454, 18 New Jersey Superior Court Reports 41, Superior Court of New Jersey March 14, 1952 (Orange, New Jersey, Protestant seminary case) (Same case as Reference Nos. 86 and 99) : xiv, 4, 269, 299, 319.

**93.** O'Brien v. City of Chicago, 105 North Eastern Reporter, Second Series 917 Case No. 2, 347 Illinois Appellate Court Reports 45, Appellate Court of Illinois, First District, Second Division, April 15, 1952 (Chicago, Illinois, Episcopal church case) : xiv, 11, 27, 39, 81, 82, 125, 150, 156, 157, 162, 230, 314.

**94.** Mooney v. Village of Orchard Lake, 53 North Western Reporter, Second Series 308, 333 Michigan Reports 389, Supreme Court of Michigan, May 16, 1952 (Orchard Lake, Michigan, Catholic combination unit case) : xiv, 27, 38, 39, 136, 195, 223, 253, 266, 279, 317, 331.

**94-A.** Sexton v. Essex County Ritualarium, 91 Atlantic Reporter, Second Series 162 Case No. 1, 21 New Jersey Superior Court Reports 329, Superior Court of New Jersey, Appellate Division, September 10, 1952 (Newark, New Jersey, Jewish ritualarium case) (Same case as Reference No. 89) xiv, 280, 319.

**95.** Anonymous: Zoning Laws and the Church, St. John's Law Review, 27:93–103, December, 1952: 9, 12, 27, 38, 53, 72, 73, 102, 103, 118, 197, 200, 224, 272, 304, 332.

**96.** Emmett Clantor Yokley: Zoning Law and Practice (The Michie Company, Charlottesville, Va., Second Edition, 1953 with supplements) : 87, 153, 263, 270.

**97.** Leo Pfeffer: Church, State and Freedom (The Beacon Press, Boston, 1953) : 165, 186, 214, 220, 221, 330, 331.

**98.** Rev. John Denis Davis, M.A., S. T. L.: The Moral Obligations of Catholic Civil Judges (Catholic University of America Press, Washington, D. C., 1953) : 225.

**99.** Yanow v. Seven Oaks Park, 94 Atlantic Reporter, Second Series 482, 11 New Jersey Reports 341, Supreme Court of New Jersey, January 26, 1953 (Orange, New Jersey, Protestant seminary case) (Same case as Reference Nos. 86 and 92) : xiv, 4, 27, 39, 73, 181, 269, 299, 301, 319, 331.

**100.** Same case, with annotation: Zoning Regulations as Applied to Schools, Colleges, Universities and the Like (E. LeFevre), 36 American Law Reports, Second Series 653: 164.

**101.** State ex rel. Anshe Cheshed Congregation v. Bruggemeier, 115 North Eastern Reporter, Second Series 65, 97 Ohio Appellate Reports 67, Court of Appeals of Ohio, Cuyahoga County, October 19, 1953 (Beachwood, Ohio, Jewish temple case) : xiv, 27, 40, 61, 63, 88, 90, 92, 94, 140, 197, 225, 226, 260, 306, 324.

**102.** Coe v. City of Dallas, 266 South Western Reporter, Second Series 181, Court of Civil Appeals of Texas, El Paso, December 16, 1953 (Dallas, Texas, Protestant evangelistic center case) : xv, 4, 84, 108, 110, 199, 204, 217, 282, 327.

**104.** Board of Zoning Appeals of Decatur v. Decatur, Indiana, Company of Jehovah's Witnesses, 117 North Eastern Reporter, Second Series 115, 233 Indiana Supreme Court Reports 83, Supreme Court of Indiana, February 1, 1954 (Decatur, Indiana, Jehovah's Witnesses' Kingdom Hall case) : xv, 27, 40, 62, 63, 69, 82, 125, 127, 131, 141, 161, 228, 229, 237, 244, 254, 270, 315.

**105.** Congregation Adath Jeshurun v. Cheltenham Township, 70 Montgomery County Law Reporter 345, Court of Common Pleas of Montgomery County, Pennsylvania, March 23, 1954 (Cheltenham Township, Montgomery County, Pennsylvania, Jewish synagogue case) : xv, 27, 40, 113, 200, 325.

**106.** State ex rel. Wisconsin Lutheran High School Conference v. Sinar, 65 North Western Reporter, Second Series 43, 267 Wisconsin Reports 91, Supreme Court of Wisconsin, June 8, 1954 (Wauwatosa, Wisconsin, Lutheran high school case) (Same case as Reference No. 120) : xv, 89, 90, 94, 101, 108, 114, 170, 171, 173, 176, 179, 201, 328, 332.

**107.** Titus St. Paul Property Owners' Association v. Board of Zoning Appeals of Town of Irondequoit, 132 New York Supplement, Second Series 148, 205 New York Miscellaneous Reports 1083, Supreme Court of New York, Special Term, Monroe County, July 7, 1954 (Irondequoit, New York, Jewish temple case) : xv, 27, 41, 83, 128, 322.

**108.** Annotation: Validity of Public Prohibition or Regulation of Location of Cemetery (C. T. Dreschler), 50 American Law Reports, Second Series 900 (following the report of a case decided September 23, 1954) : 77.

**109.** Robert E. Roeder: Constitutional Law—Equal Protection —Municipal Zoning Ordinance, Nebraska Law Review, 34:139–41, November, 1954: 168, 174.

**110.** Missionaries of Mary v. Whitefish Bay, 66 North Western Reporter, Second Series 627, 267 Wisconsin Reports 609, Supreme Court of Wisconsin, November 9, 1954: 276.

**111.** Berman V. Parker, 348 United States Supreme Court Reports 26, 75 Supreme Court Reporter 98, 99 Lawyers' Edition, United States Supreme Court Reports 27, Supreme Court of the United States, November 22, 1954: 74, 75, 76, 233.

**112.** Appeal of Catholic Cemeteries Association, 109 Atlantic Reporter, Second Series 537, 379 Pennsylvania State Reports 516, Supreme Court of Pennsylvania, November 22, 1954: 77.

**113.** James Metzenbaum: The Law of Zoning (Baker Voorhis and Co., Mount Kisco, N. Y., Second Edition, 1955 with annual supplements) (Quoted by permission) : 56, 81, 308.

**114.** Rev. Walter J. Kloetzli, Jr.: Churches in the City Plan, Address, Planning, 1955, Proceedings, American Society of Planning Officials: 3.

**115.** Roman Catholic Welfare Corporation of San Francisco v. City of Piedmont, 278 Pacific Reporter, Second Series 943, District Court of Appeals of California, First District, Division 2, January 24, 1955 (Piedmont, California, Catholic school case) (Same case as Reference No. 125) : xv, xix, 41, 176, 217, 224, 228, 236, 239, 311.

**116.** William D. Keeler: Constitutional Law—Zoning—Private High Schools Excluded from Zones in which Public High Schools Permitted, Michigan Law Review, 53:747–9, March, 1955: 28, 164, 175.

**117.** Great Neck Community School v. Dick, 140 New York Supplement, Second Series 231, Supreme Court of New York, Special Term, Nassau County, March 15, 1955: 183.

**118.** Philip G. Feder: Zoning the Church, St. Louis University Law Journal, 3:265, Spring, 1955: 28, 31, 41.

**119.** Claude Kordus: Constitutional Law—Validity of Zoning Ordinance Discriminating against Private Educational Institutions, Marquette Law Review, 38:274, Spring, 1955: 164, 174, 175.

**120.** Wisconsin ex rel. Wisconsin Lutheran High School Conference v. Sinar, 349 United States Supreme Court Reports 913 Case No. 614, 75 Supreme Court Reporter 604, 99 Lawyers' Edition, United States Supreme Court Reports 1248, Supreme Court of the United States, April 25, 1955 (Wauwatosa, Wisconsin, Lutheran high school case) (Same case as Reference No. 106) : xv, 332.

121. Gerald J. O'Reilly: Constitutional Law—Equal Protection—Zoning Ordinances, University of Detroit Law Journal, 18:434, May, 1955: 32, 164.

122. Mahrt v. First Church of Christ, Scientist, 142 North Eastern Reporter, Second Series 567, Court of Common Pleas of Ohio, Montgomery County, May 19, 1955 (Dayton, Ohio, Christian Science church parking lot case) (Same case as Reference No. 142) : xvi, 128, 263, 302, 324.

123. Diocese of Rochester v. Planning Board of Town of Brighton, 141 New York Supplement, Second Series 487, 207 New York Miscellaneous Reports 1021, Supreme Court of New York, Special Term, Monroe County, June 3, 1955 (Brighton, New York, Catholic combination unit case) (Same case as Reference Nos. 131, 138 and 149) : xvi, 229, 282.

124. Miami Beach United Lutheran Church of the Epiphany v. City of Miami Beach, Florida, 82 Southern Reporter, Second Series 880, Supreme Court of Florida, September 16, 1955 (Miami Beach, Florida, Lutheran church case) : xv, xvii, xix, 61, 68, 101, 109, 110, 124, 162, 221, 231, 232, 313.

125. Roman Catholic Welfare Corporation of San Francisco v. City of Piedmont, 289 Pacific Reporter, Second Series 438, 45 California Reports, Second Series 325, Supreme Court of California, October 27, 1955 (Piedmont, California, Catholic school case) (Same case as Reference No. 115) : xv, xix, 27, 41, 136, 158, 176, 177, 178, 180, 181, 201, 214, 215, 224, 228, 236, 239, 302, 307, 311, 330, 331.

126. Robert C. Hoover and Everett L. Perry: Church and City Planning (Department of the Urban Church, National Council of Churches of Christ in the U. S. A., New York, November, 1955) : 213.

127. Jack Economou: Zoning—Constitutional Law—Discrimination between Public and Private Schools, Notre Dame Lawyer, 31:113, December, 1955: 164, 170, 176, 333.

128. Ranney v. Istituto Pontificio delle Maestre Filippini, 119 Atlantic Reporter, Second Series 142, 20 New Jersey Reports 189, Supreme Court of New Jersey, December 12, 1955 (Morris Township, New Jersey, Catholic seminary case) : xv, 141, 142, 143, 153, 232, 233, 260, 300, 303, 320.

129. Community Synagogue v. Bates, 147 New York Supplement, Second Series 204, 1 New York Supreme Court Appellate Division Reports, Second Series 686, Supreme Court of New York, Appellate Division, Second Department, December 19, 1955 (Sands Point, New York, Jewish synagogue case) (Same case as Reference No. 148) : xvi, 144, 229, 282, 304.

130. William E. J. Listerman: Municipal Corporations—Zoning—General Welfare—Distinction between Public and Private Schools, University of Cincinnati Law Review, 24:149, Winter, 1955: 164.

**131.** Diocese of Rochester v. Planning Board of Town of Brighton, 147 New York Supplement, Second Series 392, 1 New York Supreme Court Appellate Division Reports, Second Series 86, Supreme Court of New York, Appellate Division, Fourth Department, December 29, 1955 (Brighton, New York, Catholic combination unit case) (Same case as Reference Nos. 123, 138 and 149) : xvi, 229, 282, 303, 304.

**132.** Charles Allen Rathkopf and Arden H. Rathkopf: The Law of Zoning and Planning (Clark Boardman and Company, New York, Third Edition, 1956 with annual supplements) (Quoted by permission) : 25, 81, 153, 210, 293.

**133.** Carol Aronovici: Community Building: Science, Technique, Art (Doubleday and Company, New York, 1956) (Quoted by permission) : 57.

**134.** Convent of Sisters of St. Joseph of Chestnut Hill v. City of Winston Salem, 90 South Eastern Reporter, Second Series 879, 243 North Carolina Reports 316, Supreme Court of North Carolina, January 13, 1956 (Winston Salem, North Carolina, Catholic school case) : xvi, 323.

**135.** Schwartz v. Congregation Powolei Zeduck, 131 North Eastern Reporter, Second Series 785, 8 Illinois, Appellate Court Reports, Second Series 438, Appellate Court of Illinois, First District, Third Division, February 1, 1956 (Chicago, Illinois, Jewish synagogue and school case) : xvi, 315.

**136.** Congregation Committee, North Fort Worth Congregation, Jehovah's Witnesses v. City Council of Haltom City, 287 South Western Reporter, Second Series 700, Court of Civil Appeals of Texas, Fort Worth, February 24, 1956 (Haltom City, Texas, Jehovah's Witnesses' Kingdom Hall case) : xvii, 27, 42, 83, 99, 110, 111, 128, 144, 202, 233, 260, 327.

**137.** Hoelzer v. Incorporated Village of New Hyde Park, 150 New York Supplement, Second Series 765, 4 New York Miscellaneous Reports, Second Series 96, Supreme Court of New York, Special Term, Nassau County, Part I, March 2, 1956 (New Hyde Park, New York, Jewish school case) : xvi, 322.

**138.** Diocese of Rochester v. Planning Board of Town of Brighton, 149 New York Supplement, Second Series 711 Case No. 4, 1 New York Supreme Court Appellate Division Reports, Second Series 931, Supreme Court of New York, Appellate Division, Fourth Department, March 7, 1956 (Brighton, New York, Catholic combination unit case) (Same case as Reference Nos. 123, 131 and 149) : xvi, 229, 282.

**139.** West Hartford Methodist Church v. Zoning Board of Appeals of West Hartford, 121 Atlantic Reporter, Second Series 640, 143 Connecticut Reports 263, Supreme Court of Errors of Connecticut, March 13, 1956 (West Hartford, Connecticut, Methodist church case) : xvii, 75, 76, 101, 109, 110, 112, 128, 233, 312, 313, 326.

140. Young Israel Organization of Cleveland v. Dworkin, 133 North Eastern Reporter, Second Series 174, 105 Ohio Appellate Reports 89, Court of Appeals of Ohio, Cuyahoga County, March 14, 1956 (South Euclid, Ohio, Jewish synagogue case) : xvii, 11, 26, 27, 43, 72, 84, 128, 129, 203, 222, 244, 263, 324.

141. Charles R. Currey: Constitutional Law—Due Process and Equal Protection of the Laws—Zoning Ordinance Prohibiting Private Schools, UCLA Law Review 3:387, April, 1956: 28, 35, 164, 215.

142. Mahrt v. First Church of Christ, Scientist, 142 North Eastern Reporter, Second Series 678, Court of Appeals of Ohio, Montgomery County, April 25, 1956 (Dayton, Ohio, Christian Science parking lot case) (Same case as Reference No. 122): xvi, 128, 324.

143. Dunaway v. City of Austin, 290 South Western Reporter, Second Series 703, Court of Civil Appeals of Texas, Austin, May 16, 1956 (Austin, Texas, Episcopal seminary case) : xvii, 327.

144. Anonymous: Constitutional Law—Zoning Ordinances Excluding Private Schools from Areas Where Public Schools Are Permitted Held Unconstitutional, Minnesota Law Review, 40:863, June, 1956: 28, 32, 164.

145. Re la Porte, 152 New York Supplement, Second Series 916, 2 New York Supreme Court Appellate Division Reports, Second Series 710, Supreme Court of New York, Appellate Division, Second Department, June 25, 1956: 276.

146. Anonymous: Zoning out of Private Schools Held Invalid, Stanford University Law Review, 8:712, July, 1956: 164.

147. Paul Brindel: The Piedmont Case and Restrictive Zoning, Catholic Lawyer, 2:245, July, 1956: 28, 35, 164, 177, 307.

148. Community Synagogue v. Bates, 136 North Eastern Reporter, Second Series 488, 154 New York Supplement, Second Series 15, 1 New York Court of Appeals Reports, Second Series 445, Court of Appeals of New York, July 11, 1956 (Sands Point, New York, Jewish synagogue case) (Same case as Reference No. 129) : xvi, 27, 44, 90, 94, 129, 136, 144, 201, 229, 230, 282, 283, 284, 285, 286, 304, 305, 307, 321.

149. Diocese of Rochester v. Planning Board of Town of Brighton, 136 North Eastern Reporter, Second Series 827, 154 New York Supplement, Second Series 849, 1 New York Court of Appeals Reports, Second Series 508, Court of Appeals of New York, July 11, 1956 (Brighton, New York, Catholic combination unit case) (Same case as Reference Nos. 123, 131 and 138) : xvi, xix, 2, 11, 27, 44, 63, 89, 90, 92, 94, 99, 110, 111, 129, 160, 184, 201, 229, 233, 243, 255, 270, 282, 283, 303, 304, 305, 307, 321.

150. Garden City Jewish Center v. Incorporated Village of Garden City, 155 New York Supplement, Second Series 523, 2 New York Miscellaneous Reports, Second Series 1009, Supreme

Court of New York, Nassau County, Special Term, Part II, July 23, 1956 (Garden City, New York, Jewish synagogue case) (Same case as Reference No. 154) : xvii, 27, 44, 99, 204, 234, 282, 283, 285, 322.

**151.** Reynolds Seitz: Zoning—Constitutional General Welfare Considerations in Zoning out of Private Schools, Miami Law Quarterly, 11:68, Fall, 1956: 164, 174.

**152.** Stanton G. Ware: Constitutional Law—Reasonableness of Classification for Purposes of Zoning, California Law Review, 44:775, October, 1956: 28, 37, 164, 178, 180.

**153.** P. J. McInerney: Zoning Laws Can Be Anti-Religious, Columbia Magazine, 36:12, November, 1956: 186.

**154.** Garden City Jewish Center, Application of, 157 New York Supplement, Second Series 435, Supreme Court of New York, Nassau County, Special Term, Part I, November 7, 1956 (Garden City, New York, Jewish synagogue case) (Same case as Reference No. 150) : xvii, 44, 204, 264, 282, 285, 322.

**155.** Rev. Joseph Fichter: Churches and City Planning (Address), Planning 1957 (Proceedings, American Society of Planning Officials) : 180.

**156.** Summers v. Board of Adjustment of Kansas City, 299 South Western Reporter, Second Series 883, Kansas City Court of Appeals, Missouri, January 7, 1957 (Kansas City, Missouri, Catholic church parking lot case) : xvii, 260, 318.

**157.** Stevenson v. Board of Adjustment of the City of Charleston, 96 South Eastern Reporter, Second Series 456, 230 South Carolina Reports 440, Supreme Court of South Carolina, January 17, 1957 (Charleston, South Carolina, Baptist school case) : xvii, 85, 116, 130, 264, 326.

**158.** William R. Luney: Municipal Corporations—Zoning— Exclusion of Churches from Residential Areas, Michigan Law Review, 55:601, February, 1957: 28, 33, 81.

**159.** Trustees of the Congregation of Jehovah's Witnesses, Bethel Unit, Appeal of, 130 Atlantic Reporter, Second Series 240, 183 Pennsylvania Superior Court Reports 219, Superior Court of Pennsylvania, March 20, 1957 (Application for allocatur denied, Supreme Court of Pennsylvania, May 28, 1957) (Bethel Borough, Pennsylvania, Jehovah's Witnesses' Kingdom Hall case) (Same case as Reference No. 168) : xvii, 81, 85, 86, 87, 114, 115, 116, 127, 130, 145, 148, 234, 261, 325, 333.

**160.** Walker v. City of Tampa, 93 Southern Reporter, Second Series 862, Supreme Court of Florida, Special Division A, March 22, 1957 (Tampa, Florida, Christian church case) : xvii, 37, 221, 313.

**161.** Ralph W. Crolly: Regulation of the Location of Churches by Municipal Zoning Ordinances, Brooklyn Law Review, 23:185, April, 1957: 28, 33, 35, 64, 235, 304.

**162.** O'Hara, Appeal of, 131 Atlantic Reporter, Second Series

## 354 Public Regulation of the Religious Use of Land

587, 389 Pennsylvania State Reports 35, Supreme Court of Pennsylvania, April 26, 1957 (Cheltenham Township, Pennsylvania, Catholic high school case) : xviii, 86, 92, 93, 94, 268, 269, 326.

163. William Schack: Zoning Boards, Synagogues and Bias; Religious Tolerance in the Suburbs, Commentary Magazine, May, 1957 (Quoted by permission) : 91, 191, 198, 201, 204, 305, 306.

164. Anonymous: Churches and Zoning, Harvard Law Review, 70:1428, June, 1957: 74, 78, 81, 139, 142, 146, 148, 150, 164.

165. State ex rel. Wenatchee Congregation of Jehovah's Witnesses v. City of Wenatchee, 312 Pacific Reporter, Second Series 195, 50 Washington Reports, Second Series 378, Supreme Court of Washington, June 6, 1957 (Wenatchee, Washington, Jehovah's Witnesses' Kingdom Hall case) : xviii, 27, 45, 48, 75, 131, 261, 327.

166. Paul Brindel: Zoning out Religious Institutions, Notre Dame Lawyer, 32:627, July, 1957: 29, 30, 31, 70, 164, 168, 201.

167. Gray v. Board of Supervisors of Stanislaus County, 316 Pacific Reporter, Second Series 678, 154 California Appellate Reports, Second Series 700, District Court of Appeals of California, Third District, October 25, 1957 (Modesto, California, Baptist church case) : xviii, 205, 312.

168. Swift et al., Trustees of the Congregation of Jehovah's Witnesses, Bethel Unit, v. Borough of Bethel, Pennsylvania, 355 United States Supreme Court Reports 40 Case No. 1, 78 Supreme Court Reporter 120, 2 Lawyers' Edition, United States Supreme Court Reports, Second Series 71, Supreme Court of the United States, November 12, 1957 (Bethel Borough, Pennsylvania, Jehovah's Witnesses' Kingdom Hall case) (Same case as Reference No. 159) : xvii, 127, 325, 333.

169. McKinney v. Board of Zoning Adjustment of Kansas City, 308 South Western Reporter, Second Series 320, Kansas City Court of Appeals, Missouri, December 2, 1957 (Kansas City, Missouri, Catholic church and school case) : xviii, 303, 318.

170. Anonymous: Needed Zoning Can Degenerate into Snob Restrictions, Saturday Evening Post, 230:10, December 7, 1957: 72.

171. Pelham Jewish Center v. Board of Trustees of Village of Pelham Manor, 170 New York Supplement, Second Series 136, 9 New York Miscellaneous Reports, Second Series 564, Supreme Court of New York, Westchester County, December 9, 1957 (Pelham Manor, New York, Jewish center case) (Same case as Reference Nos. 178, 179 and 220) : xviii, 27, 322.

172. Churches and Planning Control, Planning Advisory Service Information Report No. 106, January, 1958, citing Milwaukee Journal, December 13, 1957 (American Society of Planning Officials, Chicago) : 227.

173. Temple Israel of Lawrence v. Plaut, 170 New York Sup-

plement, Second Series 393, 10 New York Miscellaneous Reports, Second Series 1084, Supreme Court of New York, Nassau County, December 16, 1957 (Lawrence, New York, Jewish temple school case) (Same case as Reference No. 182) : xviii, 76, 286, 322.

**174.** Best v. Zoning Board of Adjustment of City of Pittsburgh, Pennsylvania, 141 Atlantic Reporter, Second Series 606, 393 Pennsylvania State Reports 106, Supreme Court of Pennsylvania, April 2, 1958: 75, 326.

**175.** Incorporated Village of Lloyd Harbor v. Town of Huntington, 149 North Eastern Reporter, Second Series 851, 173 New York Supplement, Second Series 553, 4 New York Court of Appeals Reports, Second Series 182, Court of Appeals of New York, April 3, 1958: 160.

**176.** Tinder v. Clarke Auto, 149 North Eastern Reporter, Second Series 808, 238 Indiana Supreme Court Reports 302, Supreme Court of Indiana, April 30, 1958: 160.

**177.** Anonymous: Zoning—Administrative Law—Denial of Building Approval to Church Held Arbitrary and Unreasonable, St. John's Law Review, 31:318, May 1957: 29, 38.

**178.** Pelham Jewish Center v. Board of Trustees of Village of Pelham Manor, 174 New York Supplement, Second Series 957 Case No. 2, 6 New York Supreme Court, Appellate Division Reports, Second Series 710, Supreme Court of New York, Appellate Division, Second Department, May 19, 1958 (Pelham Manor, New York, Jewish center case) (Same case as Reference Nos. 171, 179 and 220) : xviii, 322.

**179.** Pelham Jewish Center v. Board of Trustees of Village of Pelham Manor, 152 North Eastern Reporter, Second Series 650, 4 New York Court of Appeals Reports, Second Series 1033, Court of Appeals of New York, June 25, 1958 (Pelham Manor, New York, Jewish center case) (Same case as Reference Nos. 171, 178 and 220) : xviii, 322.

**180.** Andrews v. Board of Adjustment of Ocean Township, 143 Atlantic Reporter, Second Series 262, 51 New Jersey Superior Court Reports 69, Superior Court of New Jersey, Law Division, June 27, 1958 (Ocean Township, New Jersey, Catholic school case) (Same case as Reference No. 206) : xviii, 142, 143, 180, 181, 264, 320.

**181.** Town of Hempstead v. Merrick Woods School, Inc., 177 New York Supplement, Second Series 81, 13 New York Miscellaneous Reports, Second Series 369, Supreme Court of New York, Nassau County, Special Term, Part II, June 27, 1958: 160.

**182.** Temple Israel of Lawrence v. Plaut, 177 New York Supplement, Second Series 660, 6 New York Supreme Court Appellate Division Reports, Second Series 886, Supreme Court of New York, Appellate Division, Second Department, July 14, 1958 (Lawrence, New York, Jewish temple school case) (Same case as Reference No. 173) : xviii, 76, 322.

**183.** Russian Orthodox Church, Appeal of, 20 Beaver County Legal Journal 113, Court of Common Pleas of Pennsylvania, July 15, 1958 (Same case as Reference No. 207) : 76.

**184.** Milwaukie Company of Jehovah's Witnesses v. Mullen, 330 Pacific Reporter, Second Series 5, 214 Oregon Reports 281, Supreme Court of Oregon, September 17, 1958 (Milwaukie, Oregon, Jehovah's Witnesses' Kingdom Hall case) (Same case as Reference No. 200) : xix, 12, 27, 45, 65, 66, 76, 109, 119, 127, 131, 132, 133, 147, 206, 235, 244, 254, 262, 269, 309, 323, 324, 325, 333.

**185.** Same case, with annotation: Zoning Regulations as Affecting Churches, R. P. Davis, 74 American Law Reports, Second Series 347 : 29, 31, 35, 36, 37, 39, 44, 45, 46, 100, 109.

**186.** Minney v. City of Azusa, 330 Pacific Reporter, Second Series 255, 164 California Appellate Reports, Second Series 12, District Court of Appeals of California, Second District, Division 2, October 3, 1958 (Hearing denied in Supreme Court of California, December 3, 1958) (Azusa, California, Jehovah's Witnesses' Kingdom Hall case) (Same case as Reference No. 199) : xix, 139, 145, 149, 206, 235, 260, 262, 311, 333.

**187.** Rosenfeld v. Zoning Board of Appeals, 154 North Eastern Reporter, Second Series 323, 19 Illinois Appellate Court Reports, Second Series 447, Appellate Court of Illinois, First District, Second Division, November 6, 1958 : 161.

**188.** Believers of Islam, Inc. v. City of Chicago, 154 North Eastern Reporter, Second Series 311, 19 Illinois Appellate Court Reports, Second Series, 480, Appellate Court of Illinois, First District, Second Division, November 25, 1958 (Chicago, Illinois, Moslem temple sign case) : xviii, 205, 287, 315.

**189.** City of Miami Beach v. Greater Miami Hebrew Academy, 108 Southern Reporter, Second Series 50, District Court of Appeals of Florida, Third District, December 23, 1958 (Miami Beach, Florida, Jewish school case) (Same case as Reference No. 198) : xix, 37, 101, 163, 221, 313.

**190.** Webster's New Collegiate Dictionary (G. and C. Merriam Co., Springfield, Mass., 1959) : 65, 272, 279, 280, 281, 288, 292.

**191.** Brandeis School v. Village of Lawrence, 184 New York Supplement, Second Series 687, 18 New York Miscellaneous Reports, Second Series 550, Supreme Court of New York, Nassau County, Special Term, Part II, January 6, 1959 (Lawrence, New York, Jewish school case) : xix, 99, 184, 322.

**192.** Congregation Temple Israel v. City of Creve Coeur, 320 South Western Reporter, Second Series 451, Supreme Court of Missouri, Division No. 1, January 12, 1959 (Creve Coeur, Missouri, Jewish temple case) : xix, 11, 27, 45, 72, 203, 236, 237, 238, 266, 267, 268, 274, 293, 318.

**193.** Tustin Heights Association v. Board of Supervisors of Orange County, California, 334 Pacific Reporter, Second Series

1017, District Court of Appeals of California, Fourth District, February 6, 1959 (Orange County, California, Catholic church and school case) (Same case as Reference No. 202) : xix, 179, 261, 311.

**194.** Redwood City Company of Jehovah's Witnesses v. City of Menlo Park, 335 Pacific Reporter, Second Series 195, 167 California Appellate Reports, Second Series 686, District Court of Appeals of California, First District, Division 1, February 9, 1959 (Menlo Park, California, Jehovah's Witnesses' Kingdom Hall case) : xix, 146, 147, 261, 312.

**195.** Franciscan Missionaries of Mary v. Herdman, 184 New York Supplement, Second Series 104, 7 New York Supreme Court Appellate Division Reports, Second Series 993, Supreme Court of New York, Appellate Division, Second Department, March 2, 1959 (Clarkstown, New York, Catholic child shelter case) (Same case as Reference Nos. 210 and 213): xix, 151, 286, 322.

**196.** Parkview Baptist Church v. City of Pueblo, 336 Pacific Reporter, Second Series 210, 139 Colorado Reports 98, Supreme Court of Colorado, March 9, 1959 (Pueblo, Colorado, Baptist church sign case) : xx, 287, 312.

**197.** Schueller v. Board of Adjustment of City of Dubuque, Iowa, 95 North Western Reporter, Second Series 731, 250 Iowa Reports 706, Supreme Court of Iowa, April 8, 1959 (Dubuque, Iowa, Lutheran seminary case) : 287, 316.

**198.** Greater Miami Hebrew Academy v. City of Miami Beach, 113 Southern Reporter, Second Series 229 Case No. 1, Supreme Court of Florida, May Term, 1959 (Miami Beach, Florida, Jewish school case) (Same case as Reference No. 189) : xix, 37, 221, 313.

**199.** Minney v. City of Azusa, 359 United States Supreme Court Reports 436 Case No. 2, 79 Supreme Court Reporter 941, 3 Lawyers' Edition, United States Supreme Court Reports, Second Series 932, Supreme Court of the United States, May 4, 1959 (Azusa, California, Jehovah's Witnesses' Kingdom Hall case) (Same case as Reference No. 186) : xix, 206, 311, 333.

**200.** Milwaukie Company of Jehovah's Witnesses v. Mullen, 359 United States Supreme Court Reports 436 Case No. 1, 79 Supreme Court Reporter 941, 3 Lawyer's Edition, United States Supreme Court Reports, Second Series 932, Supreme Court of the United States, May 4, 1959 (Milwaukie, Oregon, Jehovah's Witnesses' Kingdom Hall case) (Same case as Reference No. 184) : xix, 127, 147, 333.

**201.** State ex rel. Covenant Harbor Bible Camp v. Steinke, 96 North Western Reporter, Second Series 356, 7 Wisconsin Reports, Second Series 275, Supreme Court of Wisconsin, May 5, 1959 (Lake Geneva, Wisconsin, Evangelical bible camp case) : xx, 329.

**202.** Tustin Heights Association v. Board of Supervisors of

County of Orange, 339 Pacific Reporter, Second Series 914, 170 California Appellate Reports, Second Series 619, District Court of Appeals of California, Fourth District, May 25, 1959 (Hearing denied in Supreme Court of California, July 22, 1959) (Orange County, California, Catholic church and school case) (Same case as Reference No. 193): xix, 179, 215, 259, 261.

203. John G. Hall: Zoning—Municipal Government—Exclusion of Churches from Area Zoned Residential, Villanova Law Review, 4:605, Summer 1959: 29, 31, 39, 40.

204. Anonymous: Zoning and the Exclusion of Churches, Catholic Lawyer, 5:252, Summer 1959: 63, 64, 70, 74, 100, 229, 321.

205. Allendale Congregation of Jehovah's Witnesses v. Grosman, 152 Atlantic Reporter, Second Series 569, 30 New Jersey Reports 273, Supreme Court of New Jersey, June 30, 1959 (Allendale, New Jersey, Jehovah's Witnesses' Kingdom Hall case) (Same case as Reference No. 219): xx, 81, 133, 223, 237, 320, 333.

206. Andrews v. Board of Adjustment of Ocean Township, 152 Atlantic Reporter, Second Series 580, 30 New Jersey Reports 245, Supreme Court of New Jersey, June 30, 1959 (Ocean Township, New Jersey, Catholic school case) (Same case as Reference No. 180): xviii, 142, 143, 180, 181, 320.

207. Russian Orthodox Church of the Holy Ghost of Ambridge, Pennsylvania, Appeal of, 152 Atlantic Reporter, Second Series 489, 397 Pennsylvania State Reports 126, Supreme Court of Pennsylvania, June 30, 1959 (Same case as Reference No. 183): 37, 76, 77, 111, 113, 280, 289, 290, 326.

208. In re Upper St. Clair Township Grange, No. 2032, 152 Atlantic Reporter, Second Series 768, 397 Pennsylvania State Reports 67, Supreme Court of Pennsylvania, July 2, 1959: 161, 210, 290, 291, 326.

209. Eugene Carson Blake: Tax Exemption and the Churches, Christianity Today, 3:6, August 3, 1959: 93.

210. Franciscan Missionaries of Mary v. Herdman, 162 North Eastern Reporter, Second Series 639 Case No. 1, 193 New York Supplement, Second Series 459, Case No. 1, 7 New York Court of Appeals Reports, Second Series 721, Court of Appeals of New York, October 8, 1959 (Clarkstown, New York, Catholic child shelter case) (Same case as Reference Nos. 195 and 213): xix, 151, 322.

211. Anonymous: Sees Militant Atheists Denying Christians Their Rights, Religious News Service, October 22, 1959: 118.

212. Ralph I. Yarnell, D.D.: Why Your Church Can't Be Built, American Mercury, November, 1959, page 36: 118.

213. Franciscan Missionaries of Mary v. Herdman, 164 North Eastern Reporter, Second Series 723, 196 New York Supplement, Second Series 705, 7 New York Court of Appeals Reports, Second

Series 829, Court of Appeals of New York, December 30, 1959 (Clarkstown, New York, Catholic child shelter case) (Same case as Reference Nos. 195 and 210) : xix, 151, 322.

**214.** Paul Blanshard: God and Man in Washington (Beacon Press, Boston, 1960) : 186.

**215.** Frederick H. Bair, Jr.: New Churches and the Law, Newsletter of Florida Planning and Zoning, December, 1955, reprinted in Bair Facts, the Writings of Frederick H. Bair, Jr., edited by Perry L. Norton (Chandler Davis Publishing Company, Trenton, N. J., 1960) : 335.

**216.** Yocum v. Power, 157 Atlantic Reporter, Second Series 368, 398 Pennsylvania State Reports 223, Supreme Court of Pennsylvania, January 18, 1960 (Philadelphia, Pennsylvania, Baptist church case) : xx, 194, 326.

**217.** Garden Grove Congregation of Jehovah's Witnesses v. City of Garden Grove, 1 California Reporter 65, 176 California Appellate Reports, Second Series 46, District Court of Appeals of California, Fourth District, December 11, 1959 (Hearing denied, Supreme Court of California, February 3, 1960) (Garden Grove, California, Jehovah's Witnesses' Kingdom Hall case) : xx, 147, 237, 312.

**218.** Diocese of Central New York v. Schwarzer, 199 New York Supplement, Second Series 939, 23 New York Miscellaneous Reports, Second Series 515, Supreme Court of New York, Madison County, Special Term, February 23, 1960 (Cazenovia, New York, Episcopal conference center case) (Same case as Reference Nos. 234 and 236) : xxi, 27, 46, 288, 322.

**219.** Allendale Congregation of Jehovah's Witnesses v. Grosman, 361 United States Supreme Court Reports 536 Case No. 1, 80 Supreme Court Reporter 587, 4 Lawyers' Edition, United States Supreme Court Reports, Second Series 538, Supreme Court of the United States, February 23, 1960 (Allendale, New Jersey, Jehovah's Witnesses' Kingdom Hall case) (Same case as Reference No. 205) : xx, 133, 237, 333.

**220.** Pelham Jewish Center v. Marsh, 197 New York Supplement, Second Series 258, 10 New York Supreme Court Appellate Division Reports, Second Series 645, Supreme Court of New York, Appellate Division, Second Department, February 23, 1960 (Pelham Manor, New York, Jewish center case) (Same case as Reference Nos. 171, 178, and 179) : xviii, 322.

**221.** Michael Sharff: Religion and the Zoning Laws, New York University Intramural Law Review, 15:194, March, 1960: 29, 34, 44.

**222.** William J. Gerardo, William R. Kennedy and Paul J. Schierl: Religious Institutions and Values, a Legal Survey, 1958-59, Notre Dame Lawyer 35:405, May, 1960: 70, 159, 160, 236, 238.

**223.** City of San Marino v. Roman Catholic Archbishop of

Los Angeles, 4 California Reporter 547, 180 California Appellate Reports, Second Series 657, District Court of Appeals of California, Second District, Division 2, May 5, 1960 (Hearing denied, Supreme Court of California, June 29, 1960) (San Marino, California, Catholic church parking lot case) (Same case as Reference No. 224) : xx, 4, 66, 69, 102, 147, 149, 202, 312, 333.

224. Roman Catholic Archbishop of Los Angeles v. City of San Marino, 364 United States Supreme Court Reports 909 Case No. 440, 81 Supreme Court Reporter 272, 5 Lawyers' Edition, United States Supreme Court Reports, Second Series 224, Supreme Court of the United States, December 5, 1960 (San Marino, California, Catholic church parking lot case) (Same case as Reference No. 223) : xx, 4, 66, 147, 149, 202, 312, 333.

225. Francis Biddle: Justice Holmes, Natural Law, and the Supreme Court (The MacMillan Company, New York, 1961) (Quoted by permission) : 224, 226.

226. Lewis Mumford: The City in History; Its Origins, Its Transformations, and Its Prospects (Harcourt, Brace, and World, New York, 1961) : 6, 134, 212.

227. von Kohorn v. Morrell, 172 North Eastern Reporter, Second Series 287, 210 New York Supplement, Second Series 525, 9 New York Court of Appeals Reports, Second Series 27, Court of Appeals of New York, January 12, 1961: 105.

228. Black v. Town of Montclair, 167 Atlantic Reporter, Second Series 388, 34 New Jersey Reports 105, Supreme Court of New Jersey, January 23, 1961 (Montclair, New Jersey, Catholic day school case) : xxi, 86, 116, 143, 265, 320.

229. Board of Zoning Appeals of Town of Meridian Hills v. Schulte, 172 North Eastern Reporter, Second Series 39, 241 Indiana Supreme Court Reports 339, Supreme Court of Indiana, February 7, 1961 (Meridian Hills, Indiana, Catholic church and school case) : xxi, 11, 69, 103, 104, 149, 238, 276, 277, 315.

230. Richard D. Klaber: Church Zoning in Pennsylvania, University of Pittsburgh Law Review, 22:591, March, 1961: 5, 325.

231. State ex rel. Bayside Baptist Church v. Village of Bayside Board of Trustees, 108 North Western Reporter, Second Series 288, 12 Wisconsin Reports, Second Series 585, Supreme Court of Wisconsin, March 7, 1961 (Bayside, Wisconsin, Baptist church case) : xxi, 11, 46, 47, 68, 102, 136, 150, 151, 207, 227, 238, 267, 274, 328, 331.

232. Anonymous: The Effect of Zoning Ordinances on Churches, Catholic Lawyer, 7:151, Spring 1961: 29.

233. City of Englewood v. Apostolic Christian Church, 362 Pacific Reporter, Second Series 172, 146 Colorado Reports 374, Supreme Court of Colorado, May 1, 1961 (Englewood, Colorado, Apostolic Christian church case) : xxi, 48, 312.

234. Diocese of Central New York v. Schwartzer, 217 New

York Supplement, Second Series 567 Case No. 2, 13 New York Supreme Court Appellate Division Reports, Second Series 863, Supreme Court of New York, Appellate Division, Third Department, May 9, 1961 (Cazenovia, New York, Episcopal conference center case) (Same case as Reference Nos. 218 and 236) : xxi, 288, 322.

**235.** Patrick J. McMahon: Zoning—Restriction of Church Construction in Residential Districts, Marquette Law Review, 45:306, Fall 1961: 27.

**236.** Diocese of Central New York v. Schwartzer, 10 New York Reports, Second Series 706, Court of Appeals of New York, October 5, 1961 (Cazenovia, New York, Episcopal conference center case) (Same case as Reference Nos. 218 and 234) : xxi, 288, 322.

**237.** Anonymous: Sworn Enemies (Editorial) Baptist and Reflector, October 26, 1961: 4.

**238.** Directory of Churches (National Council of Churches of Christ in the U. S. A., New York, 1962): 227.

**239.** Duallo Realty Corporation v. Silver, 224 New York Supplement, Second Series 55, 32 New York Miscellaneous Reports, Second Series 539, Supreme Court of New York, Special Term, Nassau County, Part I, January 11, 1962 (Long Beach, New York, Jewish temple case) : xxi, 323.

**240.** Ron Vernon: Zoning for Churches, Hastings Law Journal, 13:367, February, 1962: 27.

**241.** Trinity Evangelical Lutheran Church v. Board of Adjustment of the Borough of Morris Plains, 179 Atlantic Reporter, Second Series 45, 72 New Jersey Superior Court Reports 425, Superior Court of New Jersey, Appellate Division, February 19, 1962 (Morris Plains Borough, New Jersey, Lutheran school case) : xxi, 87, 182, 320.

**242.** Ralph W. Crolly and Arden H. Rathkopf: Zoning Ordinances in Relation to Churches, Colleges, Universities, Church-Conducted (Parochial) Schools and Academic Private Schools, New York Law Journal, Vol. 147, No. 38:4 and No. 39:4, February 26 and 27, 1962: 164.

**243.** William L. Church: Constitutional Law—Zoning—Regulations Excluding Churches from Residential Districts, Wisconsin Law Review, 1962: 358, March issue: 27.

**244.** Anonymous: Zoning (In Other Publications), Catholic Lawyer, 8:147, Spring 1962: 164.

**245.** Matthews v. Board of Supervisors of County of Stanislaus, 21 California Reporter 914, 203 California Appellate Reports, Second Series 800, District Court of Appeal, Fifth District, California, May 21, 1962 (Modesto, California, Jehovah's Witnesses' Kingdom Hall case): xxi, 147, 236, 312.

**246.** Columbus Park Congregation of Jehovah's Witnesses Inc. v. Board of Appeals of City of Chicago, 182 North Eastern Reporter, Second Series 722, 25 Illinois Supreme Court Reports, Second Series 65, Supreme Court of Illinois, May 25, 1962 (Chicago, Illinois, Jehovah's Witnesses' Kingdom Hall case) : xxii, 151, 161, 209, 256, 315.

247. St. John's Roman Catholic Church Corporation v. Town of Darien, 184 Atlantic Reporter, Second Series 42, 149 Connecticut Reports 712, Supreme Court of Errors of Connecticut, July 27, 1962 (Darien, Connecticut, Catholic school case) : xxii, 182, 263, 313.

248. St. Cassian's Catholic Church v. Allen, 185 Atlantic Reporter, Second Series 420, 77 New Jersey Superior Court Reports 99, Superior Court of New Jersey, Law Division, October 26, 1962 (Montclair, New Jersey, Catholic parochial school case) : xxii, 87, 182, 320.

Reference Numbers are to Chronological Table

# BOOKS

## PERIODICALS, ETC.

## ARTICLES, ADDRESSES, ETC.

Reference Numbers are to Chronological Table

# AUTHORS

Reference Numbers are to Chronological Table

## RELIGIOUS DENOMINATIONS

Reference Numbers are to Chronological Table

Reference Numbers are to Chronological Table

Reference Numbers are to Chronological Table

# MUNICIPALITIES

Reference Numbers are to Chronological Table

Reference Numbers are to Chronological Table

Reference Numbers are to Chronological Table

## STATES

Ref.

Florida:
Miami Beach:
 Jewish . . . . . . . . . . 189, 198
 Lutheran . . . . . . . . . . . 124
Tampa:
 Advent Christian . . . . . . . . . 160
 Jehovah's Witnesses . . . . . . . . 83
Georgia:
Atlanta:
 Baptist . . . . . . . . . . . . 55
 Jehovah's Witnesses . . . . . . 72, 78, 91
Decatur, Lutheran . . . . . . . . . 70
Illinois:
Chicago:
 Episcopal . . . . . . . . . . . 93
 Jehovah's Witnesses . . . . . . . . 246
 Jewish . . . . . . . . . . . 135
 Moslem . . . . . . . . . . . 188
Evanston, Episcopal . . . . . . . . 19, 23
Winnetka, Catholic . . . . . . . . . 34
Indiana:
Decatur, Jehovah's Witnesses . . . . . . 104
Indianapolis:
 Catholic . . . . . . . . . . . 62
 Methodist . . . . . . . . . . . 57
Meridian Hills, Catholic . . . . . . . . 229
Iowa:
Dubuque, Lutheran . . . . . . . . 197
Kentucky:
Louisville, Baptist . . . . . . . . . 69
Massachusetts:
Dover, Catholic . . . . . . . . . 85
Michigan:
Grand Rapids, Lutheran . . . . . . . 28
Orchard Lake, Catholic . . . . . . . 94
Portage Township, Protestant Nondenomina-
 tional . . . . . . . . . . . 60, 63, 65

## CASES

Reference Numbers are to Chronological Table

# SUBJECT INDEX

Where a particular church zoning case is discussed in connection with any subject, it is designated in this index by the place name in parentheses. This arrangement is an aid for finding the material; it should not be treated as a digest of the decisions. The reference numbers are to pages.

**385**

**PARKING SPACE.**

See Space, Light, Air and Ease of Access; Traffic.

Conditions on permits requiring, 16, (Tampa) 37, (Decatur) 40, (Melrose Park, Cheltenham Tp.) 40-41, (Haltom) 42-43, (Tampa) 60-61, (Upper Arlington) 120-21, (Louisville) 122, (Atlanta) 122-23, (Tampa) 123-24, (Decatur) 125-28, (Irondequoit) 128, (Haltom) 128, (South Euclid) 128-29, (Sands Point) 129-30, (Bethel) 130-31, (Allendale) 133, 263.

Definition of "religious uses, etc.," as including, (Dayton) 128.

Delegation to churches of sovereign power to determine, (Decatur) 228, (Garden City) 234.

Exclusion of religious uses constructively effectuated by requirements for, (Decatur) 40, (Haltom) 42-43, (Sands Point) 44.

First Amendment freedom violated by requirements for, (Haltom) 42-43, (Haltom) 233, (Garden City) 234, (Allendale) 237.

See subentry, "Traffic, etc.," under First Amendment Freedom and Allied Rights.

Nuisance arising from operation of, (San Marino) 4.

Police regulations as obviating necessity for, (Decatur) 62-63.

Public purposes served by, (Atlanta) 122-23.

"Religious uses" as including, (Dayton) 128.

Statutory authority for requiring, (Irondequoit) 41, (Irondequoit) 83, (Irondequoit) 128.

Traffic hazards abated by requirements for, (Decatur) 62-63, (Upper Arlington) 120-21, (Louisville) 122, (Bethel) 130-31, (Milwaukie) 131-33, (Allendale) 133.

Traffic problem not completely solved by, (Milwaukie) 131-33.

**PAROCHIAL SCHOOLS.**

See Catholic Church; Public Schools and Other Public Enterprises.

Public schools equated with, (Ocean) 180-81.

**PEACE AND QUIET.**

See Disturbance; Noise; Public Purpose in General.

**PEARSON, DREW, 56.**

**PENN, WILLIAM, 7.**

**PERCENTAGE OF OCCUPANCY.**

See Setback Requirements; Size of Lot; Space, Light, Air and Ease of Access.

Conditions on permits limiting, 16, (Omaha) 52-55, (Philadelphia) 79, (Dallas) 84, (South Euclid) 84-85, (Charleston) 85, (Sands Point) 90-91, 263.

Fiscal purposes and, (Sands Point) 90.

**PERIODICALS.**

Alphabetical list of, 363.

**PERMITS.**

See Conditions upon Religious-use Permits; Special Permits; Standards for Issuance of Special Permits.

**PERSONAL RIGHTS.**

See First Amendment Freedom and Allied Rights.

**PHILADELPHIA COMMISSION ON SOCIAL JUSTICE, 7.**

**PRESSURE.**

See Private Opinion.

**PRESUMPTION OF VALIDITY OF OFFICIAL ACTS.**

Generally, c. 17 (249-57).

Balancing of interests by board entitled to, (Tampa) 60-61, (Milwaukie) 65-66.

Burden of proof as corollary to, 249-50.

Discrimination against religious uses and, (San Marino) 149, 257.

Discrimination against religious, in favor of public, schools and, (Winnetka) 168-70.

Discrimination in favor of churches by manipulation of rule concerning, (Orchard Lake, Portage, Grand Rapids) 253-54.

Due process cases and, 256-57.

Equal protection cases and, 256-57.

Evidence as affected by, 249-51.

First Amendment cases and, (Atlanta) 218, (Chicago) 256-57.

General rule concerning, 251, 255-56.

Judicial approval of, (Porterville) 35-36, (Miami Beach) 101, (Bayside) 102, (Atlanta) 122-23, (Cleveland Heights) 253, (Portage, Grand Rapids) 254, (Milwaukie) 254-55, (Indianapolis) 255, (Brighton) 255.

Judicial disregard of, (Winnetka) 251, (Reno) 251-52, (Orchard Lake) 253-54, (Chicago) 256.

Judicial equivocation about, (Orchard Lake, Portage, Grand Rapids) 253-54, (Indianapolis, Brighton, Chicago) 255-56.

Judicial rejection of, (Upper Arlington) 252-53, (Sherman) 253.

Prejudice and, (Milwaukie, Azusa) 205-7, (Bayside) 207.

Preponderance of evidence and, 249-50, 257.

Property-value-depreciation ruling favored by, (Miami Beach) 101, (Bayside) 102.

Public service functions of religion treated pursuant to, (Garden Grove) 237-38.

Retroactive amendment given benefit of, (Allendale) 133.

State constitution invoked to reverse general rule as to, (Orchard Lake) 253-54.

Substantiality of purpose and, 256-57.

Traffic-hazards finding favored by, (Atlanta) 122-23, (Milwaukie) 131-33, (Allendale) 133.

United States courts and, (Atlanta) 218, (Atlanta) 266.

United States Supreme Court and, 251, (Chicago) 256.

**PRIOR NONCONFORMING USES.**

Discrimination against religious uses based on exemption of, (Decatur) 141, (Bethel) 145, (Milwaukie) 147-49.

Establishment of religion or atheism through exemption of, 2-3, (Decatur) 141.

Foreign countries and, 2-3.

Separation of church and state possibly violated by exemption of, 2-3, (Decatur) 141.

PRIVATE OPINION.
 Generally, c. 20 (293-309).
 Amicorum curiae, 177, 306-7.
 Anticlericals', 118.
 Atheists', 118.
 Attorneys', 306-8.
 Authors', (Milwaukie) 307-9.
 Clergy.
 See subentry, "Religious organizations, etc.," below.
 Discrimination in favor of religious uses by proponents of, 308-9.
 Evidence of, 301, 309.
 Judges', 306-7.
 Judicial reliance on, 301-6.
 Judicial resentment of, 309.
 National Council of Churches', 118.
 Neighbors', 105, 301, (Indianapolis) 301-2, (Dayton) 302, (Piedmont)
  302-3, (Morris) 303, (Kansas City) 303, (Brighton, Sands Point)
  303-6.
 See Consent of Neighbors.
 Politicians', 293, (Brighton, Sands Point) 303-6.
 Religious organizations', 3, (Piedmont) 177, 293, (Brighton, Sands Point)
  303-8.
 Secularists', 118.

PRIVATE PROPERTY RIGHTS.
 Balancing against other interests, (Omaha) 52-55, 55-60, (Milwaukie)
  65-66, (Meridian Hills) 69-70, (Pittsburgh) 209.
 Exclusion of religious uses sometimes necessary to protect, (Garden City)
  235.
 First Amendment freedom balanced against, (Pittsburgh, Chicago) 209.
 Police power as limitation on, 16.
 See Socialization.
 Public purpose balanced against, (Omaha) 52-55, 58-60, (Milwaukie)
  65-66.
 Public service functions of religion balanced against, (Meridian Hills)
  69-70.
 United States Supreme Court and balancing of public purpose against,
  55-60.

PROCEDURAL HARASSMENT.
 Suspicion of prejudice based on, 187-91, (Sherman) 191-93, (South
  Euclid) 203, (Creve Coeur) 203-4.

PRO-EXCLUSION RULE.
 See Exclusion of Religious Uses.

PROHIBITION OF REGULATION OF RELIGIOUS USES.
 See Statutory Prohibition of Religious-use Regulations.

PROOF, BURDEN OF.
 See Evidence; Presumption of Validity of Official Acts.

**SPAIN.**

Religious land use regulation and prior nonconforming uses in, 2-3.

**SPECIAL PERMITS FOR RELIGIOUS USES.**

See Standards for Issuance of Special Permits.

Aesthetic purpose of regulation as lessening need for, 77-78.

Definition of terms made more difficult by procedure for, 271.

Delegation of power to issue, 258-63.

See Standards for Issuance of Special Permits.

Exclusionary provision as to religious uses replaced by provision for, (South Euclid) 222, (Porterville, Azusa) 259-60.

First Amendment freedom protected by procedure for, (South Euclid) 222, (Porterville, Azusa) 259-60.

Interpretation problems increased by provision for, 271.

Standards for issuance of, 258-63.

**SPOT ZONING.**

Generally, c. 12 (153-63).

See Discrimination in Favor of Religious Uses.

Contagious character of, c. 12 (153-63).

Definitions of, (Morris) 153, 155, (Chicago) 156-57.

Judicial precautions against, (Reno) 156.

Secular, compared with religious, c. 12 (153-63).

United States Supreme Court and, (Upper Arlington) 157-58.

**STANDARDS FOR ISSUANCE OF SPECIAL PERMITS.**

Generally, 258-63.

See Special Permits for Religious Uses.

Constitutional principles requiring, 21, 258.

Due process as requiring, 21, 258.

"Hardship" as among, (San Marino) 66, (Morris, Azusa) 260.

State constitution as requiring, 258.

**STARE DECISIS.**

See Precedent.

Rule stated, 241.

**STATES, c. 21 (310-29).**

See Interpretation and Effect of State and Local Enactments.

Cases listed by, 374.

Conflict on questions of interpretation between courts of different, (Bayside, Creve Coeur) 266-67, (Cheltenham, Milwaukie) 268-69.

Constitutional principles invoked mainly against, 20.

Constitution of the United States sometimes less important than constitution and laws of, (Creve Coeur, Orchard Lake) 266.

Courts of, c. 21 (310-29).

Estoppel not properly applicable to, (San Marino) 66-67.

Exclusion of religious uses from entire, (Piedmont) 41-42, (Wauwatosa, Piedmont) 175-76, 213-14, (Piedmont) 214-15.

Police power to regulate land use vested mostly in, 20.

Presumption of validity reversed on basis of constitutions of, (Orchard Lake) 253-54.